CAMBRIDGE GREEK AND LATIN CLASSICS

D0781112

PLAUTUS

AMPHITRVO

EDITED BY

DAVID M. CHRISTENSON

Assistant Professor of Classics, University of Arizona

CAMBRIDGE
UNIVERSITY PRESS

CAMBRIDGE UNIVERSITY PRESS
Cambridge, New York, Melbourne, Madrid, Cape Town, Singapore, São Paulo

Cambridge University Press
The Edinburgh Building, Cambridge CB2 2RU, UK

Published in the United States of America by Cambridge University Press, New York

www.cambridge.org
Information on this title: www.cambridge.org/9780521454018

First published 2000

A catalogue record for this publication is available from the British Library

Library of Congress Cataloguing in Publication data

Plautus, Titus Maccius.
Amphitruo / Plautus; edited by David M. Christenson.
p.   cm. – (Cambridge Greek and Latin classics)
Based on the author's thesis (Ph.D., Harvard University).
Text in Latin with commentary and introduction in English.
Includes bibliographical references and indexes.
ISBN 0 521 45401 8 (hardback) – ISBN 0 521 45997 4 (paperback)
1. Amphitryon (Greek mythology) – Drama.   I. Title.   II. Series.
PA6568.A6   2000
872´.01 21 – dc21   99-043670

ISBN-13 978-0-521-45401-8 hardback
ISBN-10 0-521-45401-8 hardback

ISBN-13 978-0-521-45997-6 paperback
ISBN-10 0-521-45997-4 paperback

Transferred to digital printing 2005

For Alex
ambobus mihi quae carior est oculis

CONTENTS

PREFACE

My fascination with Plautus began many years ago, when, as a college sophomore with little Latin and even less acting experience, I performed in a version of *Amphitruo* directed by Gerda Seligson at the University of Michigan. In graduate school I was disheartened to discover the extent to which Plautus, whose plays were so alive for me, had become largely marginalized in American classical studies (this despite the enduring influence of Erich Segal's *Roman laughter*). With few exceptions, commentaries in English were terribly out of date, were devoted almost exclusively to technical matters, and expressed little interest in the comedies as theatrical productions. In short, there were very few inspiring pedagogical tools to introduce Latin students to Plautine theatre. In recent years Niall Slater's *Plautus in performance* has breathed new life into Plautine studies in the United States and this resurgence of interest continues to be marked not only by new scholarly publications but also by performances of Plautus at many colleges and universities. This edition adheres to the conviction that Plautus can best be appreciated as a playwright who wrote for the stage – for a particular theatre and audience – and whose comedies at the same time serve as brilliantly self-conscious exemplars of the power theatre can exert over the human imagination. In keeping with the aims of the series, considerable attention is paid here to explicating Plautus' delightful, if sometimes (to us) strangely archaic and colloquial Latin. Readers will also find much analysis and speculation as to what exactly is taking place on stage and how the actors engage the spectators of Plautus' theatre. It is also my hope that throughout this edition it is made obvious that this comedy, no less than Plautus' other extant *fabulae*, can tell us much about the Romans and their culture in the epoch in which it was first performed.

The genesis of this edition was my doctoral dissertation at Harvard University, directed by Richard Thomas, who has warmly offered encouragement over the years. Frank Romer and Marilyn Skinner carefully read an early draft of the Introduction and are responsible for many improvements there; I wish to express deep gratitude to them and to all my colleagues in the Department of Classics at the University of Arizona for their generous support. Special thanks are owed to the students who read part or all of the manuscript in connection with our Roman Comedy course in the spring of 1998: Robert Christman, Erin Corbett, Michael Crawford, Derek Halverson, Frances Maffetone, Michelle Mason, Sarah Meadows, Daniel Russell, Martha Sowerwine, and Christopher Trinacty. Their insightful criticisms and suggestions reaffirm the adage that teaching is a reciprocal process, one of whose chief rewards is learning from students. The department's Administrative Secretary, Patty Ward, also deserves hearty thanks for graciously tolerating my quirks and impositions throughout this project.

Professors Easterling and Kenney read and commented on several versions of the manuscript with their legendary acumen. Professor Easterling's broad and deep understanding of ancient theatre rescued the Introduction from many infelicities. Professor Kenney's guiding influence is present on every page; it has been a privilege to have worked closely with such an accomplished scholar and editor. Professor Kenney also provided me with proofs of John Barsby's metrical appendix to his edition of *Eunuchus*, and the organization of my section on metrics in the Introduction is largely modelled after Professor Barsby's clear and judicious presentation of this notoriously difficult subject. Pauline Hire at the Press superintended production with the utmost professionalism and care. Copy-editor Susan Moore, with her keen eye and even keener ear for the English language, was invaluable in the final preparation of the manuscript. Needless to say, any remaining errors of judgement are due to my stubbornness.

The greatest and most profound debt is owed to just a few: Robert Renehan, who showed me that Greek and Latin can indeed be living languages; members of my family (all the Christensons and Porters, quadrupeds included), who provided support in personally difficult times; and, above all, my daughter Alexandra Christenson, to whom this book is dedicated as small recompense for her esprit, love, and precocious wisdom.

Tucson, Arizona   David Christenson
June 1999

INTRODUCTION

1. PLAUTUS' LIFE AND TIMES

The biographical tradition is notoriously suspect regarding Plautus.[1] Much of what we hear ultimately descends from the Roman scholar Varro, who, working over a century after Plautus' death, probably lacked reliable sources.[2] The very dates given for Plautus' birth (254 BC) and death (184 BC, the year of Cato's censorship), though broadly accurate, are probably based on deduction rather than secure testimony. The few particulars given for his life read much more like fiction than fact. His alleged unsuccessful venture in trade abroad and subsequent employment in a mill in Rome recall stock situations of New Comedy. And Gellius' report (*NA* 3.3.15) that Plautus wrote two plays while imprisoned for slander suspiciously recalls a similar event in the biography of Naevius. The designation of Sarsina in Umbria as Plautus' native land may be only an inference drawn from an obscure jest at *Mos.* 770. Most suspicious of all is the playwright's implausible name (Titus Maccius Plautus): it appears to be a comic formation modelled on the *tria nomina* used by prominent Roman families (and freedmen) in this period, with the transparent meaning 'Phallus son of Clown the Mime-actor'.[3] Each element suggests a form of (unscripted) native Italian comedy, and so we reasonably may suppose that Plautus began his theatrical career here.[4] This also would accord with the plausible report that Plautus had made money *in operis artificum scaenicorum* (Gel. *NA* 3.3.14); 'in the employment (or service) of stage-artisans' is a vague description which could signify that he was a stage-worker, actor,[5] writer of

---

[1] *CHCL* II 808–9.

[2] For his scholarly methods see Lehmann (1995).

[3] Gratwick (1973) 83.

[4] I.e. in Atellan farce and/or Mime: see pp. 8–11 below. How he came to learn Greek and ultimately became active in Roman theatrical productions based on Greek scripts is unknown.

[5] If the genitive denotes possession. Leo (1912) 63–86 suggested that Plautus' career as an actor in Atellan farce is what originally brought him to Rome. If he continued to act in his own plays in Roman theatre – as Livy

scripts, or even a producer. Versatility is at the highest premium in a small improvisatory company, and perhaps Plautus began his theatrical career 'from the ground up' in such a troupe; direct experience in all aspects of theatre agrees with the current view of Plautus as a playwright 'who takes a performer's-eye view of comedy'.[6] Thus it is not unlikely that after achieving some notoriety in Rome he assumed this name (if it was not bestowed upon him by posterity) in recognition of his earlier days in Italian popular theatre. This also suggests that he was by birth a slave or person of low status who attained a social identity only as the result of his theatrical success; his attainment of a name curiously mirrors the claims to identity staked by Plautine slaves, who, despite being social ciphers and legal non-entitities from a Roman point of view, scurrilously vaunt their ancestry.[7]

Didascalic notices provide two dates: the performances of *Ps.* in 191 and *St.* in 200. These indicate that the high point of Plautus' career coincided with that of Cato the Elder (239–149 BC) in Roman political life. The demand for theatrical performances in Rome seems to have increased dramatically during the Second Punic War, and Plautus' career as a comic playwright may have begun in these closing years of the third century BC. Thus, the entire *œuvre* probably

(7.2.8) asserts playwrights universally did in the time of Livius Andronicus – one supposes that he played the role of Jupiter in *Am.* This hypothesis would explain why Amphitryon at the play's end asks the audience to applaud for Jupiter in particular and also gives additional point to Mercury's designation of Jupiter as an *architectus* in the prologue (45); the scheming slave in Plautine comedy is conventionally described in such terms (e.g. *Mil.* 901), and Plautus may have been well known for playing this role in previous plays (for the view that Plautus performed in *Ps.* see Slater (1985) 118–46 and Hallett (1993)). The analogy between the playwright and the *architectus doli* is made explicitly in the plays, e.g. *Ps.* 401–5. Evidence for playbills is lacking, but advance notice that Plautus was to perform in *Am.* could have circulated by word of mouth, and so the audience would catch Mercury's meaning.

[6] Handley (1975) 129.

[7] See 28, 365nn. Conversely, it seems less likely that Plautus used this pseudonym to disguise his high birth because of aristocratic prejudice against the comic theatre; given his enduring fame, the scholarly tradition would have attempted to ferret him out, as it did, e.g., Catullus' Lesbia. The broader issues of identity so prevalent in Plautine theatre merit further investigation; for some reflections on identity in *Epid.* see Gruber (1986) 42–65.

spans a period of approximately thirty years (*c.* 215–185 BC). The latter half of Plautus' career postdates the defeat of Hannibal at Zama (202 BC) and the end of the Second Punic War, and coincides with Roman intervention in the affairs of the eastern Mediterranean. The first production of *Am.* most probably falls within this dynamic period of military expansion marked by increased foreign influences, institutional stress, and social tensions in Rome and Italy. No definitive historical markers can be found in the text. Identifications of covert allusions to figures such as M. Fulvius Nobilior or to specific battles prove to be illusory.[8] Sosia's characterization of Alcmena as a raging Bacchante (703) has been taken as a topical reference pointing to a date close to the state's sudden suppression of this imported orgiastic cult through the *senatus consultum de Bacchanalibus* of 186 BC. A related reference at *Cas.* 979–80 has helped to secure a consensus on that play's lateness.[9] Moreover, *Cas.* and *Am.* are strikingly similar sex farces and share an abundance of thematic correspondences;[10] in both plays 'Jupiter'[11] schemes to enjoy an extramarital affair, though in *Cas.* the *senex* is foiled by his clever 'Juno'. And both plays feature an elaborate play-within-the-play that in each case is performed with the utmost theatrical self-consciousness. Approaches to Plautine chronology based on dramatic technique, style or metre have yielded drastically different dates for *Am.* (as for other plays), though several have placed it somewhere around 190 BC,[12] where it would fall among a group of plays that usually includes *Rud.* The chronological proximity of *Rud.* could account for Plautus' decision to present his mythical travesty, in that a character in this play apparently refers to a recent performance of Euripides' *Alkmene* on the Roman stage.[13] If at the time of

---

[8] Sensible statement of methodology in identifying historical allusions in Plautus in Harvey (1981) and (1986). Cf. Gruen (1990) 124–6.

[9] MacCary and Willcock (1976) 11.

[10] Leadbeater (1986).

[11] The *senex* Lysidamus in *Cas.* is frequently so designated, e.g. 331–2. The repeated references themselves perhaps suggest that the début of *Am.* was recent.

[12] E.g. Sedgwick (1949); for the difficulty of establishing an accurate chronology in general see Duckworth (1952) 54–6.

[13] Jocelyn (1967) 6–7. See further p. 54 below.

the first production of *Am.* an adaptation of Euripides' tragedy had been staged within recent memory, this performance would provide a point of reference for a Roman audience to appreciate a travesty of the Jupiter–Alcmena–Amphitryon myth. If this is correct, Mercury's mention (91–2) of Jupiter's appearance on the Roman stage in the prior year, presumably as *deus ex machina*, would refer to an adaptation of Euripides' play. Thus, we can with some confidence settle on an approximate date of 190–185 BC for *Am.*

2. ROMAN COMEDY

(a) *Greek background*

Already within the lifetime of Aristophanes, the bawdy, interactive, and fantastical style of comedy of fifth-century Athens later to be designated 'Old Comedy' began to take a new direction. In the last plays of Aristophanes, the role of the chorus that had figured so prominently earlier in his career is noticeably curtailed, and signals a general trend toward suppression of music and dance as organic features of comedy.[14] His *Ec.* and *Pl.*, both dated to a period within ten years of his death in 386 BC, by convention mark the transition to the so-called 'Middle Comedy', a term that conveniently describes the forms of comedy that evolved over the first three-quarters of the fourth century.[15] Change of course was gradual rather than instantaneous, and very different syles of comedy must have co-existed for much of this century. The use of masks, for instance, persisted into New Comedy, though the particular types evolved as comic plots changed. In general, it is clear that the political and intellectual life of Athens ceased to occupy centre stage in this period as comedy became more international and more universal themes found acceptance. Though Middle Comedy survives today only in the form of titles and mostly short quotations, these suggest a lively and versatile

[14] Recent work rightly questions overly schematized models of comic development in the fourth century based on such assumptions as the precipitous decline of the chorus: for this particular question see Rothwell (1995) and for a concise summary of the larger issues Henderson (1995).

[15] The most comprehensive study of comedy in this period is Nesselrath (1990).

repertoire, even if such trademarks of Aristophanic theatre as unrestrained obscenity, imaginative and grossly padded costumes (outfitted with phalli), exuberant song and dance, and relentless satire
were diminished or disappeared altogether. Apropos of *Am.*, the
period of Middle Comedy clearly was one in which both doubles-
plays and travesties of myth were commonly staged.[16] Mythological
burlesque eventually seems to have disappeared in favour of plays
on more mundane subjects featuring stock characters such as pimps,
prostitutes, parasites, clever slaves, cooks, and lovesick young men;
some of these types were inherited from Old Comedy, but all were
figures from everyday life as well. With this growing movement away
from the fantastical conceptions of Old Comedy, comedy had
reached a transitional, more 'realistic' phase.[17] At the same time,
fourth-century comedy was much affected by the enduring influence
of Euripides, whose plays had blurred generic distinctions by largely
'demythologizing' tragedy and refocusing it on everyday domestic
life, while placing a new emphasis on psychological realism. Specific
elements such as recognition scenes seem to have been taken over by
comic poets from Euripides.[18]

New Comedy,[19] which flourished from *c.* 325 to 250 BC, was to exert
the most direct Greek influence on Roman comedy. Up until the
twentieth century, it was known, save for scattered snippets mostly
quoted by ancient grammarians, only indirectly through the versions
of Plautus and Terence. All the latter's extant plays are adaptations
of Greek New Comedy, while about half of the former's surviving
works are known to be adapted from this genre. Twentieth-century
papyrus finds have yielded an almost complete play of Menan-

---

[16] Reinhardt (1974) 95–8. Mythological burlesque had also been popular in
Old Comedy, as citations and titles of Cratinus' plays suggest, and seems to
have been standard fare (albeit in more restrained form) in the satyr-plays of
the tragic festivals. In the early fifth century Epicharmus produced mythological burlesques in Sicily.

[17] See further Slater (1995).

[18] Quintilian (*Inst.* 10.1.69) considered Euripides to be Menander's chief
model. For the latter's metatheatrical reworking of Euripidean drama see
Wiles (1991) 5–6.

[19] For the genre in general, as it is represented primarily by Menander, see
Goldberg (1980), Hunter (1985) and Zagagi (1994).

der (*Dysk.*), as well as significant fragments of several others. In Menander an aesthetic wholly different from Aristophanes' is immediately recognizable. His plays are usually set in contemporary Athens or an Attic deme, but given the cosmopolitan nature of their plots could just as easily take place in any urban centre of the Hellenistic world. The plays are rooted in domestic rather than political life, and the same stock characters that moved to the forefront in Middle Comedy predominate. Certain stereotypical situations recur, e.g. children separated at birth are reunited through an incredible series of coincidences, or a slave connives against his elderly master to aid and abet the amours of the latter's son.[20] These five-act plays are carefully constructed, employ sub-plots, skilfully provoke suspense, demonstrate psychological subtlety, and, despite some of their absurd premises, strive to sustain the illusion of presenting a picture of real (especially emotional) life by providing probable and ethical motives for action.[21] Menander's characters behave plausibly according to their particular situation and generally respect the norms of everyday experience. Outside of prologues and epilogues,[22] the actors sometimes acknowledge the (apparently) all-male audience through the formula ἄνδρες, 'gentlemen' (e.g. *Dysk.* 194, 659, 666, *Sam.* 329, 447, 683), which is used sparingly in (usually) monologues to encourage the spectators to identify with a character's emotional perspective. The language of Menander's characters is simple but elegant, and little trace remains of the inventive verbal effusiveness of Old Comedy. The immediate and robust humour in which Aristophanes abounds is mostly lacking, and much of

---

[20] Menander treats these situations, like his stock characters, with considerable variety and invests them with surprising humanity. Cf. Zagagi (1994) 15–45.

[21] Since antiquity – cf. Aristophanes of Byzantium's famous exclamation 'O Menander and Life, which of you imitated the other?' – Menander has been praised for his realism, but we should avoid indiscriminately ascribing facets of modern naturalistic theatre to his plays. For the considerable artifice of Menandrian theatre, which continued the tradition of masked comedy and featured rigidly codified costumes, see Wiles (1991) 63–7 (and *passim*). Cf. also Goldberg (1980) 109–21.

[22] And here the familiar second person is only rarely found (e.g. *Asp.* 113, *Dysk.* 965–7); cf. 'prologue' below. The audience is addressed as θεαταί, 'spectators' (cf. 998n.), only at *Perik.* 171.

Menander is not humorous at all. The texts suggest that music played a much less prominent role in Menander. Nearly all lines are delivered in the metre most closely approximating everyday speech, the iambic trimeter, with a few recitative (?) trochaic and iambic tetrameters mixed in.[23] The traditional comic chorus was restricted to supplying what appears to be a non-integral musical interlude between acts, indicated in the text by the notation ΧΟΡΟΥ, '[song] of the chorus'.[24] We are totally ignorant of the nature of these *entr'actes*, but the stereotypical characterization of the approaching chorus as a drunken and youthful band of revellers at the end of Act 1 (e.g. *Asp.* 246–8, *Dysk.* 230, *Epitr.* 169–70, *Perik.* 261–2) suggests a light sideshow rather than an elaborate choral production that enriched or commented on the drama. Perhaps the main effect of the choral interludes was to suggest – in keeping with the general trend toward naturalism – the passage of time. Thus we may describe the comedy of Menander in the most general terms; but we should not assume that Greek New Comedy was homogeneous, as the sands of Egypt may yet yield further papyri that will revise our overall picture.

Menander died in 292/1 BC, a century before Plautus' *floruit*, but some of his plays, like those of his rivals Philemon and Diphilus, seem to have become instant 'classics' and enjoyed enduring success through revival performances in Athens (it is also supposed that some of Menander's plays were originally performed outside Athens). After his death, a sizeable repertoire became known throughout the Hellenistic world owing to performances by itinerant acting companies. The earliest Roman playwrights most probably were introduced to Greek drama in southern Italy or Sicily, where, in addition to the comic repertoire, they were likely to see performances of Euripides and others by the 'Artists of Dionysus'. Tradition maintained that on the heels of the Roman victory in the First Punic

---

[23] It is not known if these latter measures were always accompanied by music, as are the iambic tetrameters (catalectic) in the final scene of *Dysk.* (880–958), where the notation αὐλεῖ, 'the piper plays', on the papyrus makes this explicit. Cf. Gomme and Sandbach (1973) 36–7.

[24] 'Hellenistic comedy deals with the actions of individuals, not with the actions of communities, and it is no longer the property of Hellenistic choruses to be "doers"' (Wiles (1991) 39).

War[25] Livius Andronicus, a freedman from Tarentum, instituted
dramatic performances at the *ludi Romani* of 240 BC, when he may
have presented both a comedy and a tragedy. But early Roman
comedy involved much more than simply translation or close adaptation of Greek models: here the influence of distinct forms of native
Italian drama was instrumental.

(b) Italian background

Some of the qualities that immediately distinguish Plautus' comedy
from Menander's were present from the beginnings of Roman comedy. Most significantly, Andronicus' comedies featured *cantica*: music
appears to have been an integral feature of Roman drama based on
Greek models from its very inception. Naevius, who made his theatrical début in 235 BC, seems to have exercised considerable influence
on Plautus.[26] The fragments of Naevius reveal a vigorous diction
that in its playfulness, repetition, and awareness of its own expressive capabilities immediately calls to mind the verbal exuberance of
Plautus. One suggests the direct method of control Plautine prologists typically exert over their audiences: *com.* 1 R = 1 W *Acontizome-
nos fabula est prime bona.* In this forthright promotion of the play, we
recognize a style more reminiscent of the parabases of Old Comedy
than of anything we find among the remains of Greek New Comedy.
Titles (e.g. *Stalagmus*) attest to the prominence of lead-slaves and
suggest that the centrality regularly assumed by deceptive slaves in
the plots of extant Roman comedy was not entirely Plautus' doing.
We should also guard against overestimating the innovative genius of
Naevius; presumably, he and other early Roman playwrights sought
to win their audiences' acceptance of an essentially foreign entertainment by introducing elements familiar to them from popular Italian
drama. Though these performances would have been unscripted at

---

[25] 'Victory in the First Punic War not only confirmed Roman ascendancy
in Hellenic south Italy but extended it to Hellenic Sicily. The accomplish-
ment would be marked by elevation of the Ludi to a cultural event that
announced Rome's participation in the intellectual world of the Greeks. The
national ceremony acquired an international dimension' (Gruen (1990) 84).

[26] Wright (1974) 33–59.

this time, and so our understanding of them is deficient in the details, it is possible to sketch a general picture. Italian popular entertainment emphasized variety and improvisation, staging was transitory and 'theatres' fostered intimacy between actors and audiences. Song and dance no doubt figured prominently in these performances.

As its name suggests, Atellan farce[27] originated in Atella in Campania. The stock characters all wore masks; we hear of such figures as Bucco ('Fool'), Pappus ('Grandpappy'), Dossenus ('Glutton'), Manducus ('Chomper'), and Maccus ('Clown'), the last of which presumably provided Plautus with one element of his comic pseudonym.[28] The names themselves suggest a highly farcical entertainment generated by the interaction of these universal comic stereotypes. Performances, which remained unscripted until the time of Sulla, would have required the players to develop conventional situations only broadly sketched ahead of time through their improvisatory skills. Though much of these brief impromptu pieces would have been given over to jokes, slapstick, and banter, some of the titles of literary farces that come down to us suggest more elaborate plots: *Maccus Virgo* presumably featured a transsexual impersonation (cf. *Cas.*); there were doubles-comedies (*Duo Dossenni*, *Macci Gemini*); *Satura* may have been some sort of 'Medley' or perhaps a sketch involving a pregnant woman.[29] There were also burlesque treatments of myth.[30] Suetonius (*Nero* 39.3) provides direct evidence for song in Atellan farce of the first century AD.[31]

Mime[32] has a long history in Italy and seems to have been an enormously popular form of street entertainment well before

[27] Beare (1964) 137–48.

[28] Cf. p. 1 above. That Plautus was familiar with Atellan farce is also shown by jokes at *Bac.* 1088 and *Rud.* 535–6.

[29] Cf. pp. 38–9 below.

[30] Höttemann (1993) 93–6 argues that these were introduced to Atellan farce by Lucius Pomponius (first century BC).

[31] Other native performances probably featured song and dance as well. In his problematic account of the origins of Roman drama Livy (7.2.3–13) notes the importation of a form of Etruscan dance accompanied by the pipe in 364 BC, out of which Roman youths first developed jesting dialogues loosely set to music and subsequently more elaborate medleys (*saturae*).

[32] Beare (1964) 149–58.

Plautus' time. In contrast to Atellan farce, it was unmasked. Italian
mime originally was purely improvisatory, but in the first century BC
mimes began to be scripted. Troupes organized by a lead-mime (an
archimimus or *archimima*, as both women and men performed) enacted
stock scenes, such as the racy tales of adultery attributed to Decimus
Laberius. The title of Novius' *Gemelli* demonstrates that doubles-
comedy also was part of the repertoire. The genre earned a reputation for bawdiness: the actors' costumes featured phalli, and actresses
appeared nude in performances at the festival of the goddess Flora.
The mime actor, who performed barefoot, was nicknamed *planipes*
('flat-foot'); as *plaut-/plot-* means 'flat' it is likely that Plautus' pseudonym betrays experience in mime as well. At any rate, it cannot be
doubted that the influence of mime played a role in the early Roman
comic playwrights' transformation of Greek New Comedy into something significantly more burlesque and boisterous. Mime was also to
provide themes for Roman satire and elegy; it seems to have sub-
sumed Atellan farce in the late empire, and persisted in sub-literary
forms for centuries, undergoing only superficial transformations, and
resurfacing as, e.g., the *commedia dell'arte* of the sixteenth and seventeenth centuries.

Further influences on early Roman comedy no doubt came from
Sicily and southern Italy. Comedy was well established in Sicily at
least as early as 500 BC, when Epicharmus produced plays that
roughly fit the mould of Attic Old Comedy (several titles suggest
mythological burlesque). Though it is unlikely that Horace had
access to a reliable account of early theatre in Rome or Italy, he
asserted (*Ep.* 2.1.58) that Epicharmus was the main influence on
Plautus. The so-called *phlyax* plays of southern Italy are known to us
primarily through pictorial evidence belonging to the fourth century
BC.[33] Most of the vases assigned to this obviously farcical genre depict scenes of mythological burlesque, with Herakles being the most
popular subject. One curious vase,[34] taken to represent Antigone being led off to Creon, features the unmasking of the male actor playing her, who wears a phallus and is revealed to be bald and bearded.

---

[33] Bieber (1961) 129–46, Trendall (1967), Taplin (1993) 48–54.
[34] Fig. 490 in Bieber (1961) 134.

Stock scenes drawn from everyday life also are portrayed; a slave is beaten in one,[35] while in another a father and son apparently wrangle over a woman (cf. *As.*, *Cas.*, *Mer.*).[36] Terracotta models of stages suggest a means of staging not unlike that of *Am.*[37] The players are masked and their costumes resemble those of Old Comedy, and it may be the case that some of these vases taken to depict *phlyax* drama actually represent scenes of Attic comedy.[38] Though we can reasonably assume some influences on Roman comedy from South Italy, we cannot trace any direct lines. We recall that Andronicus was a native of Tarentum and that Naevius served in the first Punic War, and so he, like a considerable portion of the Roman citizenry in the third century, could have been introduced to dramatic performances in South Italy while on military campaign.

(c) *The* fabula palliata

Thus, the *fabula palliata*, or 'play in Greek costume' as the comedies were called, was a truly hybrid genre from the start. Whereas playwrights such as Terence adhered closely to the Attic heritage, Plautus like Naevius completely refashioned his models by incorporating elements of stagecraft from Italian popular farce. The result was a form of comedy that constantly declares its status as artifice. It is difficult to grasp the full force of this spectacle through written texts. Still, it is immediately evident that Plautine characters are drawn in much broader and louder strokes than they ever seem to have been in Greek New Comedy, and characterization is as fluid as it had been in Aristophanes. In Plautus' plays, flamboyant slaves carry out schemes of unprecedented deviousness, the parasite's clamour for a meal becomes raucously baroque, and pimps and prostitutes are absurdly greedy. Intricacy of characterization is shelved in favour of more elastic plots squarely fixed on trickery and the tricksters who direct ingeniously improbable plays-within-plays. Plots may be fraught with inconsistencies, but the action proceeds swiftly and relentlessly, with the actors creating the appearance of seamless im-

---

[35] Fig. 513 in Bieber (1961) 140.   [36] Fig. 504 in Bieber (1961) 138.
[37] See p. 52 below.   [38] See pp. 51–2 below.

provisation throughout.[39] Absent are the act-divisions and chorus of Greek New Comedy:[40] dramatic pace is greatly accelerated and the richly varied music is an integral part of the action. Language in Plautus' hands becomes unrealistically prolix, and profuse alliteration, assonance and other kinds of parallelism combine to create discourse that is largely non-referential; in Saussurian terms, Plautine language privileges signifier over signified. Characters speak in fantastic hyperbole, develop the most elaborate conceits and the most extravagant imagery or simply assail each other in a coarse (though rarely obscene) kind of vaudeville banter saturated with puns.[41] Actors speak directly to the audience as much as they do to each other. The pretence of a Greek setting is not scrupulously maintained, and Roman places, customs and persons, who are referred to as *barbari* in the plays, regularly intrude. Literary parody is pervasive, and Roman institutions are also burlesqued. In short, the entire Plautine spectacle has much more in common with the festive comedy of Aristophanes than the quiet domesticity of Menandrian drama: it is hard to conceive of a form of comedy that could more deliberately subvert its primary models.[42] The result of this subversive process was the creation of something delightfully farcical and fresh.

[39] 'The plots are loosely organized and open in structure. The performance is not the *mimesis* of an action, but is, rather, in itself an action, an integral part of the Roman *ludi* (the games or festival)' (Wiles (1991) 7–8). For improvisation in Plautine theatre see further Slater (1993).

[40] The *piscatores* at *Rud.* 290ff. and the *aduocati* at *Poen.* 515ff. are generally regarded as vestigial choruses.

[41] Speech seems to have been much more restricted in Republican Rome (cf. the famous account of Naevius' imprisonment for insulting the Metelli) than it had been in fifth-century Athens and the open satirizing of public figures so prominent in Aristophanes is altogether lacking in Plautus.

[42] The 1968 discovery of a portion of Menander's *Dis exapaton* ('The Double Deceiver'), the source play for *Bac.*, provides a concrete demonstration of Plautus' methods of adaptation. The Greek text has been edited by E. W. Handley in *P.Oxy.* 64 (1997) 14–42; for the enormous bibliography on the fragment and its relation to *Bac.* 494–562 see (e.g.) Barsby (1986) on *Bac.* 494–9. For Plautus' subversion of Greek New Comedy in general see Anderson (1993).

3. THE PLAY'S THE THING

(a) *Theme, structure, and movement*

Am. is one of three extant Plautine doubles-comedies. It is immediately distinguishable from its congeners (*Bac.*, *Men.*) by the mythical dimension of its plot and the fact that this plot calls for impersonation rather than identical twins. But more significant than these superficial distinctions in defining the uniqueness of *Am.* is its self-conscious development of the theme of gemination. A primary impulse of any comedy featuring at least one pair of precise doubles is to create as many permutations of characters and situations as possible, so as to exploit every opportunity for humorous confusion. Typically, a climactic scene brings the doubles face to face, whereby the issue of identity is resolved. To examine how Plautus articulates this conventional framework of doubles-comedy in *Am.*, we must first catalogue the seventeen scenes that follow the prologue:

  (Mercury's prologue (1–152))
 1. Sosia, Mercury (153–462)
 2. Mercury (463–98)
 3. Jupiter, Alcmena, Mercury (499–550)
 4. Amphitryon, Sosia (551–632)
 5. Alcmena, Amphitryon, Sosia (633–860)[43]
 6. Jupiter (861–81)
 7. Alcmena, Jupiter (882–955)
 8. Sosia, Jupiter, Alcmena (956–83)
 9. Mercury (984–1008)
10. Amphitryon (1009–20)
11. Mercury, Amphitryon (1021–fr. 6)
12. Alcmena, Amphitryon (frs. 7–10)
13. Amphitryon, Blepharo, Sosia (frs. 11–14)
14. Jupiter, Amphitryon, Blepharo (fr. 15–1052)
15. Bromia, Amphitryon (1053–1130)

---

[43] It is assumed here that Amphitryon and Sosia remain on stage for Alcmena's monody, perhaps miming their journey from the harbour during the song (which they are presumed not to hear): cf. 551–632, 628, 654–86onn.

16. Jupiter, Amphitryon (1131–43)
17. Amphitryon (1144–6)[44]

Am. is organized according to a flexible network of (mostly) binary parallels and oppositions.[45] The core of the doubles-drama, scenes 1–14 ('Act v', i.e. scenes 15–17, stands apart as the denouement), is framed by the corresponding scenes in which the two pairs of doubles confront each other. In each encounter, the human character, Sosia in 1 and Amphitryon in 14, suffers verbal and physical mistreatment, and ultimately comes to doubt his own identity.[46] In performance, the parallelism is made obvious by the bold but unsuccessful rush toward the palace[47] each human character makes as the scenes reach their climaxes (449, 1052). Within this outer frame, four scenes (3, 5, 7, 12) feature Alcmena, who appears in alternation with her counterfeit (3, 7) and real (5, 12) husband, so that harmonious and turbulent scenes alternate: at 938–40 Jupiter metatheatrically describes the rhythm of these scenes when he parodies Alcmena's earlier song (633–40). Other relationships between these scenes are immediately recognizable. Scene 3 is a departure scene, 5 one of arrival. Despite the scant remains of scene 12, it is apparent that Alcmena there counters Amphitryon's repeated claim that she is insane in scene 5 (e.g. 696, 777) with similar accusations against his sanity (fr. 8); it is likely that the scenes corresponded to each other in further ways. Similarly, there are four scenes (4, 8, 11, 13) in which the confused and constantly shifting relations of master and slave are brought to the forefront. In both 4 and 13, the real Sosia is unjustly accused by Amphitryon and threatened with violence (556–64, fr. 12) as the result of Mercury's machinations. In scene 8 the real Sosia is made the dupe (974–5) of his supposititious master, while in 11 the

---

[44] Division into acts and scenes is dispensed with here, not only because these are Renaissance accretions to the MSS, but also because they disguise the continuous nature of Plautine performance and may create a false sense of dramatic structure and unity.

[45] Cf. Reinhardt (1974) 120.

[46] With Sosia's *ubi ego perii?* (456) compare Amphitryon's *perii, miser* (1039), where the literal meaning of the colloquial exclamation is apropos. Cf. 295, 1076nn.

[47] See pp. 19–20 below.

counterfeit slave deludes the real Amphitryon. The roles of Mercury and Sosia mirror each other in two other scenes (3 and 5, respectively), where each plays the typically Plautine interloper who comments peripherally on an exchange between two other characters. Three scenes (2, 6, 9) feature one of the gods, alone on stage, addressing the audience directly. These addresses stand apart from the doubles-comedy and comment on it, and in effect further the intimacy Mercury establishes with the audience in the prologue; together with it they offer the clearest evidence of Plautus' overwhelming desire to control his audience's reception of this 'passing strange' play. Even these four 'prologues' exhibit binary relationships among themselves, for example when Jupiter in scene 6 draws attention to his status as an actor in costume (861–7) just as Mercury had done in his opening (115–19). In fact, only one scene (10), Amphitryon's appearance on stage to report his failed search for Naucrates in the city, does not seem to be integrated into this complex structure of binary relations. Its practical function is to give Mercury sufficient time to climb up to the roof of the stage building from where he will delude Amphitryon in the next scene. There is, however, a link with the immediately preceding and similarly short monologue of Mercury. There Mercury in detail informs the audience (997–1008) of his immediate plan to keep Amphitryon away, to be fulfilled in scene 11, while in 10 Amphitryon closes his monologue by confidently stating his naïve desire to enter the palace (1015–20). Taken together, the monologues advertise the enormous imbalance of knowledge and power between the divine and human characters that is central to the play.

Motifs of doubling pervade *Am.* to an absurd degree.[48] The mythical tradition provided the pair of Amphitryons, the birth of twins, and Hercules' precocious slaying of the two snakes as related in Bromia's report. But Plautus' play also features a second pair of doubles (Mercury and Sosia), two messenger's speeches (197–262, 1053–1124), two searches for characters off-stage (Naucrates and Blepharo: cf. 949–51), and a second sexual encounter (cf. 112, 976–81) between Alcmena and the false Amphitryon. A fascinating artic-

---

[48] Cf. Dupont (1976).

ulation of the gemination theme involves language. Though various
types of linguistic doublets are not uncommon in Plautus and archaic Latin in general, the frequency of these is greatly pronounced
in *Am.* This is especially evident in the prologue.[49] As part of the
process of inducting the audience into the world of the doubles-
comedy Mercury frequently employs doublets of the same word
(repetition or polyptoton): 7 *quasque … quasque* and *incepistis … inceptabitis*, 9 *ea … ea*, 17 *cuius … quam* and *uenio … uenerim*, 28 *humana
… humano*, 32 *pace … pacem*, 39 *uelle … uelimus*, 47 *bonis … boni*, 46
⟨*ille*⟩ *illi*, 49 *facere … facit*, 80 *est … est*, 86–7 *mirari … miremini*, 98
Argis … Argo, 111 *ex … ex*, 134 *illa illum*, 147 *uidere … uidebitis*. The
coupling of semantically similar words[50] is especially common: 3 *adficere atque adiuuare*, 6 *bono … amplo*, 9 *adferam … nuntiem*, 11 *concessum et
datum*, 16 *aequi et iusti*, 18 *dicam … eloquar*, 23 *uereri … metuere*, 37 *ignorant neque tenent*, 118 *ueterem atque antiquam*, 129 *seruom et conseruom*. We
also find word-roots repeated in close proximity: 1 *uos in uostris* (cf. 8),
137 *donis donatus*; and antithetical pairs: 2 *emendis uendendisque*, 5 *peregri
et domi*, 35 *iniusta … iustis* (cf. 36). The god twice describes the play
itself as a blending of two genres: 59, 63 *tragicomoedia*. Linguistic
gemination is found throughout the play, though never so pronounced as in the prologue. Plautus is especially playful when referring to Alcmena's pregnancy and parturition: 487–8 *uno ut fetu … uno
ut labore*, 681 *grauidam … plenam*, 878–9 *grauida est … grauidast* (cf.
1136–7), 1089 *geminos :: geminos*. Sosia, in voicing his sense of foreboding-
ing with regard to the *patera* Amphitryon has taken as a spoil of war
not only covertly references the birth of the twins through repetition
of the verb *parere*, but also captures an essential theme of the play:

> tu peperisti Amphitruonem ⟨alium⟩, alium ego peperi Sosiam;
> nunc si patera pateram peperit, omnes congeminauimus!   (785–6)

---

[49] By comparison, in the prologue of *Men.*, an earlier and less sophisticated
doubles-comedy, there is the pointed *puerorum, puerum* (38), but only eight other
(certain) instances of linguistic doubling over the 76 extant lines: 10 *dicam …
dicitur*, 72 *haec … haec*, 73 *alia … aliud*, 15 *modio … trimodio*, 42 *illius … illi*, 51
quis quid, 54–5 *qui … dederit, nugas egerit | qui dederit … nugas egerit*, 65 *rapidus
raptori*. *Men.* 13 has *huic … hoc*, but the text is suspect.

[50] Haffter (1934) 68 notes the unusually high number of semantic pairs in
the *Am.* prologue, but regards this merely as a means of stylistic elevation and
does not explore any thematic implications.

Language itself thus assumes a quasi-magical role to assist in the creation of the duplicitous world of *Am*. Sometimes, however, for the bedazzled human characters the conventions of language break down and cannot adequately describe the situation, as when Sosia recounts his strange experience with his double to Amphitryon:

> neque, ita me di ament, credebam primo mihimet Sosiae,
> donec Sosia illic egomet fecit sibi uti crederem.   (597–8)

> nec lac lactis magis est simile quam ille ego similest mei.   (601)

But all in all the world of the play is one in which the possibilities for mirroring – to use a metaphor Sosia himself suggests (442) – appear infinite with respect to characters, scenes, motifs, and language. And mirroring, along with such related concepts as duplication, deception and illusion, is a fundamental aspect of dramatic mimesis.

The final resolution of all the confusion wrought by the gods' impersonations calls for fantastical measures, which Plautus readily delivers. As no denouement occurs in the climactic scene (14) in which Amphitryon and Jupiter finally meet,[51] the play is brought to its conclusion through divine intervention and revelation. First we hear of the miraculous events attending the birth inside the house through the ecstatic report (scene 15) of the appropriately named Bromia.[52] Her revelation that Alcmena has painlessly given birth to twins, one of whom is Jupiter's son, instantly placates Amphitryon, who orders a sacrifice for the god and declares that he will consult Tiresias (1124–9). But before Amphitryon can leave the stage, Jupiter makes a thundering appearance (scene 16) as *deus ex machina* – and so presumably in changed costume and mask – to help alleviate any lingering doubts or tensions.[53] Jupiter informs Amphitryon that he 'borrowed Alcmena's body' and sired a son who someday will bestow immortal glory upon the Theban general (1131–43). Following the god's announced 'migration' into the sky, Amphitryon reiterates his acceptance of everything (1144–5) and calls for the final *plaudite*.

---

[51] Cf. the recognition scene at *Men.* 1059–1162, where by contrast it is a matter of having the brothers discover their true relationship to one another.

[52] 1077n.

[53] Jupiter in effect delivers the play's epilogue, which with Mercury's opening prologue posits another binary opposition.

In this way the state of outward harmony toward which comedy is commonly said to move is achieved. The play is concluded precisely in the arbitrary, but quintessentially comic, manner described by Aristotle: '... [in comedy] the most bitter enemies in the plot, such as Orestes and Aegisthus, walk off as friends in the end and nobody is killed by anyone'.[54] The magical world of doubling and duplicity had begun to fade when Jupiter dropped his mask as Amphitryon and donned the paraphernalia of his divinity, and when the god by some mechanism rises above the stage, which is occupied only by Amphitryon, the audience is visually reassured that the human and divine orders have been properly restored. And if the actor playing Jupiter subsequently returns to the stage and removes his mask when Amphitryon asks the audience to applaud *Iouis summi causa* (1146), this spectacle clearly signals the end of the ludic pageant.[55]

(b) Performance

> O body swayed to music, O brightening glance,
> How can we know the dancer from the dance?
> (Yeats, *Among school children*)

Yeats's question could just as easily be posed of the ancient theatre: how can we know the play apart from the performance? Performance criticism suggests that our attempt to understand and appreciate Plautine theatre from the mere words of (manu)scripts has traditionally been misguided:

> Even at the level of clothes and paint and noise, the theatre bombards its audience with a hundred simultaneous capsules of information, anything capable of reaching the mind and imagination through the eye or ear. The critic, equipped with literary

[54] *Poet.* 1453a36ff. Cf. Kerr (1967) 57: 'We are accustomed to calling the endings of comedies happy endings, but that is simply a polite convention we have agreed upon. A moment's closer inspection would show us – perhaps to our astonishment – that the cheerful doling-out of futures which takes place at the end of most comedies is not in any secure sense "happy". Rather, it is sublimely arbitrary.'

[55] See 1131–43, 1144, 1146nn. and p. 1 n. 5 above.

apparatus, the linear logic of cause and effect, cannot cope with such an assault. Yet dramatic simultaneity, the synaesthesia of the senses and perceptions, is the object of study; for from it come the concepts by which the experience is to be judged, and by no other way.[56]

We cannot in fact offer an unambiguously positive response to Yeats's query when it is reformulated *vis-à-vis* Plautine theatre. The enormous gulf in culture, language and theatrical convention that separates us from Plautus and his audience prevents us from testing our hypotheses about his plays in the most meaningful way, i.e. in his theatre, before his audience. Still, it remains the challenging task of classicists equipped only with such not fully adequate tools as philology, archaeology, and comparative analysis to strive to muster something of the imagination of a stage-director; in this way alone can we gain a better sense of Plautus' performances and his audience's reception of them. In recent years, this effort has been aided by Slater's (1985) pioneering study of Plautine performance.[57]

Plautine theatre was highly stylized, both in its physical structure and its techniques and conventions.[58] The ruling class at Rome long resisted the construction of permanent theatres, either, as is often claimed, to deny a possible outlet for political protest,[59] or out of fear that construction of a massive stone structure 'would enshrine the drama as an unshakable institution, no longer dependent upon the resolve of magistrates and the verdict of the aristocracy'.[60] It was not until the construction of Pompey's theatre in 55 BC that the Roman people enjoyed a fixed venue for drama. Up to that time, theatres were set up only temporarily, most probably in the forum,

---

[56] Styan (1975) 4–5. Cf. Barthes's description of theatre as a 'cybernetic machine' (1972) 261–4 and Elam's (1980) more formal study of theatrical sign-systems.

[57] Barchiesi (1970) was also instrumental in reinvigorating Plautine studies. Cf. now Moore (1998).

[58] For the contrasting uses of theatrical space in Greek and Roman Comedy see Wiles (1991) 55–62.

[59] This motive could be cloaked in moral disapproval; for the stereotypical view of spectating in the theatre as a decadent activity see Tac. *Ann.* 14.20.

[60] Gruen (1992) 209–10.

the circus or before a temple on certain occasions.[61] Contemporary visual evidence for Plautine theatre is lacking, but it is certain that in comparison with the great stone structures associated with Hellenistic drama, the layout of the open-air theatre of *c.* 200 BC at first glance must have seemed unimpressively simple.[62] For the most part, the action is imagined to be taking place in a street in front of a background depicting one to three houses; *Am.* requires only a single domicile, which, given Amphitryon's heroic status, was probably designed to suggest a palace. The actors could move in and out of this background structure through any one of up to three doors. Later paintings of Roman theatre settings show partially enclosed porches in front of these, which could have been put to good effect by eavesdropping characters. There are also two side wings, one of which by convention leads to the forum and the centre of town, the other to the harbour or country. *Am.* is unique among the extant comedies in that the action takes place on two tiers (yet another instance of gemination!); presumably, a ladder behind the façade led to scaffolding near the top. The upper tier is used only by the gods – Mercury in scene 11 and (perhaps) Jupiter in the finale[63] – and so visually reinforces the hierarchical distinction between the characters. An altar apparently always stood in front of the stage building.[64] There was no curtain in early Roman theatre, and the audience, which sat on (probably) wooden benches by Plautus' time, seems to have been separated from the slightly raised platform of the stage by only a small space. Since Roman playwrights had dispensed with the choral interludes of Greek New Comedy and instead featured songs (*cantica*) performed on stage by individual characters, no orchestra separated actors and audience; instead, this area immediately in front of the stage could be taken up by seats, which were formally reserved for

---

[61] Discussion of evidence in Saunders (1913). Plays were performed during at least four festivals in the time of Plautus: the *ludi Romani* and *ludi plebeii* in honour of Jupiter, the *ludi Apollinares*, and the *ludi Megalenses* in honour of the *Magna Mater* (Cybele).

[62] Beacham (1992) 56–85 reconstructs an early Roman theatre.

[63] 1131–43n.

[64] The altar is most often said to be Apollo's, but sometimes belongs to other deities: Duckworth (1952) 83–4. It is not known if a single deity presided over drama at Rome as Dionysus generally did at Athens.

senators from 194 BC on.[65] We do not know precisely how large the stage or the seating area was. Evidence for props in Plautus is fairly scarce; in *Am.*, we hear of a *lanterna* (149), a *patera*, and a *cistellula* (769–78). The artifice and arbitrariness of such a theatrical space is underscored by the prologist at *Men.* 72–3: *haec urbs Epidamnus est dum haec agitur fabula* | *quando alia agetur aliud fiet oppidum.*[66] Thus, there was no concerted effort to create the sense of realistic space to which we are accustomed in the tradition of naturalistic theatre. Instead, Plautine theatre is particularly suited to intimate communication between actors and audience, as well as various improvisatory techniques.[67] Asides to the audience occur with unprecedented frequency in Plautus; the design of the temporary Roman theatre greatly facilitated these, whereas the structure of the Greek theatre itself had encouraged greater distance between actor and audience.[68]

The actors all (probably) wore masks.[69] In the absence of a full visual record, it is difficult to assess the forms and functions of the individual masks. Evidence gleaned from Plautus' plays suggests that the complex and subtle system of masks employed in Greek New Comedy was greatly simplified, with a single, highly caricatured mask being used for each character-type (e.g. *senex*, *leno*, *adulescens*).[70] Thus the audience would instantly recognize boundaries of expected behaviour within which a character might move, though Plautus sometimes deliberately subverts these expectations. And although an actor might invest his mask and role with any number of alluring qualities, the masks, especially grotesque ones like those probably used in Plautine theatre, serve as omnipresent visual reminders of the disjunction between the character and the actor beneath the mask, and therefore of the play's artifice. Costumes also were taken over from Greek New Comedy and a distinct costume was associated with each character type. Style, length, and colour of dress, as well as any accoutrements, were codified according to gender, social

---

[65] Livy 34.44.4–5, 34.54.4; cf. Val. Max. 2.4.3, 4.5.1.

[66] Cf. *Truc.* 1–3 *perparuam partem postulat Plautus loci* | *de uestris magnis atque amoenis moenibus,* | *Athenas quo sine architectis conferat.*

[67] Cf. Slater (1987) 6–8.

[68] Wiles (1991) 52–3.

[69] *CHCL* II 83–4.

[70] See further Wiles (1991) 133–40.

status, and age.[71] For example, the *senex* wore a long white cloak, which stood in sharp visual opposition to the richly coloured one of the *adulescens*, and usually carried a walking-stick (cf. 520). Special measures were taken to accommodate exigencies of specific plots: padding, which probably was not part of the standard costume of the *matrona*, no doubt was used to signal to the audience that Alcmena in *Am.* is pregnant (cf. 667).

These physical circumstances alone suggest that Plautus did not seek to seduce his audience into believing that it was watching a consistent representation of real life. Plautine theatre is an extreme example of drama which can be classified as predominantly 'non-illusory', a term which to varying degrees describes virtually all European theatre up until the naturalistic movement of the late nineteenth century.[72] Judged according to the anachronistic standards of modern theatrical naturalism (which, despite many innovative theatrical movements in the twentieth century, still predominates in popular theatre, film, and television, whether comic or serious), Plautus traditionally has come up short in many critics' estimation:[73] those who bring only 'the linear logic of cause and effect'[74] to Plautus or crave plausible motivation and psychological realism are bound to be disappointed. Plautine theatre is instead driven by a dynamic complex of shifting relationships between the actors themselves, the actors and the audience, and the actor and his role. At the core of these relations is a markedly self-reflexive theatre that constantly looks inward to find humour at its own expense as it simultaneously exposes and exploits its own artifice and convention. As we have seen, the improvisatory and self-conscious techniques of Plautus may owe much to native Italian forms of drama such as Atellan farce and mime.[75]

Before turning to closer analysis of performance in *Am.*, one ele-

[71] See further Duckworth (1952) 88–92 and Wiles (1991) 188–92.

[72] Cf. Styan (1975) 180–223 and Slater (1985) 10–11.

[73] Cf. the notorious condemnation of Norwood (1932) 4. For the persistence of the notion in Plautine scholarship that drama *should* feature consistent characterization and offer moral enlightenment see Wiles (1988) 262–3.

[74] See pp. 18–19 above.

[75] This is not to imply that the Greek dramatic tradition, as Plautus knew it, was not itself theatrically self-conscious. Recent work on Greek tragedy has identified self-reflexiveness as a pervasive feature of the genre and called into question the very notion of a 'dramatic illusion' there: see Easterling

ment merits special consideration: music. In some Plautine manu-
scripts, the headings of scenes include the notations 'DV' (or 'D')
and 'C', abbreviations for *diuerbium* (speech) and *canticum* (song).
These are presumed to reflect an ancient dichotomy between scenes
with and without musical accompaniment. The testimony of ancient
writers about musical presentation is confusing and contradictory,
but there is a modern consensus that three distinct types of delivery
fall within these two groups: spoken verse (iambic senarii), some sort
of 'recitative' (longer iambic and trochaic measures 'chanted' in
company with the *tibia*), and polymetric song (various types, usually
referred to as *mutatis modis cantica*).[76] Thus, as noted above, it appears
that Roman comic playwrights before Plautus converted the plain
trimeters and relatively rare tetrameters of Greek comedy into a
versatile musical system which in and of itself suggests a theatre of
energetic movement. In Plautus, the spoken *senarii* occur less frequently than the recitative trochaic septenarii, the single most common metre, while in Terence the former outnumber the latter
almost 3 : 1. The piper (the Roman *tibia*, like the αὐλός, was played
with a reed and so probably sounded more like a clarinet or oboe
than a 'flute' as it is usually described) who accompanied the recitative and sung measures must have made a considerable aural and
visual impact. A passage in Cicero (*Mur.* 26) suggests that the *tibicen*
moved with the actors on stage. Presumably, stereotyped modes of
playing were associated with specific character-types and scenes.[77]
Plautus' variously constituted polymetric songs are put to a number
of different uses, as those of *Am.* illustrate, where the *cantica* include

(1997) 165–73. But the unmasking of convention and the overt reminders of
the play's fictiveness in which Plautine theatre revels sharply distinguish the
Roman playwright from Menander and bring to mind the theatre of Aristophanes (Plautus apparently lacked access to scripts of Old Comedy). For the
metatheatrical character of popular Italian theatre see pp. 8–11 above.

[76] With the present state of our knowledge there can be little certitude
about even the most general aspects of Plautine music; some doubt the existence of recitative in Roman comedy altogether. Further dispute surrounds
the manner in which the *cantica* were delivered. Some scholars, e.g. Dupont
(1985) 79–80, accept ancient testimony that professional *cantores* came on
stage to sing the *cantica*, presumably leaving the actors to dance or perform
a kind of pantomime. Others, e.g. Duckworth (1952) 363–4, question the
sources and emphasize the awkwardness of staging scenes in this manner.

[77] Dupont (1985) 90.

Sosia's bombastic entrance (153–79), the brilliant messenger's 'speeches' delivered by both Sosia and Bromia (219–47, 1053–73), the so-called *uirtus* monody of Alcmena (633–53), and the contentious duet of Amphitryon and Sosia (551–85b). In the absence of any firm evidence as to the nature of Plautine music and singing techniques, and how these coloured individual scenes, we can only conceive of broad analogies with modern musical comedy or opera. We suspect but cannot prove that dance also was a regular feature of Plautine performance.[78] At any rate, in their musical virtuosity alone Plautus' performances immediately distinguish themselves from the relatively quiet drama of a Menander or a Terence.

In *Am.*, the character of Mercury best illustrates how impersonation, role-play, and theatricality itself move to the forefront in Plautine theatre. In the persona but not the expected costume of the Olympian god of messengers, businessmen, travellers, and tricksters, the actor playing Mercury begins the prologue by entering into negotiations with the audience that are quickly revealed to be aimed at securing a fair hearing for the play (15–16). In this guise he pretends to have been sent by his father 'Jupiter' (19–20), but it is immediately obvious that he is present primarily as the playwright's mouthpiece and the play's advocate. A central concern is the play's genre (50–63):[79] *Am.* was not the sort of comedy to which the audience of the *palliata* was accustomed, and Plautus' *tragicomoedia* may well have been the first performance of a mythological travesty on a Roman stage. By specially preparing the audience for the unusual fare, Mercury seeks to anticipate any possible confusion caused by this exotic form of comedy, which will even take the unusual step of putting Jupiter on stage as a character (86–95). The actor is similarly preoccupied with matters belonging to the province of the theatre rather than the action of the play when he issues a lengthy

---

[78] Cf. *St.* 644–772, *Pers.* 753–858.

[79] A general parallel for Mercury's (re)negotiation of the play's genre is found in Men. *Asp.*, where, following Daos' mistaken report of Kleostratos' death, Tyche enters to assure the audience that in reality nothing 'tragic' (δυσχερές) has occurred (97–8). The issue there is the (apparently) inappropriate seriousness of the subject matter; in *Am.* Mercury explains why figures whose status normally associates them with tragedy ('regal personages and gods') are to appear in a Plautine comedy. See 51–63n.

comic decree against claques (64–85). He does eventually get around to narrating (97–152) the *argumentum* and informs the audience of the circumstances under which he and Jupiter are impersonating Sosia and Amphitryon, though not without drawing special attention to this impersonation as a kind of play-within-the-play (116–19). Towards the end of the prologue, when Mercury assumes his audience's acceptance of the arbitrary conventions used to distinguish the doubles visually (i.e. the *pinnulae* and *torulus* 142–5), he also assumes their complicity in the deception to be carried out against Amphitryon's household. And with his closing assertion that it will be 'worthwhile' for the audience to watch the gods perform as actors (152), Mercury goes beyond merely assuming their sympathies to highlight the larger theatrical frame.[80] Thus, already in the prologue, 'Mercury' has introduced three distinct personae, none of which is ever submerged completely, and whose relative prominence shifts constantly as the play unfolds: that of the Olympian god as known in myth and cult, the god as impersonator of the comic slave Sosia, and the actor who in creating these personae often reflects upon the act of playing itself.

The prologue establishes Mercury as a character who in conjunction with Jupiter relentlessly controls not only the action of the play but also the audience's interpretation of it. Mercury retains this superior vantage-point as the uniquely long opening scene with Sosia (153–462) commences. His presence as an eavesdropper there creates an ideal audience that regards the human characters with ironic detachment and completely undermines any attempt by Sosia to gain the spectators' confidences. Thus, Sosia's initial attempt to win over the audience through the mock-bravado and bombast typically associated with comic slaves is hopelessly doomed: the audience is well

---

[80] The disjunctive humour in associating Olympian gods with the humble art of acting (as it was generally perceived in ancient Rome) is largely lost on modern readers; for Mercury's earlier reference to the lowly status of actors see 26–7n. Neither actor nor audience is allowed to forget their interdependent roles in the making of Plautine performance, as, for instance, when Jupiter reports (867–8) that he has returned for the audience's sake to bring the *comoedia* to an appropriate conclusion, and when Mercury assures the *spectatores* (998) that they will enjoy his mockery of Amphitryon if they are attentive (1006).

aware that an *audacior homo* (in this case a god playing one) lurks in the background and that Sosia surely is not *solus* (153–4) as he believes.[81] Until he finally engages Sosia in the scene, Mercury's asides, which often take the form of stage directions for the benefit of the audience (e.g. 263–4, 295), foil any attempt by Sosia to win sympathy. Mercury remains continuously on stage until verse 543, i.e. for almost the first half of the play; it is not until 551 that the human characters hold the stage by themselves when the hoodwinked slave and incredulous master make their heated entrance.

As we have seen, Mercury's prologue initiates a framework in which the audience is exhorted to act as co-conspirator against the human characters. This is similarly the case when the gods appear alone on stage to address the audience: in each instance, Mercury (scenes 2, 9) and Jupiter (scene 6), like stage-directors, carefully map out each phase of the evolving deception, sometimes as if to reassure the audience that the comedy will reach a 'happy ending' (477–95, 876–9). But beyond this controlling function, Mercury shows himself to be an exceptionally versatile player who can assume virtually any role in the comic repertoire. In the departure scene of Alcmena and Jupiter he attempts, albeit unsuccessfully, to play the role of the *parasitus* (515–21), who in this instance is to assist his 'patron' in his amours.[82] He maniacally parodies the stereotypical comic *seruus currens* (984–90),[83] and then the *seruus frugi* (992–6), the latter instance in mockery of Sosia's similar outburst in the preceding scene (958–61). In the fragmentary scene 11, by abusing the real Amphitryon in the guise of Sosia, Mercury enacts the 'Saturnalian' rout of slaves who (temporarily) triumph over their masters in several Plautine comedies.[84] In the course of the lengthy opening scene he states his in-

---

[81] As the scene continues, Plautus preserves this distance between Sosia and the audience through the frequent use of irony, as when the slave declares (180–4) that the gods have every right to appoint a man to beat him.

[82] For the role see Guilbert (1963).

[83] Mercury's disdain for the *seruolus in comoediis* (987) takes on additional point when we recall that the actor playing the god is probably a slave himself. See further 984–90n.

[84] Cf. Segal's classic study (1987) 99–136, which, despite due criticism of some of its methodology and its excessive dependence on suspect Freudian psychoanalytical models (cf. Wiles (1988) 263–5), remains the most enlightening introduction to the carnival aspects of Plautine theatre. See further pp. 33–6 below.

tent to drive Sosia from the house by employing the conventional resources of the clever slave of New Comedy:[85]

> itaque me malum esse oportet, callidum, astutum admodum,
> atque hunc telo suo sibi, malitia, a foribus pellere.   (268–9)

At this point, an additional frame of play-within-the-play is launched when he frightens Sosia by posing as a street-thug broadcasting his desire for a brawl (300–25). This in turn is followed by his face-to-face impersonation of Sosia, where he finally plays the role of Amphitryon's slave; here he is so adept that he convinces the slave of his own death.[86] Thus, the extent to which *Am.* is ultimately centred on role-playing and stagecraft is well illustrated by these various transformations of role effected by Mercury.[87] In his seemingly boundless energy and movement, and unabating craftiness, the god successfully embodies the quintessential Plautine slave (e.g. Pseudolus), the subaltern who tirelessly furthers the interests of his social betters with little or nothing to gain for himself save enjoyment of the theatrical game.[88] Such esprit is endemic to Plautine comedy, where 'we are constantly invited to see a play about a play'.[89] From a practical standpoint, Mercury's role is an especially challenging one that calls for an actor of unusual comic expertise and versatility, who is able to create the impression of constant improvisation – the sort of role playwrights develop with an accomplished actor in mind.[90]

It should now be evident that *Am.*, like all of Plautus' plays, displays a general indifference to character (in the modern sense), psychology, and strictly symmetrical and logical development of plot.

---

[85] For the typology see Duckworth (1952) 249–53.

[86] See p. 14 above.

[87] Aristophanes was similarly preoccupied with the fictive devices of his comic theatre and not infrequently made these the subject of his plays, as is most clearly seen in *Thesm.* (cf. Zeitlin (1996) 375–416; more generally, Muecke (1977)). Among extant tragedies, Euripides' *Bacch.* best illustrates how theatricality and the power of illusion could become central issues in Attic tragedy (cf. Segal (1997) 215–71).

[88] Cf. Bettini (1991*b*) 24–6.

[89] Muecke (1986) 224.

[90] Such as the famous Roman actor–impresario T. Publius Pellio. Giraudoux fashioned the role of Mercure in *Amphitryon 38* to suit the comic genius of Louis Jouvet (cf. p. 74).

These Plautine tendencies, which constitute deliberate distortions of his Greek models, have traditionally been chalked up to dramaturgical incompetence, or, as Plautus has risen in critical esteem in recent years, the playwright's obsessive desire to secure immediate laughter.[91] The latter view is closer to the mark, though we should also consider Plautine performance within the broader context of non-illusory theatre:

> The drama of logical cause and effect, character and motivation, with which Ibsen is associated, is atypical of what the theatre traditionally has done. The plays of the Greeks, of Shakespeare, of the *Commedia* and Molière were plays of hidden forms, magical results and inner causes, and were thoroughly caught in the seamless web of superstition. Today, with the renewed impulse towards 'poetry of the theatre', the theatre of the absurd, the theatre of cruelty and other manifestations, the stage is assuming its accustomed, illogical role.[92]

One could just as aptly cite the comedies of Plautus as 'thoroughly caught in the seamless web of superstition'. *Am.* is one of the most farcical specimens in the Plautine corpus, and farce is a comic sub-genre that is predisposed to subvert logic, causality, and the norms of everyday life at every possible turn.[93] An illustrative example of how farcically a scene may develop occurs when Amphitryon first arrives home after successful completion of the war against the Teleboans. As he approaches the palace he loudly stresses to Sosia that his wife doubtless will be overjoyed to see him: 654–8 *edepol me uxori exoptatum credo aduenturum domum ... certe enim med illi expectatum optato uenturum scio.* He eventually meets Alcmena and following a bloated third-person salute addresses her directly: 677–9 *ualuistin usque? expectatun aduenio?* Whereas the first query is natural enough, the second is obviously intended to flag for the audience the central conflict around which the scene is to be constructed: Amphitryon will not receive the warm welcome he anticipates because his wife believes he has already returned on the previous night, and this is the critical factor that leads to the charge of adultery. Plautus probably gave no thought to whether or not a husband in real life would

---

[91] E.g. Arnott (1975) 34–7.   [92] Styan (1975) 54.   [93] Cf. Nelson (1990) 157.

place so much emphasis on his wife's anticipation of *his* arrival. Instead, this exchange demonstrates the tendency of Plautine drama to keep the audience's focus on situation rather than character. If it reveals anything about Amphitryon as a character, it is that he is being sketched in typically broad strokes as the conventionally vain comic soldier.[94] In no less typical Plautine fashion, the welcoming motif is rounded off with a joke from Sosia: 680 *expectatum eum salutat magis haud quicquam quam canem.*[95]

The characters of *Am.* themselves frequently acknowledge that they are caught in a confused tangle of wonder and magic. The *mir*-root takes on an incantatory force as it is repeated, primarily by the human characters, twenty-eight times in the play,[96] as, e.g., when Amphitryon fears that the *patera* he was awarded after the battle has somehow found its way to Alcmena:

> enim uero illud praeter alia mira miror maxume,
> si haec habet pateram illam.   (772–3)

Mercury had introduced the theme of wonder in the prologue, where his concern was the audience's reception of a peculiar play featuring Jupiter as a character (29, 86–9) and Mercury in the unusual role of a slave (116). To a limited extent, the audience's state of wonder mirrors that of the human characters, though they by contrast enjoy the guidance of the gods' prologizing addresses throughout the play. The theme of (literal) magic runs throughout *Am.* The classification of the play itself as a *tragicomoedia* is articulated in terms analogous to magic when Mercury jests that he will use his divine powers to transform a tragedy into a comedy, miraculously 'with all the same verses' (53–5). In the magical world of the play, the divine characters, one of whom is a notorious *uorsipellis* or 'skin-

---

[94] 504–5, 655–7nn.

[95] Other examples in which a similar disregard for verisimilitude is evident are numerous. With reference to Sosia's designation of himself as a *uerna* (180) immediately after being termed thus by the eavesdropping Mercury in an aside (176–9), Slater (1990) 109 writes 'the action does not take place within a plane of illusion, but appeals directly to the spectator for approval'.

[96] 29, 86–9, 116, 283, 319, 432, 594–6, 616, 750, 765, 772, 828–9, 858, 954, 1036, 1057, 1080, 1105, 1107, 1117. By contrast, in the other doubles-comedies, *Bac.* and *Men.*, there are only six and nine instances, respectively.

changer' (123), are said to assume (121, 124, 141, 265) and even steal
(458) the *imagines* of their human counterparts; Mercury's assumption of the form and character-type of Sosia in particular is accomplished according to ancient magical belief.[97] Amphitryon accuses
Sosia (605) and Alcmena (777) of being bewitched, and the same
accusation is levelled at him by Mercury as Sosia (fr. 6) and Alcmena
(fr. 8). Plautus cleverly names Alcmena's mute attendant Thessala to
evoke the region of Greece traditionally associated with magic and
witchcraft,[98] and Jupiter gives instructions (976–83) to the absent
Mercury in the manner of a sorcerer.[99] All such instances obviously
underscore the supernatural aspect of the events that take place in
the household,[100] but are also emblematic of Plautine theatre itself,
where deception and enchantment figure so prominently. Amphitryon to a degree beyond all other characters is actively resistant
to the gods' wizardry. In his first entrance, he establishes himself as a
rigorously logical figure who refuses to accept the strange story told
by his more flexibly minded slave:

> quia id quod neque est neque fuit neque futurum est
> mihi praedicas.   (553–4)

> tun me, uerbero, audes erum ludificari?
> tune id dicere audes, quod nemo umquam homo antehac
> uidit nec potest fieri, tempore uno
> homo idem duobus locis ut simul sit?   (565–8)

Amphitryon never discovers by himself the true source of the *ludus*
against him, and although, as we just saw, he in anger occasionally
claims that some form of enchantment is behind all the confusion,
he clings steadfastly to logic and the norms of everyday experience
in insisting to the end that he is merely the dupe of another man's
trick (cf. 1041, 1047). His resistance to the supernatural befits his role
as the play's chief 'blocking character' standing firmly in opposition
to the gods' sexual ruse. The final scenes of *Am.*, in which we learn
of the miraculous birth of the twins and Jupiter appears spectacu-
larly as *deus ex machina*, provide fitting closure to a drama permeated

---

[97] Bettini (1991c) 25–36.   [98] 770n.
[99] Cf. his dismissal of Night at 546–50.   [100] Cf. also 782, 830, 1043.

by magic and miracles, which constantly challenges normative assumptions about appearance and reality.

This pervasive sense of wonder and steadily weakening grasp of what is real are reinforced by a cluster of related ideas repeatedly expressed by the characters. Accusations of madness and desperate claims to sanity become especially rampant (386, 402, 448, 582, 585b, 604, 703–4, 719–20, 727, 730, 753, 789, 844, 904, 929, 1084). The extent to which reason and madness have been confused perhaps is best seen in Amphitryon's assertion that the frantic and bacchantic Bromia alone has a 'sound mind' (1083). In a similar way, conventional distinctions between truth and lying are blurred as characters repeatedly insist that they speak the truth and others are fabricating (366–7, 369, 410–15, 562, 573, 589–91, 687, 736, 901). For Sosia, confusion of fact and fiction involves theatrical metaplay. By his own admission, and in keeping with the stock ethos of the slave of New Comedy, he is a master at deceit and fabrication (197–8, 265–9), and his battle narrative (203–62) neatly illustrates his improvisatory skills;[101] in a Plautine comedy enacted on the purely human plane he and not Mercury would be expected to direct some kind of deception. Still, in the intricate poetic fiction that is his messenger's speech, he manages to hit upon an accurate account of the battle, as Mercury must acknowledge (248–9). But when Sosia reappears with Amphitryon (551–632), the master dismisses as pure fiction all the slave reports as having happened at the house in the opening scene. Though on this occasion Sosia is truly behaving as the *seruus bonus* he claims to be (590), the more insistently he vouches for the veracity of his account, the more vehement become Amphitryon's charges that he is lying. Amphitryon's reaction reflects the conventional relations between master and slave in Plautine comedy: Sosia, he assumes, must be launching some scheme against him (cf. 565, 571, 585a). Thus, the humour in Sosia's predicament here and elsewhere depends upon the manipulation and inversion of comic stereotypes. Other related motifs that recur in the topsy-turvy world of the play include confusion between sleep and/or dreams and wakefulness (297–8, 620–4, 697, 701, 726, 738), drunkenness and sobriety (574–6, 631, 999–1001), and seriousness and jest (906, 920–1, 963–4).

[101] 197–202n.

Irony takes on an important function in a non-illusory performance such as *Am.*; it no less than the more direct forms of audience address (i.e. asides and the various 'prologues' in *Am.*) amounts to privileged communication. Irony is most frequently employed to strengthen the conspiracy against the human characters, while also encouraging the audience to maintain a comic perspective. In reading we may forget that the actor's intonation and gestures would be used to convey irony as explicitly as possible. Most frequently, the gods make a vow or wish, or swear an oath or curse by their own divinity (392, 436–7, 450–1, 933–4). Similarly, the human characters often name Jupiter, Mercury, or the gods collectively (435, 455, 461–2, 569–70, 1022, 1051–2, 1073–4, 1077) in their own oaths and exclamations; examples of this type also occur frequently (739, 780, 799, 822) in what critics have perceived to be the most 'serious' of the extant scenes, the first confrontation between Amphitryon and Alcmena. At a climactic moment there Plautus has Alcmena swear that she has not committed adultery:

> per supremi regis regnum iuro et matrem familias
> Iunonem, quam me uereri et metuere est par maxume,
> ut mi extra unum te mortalis nemo corpus corpore
> contigit, quo me impudicam faceret.   (831–4)

The oath, with all its playful alliteration and assonance, helps the audience preserve the requisite emotional distance on which this farce depends. Alcmena's asseveration of innocence here by Juno and Jupiter, as well as her technically correct and humorous assertion that 'no mortal' except Amphitryon has defiled her body[102] are loud reminders of the central play-within-the-play, and of the fact that this scene no less than any other is part of the gods' intricate theatrical game in which the audience is colluding.[103] Indicative of

---

[102] Jupiter continues this by-play in the subsequent scene of reconciliation between Alcmena and himself when he swears to her that his *uxor* (he avoids the second person pronoun altogether) is *pudica* (932).

[103] Cf. Jupiter's absurd oath (931–4) precisely at the moment Alcmena proposes a divorce (928n.); Amphitryon similarly will bring the house down when he asserts (1051) that neither Jupiter nor all the gods can stop him from entering the palace.

the sophistication of Plautine theatre, irony is taken to further extremes and even occurs at the expense of a god. During the opening scene, Mercury vehemently objects to Sosia's imputation of drunkenness to the celestial divinities allied in the lengthening of the night and expostulates to the audience: 284 *ain uero, uerbero? deos esse tui similis putas?* As readers, we recognize that the chief irony here is that the gods of mythological burlesque are indeed extravagantly human in all their appetites. But from the visual perspective of an audience, the joke is more immediate in that the line is delivered by a divine character, who in his mask, costume, and mannerisms is, save for the *pinnulae* (143), the precise equivalent of the mortal near by on the stage.

In sum, within the intimate confines of Plautine theatre, members of the audience are constantly reminded that they themselves have an essential role in the dynamics of performance, that the play is mere artifice (most often a play about a play), and they are directed to enjoy it from an amoral, comic perspective. The plays themselves and the experience of watching them closely mirror the festival contexts in which they were usually performed. Roman festivals, at least before they themselves became virtually everyday events (as in the empire), seem to have been truly special occasions that indulged the fundamental human desire for imaginative play. During festival time, even the lowest-ranking members of Rome's rigid social order enjoyed some form of empowerment to the extent that hierarchical distinctions might be relaxed; the very fact that the ruling elite held entertainments for the entire populace was an acknowledgment that certain obligations were owed to the lower classes, and that the latter were politically relevant.[104] Plautus warmly embraced the festival licence temporarily granting freer reign to the Roman populace's social fantasies, and his plays are rife with social inversions, the slave's outwitting of his master being one of the most common of these. Signs of the normal hierarchy were not, however, entirely elided in the theatre. Members of the ruling class, outfitted as they were in the trappings of their offices, were highly visible, all the more so

---

[104] Cf. Dupont (1985) 44–5 and Wiles (1991) 60.

after senators were granted special seating.[105] The aggressively self-reflexive style of Plautine theatre ultimately may have had a similar effect. By constantly exposing its theatrical underpinnings, Plautine comedy reminds the audience that the events enacted on stage are only a playful manifestation of the larger *ludi* and have little or no resonance beyond the festival: 'There is no future in Plautus' world, and characters act only for present gratification'.[106] In the final analysis, Plautine comedy seems not to have seriously challenged the conservative Roman social order.[107] In the case of *Am.*, the audience is exhorted to identify with the gods on stage, their co-conspirators, with whom they share and should revel in a position of superior knowledge for the duration of the play. They are invited to enter a thoroughly magical space, a complexly framed and socially fluid world in which an actor of the lowest status[108] may even impersonate the most powerful Roman god, in order to delude a distinguished general and his virtuous wife: 151–2 *erit operae pretium spectantibus | Iouem et Mercurium facere histrioniam*. The blatant transience and self-proclaimed artifice of this theatrical game doubtless made the experience more palliative for the elite to whom Plautus' theatre owed its continued existence, and who under different conditions might have felt threatened.

(c) *Reception and reaction*

Any discussion of how Plautus' audience might have received one of his plays, i.e. why they might have found it to be humorous (or un-

---

[105] Cf. pp. 20–1 above. Seating arrangements probably reflected social stratification long before the formal segregation of 194 BC: Gruen (1992) 205. Cf. also Moore (1994).

[106] Wiles (1991) 62.

[107] Thus the overall conclusion of Segal (1987), but the issue is by no means closed. Sutton (1993) 68 sees a 'sustained subversive attack on Roman paternalism' in Plautus. The degree to which festive comedy can be a socially disruptive force is greatly disputed in anthropological literature, as the rich body of festive comedy found in different societal contexts resists monolithic theorizing. For the issue as it pertains to Old Comedy in democratic Athens see Goldhill (1991) 176–88 (with further references).

[108] Cf. p. 2 above.

humorous), should be prefaced with some precautionary remarks regarding the composition of that audience. References in prologues[109] suggest an extremely diverse body made up of both women and men, slaves and free persons, the socially prominent and the nonentities of Roman society, old and young, rich and poor, married and unmarried: it is obviously misleading to use a monolithic expression such as 'the Roman audience'. The individuals comprising these various groups might have laughed in unison at some aspects of Plautus' plays, though perhaps for different reasons, while on other occasions reactions were mixed. Audience reactions cannot be sorted out systematically here, though the reader is encouraged to consider these on his or her own. The focus will be on aspects of *Am.* that were likely to meet with the broadest crowd approval. If Arnobius' and Prudentius' testimony to revival performances of *Am.* in the late empire is to be trusted, the play must have been a perennial favourite in the Roman comic repertoire.

Theoretical discussions of comedy and laughter have often argued that the great majority of human beings derive pleasure from observing the follies and misfortunes of others, and that perhaps even something in our physiological programming encourages us to enjoy a position of relative superiority.[110] Our experience suggests that there is much to recommend this unflattering hypothesis about ourselves, but we also must realize that such over-simplified formulations cannot account for all types of humour. Other approaches (as Freud's) privilege the cathartic nature of humour. According to such views, some of the favourite targets for laughter tend to be our most sacred institutions and most deeply held cultural values, and an occasional jest at the expense of these brings much-needed release from the everyday anxiety associated with adhering to their supporting morality and ideologies. This human desire to be free from social control probably accounts for much of the psychological appeal of festive comedy. Apropos of *Am.*, the fundamental institution of marriage has been a seemingly universal target of humour throughout

---

[109] See esp. *Poen.* 16–35.
[110] Concise discussion in Nelson (1990) 1–18.

the world. As noted above,[111] theorists debate whether this type of laughter is socially destructive or simply reinforces the existing social order. Both are possible in given situations and societies, but the latter seems to apply more accurately to Plautine comedy, which within the festival context of the Roman *ludi* revels only in a temporary 'flouting of the rules':[112] few would argue that *Am.* contributed directly to soaring rates of adultery and divorce in Rome. Instead, it is more productive to approach *Am.* as a kind of cultural mediation with respect to the institution of marriage.

Critics have long tended to exaggerate the uniqueness of *Am.* But readers only casually acquainted with Plautus will immediately recognize the same sorts of verbal exuberance, comic motifs, and techniques as those found in his other plays. Furthermore, the plot, despite its unparalleled mythic dimension, diverges far less from a fundamental Plautine storyline than is usually assumed. In a stimulating narratological study of Plautus following the model of Greimas, Bettini argues that a basic opposition between possession and desire is played out in the comedies,[113] and the plots can be reduced to a pattern whereby goods are to be transferred from one party to another. The plays may thus be said to articulate two basic themes: 'the distribution of women' and the 'distribution of wealth'. In several plays a female character is to be 'transferred' from an 'opponent' (or antagonist) to a 'receiver', usually an *adulescens* who plots with his 'helpers' (whose cohort includes the clever slave) to 'confiscate' a beloved *meretrix* from an opponent, usually a pimp or a soldier. The transfer is often effected by means of a calculated deception that involves the transgression of social norms, e.g. a sum of money is extorted from a *senex*. *Am.* immediately presents several

[111] P. 34 n. 107.

[112] Segal (1987) 14.

[113] Bettini (1991*b*); for his analysis of the plot of *Am.* (slightly different from that here) see Bettini (1991*b*) 43–5. Though Bettini's pursuit of an underlying 'anthropology' of Plautine comedy informed by Roman cultural codes and ideologies is often illuminating, it has rightly drawn criticism, especially in its treatment of individual plays (cf. the review of Lowe (1994)), and as Wiles (1991) 32 notes, generally suffers from its 'failure to distinguish text from performance'.

challenging variations of this pattern. First, the *meretrix* is replaced by a *matrona* whose husband functions as the antagonist in resisting Jupiter's desire to enjoy an adulterous relationship with his wife. Critics usually assume that Jupiter, in imitation of Amphitryon and his warrior ethos, is costumed as a vigorous young *miles*, but references in the text clearly indicate that the doubles wore the mask of a *senex*.[114] The apparent anomalies raised by the pair's costuming are obviated somewhat when we note that the audience has been encouraged to imagine (104–6) a more youthful Jupiter beneath his mask, and Amphitryon, like the stereotypical *senex* of many other Plautine comedies, effectively functions as the 'enemy of pleasure' in resisting Jupiter's seduction of Alcmena. Mercury's role in the plot is less problematic; as we have seen, he serves as a ready helper in Jupiter's amorous pursuit. So although the presence of a god – a critical element in making the act of adultery palatable – and the pursuit of a legitimately married woman rather than a *meretrix* complicate the particulars here, the audience would at least recognize a recurring plot structure built around 'the distribution of women'. But this is not to imply that the variations in *Am.* are without significance. While it is true that both Alcmena and Amphitryon receive compensation – painless parturition, as well as fame and glory through association with Jupiter and Hercules – the play does in fact portray the single (extant) instance of successfully consummated adultery in the *palliata*. How exactly is this potentially discomfiting subject moulded into the stuff of a successful comedy? To address this question, let us turn from abstract structures to concrete aspects of performance.

The character of Alcmena is critical to any assessment of the play's reception. As there is inherent unfairness in the gods' treatment of her (as is also the case for Amphitryon), modern critics have tended to sentimentalize her role, even going so far as to regard her as an Antigone among buffoons: 'Whenever Alcmena appears, P. forgets his clowning and the tone changes to something not unworthy of tragedy, a high seriousness such as would befit a Roman ma-

---

[114] See further 1072n.

tron. P. makes free with the gods and the general, but is overawed
by the ideal wife and mother.'[115] Such a view seems utterly foreign to
the spirit of this sex farce. First of all, deprived as we are of the
spectacle of performance, we must never forget that Alcmena is
pregnant: 'On stage, the pregnant woman is an irresistibly comic
figure; nature has caught her out.'[116] Before she ever appears, Mercury repeatedly apprises the audience of her condition (102–11, 479–
80), and at her entrance Jupiter's words sharply focus the audience's
attention on what is visually obvious:

> bene uale, Alcumena, cura rem communem, quod facis;
> atque inperce quaeso: menses iam tibi esse actos uides.

(499–500)

Plautus' Alcmena is the only character in extant Greek and Roman
drama to appear pregnant on stage. According to a well-attested
convention of New Comedy, pregnant women are not seen but only
heard as they are imagined to give birth offstage. And Plautus' audience was cognizant that the role of the pregnant Alcmena was being
played by a man (as were all female roles).[117] Even if the use of
masks largely neutralized the disjunction between the actors' gender
and that of the female characters portrayed, the spectacle of the
male actor extending the usual bounds of cross-dressing in Roman
comedy in order to simulate female fecundity itself probably coloured the audience's view of the character. It is easy to imagine the
male actor embracing this unusual role with gusto, as would be im-

[115] Sedgwick *ad* Act II, sc. ii (p. 103); in *CHCL* II 109–10, she is said to be
'presented powerfully as a tragic heroine'.

[116] Nelson (1990) 58–9; cf. Phillips (1985).

[117] In addition to comparing our own experience as spectators of comedy
in which males assume female roles, we should recall that the representation
of women by men is explicitly made a source of (mostly obscene) humour in
Plautus when Chalinus impersonates Casina in the famous play-within-the
play of *Cas.*: see further Gold (1998). For the controversial thesis that the portrayal of women by men in Aristophanes was not simply an accepted convention but constituted a kind of self-conscious 'drag-show' see Taaffe (1993),
along with the circumspect review of Gilbert (1995). Comparisons with the
Elizabethan stage, where Shakespeare's actors sometimes explicitly draw attention to the transvestism of their roles (e.g. Rosalind in *As You Like It*), are
also instructive.

mediately evident in his intonation and gestures.[118] Not content with
the visual effects of a grotesquely padded figure on stage, Plautus
keeps his audience focused on the pregnancy through a barrage of
jokes that turn on Alcmena's condition.[119]

Plautus did not want his audience to reflect on any possible 'tragic'
implications of Alcmena's situation; controlling dramatist that he is,
he leaves little doubt on this point. The gods cavalierly and crudely
describe Jupiter's sexual dalliance in the language of finance, as
when both Jupiter (980–1) and Mercury (498) designate her as the
supreme god's *uxor usuraria*, his 'wife on loan'. In the prologue, Mercury tells the audience that Jupiter 'has borrowed her body' (108),
and the king of the gods says the same (1135–6) to Amphitryon at the
play's conclusion. Finance was central to Roman life, and many
Plautine protagonists, in keeping with the topsy-turvydom of festival-
time, display an irreverent and atypically Roman attitude towards
money.[120] Not surprisingly, the language of finance permeates Plautus' plays. The prologue of *Am.* in fact opens (1–16) with an elaborate *quid pro quo* in which Mercury promises continued *lucrum* in
exchange for the audience's granting the play a fair hearing. The
theme of finance thus is put in the foreground from the very opening. But in the fantasy world of *Am.* everyday transaction is magically transformed into divine seduction; while the forum is closed
during the festival, on the Plautine stage Jupiter conducts erotic
business of the most ridiculous sort. And critics who see genuine
tragedy in Alcmena's situation should also note that in the play there
looms the prospect of divorce, not death, as in the tragic tradition,[121]
and Roman-style divorce was fundamentally an exchange of property: 928 *tibi habeas res tuas, reddas meas*. In a similar vein, Amphitryon
in the end assesses the whole situation as a kind of financial exchange in which he bears no resentment at sharing 'half his largess'

---

[118] He might, for example, proudly stroke his belly as Jupiter speaks at
499–500 (quoted immediately above). Elsewhere in Plautus, pregnancy is a
vehicle for absurd and no doubt highly visual humour, as when the conventionally plump *leno* Cappadox asserts that he must be carrying twins (*Cur.* 221)
and the voracious and imaginative parasite Gelasimus paradoxically claims
that an 'enormous hunger' has been gestating inside him for over ten years
(*St.* 155–70).

[119] 654–86on.   [120] Segal (1987) 53–69.   [121] See pp. 47–9 below.

(1125 *boni dimidium*) with Jupiter. But while the play temporarily distracts the audience's minds from 'business as usual', the actors themselves may have been engaged in fierce competition for remuneration: this would explain the urgency of Mercury's lengthy decree against actors who organize claques (64–85). The same may be true for the playwright and producer, who, even if not rewarded directly for success, certainly held vested interests in securing future contracts with the aediles who sponsored the public festivals.[122]

Plautus not only sharply highlights the carnal nature of the affair from Jupiter's perspective, but also endows the character of Alcmena with an interest in sexuality that directly conflicts with the public persona of a *matrona*; by Roman standards she is a voluptuary.[123] In the prologue the audience learns that the night has been artifically lengthened so that Jupiter may maximize his sexual pleasure (113–14). In the opening scene Sosia had quipped (287–8) that the hiring of an expensive prostitute on such a night would turn out to be a good bargain; Mercury's immediate approval (289–90) of Jupiter's dalliance with Alcmena clearly places the affair in the context of just such a transaction. Yet in her first appearance Alcmena melodramatically laments the false Amphitryon's imminent departure: 'you're leaving me before the place on the couch where you were lying had a chance to heat up' (513). This was in response to Jupiter's exasperated and ironic question, 'Isn't is enough for you (509 *satin habes ...?*) if there's no woman whom I love as much as I do you?' The notion of sexual satiety, up to this point relevant to Jupiter alone (472), develops into a leitmotiv for the pregnant Alcmena. She next appears to deliver her famous song (633 *satin parua res est uoluptatum ...*), which critics have almost universally judged to

---

[122] For matters of production see *CHCL* II 80–4; for financial opportunites Lebek (1996) 29–48. We know regrettably little about the competitive and remunerative aspects of early Roman theatre, which, as suggested by both the prologues of Plautus (in their aggressive promotion of the plays) and Terence (in their constant dialogue with other playwrights), were probably considerable.

[123] Noted by Segal (1987) esp. 180–4. For the figure of the *matrona*, traditionally idealized as chaste, faithful, and obliging to her husband, focused on the home, and always dignified in public see Treggiari (1991) 229–61. Women are stereotypically described as sexually insatiable in Aristophanes, e.g. *Ec.* 225–8, *Lys.* 21–5.

rival sublime passages of Greek tragedy.[124] As readers, we must take care not to be overly impressed by the broad generalizations of 633–41 and lose sight of the context. Alcmena's primary topic is the relative infrequency of 'pleasures'[125] in life. She quickly reveals that her general reflections arise from her particular situation: she has been granted *uoluptas* for only a short while (638), since she has been able to be with her 'husband' *for one night only* (639), i.e. the extraordinarily long night of sex with Jupiter. So while the rhetorical form of her reflections may evoke tragic models, the content certainly does not. The central motif of *satietas* continues in the second half of her song when she asserts that she would be satisfied (646 *satis mi esse ducam*) at her husband's public acclamation. She then launches into enthusiastic praise of *uirtus*, which (reflecting Plautus' love of wordplay) is prompted by her use of the word *uir* in the previous verse.[126] The words printed on the page do not necessarily suggest satire, but here as much as anywhere else in the play we rue our ignorance of delivery and music (and dance?). What kind of tone was the actor to lend to the key word *uirtus*, a concept exceedingly familiar to the audience from aristocratic memorials and so possibly ripe for parody?[127] Did the musical syntax and the playing of the *tibicen* by themselves undermine any conveyance of genuine *grauitas*? But however one construes the tone of the song, Alcmena's reflections on *uirtus* have a pointed comic purpose, for she is exalting the very sort of military valour her returning husband can claim as his own thanks to his success against the Teleboans. Amphitryon confirms this immediately after her song ends:

> edepol me uxori exoptatum credo aduenturum domum,
> quae me amat, quam contra amo, praesertim re gesta bene,
> uictis hostibus: quos nemo posse superari ratust,
> eos auspicio meo atque ductu primo coetu uicimus.   (654–7)

---

[124] E.g., Oniga *ad loc.*, Hunter (1985) 126; the chief dissenters are Perelli (1983) 388–91 and Phillips (1985).

[125] A form of *uoluptas* occurs four times in the space of nine verses. Previously in the play, the noun had been used only to refer to Jupiter's sexual gratification (114).

[126] For possible punning on *uirtus* see 648–53n.

[127] See 75n.

Once again, we see Plautus giving loud notice of the central conflict of the scene to follow:[128] the *uirtus* encomium further highlights the fact that Amphitryon can reasonably expect his wife's welcome to be all the warmer because of his victory. But he cannot know that Jupiter has stolen all his thunder by impersonating him on the previous night. This last part of Alcmena's song, then, is designed primarily to set up, in typically broad and farcical Plautine strokes, the pivotal scene built upon the imperfect homecoming. This becomes all the more evident when we recall that Amphitryon (with Sosia) remains on stage during her song and so the immediate effect of Alcmena's celebration of *uirtus* is to underscore the expectations of the triumphant general as he approaches his palace. As husband and wife prepare – with sharply contraposed degrees of enthusiasm – to meet (654–75), the effect is not unlike that achieved in cinema and television through the use of a split screen. And here finally the motif of *satietas* is playfully capped with Sosia's jest about Alcmena's pregnancy when he quips that he and Amphitryon must have missed the midday meal: 667 *Alcumenam ante aedis stare saturam intellego.*

Alcmena is caricatured as no less a voluptuary when she recounts to Amphitryon the intimate details of her evening with Jupiter, at times employing some of Plautus' most playful language, e.g. 735 *immo mecum cenauisti et mecum cubuisti* (cf. 799–808). And there are unmistakable comic ironies even when, in the course of her defence, she appears as a spokesperson for the values traditionally associated with the idealized *matrona*:

> non ego illam mi dotem duco esse, quae dos dicitur,
> sed pudicitiam et pudorem et sedatum cupidinem,
> deum metum, parentum amorem et cognatum concordiam,
> tibi morigera atque ut munifica sim bonis, prosim probis.

(839–42)

Though under entirely innocent circumstances, technically Alcmena has compromised her *pudicitia et pudor* in her relations with Jupiter, whom Mercury proudly acclaims a *moechus* in the prologue (135; cf. 1049 *adulterum*). And we have just seen to what lengths Plautus goes to show that her *cupido* is anything but restrained. Mention of rever-

---

[128] Cf. pp. 28–9 above.

ence for the gods in this context is patently ironic, especially after her recent oath (831-4).[129] Alcmena's traditional assertion of her indulgence toward her husband (842 *morigera tibi*) echoes language Mercury had used regarding Jupiter's own sexual gratification: 131 *pater nunc intus suo animo morem gerit* and 277 *gere patri morem meo.*[130] Moreover, the interloping Sosia's immediate comment (843), which Nixon translates 'My word! She's a regular pattern of perfection, if she's telling the truth', seems to undermine any possible *grauitas* here and suggests that her lines were melodramatically delivered. We do not know for certain that the male actors who portrayed women in Roman comedy employed falsetto, but a passage in Quintilian (*Inst.* 11.3.91) criticizing comic actors for using an *effeminata uox* in inappropriate circumstances suggests that this may have been a normal practice.[131] In short, it is difficult to see how Plautus' Alcmena is meant to be portrayed as a heroine of tragic proportions who straightforwardly embodies the highest ideals of female *pietas*. There is simply too much irony and cross-chatter – and, probably, stage business – to support the idea that her words here 'far transcend the limits of comedy'.[132] When Mercury dubbed the play a *tragicomoedia*, the primary sense was that the play is a mythological travesty and therefore will combine characters associated with both genres (*reges, di*, and a *seruos*), not that serious and comic elements will be uncomfortably fused together.[133] Alcmena does not somehow stand apart from Plautus' festive assault on Roman marriage; female marital fidelity was regulated by the most severe social strictures in Rome, and by appointing a sexually caricatured figure such as Alcmena to

[129] See p. 32 above.

[130] In a later scene, Jupiter again picks up the motif: *uolo deludi illunc, dum cum hac usuraria | uxore nunc mi morigero* (980-1). See further 842n.

[131] Cf. the two courtesans' discovery of each other at *Rud.* 233-4 as the result of hearing a *uox muliebris*. We can easily imagine Chalinus (as Casina) using falsetto in such a line as *Cas.* 978 *non amas me?* (addressed to Lysidamus).

[132] Sedgwick on 839-42.

[133] See 51-63n. This is not to suggest that serious and comic elements could not coexist in New Comedy (as they most clearly do in several plays of Menander and Terence) and that Romans could not have come to the theatre with the expectation that such a fusion was possible. The present discussion maintains that the persistent identification of tragic elements in *Am.* may simply be the result of the failure of modern scholars to consider all aspects of performance.

champion its cause, Plautus invites his audience to ease their anxi-
eties through laughter.

The cuckolding of Amphitryon has also disturbed post-classical
readers, and some of the play's adapters made him far less amenable
than Plautus' character at the end of the play.[134] But Plautus actively
discourages his audience from seriously pondering the couple's
future: Jupiter twice reassures them (867–72, 1141–2) that husband
and wife will reconcile and resume their accustomed *concordia*, and,
whereas Amphityron had earlier denied being her *uir* (813; cf. 729n.),
in the last line of the play he explicitly acknowledges Alcmena as his
uxor (1145). Thus the play exploits an ambiguous, divinely determined situation where adultery is and still is not quite adultery; as a
god Jupiter is able to realize the fantasy of Lysidamus in *Cas.* with
impunity. And the mythic couple, clearly assimilated by Plautus to
some of the most distinguished personages of Roman society (i.e. the
ambitious aristocratic general and the noble *matrona*) can be sub-
jected to the erotic escapades of an openly lecherous (cf. 104–6, 113–
14, 891–2, 980–1) god. The audience, though members of a society
with notoriously strong sanctions against acts of adultery involving a
free citizen's wife, can temporarily revel in the violation of one of its
strictest taboos. Marriage once again finds itself as the target of malicious laughter: 'In ... bedroom farce, we savour the adventure of
adultery, ingeniously exaggerated in the highest degree, and all
without taking responsibility or suffering the guilt.'[135] Mercury even
goes so far as to recommend his father's behaviour to the audience:

> amat: sapit; recte facit, animo quando obsequitur suo,
> quod omnis homines facere oportet, dum id modo fiat bono.
>
> (995–6)

Surely, this is a carnival fantasy, and Mercury is not sincerely advocating adultery in the Roman sense of the concept.[136] In the end,

---

[134] See p. 72 below.   [135] Bentley (1966) 229.

[136] In the Roman moral tradition, extra-marital relations between a married man and a slave or prostitute were acceptable, provided he did not incur
significant financial losses and damage his reputation as a result. This is
probably the point of Mercury's vague qualifier *dum id modo fiat bono*; cf. *Cur.*
34–8, *Mer.* 1021–3, and Hor. *S.* 1.2. For the Roman 'double-standard' in general see Treggiari (1991) 299–319.

Jupiter steps away from his dalliance and suggests that all has un-
folded with a view to the procreation of the heroic Hercules, though
he cannot resist one last reference in Amphitryon's presence to the
carnality of his affair with Alcmena (1135–6). It may seem incredible
to some readers that Amphitryon acquiesces so easily and promises
to perform a sacrifice to his former rival, but the entire focus of the
performance is on the farcical (and festive) situation, not the exploration of discordant undertones; we also have seen that harmonious
yet arbitrary endings are paradigmatically comic.[137] Though this
discussion has deliberately emphasized the farcical character of
Plautus' presentation, the question of whether or not some members
of an ancient audience might have found certain elements in the
play troubling should remain open; centuries later adapters such as
Kleist virtually turned *Am.* into a tragedy.[138] It is none the less hoped
that it has been convincingly argued here that at least some of the
serious elements perceived by modern scholars to exist in the play
may be illusory, and have arisen from readings of the play too far
removed from the original spectacle of performance: 920–1 *si quid
dictum est per iocum,* | *non aequom est id te serio praeuortier.*

4. BACKGROUND AND SOURCES

(a) *The myth*

The story of Zeus's impregnation of Alkmene and the subsequent
birth of Herakles is of great antiquity, and belongs to the densely
populated catalogue of Zeus's amours. These myths in general reflect the desire of various localities to establish a connection with the
Indo-European sky god[139] and also illustrate 'the rules of an extreme
patriarchal family order which permits the dominant male all freedom'.[140] The story is referred to (in an allusive manner suggesting its
familiarity) by Agamemnon at *Il.* 19.95–133 within a speech intended
to illustrate that even Zeus is subject to *Ate.* At issue there is the

---

[137] See pp. 17–18 above.   [138] See pp. 73–4 below.

[139] The story of the warrior Herakles' conception by divine visitation may
owe its ultimate origin to Egyptian royal legitimacy myth: cf. Stärk (1982)
285–7 (with further references).

[140] Burkert (1985) 129.

deception of Zeus by Hera, who manages to ensure the eventual
sovereignty of Eurystheus over Herakles by delaying Alkmene's parturition and accelerating that of the unnamed 'wife of Sthenelos',
who gives birth to Eurystheus prematurely at seven months. An even
briefer notice occurs at *Od.* 11.266–8 when Odysseus recounts that in
Hades he saw Alkmene, 'the wife of Amphitryon, who bore mighty,
lion-hearted Herakles after she lay in the arms of great Zeus'.[141]

It is the *Scutum* attributed to Hesiod but usually dated to the sixth
century that provides the first detailed narrative (1–54) of the affair of
Zeus and Alkmene.[142] Here we learn that after he killed Alkmene's
father in some sort of dispute over oxen, the Argive Amphitryon
took refuge in Thebes with her, though she refused to consummate
their marriage until he had avenged the death of her brothers at the
hand of the Taphians and Teleboans, and so Amphitryon launched
an expedition against them. Zeus meanwhile, according to the [*Sc.*]
account, has developed a powerful passion (31) for Alkmene, who is
outstanding among mortal women in beauty, stature, and intellect
(4–6). He therefore devises a stratagem one night (30–4) to gain
access to Alkmene's bed, presumably appearing in the guise of
Amphitryon, though this is not stated explicitly. Zeus sleeps with
Alkmene on the same night that Amphitryon is to return from the
successfully completed campaign against the Taphians and Teleboans (35–8). Amphitryon is portrayed as being most eager (39–45)
to reach Thebes and reap the benefits of his success. There, without
any mention of the confusion that would arise from his arrival for a
second time, Amphitryon spends the rest of the night (46) with his
wife. As a result of this busy night Alkmene is impregnated by both
Zeus and her husband. After an unspecified time (presumably the
usual ten months by the ancient manner of reckoning)[143] she gives

[141] Cf. Hes. *Th.* 943–4.

[142] The discovery, in the Forum Boarium, of a terracotta statue group (*c.*
530 BC) depicting Athena and Herakles suggests that the latter's myths may
also have found their way to Rome at a very early date: see Feeney (1998) 51.

[143] The early fifth-century historian Pherecydes of Athens is credited with
a version of the birth in which both Herakles and Iphikles were delivered
prematurely at seven months (*FGrH* 3 F 13c). Typically, Herakles is a ten-
months baby, and apart from the passage just noted, is said to be born after a
pregnancy of seven months only at *Am.* 482. Cf. n. 146 below.

birth to twins: from Zeus's seed Herakles, and by Amphitryon Iphikles, who is destined to be a weaker and lesser man than his half-
brother (50–2). We hear nothing from the [*Sc.*] poet regarding the
circumstances surrounding the birth, but a full account of the snakes
sent by Hera and their strangulation by the baby Herakles is found
first at Pind. *Nem.* 1.33–50.[144] Other motifs of the story are attested
in early classical authors: the means of deception by impersonation
is explicit in Pindar (*Nem.* 10.10–17) and Charon of Lampsacus (*FGrH*
262 F 2); Charon also attests to a cup presented by Jupiter to
Alkmene in the course of the impersonation;[145] the lengthening of
the night is attested first in Pherecydes.[146]

(b) *Prior dramatic treatments*

Thus, by the fifth century the well-known Zeus–Alkmene–
Amphitryon story had much to recommend it to dramatic poets,
both tragic and comic. A tragic poet could focus on such elements as
Alkmene's fidelity, and explore such themes as divine intervention in
human affairs, and appearance and reality. By contrast, the nocturnal visitation of an amorous Zeus to Alkmene's bed would readily
lend itself to the comic stage, where deception and adultery are
familiar topics.[147] Each of the three most famous Athenian trage-

[144] The event seems to follow immediately upon Herakles' birth in Pindar
(as in Plautus); elsewhere, several months separate the birth and the killing of
the snakes, e.g. Apollod. *Bibl.* 2.4.8.

[145] Cf. Pausanias 5.18.3. Pherecydes may have recounted a version (*FGrH* 3
F 13 b/c) of the story which included the impersonation, the gift, and the
lengthened night, though the interpretation of his account is fraught with
difficulties: see Stärk (1982) 280–1.

[146] *FGrH* 3 F 13. If *Am.* 481–2 are not interpolated, then Plautus' play assumes that Jupiter visited Alcmena seven months before (cf. 107–9) and that
the traditional long night of the hero's conception has been transferred to the
one prior to his birth, i.e. the dramatic time as the play opens. The conflation
of the two nights allows Plautus to put an extremely pregnant Alcmena on
stage and renders the lecherous character of Jupiter all the more farcical (but
see 481–2n.).

[147] One should avoid dogmatism, however, in distinguishing the tragic and
comic elements. For the range of possible treatments in ancient drama see
Prescott (1913) 15–18.

dians may have treated the myth.[148] For the existence of Aeschylus'
Alkmene we have only the testimony of Hesychius (*s.v.* ἀποστάς), but
since the play is not included in the list given by the Medicean
manuscript, he has been doubted. Nor do the scant remains of
Sophocles' *Am.* (122–4 Radt) provide us with any indication at all as
to its subject matter. And if Accius' *Am.* was adapted from this play,
there is no consensus regarding its plot.[149] Much more can be determined about Euripides' *Alkmene* and we are in a much better position
to assess its possible relevance to Plautus. A general outline of Euripides' play is made possible through its relatively substantial fragments (88–104 Nauck), which are supplemented by vase evidence.[150]
The plot may be summarized as follows: Amphitryon somehow becomes convinced of his wife's infidelity and violently confronts her,
whereupon she seeks sanctuary at an altar. With a companion identified as Antenor on one vase he pursues Alkmene there, creates a
pyre around the altar, and ignites it.[151] At this climactic moment a
rainstorm[152] is sent to extinguish the flames and Zeus appears as *deus
ex machina* in order to resolve the conflict. From this outline, it can
be deduced that Euripides' *Alkmene* took place upon Amphitryon's
return from the battle with the Taphians and Teleboans, either on

[148] There is also testimony for plays entitled *Alkmene* by Ion of Chios, Dionysius the Elder, and Astydamas the Younger, but nothing substantive is
known about these treatments.

[149] Cf. 45–61 W = *TRF* 169–72. Ribbeck (1875) 553–60 noted that there
are at least three possibilities: (1) the wooing of Alcmena by Amphitryon and
the death of her father; (2) the episode (cf. Apollod. *Bibl.* 2.4.7) in which Comaetho betrayed her father Pterelaus to Amphitryon, who then put her to
death; (3) treatment of the *Herakles Mainomenos* theme. None the less, Webster
(1953) 86–97 assumed a central role for Sophocles' play in the creation of
Plautus' Greek original, a view that Sedgwick (Intro. pp. 2–6) embraced with
only a small measure of reluctance.

[150] For the pictorial evidence see Trendall and Webster (1971) 76–7.

[151] In connection with the vase evidence see fr. 90 Nauck.

[152] That such a storm was somehow represented on stage and not simply
described in a messenger's speech is suggested by the metatheatrical jest at
Rud. 85–7 *detexit uentus uillam – quid uerbis opust?* | *non uentus fuit, uerum Alcumena
Euripidi,* | *ita omnis de tecto deturbauit tegulas.* Presumably, the speaker refers to a
recent adaptation on the Roman stage, whose storm scene had made a lasting
impression. For the view that the adaptation was Ennius' see Skutsch (1968)
179–81.

the long night of Herakles' conception or on the next morning, as the appearance of Eos on one vase strongly suggests. Alkmene would have incurred her husband's wrath in one of two ways: either she failed to greet him in the warm and congratulatory manner he expected, and upon further questioning mentioned that she had already slept with him,[153] or she surprised him by appearing pregnant (the pictorial evidence is inconclusive on this point). If the latter scenario is correct, we must assume that Euripides followed the version as in [Sc.], according to which Alkmene and Amphitryon had not yet consummated their marriage.

Two comedies, *Nyx makra* (frs. 89–94 K–A, *PCG* vii 469–71) by the Athenian comic playwright Plato, and Rhinthon's *Am.*,[154] have received serious consideration as immediate or remote influences on Plautus.[155] On the basis of the title and a fragment (90 K–A) which has suggested to some the lantern that Sosia carries in the opening scene of *Am.*, it has been argued that Plato's play, if not the original itself, was the inspiration for a later Greek comic poet whom Plautus followed.[156] The fragments, however, do not even demonstrate that the conception of Herakles was the subject of Plato's play. One (91 K–A) seems to describe a procession at night which does not readily harmonize with the mythical night of Herakles' conception, but instead suggests an Attic nocturnal festival; the latter was a regular setting in classical Greek Comedy.[157] Our knowledge of Rhinthon's *Am.* is even more limited.[158] The Suda (*s.v.* 'Ρίνθων) describes the playwright as follows: 'of Tarentum, comic poet, founder of the

[153] Cf. Apollod. *Bibl.* 2.4.8.

[154] Testimony in Olivieri (1946–7) 8–10 = *CGF* i 185. Rhinthon's *floruit* is set at the beginning of the third century.

[155] A third play that has been mentioned in connection with Plautus is the *Am.* of the Old Comedy poet Archippus (frs. 1–7 K–A, *PCG* ii pp. 539–40). The fragments reveal almost nothing; from a citation by Athenaeus (499b) we may possibly infer the role of a cup such as the *patera* in Plautus' play.

[156] Thus Sedgwick, Intro. pp. 4–6.

[157] Cf. Stärk (1982) 300–1. In New Comedy, Athenian virgins are raped typically in connection with nocturnal festivals (e.g. *Sam.* 38–49), a nod to verisimilitude in that these afforded one of the few opportunities for them to leave the house in everyday life.

[158] For the popular *phlyax* drama of southern Italy, which is broadly reconstructed through the evidence of vases, see pp. 10–11 above.

genre called *hilarotragoedia*, which is a *phlyax* composition ...', while
Stephanus Byzantius (*s.v.* Τάρας) records, 'Rhinthon of Tarentum,
phlyax-playwright, remodeller of tragic subjects into something
comic'. Since mythological burlesque long predates Rhinthon, either
he is incorrectly labelled the *primus inuentor* of the genre or he composed a distinct form of 'mixed' drama about which we can only
hazard guesses. Titles attributed to him suggest he regularly burlesqued Euripides. The assertion that he refashioned tragedy into comedy none the less is possibly relevant to Plautus' *Am.*, and, not surprisingly, Rhinthon's description of *hilarotragoedia* has been associated
with Mercury's coinage of the term *tragicomoedia*. Unfortunately, the
single extant citation from Rhinthon's *Am.* reveals nothing about his
treatment of the story. If, however, a South Italian vase depicts a
scene from this or a similar *phlyax* play,[159] we can get some idea of
the nature of the performance. There a grossly padded Hermes
holding a lantern guides an elderly Zeus, who supports a ladder,
toward an upper-storey window in which can be seen a majestic
female figure, often assumed to be Alcmena.[160] Rather than using
impersonation to reach the figure, Zeus in this scene apparently
launches a direct nocturnal assault: on the face of things, this play
would be very different from Plautus'.

(c) The theories

We can assume that in both Attic and southern Italian theatre
there were many more dramatic treatments of the Zeus–Alkmene–
Amphitryon story than those just outlined. Virtually all the latter
prove to be very unpromising candidates as sources for Plautus' *Am.*:
a responsible account of possible sources for *Am.* should stress that
the issue is far from settled. The problem of sources has been rigorously pursued, generally on the grounds that it is an important
one for literary history, though the value of the research has varied
tremendously. Whereas earlier scholarship focused more on re-

---

[159] Fig. 484 in Bieber (1961) 132. On the basis of chronology alone, the
identification is by no means certain.

[160] The figure is not labelled, and could be any one of a number of
heroines, e.g. Danaë as Stewart (1958) 369–70 suggests.

constructing the lost Greek originals, contemporary inquiry into Plautus' sources aims at further illuminating his *modus operandi* as an adapter. The discussion here will outline and assess the major trends, while still maintaining that with our present knowledge there can be little certitude regarding Plautus' manner of composing *Am.*

The most common assumption is that *Am.*, like all of Plautus' plays, must be based on a text (or texts) of Greek New Comedy.[161] It is the case that when, in eight of the plays, the audience is informed of the author and/or title of the source play in the prologue, these do belong to Greek New Comedy. A few other Plautine plays are plausibly matched with Greek New Comedy sources, and the sources revealed for Terence's plays likewise belong to this genre. In fact, the names of Menander, Diphilus, and Philemon recur most frequently as sources for the Roman comedies. For several of Plautus' plays, however, we do not know his specific sources. Though a full-scale mythical travesty such as *Am.* is otherwise unattested in extant New Comedy, those advocating the *communis opinio* that its source should belong here stress broad similarities in dramatic technique, humour, etc. between *Am.* and other Plautine plays. But this sort of observation has little bearing on the question of sources and only says that, when finished products are compared, Plautus is like Plautus. Still, there remains a statistically based comfort in the conservative view that Plautus used only New Comedy sources.

The unusual plot of *Am.* has led some to locate its source in Greek Middle Comedy, as mythological burlesque and doubles-comedies were popular in this period. Parodies built around the birth of the gods in particular became fashionable in the transitional period between Old and Middle Comedy.[162] Thus, the view that Plautus used a comic script that had already combined the themes of Herakles' conception and birth has found some acceptance: 'In default of other evidence the *Amphitruo* should belong to the Middle Comedy.'[163] It remains unclear how Plautus might have obtained such a script or seen a performance of a Middle Comedy, as we are ignorant of the extent of the travelling artisans' repertoire in his day. But

---

[161] E.g. Beacham (1992) 29–30.
[162] Nesselrath (1995) 1–27.
[163] Webster (1953) 5. Cf. the more cautious view of Hunter (1987).

a recent reassessment of fourth-century South Italian vase-painting convincingly argues that at least some specimens depict scenes from Attic Old and Middle Comedy rather than ones from local drama, as had generally been assumed.[164] Mythical burlesque is well represented on these vases; their production was most probably inspired by performance rather than the reading of comic scripts, but these might also have found their way to southern Italy as an aid to performance. Consequently, there is provisional evidence for a wider repertoire in South Italian theatre in the fourth century, which perhaps suggests that it was still possible for Plautus to encounter Middle Comedy there in some form more than a century later.

A third possible source for Plautus' *Am.* is the native dramatic tradition in southern Italy itself, where Rhinthon's *Am.* is put forward as the most likely candidate. Fullest support for this thesis is given by Chiarini,[165] who argues that *Am.* presents several problematic elements that cannot be paralleled in Attic (or Roman) comedy: *Am.* is the only extant New Comedy with a change of scene;[166] in this play alone is the action played out on two levels, as seems to have been the case in southern Italian drama; the appearance of a pregnant character on stage is unparalleled; finally, Plautus' play posits the existence of a harbour at Thebes, an inconceivable blunder for an Attic playwright. Chiarini also asserts that in contrast to extant mythical burlesque the tragic story behind *Am.* is not sufficiently distorted and there is much in the play that could stand in a tragedy.[167] These observations, however, do not seem decisive enough to determine a non-Attic source with certitude. Though the small sample of plays by Menander, Plautus, and Terence that we possess does not present a similar change of scene, shifts of setting occurred in Attic tragedy and Old Comedy and seem natural where warranted by exigencies of plot. We have seen that the two-tiered action is both

---

[164] Taplin (1993) esp. 32–54, 89–98.

[165] (1980) esp. 106–15.

[166] I.e. scenes 1–3 take place before the palace, while in scene 4 Amphitryon and Sosia are at an undesignated location on their journey to the palace; in the next scene (5) they appear with Alcmena in front of it. Cf. p. 13 above and 551–632, 633–53nn.

[167] (1980) 99–106.

practical and thematic in *Am.*,[168] and the temporary nature of Plautus' theatre could readily accommodate such alterations. It may be only an accident of transmission that no other character in ancient comedy appeared pregnant on stage and we should not assume the operation of a strict taboo.[169] And regarding the Theban harbour, Plautus may be carelessly following stage convention.[170] As for the play's presumed non-Attic quality as mythical burlesque, we should recall that very few specimens of this genre survive, and it is perilous to establish generic expectations; at any rate, a comedy centred on an adulterous ruse of the lusty supreme god does constitute significant reworking of a myth best known from tragedy. In sum, with the evidence currently available, any connection between Plautus' *Am.* and Rhinthon's is tenuous; this is not to deny, however, that Plautus may have been influenced by native drama in southern Italy in other more general ways, as has often been supposed.

In 1917 Westaway argued that *Am.* betrayed a Euripidean structure and concluded 'it is a direct burlesque of Euripides by Plautus'.[171] Westaway's supporting arguments were sketchy and impressionistic, and her thesis attracted little attention.[172] But in recent years the possibility of Plautus' direct reworking of a tragic source has come to the forefront, with two studies that employ vastly different methodologies reaching similar conclusions. The first, a traditional analytical approach, sets out to separate what is Plautine from what is Greek.[173] It is argued that the comic figure of Sosia is a Plautine innovation, as is the appearance of Jupiter on stage. Thus, virtually all the comic elements of the first four 'acts' are likely to be Plautine.[174] Once the scenes of Plautine origin are identified, there remains a central kernel, the long scene of conflict between Alcmena

---

[168] P. 20 above.

[169] We would hardly expect to find such a farcical figure in the more genteel comedies of Menander and Terence.

[170] 149n.

[171] (1917) 15.

[172] The same conclusion was reached independently by Caldera (1947), who stressed the two apparent geographical absurdities in *Am.*: the harbour of Thebes and the *portus Persicus* (404n.).

[173] Lefèvre (1982).

[174] Lefèvre (1982) 8–19, 26–7.

and Amphitryon (633–860). This scene, minus Sosia's humorous
interjections, points to a Greek tragedy of the long-night type, which
Plautus is presumed to have adapted directly. For the fifth 'act',
Plautus has used another source; in this tragedy Tiresias (cf. *Am.*
1128–9) will have appeared at the end to clarify the situation and
forecast the birth of the twins. Finally, the tragedy which Plautus has
converted into a *tragicomoedia* over the first four 'acts' could have
been Euripides' *Alkmene* or, more likely, a Roman version of it.[175]
Critics of the analytical method have long maintained that this
approach is only a fragile house of cards built on dual presumptions
as to what Plautus was capable of and what a hypothetical Greek
playwright was not.[176] Still, this particular analysis is often illuminating, as is Lefèvre's interpretation[177] of Mercury's description of the
play in the prologue, where it is argued that Mercury is bluntly in-
forming the audience that Plautus has taken a tragedy directly and
deformed it into a mythical burlesque (51–63 *tragoedia ... comoedia ...
tragicomoedia*), that Sosia is an instrumental figure in this deformation
of serious drama (60–4), and that the god's assumption of a slave's
costume and role is an innovation in the dramatic tradition (116–19).

The second study[178] presents a brilliant analysis of the play in
performance and concludes not only that Plautus himself has reworked a tragedy, but that the work in question is Euripides' *Bacchae*.
The central thesis is that the two plays exhibit 'strong similarities
of metatheatrical structure'.[179] In both Theban-based plays gods
in human disguise create and direct, with extreme theatrical self-
consciousness and irony, highly deceptive plays-within-the-play.
There are visual links between the two plays, such as the setting
before a palace and the two-tiered staging, and deeper connections
such as exploration of the nature of illusion itself.[180] The thesis that
Plautus has reworked *Bacchae* probably will not convince all. On the

[175] Lefèvre (1982) 29–38.
[176] Cf. Duckworth (1952) 202–8 and Arnott (1975) 37–8.
[177] (1982) 22–6.
[178] Slater (1990), who further develops the work of Stewart (1958).
[179] Slater (1990) 123.
[180] Slater (1990) 117–21.

most immediate level of plot and performance, the two plays present far more drastic differences than similarities, whatever themes they share: we would expect to find more tell-tale marks of direct reworking, especially on the verbal level.[181] None the less, this study both enriches our understanding of the play, and also presents provocative new arguments to bolster the notion that Plautus may have recast a tragedy directly, whether Euripides' *Bacchae* or some other tragic script (or performance) to which he had access.

While none of the hypotheses discussed in these pages can be rejected outright, the evidence suggests to this editor that the question of sources best reduces itself to a pair of closely related alternatives: Plautus most probably either adapted a mythical travesty belonging to the period of Middle Comedy or converted a tragedy into one himself. The former view assumes at least one Greek comic playwright as intermediary in the process, the latter maintains that the accomplished Roman playwright, working in his mature years, could be just as original as this hypothetical Greek intermediary. Under the latter scenario, Italian sub-literary theatre could have furnished Plautus with models of mythical burlesque on at least a small scale. The view of Plautus as a hack translator of Greek comedies presumed to be in every way superior was for ever shattered by Fraenkel's monumental study of Plautine originality.[182] Subsequent discoveries of Menander, which fostered greater appreciation of Plautus' deliberately farcical distortion of his models, and the recent application of performance criticism to Plautus have demonstrated that the Roman poet perhaps was even more original than Fraenkel had supposed. The idea that Plautus may have worked directly from a tragedy, whether in Greek or a Roman adaptation, should no longer be dismissed out of hand.

---

[181] Our best available evidence for Plautus' method of composing, the parallel texts of *Bac.* and Menander's *Dis exapaton*, demonstrate that Plautus, while capable of the freest adaptation, could at times translate quite literally; cf. Handley (1968) and Hunter (1985) 16–18. To account for the almost complete lack of verbal correspondences, Slater (1990) 123 suggests that Plautus could have seen a performance of Euripides' play and worked from memory rather than a script.

[182] (1922/1960).

5. MUSIC, METRE, AND SCANSION

(a) Overview

There seem to have been three distinct modes of delivery in Roman comedy: spoken verse, recitative, and song, which we designate here by S, R, and C, respectively. Repeated sequences of (S)CR (*Am.* opens SCRCR, 1–462) and of SR unbroken by C (e.g. *Am.* 861–1053) were expected patterns, but Plautus' plays show much variation. In accordance with established conventions, *Am.* commences in S, the metre of prologues, and ends in R (the final call for applause is invariably delivered in trochaic septenarii). Within the body of *Am.*, R (usually the trochaic septenarius) is frequently used in scenes featuring lively and combative discourse between two characters (e.g. 263–462, 586–632, 654–860, 1009–fr. 6).[183] And, as is also typical, examples of C in *Am.* coincide with the entrance of a character. The total number of songs in the play (five) is about average for Plautus; the percentage of spoken lines (27%) is slightly lower than is usual, but at least one scene in senarii falls within the lacuna. Beyond the conventions just noted, we cannot posit hard-and-fast rules regarding what kinds of situations and character-types tend to be associated with S, C, or R in Plautus, whose musical practice is fluid and flexible. Significantly in *Am.*, the gods address the audience almost exclusively in spoken senarii. This no doubt is due to the prologizing function of these addresses, where the gods discuss both scenes enacted and scenes to come in an effort to control the audience's reception of the play (463–98, 861–81, 974–83). Similarly, Jupiter, once his impersonation of Amphitryon is ended, explains the mysterious events one last time as *deus ex machina* in unaccompanied senarii (1131–43). Such instances demonstrate how the cessation of musical accompaniment might be used to seize the audience's attention. Other cases are less straightforward. When Mercury bursts on to the stage playing the *seruus currens* (984ff.), he does so in recitative iambic

---

[183] Scholars debate whether the septenarius is simply an adaptation of its Greek equivalent (the trochaic tetrameter catalectic) or predates Roman theatre, as its use in triumphal songs *et sim.* suggests. Cf. Jocelyn (1967) 33–4.

octonarii, the standard measure for this stereotypical comic scene.[184] Though he shortly assumes a prologizing persona here as well (997–1005), he continues in recitative, but rounds off the scene with three senarii when he explicitly reminds the spectators of their role in the making of performance – i.e. they must pay close attention (1006) – and restates his plan to befuddle Amphityron from the roof in the next scene. The remaining senarii in *Am.* occur in two scenes that are almost diametrically opposed in tone and content: Jupiter's wheedling pacification of Alcmena (882–955) and the lost, but doubtless strident (and unresolved) second confrontation between Alcmena and Amphitryon (frs. 7–10). Thus, though some general tendencies of musical patterning are recognizable, a simple dichotomy in association with the divine and human characters cannot be established, and attempts to impose rigid patterning must constantly explain away perceived exceptions.[185] Perhaps the simple desire for constant musical variety and diverse pacing governed Plautus' choices as much as comic typology and emotional colouring.

(b) Basic principles

(i) Quantity of syllables

Short ($\cup$ = one time-unit) and long ($-$ = two time-units) syllables[186] may be determined as in (e.g.) Virgil with only minor qualifications. According to the rules of syllable division in Latin, a single consonant between two vowels belongs to the latter vowel (*fa-ci-lis*). When two consecutive consonants occur between vowels, whether within or between words, the first normally belongs to the preceding vowel and the second to the one following (*mit-to*). However, successive consonants of the type mute + liquid (*c, g, p, b, t, d + r* or *l*) are not split between syllables in Plautus (*pa-trem*), except in compounds (*ab-ripio*) and in closely related word groups (*et-res*). A syllable ending in a consonant is said to be 'closed' and counts as long regardless of

---

[184] Examples in Duckworth (1936) 95.

[185] As Dupont (1987).

[186] These are alternatively designated 'light' and 'heavy' syllables, respectively; cf. Allen (1978) 89–92.

the quantity of its vowel; one ending in a vowel by contrast is 'open' and scans long only if that vowel is long by nature or a diphthong; *x* and *z* are double consonants and *h* is a mark of aspiration and so not a consonant at all. Plautus preserves the original long quantity of certain final syllables that are scanned short in classical Latin: in the third person singular of verbs, *-at*, *-et*, and *-it* are usually long except for futures in *-bit*, the future perfect, and the present indicative of the third conjugation; final syllables in *-ar*, *-er*, *-or*, and *-al* are usually long in the case of nouns and comparative adjectives as well as verbs.[187] But in certain conditions, these long final syllables may be subject to iambic shortening.[188]

(*ii*) *Word accent*

Because of the prevalence of iambic shortening in Plautus, it is important to be aware of the rules for Latin stress accent. Monosyllables are accented only if they are truly independent words (i.e. not prepositions, enclitics, etc.). Disyllables are normally accented on the first syllable. In words of three or more syllables, if the penult (second-last syllable) is long, this syllable usually receives the accent; if it is short, the accent falls on the antepenult (third-last syllable). However, words of four syllables configured ∪ ∪ ∪ × (× here designates the *anceps* or 'doubtful' syllable, realizable as long or short) are accented on the fourth-last syllable (*stúltitia*, *fámilias*). It is conventionally assumed that words of more than four syllables received secondary accents by reapplication of the Penultimate Law (*expúgnauísses*). The attachment of enclitics (e.g. *-que*, *-ue*, *-ne*, *-ce*) naturally affects accent (*ánimum* but *animúmque*), as also is the case in closely connected word groups (*operám dare*, *uoluptás mea*). Some words accented on the penult retained this accent even after a final vowel was dropped (e.g. *illíc(e)*, *istúc(e)*, *tantón(e)*).

(*iii*) *Elision*

A final open syllable with a short or a long vowel (diphthongs included), or a final syllable ending in *m*, was melded with the following word beginning with a vowel or *h*. Whether or not this final

---

[187] Questa (1967) 9–10.   [188] See p. 63 below.

elided syllable was completely lost in pronunciation,[189] it does not count in scansion: *Am.* 3 *adficere atque adiuuare in rebus* = *ad-fi-ce-r(e)at-qu(e)ad-iu-ua-r(e)in-re-bus*, 19 *quam rem oratum huc* = *quam-r(em)o-ra-t(um)-huc*. Syntactical breaks or changes of speaker do not prevent elision.

(iv) Feet

The stichic metres most commonly used by Plautus are traditionally divided into 'feet': 'senarii' of six feet (twelve elements), 'octonarii' of eight feet (sixteen elements), and 'septenarii' of seven and a half feet (fifteen elements). The basic foot of all these lengths is the iamb ($\cup -$) or the trochee ($- \cup$), but early Latin verse is so flexible in its treatment of the odd elements of iambic verse and the even ones of trochaic that these 'pure' forms are obligatory only at line-end. Elsewhere in the line, each of the (expected) short positions is *anceps*, and thus may be filled by a short or a long syllable or the two resolved shorts of a long ($\cup \cup$ being temporally equivalent to $-$). The even elements of iambic verse and the odd ones of trochaic must be realized as a long or two resolved shorts in all positions except at line-end, or positions analogous to line-end, where by the substitution known as *brevis in longo* a single short is also admissible. Thus, in addition to their pure forms, the individual feet of iambic and trochaic verse may be shaped as follows: **spondee** ($- -$), **dactyl** ($- \cup \cup$), **anapaest** ($\cup \cup -$), **tribrach** ($\cup \cup \cup$), and (rarely) **proceleusmatic** ($\cup \cup \cup \cup$); the final foot of an iambic verse may also be a **pyrrhic** ($\cup \cup$). This extreme flexibility leads to a staggering number of possible metrical configurations of lines and seemingly threatens to mask any predictable sense of rhythm.[190]

(c) Podic schemes of common metres

(i) Iambic senarius

$$\times - \mid \times - \mid \times \mid\mid - \mid \times - \mid \times - \mid \cup \overset{\wedge}{}$$

[189] See further Soubiran (1966), Allen (1978) 78–82 and Gratwick (1993) 251–3.

[190] Cf. Cic. *Orat.* 184 *at comicorum senarii propter similitudinem sermonis sic saepe sunt abiecti, ut nonnunquam uix in eis numerus et uersus intellegi possit.* For Horace's lack of appreciation of early Latin verse see Gratwick (1993) 40–1, 58–9.

With the exception of the pure iamb at the end of the line (whose final syllable may be *brevis in longo*, here noted by ^), each foot of the senarius consists of an *anceps* followed by a *longum*. Word-end (here marked | |) regularly falls after the fifth element, and divides the line into two distinct parts or 'cola'. Alternatively, word-end is sometimes found after the seventh element, in which case there is also word-end after the third (× — | × | | — | × — | × | | — | × — | ∪ ^).[191]

Am. 14 lŭ-cr(um) ūt | pĕrēn- | nĕ | | uŏ- | bīs sēm- | pĕr sūp- | pĕtāt

Am. 2 ēmŭn- | dīs | | uĕn- | dūndīs- | quĕ | | mē | laĕtŭm | lŭcrīs

(*ii*) *Iambic octonarius*

× — | × — | × — | × ^ | | × — | × — | × — | ∪ ^

Again, *ancipitia* and *longa* alternate and the final foot is subject to the same treatment as in the iambic senarius (see immediately above). The majority of Plautine octonarii have word-end after the eighth element, which sharply divides the verse into two half-lines, with the result that the fourth foot must be a pure iamb (*brevis in longo* is allowed in the eighth element). Other octonarii have word-end after the ninth element (× — | × — | × — | × — | × | | — | × — | × — | ∪ ^), in which case the fourth foot is no longer analogous to the final one.

Am. 206 sī sĭnĕ | u(i) ēt sĭnĕ | bēllō | uĕlīnt | | rāpt(a) ēt | rāptō- |
res trā- | dĕre

Am. 251 uŏrtēn- | tĭbŭs | Tĕlŏbō- | īs tĕ- | līs | | cōm- | plēbān- |
tūr cōr- | pŏra

(*iii*) *Trochaic septenarius*

— × | — × | — × | — × | | — × | — × | — ∪ | ^

This measure is said to be a 'catalectic' version of the relatively rare trochaic octonarius in that its movement is essentially identical with the octonarius until the last foot, where the final element has been

---

[191] Cf. Questa (1967) 169–70.

suppressed. In direct contrast to iambic measures *longa* precede *an-cipitia*, with which they alternate, in trochaic verse. Comparison with the schematization of the iambic senarius demonstrates that the septenarius may also be regarded as a senarius with an additional cretic unit ($-\times-$) at its head. Word-end is regular after the eight element (corresponding to the fifth element of the senarius), which is indifferently long or short. A pure trochee is obligatory in the seventh foot and the final element may be *brevis in longo*.

$$Am.\ 276\ \text{ĭtă stā-} \mid \text{tĭm stănt} \mid \text{sīgnă,} \mid \text{nĕquĕ nŏx} \mid \mid \text{quŏquăm} \mid \text{cōncē-} \mid$$
$$\text{dĭt dĭ-} \mid \bar{e}$$
$$Am.\ 277\ \text{pērgĕ,} \mid \text{Nōx, ŭt} \mid \text{ōccē-} \mid \text{pĭstī;} \mid \mid \text{gĕrĕ pă-} \mid \text{trĭ mŏ-} \mid$$
$$\text{rĕm mĕ-} \mid \bar{o}$$

(d) Plautine prosody

The following is an outline of some of the most important features of early Roman verse. The most complete treatments of Plautine metre are Questa (1967) and Soubiran (1988). Shorter but instructive accounts in English of archaic prosody can be found in the editions of Willcock (1987) 141–61, Gratwick (1993) 40–63, 248–60, and Barsby (1999) 290–304. For the most basic rules of prosody Raven (1965) is helpful.

(i) Synizesis (Questa (1967) 79–85, Soubiran (1988) 179–84)

Two contiguous vowels within a word may (or may not) meld together to produce a single syllable, e.g. *mei* is set as a single long in *Am.* 31, but *duas* is iambic in 488. The possessive pronouns and the genitive singular of the relative and demonstrative pronouns very frequently undergo synizesis, as do most oblique forms of *is*, and forms of *deus*. In the case of iambic words, it is often impossible to determine whether a prosodic reduction is due to synizesis or to iambic shortening or prosodic hiatus,[192] though synizesis is generally assumed as the simplest explanation wherever possible.

----

[192] See pp. 63–4 below.

(ii) Prodelision (Questa (1967) 23–5)

A preceding word may (or may not) coalesce with a following *es* or *est*, thereby causing the initial vowel of these words to be lost in scansion. In Plautus, this may occur not only after final vowels or-*m*, as in Classical Latin, but also after -*us* (e.g. *Am.* 88 *acturust*, but 296 *accepturus est*) and -*is*, for which the MSS give the spelling -*est* (e.g. *Am.* 443 *consimilest*, 601 *similest*).

(iii) Apocope (Questa (1967) 13–21)

A final syllable with a short vowel and ending in *s* which is followed by a word beginning with a consonant sometimes counts as long,[193] sometimes short, e.g. *minus* is pyrrhic at *Am.* 27, while the -*s* of *minus* 'makes position' before *liceat* in 986. Some editions, but not this one, visually indicate the loss of *s* in scansion with an apostrophe. By contrast, the frequent pyrrhic scansion of certain disyllables (e.g. *satis, nimis*) before consonants may be due to iambic shortening. Similarly, in cases where elision is not possible, a final short *e* is very often eliminated altogether in prosody; this occurs most frequently in words such as *ille, nempe, proinde, deinde, unde,* and *inde* and is usually readily detectable in scansion, e.g. *Am.* 988 *ille* scans as a single long.

(iv) Resolution (Questa (1967) 125–44)

Plautus is very strict with regard to the resolution of long syllables. Two resolved shorts cannot fall in the last two syllables of words of three or more syllables, i.e. the final resolved syllables must stand in a pyrrhic word. Outside of the first foot, exceptions are few, and instances such as *Am.* 55 *ōmnĭbŭs* are suspect; this law does not apply where elision occurs, e.g. 956 *Āmphĭtru(o) adsum*. Nor should word-end fall between these two shorts if each belongs to an accented word, i.e. the resolved syllables must stand in the same word or word-group; prepositions, conjunctions, enclitics, and other 'weak' types of words such as pronouns are not treated as separate entities, e.g. *Am.* 8 *ĕt ŭti*, 23 *ĭt(a) ŭt* . This law against 'split resolution' is sometimes broken in the first foot, provided the foot is a dactyl.

---

[193] For the conditions under which the long scansion occurs see Gratwick (1993) 50.

(v) Iambic shortening (Questa (1967) 31–70, Soubiran (1988) 242–52)
From an early date, there was a natural tendency in Latin for disyllables of the type ∪ − to become ∪ ∪ (e.g. *ego* > *ego*, *bene* > *bene*,
modo > *modo*), where the shortening (or 'weakening') of the long syllable is apparently due to the accent on the preceding syllable. In
Plautine metre of virtually all types, this process of iambic shortening occurs quite freely, and iambic words often scan as pyrrhic, e.g.
Am. 344 *enim*, 353 *abi*. In longer words or word groups, ∪ − × may
become ∪ ∪ ×, e.g. *Am.* 74 *magistrátum*, 939 *uoluptátes*, 1021 *quis ad
fóres*, 964 *an id ióco*. Disyllabic forms of *ille, iste,* and *ipse* were originally accented on the last syllable and so we find, e.g., *Am.* 270 *quid
illíc*, 415 *et ipsús*. In all cases, the two consecutive shorts that result
from iambic shortening serve as a resolved long. Instances of iambic
shortening are noted in the commentary.

(vi) Hiatus (Questa (1967) 86–97)
The option of *not* melding words in the circumstances described
above,[194] utilized only in rare cases in classical poetry (e.g. as a
Graecism in Virgil), occurs with more freedom in Plautus than in
any other Latin author. Traditionally, most editors have accepted
hiatus only in conjunction with breaks in sense or syntax such as
change of speaker, interjections, the main cola break or some other
pause in speech. The extent to which hiatus is to be tolerated is still
contested, and many transpositions and emendations have arisen out
of intolerance for cases other than those just noted, even when the
text seems beyond suspicion. This edition will follow a primarily
metrical approach to hiatus,[195] and all instances are noted in the
commentary.

(vii) Prosodic hiatus
In early Roman verse, words normally subject to elision are sometimes not completely elided in scansion. Typically, a long monosyllable followed by a word beginning with a short vowel counts as a
single short in scansion, e.g. *Am.* 450 *quo agis*, 863 *qui habito*, 1038
qui utri; similarly treated are short monosyllables ending in *m*, e.g.

---

[194] Pp. 58–9.   [195] See pp. 68–9 below.

Am. 473 quăm ămat. The monosyllable in prosodic hiatus regularly serves as the first short of a resolved long, as in all the examples immediately above; less frequently it is the second short of a resolved pair, and sometimes it is neither, e.g. *Am.* 498 cŭm Ālcumena.

(*viii*) *Enclisis (Questa (1967) 71–8)*
Some long monosyllables are scanned as short when they are combined with *quidem, quis* or *quid,* e.g. *Am.* 660 hĭcquidem.

(*ix*) *Loci Jacobsohniani (Questa (1967) 151–6)*
Certain places within iambo-trochaic verse are analogous to line-end and so may regularly admit *breuis in longo* (as they do hiatus), as was seen to be the case for the eighth element of the iambic octonarius. Jacobsohn (1904) demonstrated that this licence is also extended to the eighth element of the iambic senarius (e.g. *Am.* 94 Iuppitĕr, 882 aedibŭs), and to the third (e.g. *Am.* 797 dĕdisti) and eleventh (e.g. *Am.* 345 dicerĕ, 438 Sosiă) elements of the trochaic septenarius.

(*x*) *Luchs' law (Questa (1967) 188–94, Soubirin (1988) 383–9)*
Plautine iambo-trochaic verse is also especially strict about the metrical configuration of words at line-end and at places analogous to line-end. According to Luchs' law an iambic word ending an iambic line (or half-line) or a trochaic septenarius should not be immediately preceded by another iambic word or a word of three or more syllables ending in an iamb.

Am. 21 ta(m) ēt- sĭ | pr(o) īmpĕrĭ- | ō uo- | bīs quŏd | dīctum | fŏrēt

Am. 31 cōntā- | gĭo- | nĕ mēĭ | pātrĭs | mētuo | mălum

Am. 286 āccĭpĭ- | ām mŏdŏ | sīs uen(i) | hūc ĭn- | uĕnĭēs | īn fŏr- | tunĭ- | um

Cases such as *Am.* 1058 ănĭmō | mălēst | āquăm | uĕlĭm | | (the first half of a trochaic septenarius) are suspect or exceptional.

(*xi*) *Meyer's law (Questa (1967) 194–206, Soubiran (1988) 337–68)*
This establishes that a word whose ending corresponds with the end of a foot must be a pure iamb at the following places: the second and fourth feet of the iambic senarius and the corresponding places

of the trochaic septenarius, and (usually) the second and sixth foot of
the iambic octonarius.

Am. 30 ātqu(e) ĕgŏ | quŏqu(e) ĕtĭ- | ām, quī | Iŏuīs | | sūm fī- | lĭūs

Am. 40 ĕt ĕg(o) ēt | pătēr | | dē uŏ- | bīs ĕt | rē pū- | blĭca

Am. 434 tū nē- | gās mēd | ēssĕ | quĭd ĕgŏ | nī nē- | gĕm qu(ĭ) ĕgŏ- |
mēt sĭ- | ēm

Am. 215 prŏpĕrĕ | suīs | | dē fĭ- | nĭbŭs | ēxēr- | cĭtūs | | dēdū- |
cĕrĕt[196]

Viewed differently, the breaks at these places should be approached
with a cretic; in fact, the ultimate effect of the operation of both
Meyer's and Luchs' law is to promote the pure cretic $(- \cup -)$ as a
definitive cadence in both iambic and trochaic verse.

(e) Analysis in metra

Though the 'podic' analysis above is rooted in antiquity, it is more
instructive to regard the metron rather than the foot as the basic
unit of Plautine iambo-trochaic verse. Metrical cadence is defined
by the way a line ends rather than how it begins, and podic analysis
obscures the identical manner in which iambic and trochaic rhythms
fall out. To take a well-known example, the last three metra (i.e. six
feet) of the trochaic septenarius are identical to the iambic senarius,
with the former differing from the latter only in the three additional
elements at its head:

$$\times - \times - \times \,|\,| - \times - \times - \cup - \text{ (senarius)}$$
$$- \times - \times - \times - \times \,|\,| - \times - \times - \cup - \text{ (septenarius)}$$

The laws and tendencies discussed above usually apply to precisely
the same places in the verse-cadence of both iambic and trochaic
measures, a fact that is largely disguised by analysis in terms of feet
or by counting elements from the beginning of lines. Similarly, cola

---

[196] Meyer's law is not violated where elision with a word following occurs,
e.g. *Am.* 85 ĕĭŭs ōr- | nāmēnt(a) | ĕt cŏrĭ(um) | ŭtī | cŏncĭ- | dĕrent.

can be more clearly marked by analysis in terms of metra. Podic analysis also obscures the significance of the cretic ($-\cup-$) as a final cadence in both iambic and trochaic verse by assigning this sequence to two different feet; the same is true for the various places within lines where, as we have seen, the operation of Luchs' and Meyer's laws and other factors combine to promote the cretic as the proper cadence with which to define colon boundaries. Statistical data also demonstrate that the movement of Latin iambo-trochaic verse was in metra (though less obviously so than that of its Greek conterparts) and that therefore it is very misleading to regard these measures as made up of undifferentiated sequences of feet shaped $\times-$ (the fixed final foot exempted).[197]

(f) Notation in this edition

A notation has been developed to capture the identical character of iambic and trochaic verse and to meet the objections to podic analy-sis noted above,[198] according to which the iambic senarius can be schematized as

A B C D A B C D A B c D

Here, A B C D constitute a metron, with the A's and C's representing the *ancipitia*, and the B's and D's the *longa*. The *anceps* may be real-ized as a long (A, C), the two resolved shorts of a long (aa, cc), or a single short (a, c; c always in the final metron). The *longa* appear as either B, D, or their resolved equivalents (bb, dd); as we have seen, the final D always scans long and therefore will be marked D re-gardless of the 'actual' quantity of the syllable. Where *brevis in longo* occurs other than at line-end, the convention d+ is used. The sym-bol / is used to mark significant word-end (i.e. colon boundary)

---

[197] Alternate *ancipitia* of the senarius and septenarius show strikingly simi-lar statistical preferences in their realization as a *longum* (a long or pair of re-solved shorts) as opposed to a single short. And the even feet of the senarius and the odd feet of the septenarius, while tending to be spondaic (or the temporal equivalent of a spondee) overall, are far more likely to be pure iambs than the remaining feet in each line. See Gratwick (1993) 44, 54–6, 257–60.

[198] Used by Gratwick (1987) and (1993) after Handley (1965).

within lines. Using the notation, the first four senarii of *Am.* are scanned as follows:

Vt uos in uostris uoltis mercimoniis
A B C D A / B C D a B c D
emundis uendundisque me laetum lucris
A B C / D A B c / D A B c D
adficere atque adiuuare in rebus omnibus,
A bb C D a B C D a B c D
et ut res rationesque uostrorum omnium
a B C / dd A B c / D A B c D

Similarly, the iambic octonarius can be schematized thus:

A B C D A B c D / A B C D A B c D;

whereas octonarii that have word-end after the ninth element are patterned:

A B C D A B c D A / B C D A B c D.

Examples:

Am. 212 Amphitruo, magnanimi uiri freti uirtute et uiribus
A bb C D aa B c D / A B C D A B c D
Am. 259 in dicionem atque in arbitratum cuncti Thebano poplo
A bb C D a B c D A / B C D A B C D

The affinity between the trochaic septenarius and the iambic senarius can be grasped instantly through the notation adopted for the former:

B C D A B C D A / B C D A B c D

The trochaic measure follows the movement of the senarius with the addition of three preceding elements, B C D. This initial unit of the septenarius is readily identifiable as a cretic ($- \cup - = $ B c D), though the *anceps* may of course be realized as a long (C) or two resolved shorts (cc); initial difficulties in scansion may also arise from the resolution of the B and D elements into two shorts. The remainder of the line, A B C D A / B C D A B c D, is a senarius, with regular word-end after the second A, in this case, the eighth rather than the fifth element as in the senarius. For the more difficult lines, readers are advised to scan by working backwards, first establishing the three *metra* akin to those of the senarius, and then the initial 'cretic' unit. The final septenarii of *Am.* are thus scanned as follows:

> faciam ita ut iubes et te oro promissa ut serues tua.
> bb c D a B C D A / B C D A B c D
> ibo ad uxorem intro; missum facio Teresiam senem.
> B c D A B C D A / bb C D aa B c D
> nunc, spectatores, Iouis summi causa clare plaudite.
> B C D A B cc D A / B C D A B c D

The use of this notation proves advantageous for other reasons. For example, Luchs' and Meyer's laws may be succinctly reformulated and generalized:

Meyer's law: if unaccented word-end falls in D/, then it should be approached

$$\ldots B c D / \text{not} \ldots B C D /$$

Luchs' law: if unaccented word end falls in B /, then it should be approached

$$\ldots D A B / \text{not} \ldots D a B /^{199}$$

Scansion of a few verses will confirm that these tendencies become strongest as line-end is approached, but statistically predominate throughout verses except at line-opening. The combined implication of these laws, as reformulated here, is that cretics are most likely to be configured as B c D/ rather than D a B/, and the notation most clearly marks this fundamental cretic cadence of iambo-trochaic verse. This editor has tested Gratwick's proposition that metrical hiatus is primarily associated with colon boundaries and his formulation of this phenomenon is generally followed here: 'Plautus ... frequently allows himself metrical hiatus between *cola*, that is **at any inner juncture ... A/B ... or ... D/A ..., but *not* normally at the junctures ... B/C ... or ... C/D ...**; where, if hiatus occurs, it is ... a definite licence, or corrupt.'[200] The notion that hiatus is always permissible at any such A/B or D/A juncture is a useful guide to editing Plautus, but there remain problematic cases

---

[199] Gratwick (1993) 56.   [200] Gratwick (1993) 253; cf. ibid. 52–4.

of hiatus within these boundaries; these are taken up in the commentary as they occur.

(g) Reading Plautine verse aloud

It is assumed here that Plautus' iambic and trochaic verse is ordered on purely quantitative principles, that respect for word accent is not a primary determinant of word position, and that the notion of regularly spaced beats – i.e. the ictus about which modern scholars still debate, often along national lines – may be entirely anachronistic.[201] The relative unpredictability with which the *ancipitia* are realized as short or long prohibits the imposition of regularly spaced beats, whether these are supposed to coincide with each *longum* or alternate *longa*, i.e. all B and D positions, or D positions only, respectively. Nor does the observation that natural word accent frequently coincides with this putative ictus support the operation of the latter; the rules of Latin word accent[202] naturally promote the coincidence of *longa* and word accent, and Plautine verse does not require this correlation at line-end, where long monosyllables are altogether avoided and disyllabic words, which are necessarily iambic, normally defy it. Native speakers of languages whose verse is accentual will nonetheless find it convenient to impose some sort of stress at more or less regular intervals, as long as this is acknowledged to be a matter of convention rather than actual Latin practice. Thus, readers may choose to give additional stress to B and D or (better) simply D positions (or to the first short where these *longa* are resolved) when reading Plautine verse aloud. Such a convention is useful in signalling colon boundaries and final cadence. Readers so inclined may follow the example of recent editions in this series[203] and devise a system of sublinear dots to mark the onset of *longa* in their texts. In this edition, the more difficult lines are scanned in the commentary using the notation described above, and the more challenging points of prosody are taken up there (*ad loc.*) as well.

---

[201] The arguments of Gratwick (1993) 40–8, 59–62 are followed closely here.

[202] See p. 58 above.

[203] Gratwick (1993) and Barsby (1999).

(h) *The* cantica

We do not know precisely why the Roman comic playwrights made such extensive use of song, though it is likely that native Italian drama played an influential role. Though Greek New Comedy featured some kind of choral interlude between acts,[204] the extant work of Menander yields only a single instance of lyric song (from the *Theophoroumene*) and otherwise shows only the opposition of spoken verse (83%) and recitative (17%). We do, however, hear of itinerant companies performing scenes from classical tragedy throughout the Greek world in the third century BC, for which they converted scenes orginally spoken to song,[205] a practice that might possibly have influenced Roman comedy. Another hypothesis is that the comic poets followed what were probably scaled-down productions of choral lyrics in the Roman adaptations of Greek tragedies; playwrights such as Naevius and Ennius in fact wrote both tragedies and comedies.[206] It may be that Roman comic playwrights were simultaneously influenced by all these factors.

The various sung measures in Plautus reveal a considerable musical virtuosity, though somewhat less than Aristophanes'; an anonymous epigram known to Varro (Gel. *NA* 1.24.3) declared not only that *Comoedia* herself wept at Plautus' death, but that 'Laughter, Play, Jest and *numeri innumeri* all mourned together.' The analysis of particular songs is fraught with difficulty owing to our almost complete ignorance of musical performance. **Bacchiacs** ($\times--$ e.g. 173ff.) and **cretics** ($-\times-$ e.g. 219ff.) are very common in Plautine song and occur in various lengths; they usually pose little difficulty in scansion if the reader bears in mind that the *longa* are subject to resolution. Both may occur in catalectic or syncopated (i.e. a metron may be curtailed by a syllable internally) form. In addition to these and the various iambic and trochaic lengths that fall within *cantica*, we encounter only the following measures in *Am.*:

Anapaest: properly $\cup\cup-$ but replaceable by either a **spondee** ($--$) or a **dactyl** ($-\cup\cup$), with resolution of any *longum* possi-

---

[204] See p. 7 above.
[205] Gentili (1979) esp. 15–41.
[206] See further Fraenkel (1960) 307–53.

ble. In *Am.*, there are two dimeters (166–7), with each metron consisting of two anapaests, and a single tetrameter (1062);

Sotadean: a rare Ionic metre that occurs in comedy only at 168–72,[207] most commonly of the type $- - \cup \cup - - \cup \cup - \cup - \cup - -$;

Colon Reizianum: $\times - \times - -$ (e.g. 653).[208]

In some places, colometry and precise identification of measures are in doubt (e.g. 161ff.), and textual corruption creates further problems in interpreting runs of syllables. Schematization and discussion of individual songs are reserved for the commentary *ad locc.*

6. PLAY WITHOUT END

Limitations of space allow for only the briefest survey of the remarkable influence *Am.* has enjoyed in European literature.[209] Regular revivals of it and other perennial Plautine favourites were staged at least into the Augustan Age, whereafter the plays were primarily read. As the empire became Christian, Plautus' plays met with increasing censure and Terence's, which could be culled for their moral maxims, garnered increased respect; St Jerome (*Ad Eust.* 30), however, confessed to a fondness for the more boisterous comedies of the elder playwright. We do not hear of a medieval adaptation of *Am.* prior to Vital de Blois' *Geta*, which no doubt was read rather than performed in the early twelfth century. Here the basic love-triangle of Plautus' play is preserved, though it is subordinated to new material. Mercury appears under the name Archas, but the main focus is on Geta (= Sosia), a slave who has taken on intellectual airs as the result of accompanying Amphitryon on a philosophical pilgrimage to Greece. Geta is eventually put in his place by more accomplished scholastic debaters.

The Palatine branch[210] of the tradition was at some point split up

---

[207] Questa (1967) 259–60.

[208] Questa (1967) 245–9.

[209] Accounts of the play's history can be found in Shero (1956), Lindberger (1956), and Riedel (1993).

[210] See pp. 75–6 below.

for ease of copying into two parts consisting of eight (*Am.*, *As.*, *Aul.*, *Capt.*, *Cas.*, *Cist.*, *Cur.*, *Epid.*) and twelve (*Bac.*, *Men.*, *Mer.*, *Mil.*, *Mos.*, *Per.*, *Poen.*, *Ps.*, *Rud.*, *St.*, *Trin.*, *Truc.*) plays; the latter group all but perished in the late Middle Ages until their rediscovery by Nicolaus Cusanus in 1429. This exciting find kindled new interest in Plautus, resulting not only in scholarly Latin editions, but in translations and performances as well. In 1487 Pandolfo Collenuccio produced an Italian translation of *Am.* which was subsequently produced and grandly staged on two separate occasions under the patronage of Duke Ercole I. At the end of this play, Anfitrione confides his displeasure at being a cuckold to the audience. Around this time, someone composed 175 lines of Latin to fill the large lacuna of *Am.* Credit for these *scenae suppositiciae* has traditionally gone to Hermolaus Barbarus, but his authorship has been called into question.[211] These appeared in Latin editions well into the nineteenth century and generally were regarded as genuine by adapters. Interest in *Am.* spread throughout Europe in the sixteenth century, with (e.g.) Lodovico Dulce's *Il Marito* (1545), an openly lewd play in which the gods are replaced by mortals, and *Os Enfatriões* by the renowned Portuguese epic and lyric poet Luiz Vaz de Camões, a play that once again leaves the audience with the distinct impression that Amphitryon is a disgraced cuckold. Shakespeare's *Comedy of errors* (1591), though based primarily on *Men.*, borrows from *Am.* as well.[212]

The seventeenth century saw two vastly different adaptations: the sobering *Sacri Mater Virgo* by the German priest Johannes Burmeister in 1621 and Molière's comic masterpiece of 1668, in which he himself played the role of Sosia. Burmeister observed the parallels between the myth of Hercules' birth and the Christian account of immaculate conception, and, sometimes following Plautus closely, produces his own Latin 'comedy' with the simple substitutions Alcmena > Mary, Jupiter > Holy Ghost, Amphitryon > Joseph, Hercules > Jesus. Molière's *Amphitryon*, much influenced by Rotrou's highly successful *Les Sosies* (1638), is in a sense more 'classical' than Plautus',

---

[211] In a letter he claims to have supplemented a lacuna in Plautus, but does not give the title of the play. Braun (1980) 83–91 believes that he is referring to a supplement of *Aul.*

[212] Duckworth (1952) 417–18.

with its tidy structure and concentration of the action on a single night just after Alcmène and Amphitryon are married.[213] Among Molière's many innovations are the replacement of the prologue with a witty and fantastical exchange between Night in her chariot and Mercury, who reclines on a cloud (the staging of the scene reflects a fascination with mechanical contrivances in seventeenth-century French theatre); an intriguing sub-plot in the marriage of Cleanthis and Sosie (perhaps suggested by Sosia's mention of his *amica* at *Am.* 659); and Sosie's rehearsal of his messenger's speech directly to his lantern, which is made to represent Alcmena, resulting in a monologue no less brilliant and metatheatrical than its Plautine forebear. Molière's Jupiter is a seventeenth-century gallant, utterly smitten by Alcmène, and resentful of the fact that he wins her affection only through impersonation of her husband; his attempt to force her to make a distinction between lover and husband stimulated subsequent adapters. In the wake of Molière's phenomenal success, Dryden produced his *Amphitryon, or The Two Sosias* in Restoration England (1690), which while lacking Molière's wit and ingenuity featured the music of Henry Purcell, with singing and dancing, and the introduction of several new characters.

Various plays, operas, and ballets, mostly inspired by Molière, followed in the eighteenth century, but the next decisive moment in the tradition is marked by Heinrich von Kleist's *Amphitryon* of 1807. This disconcerting and haunting Romanticist play, a true tragicomedy in the modern sense, focuses on the profound emotional suffering of an Alkmena coming to suspect her own infidelity, as when, for example, the diadem (cf. King Pterelas' bowl in Plautus) which the disguised Jupiter gives her engraved with the letter 'A' later mysteriously bears a 'J'. Her suspicion is cruelly fed by a Jupiter who seems entirely alienated from his divine existence and is obsessed with the idea of being loved as himself rather than as Amphitryon. Kleist has introduced an intense and modern interest in psychology to the drama, and at the same time raises fundamental epistemological questions. Not surprisingly, his *Amphitryon* has evoked a plethora of wide-ranging interpretations, but, despite all this critical attention,

---

[213] Alcmène thus does not appear pregnant on stage, as seems to be the rule in the post-Plautine tradition.

to most readers perhaps Alcmena's final cry of '*Ach!*' neatly captures the play's enigmatic quality.[214] Caught up in the swell of the Romanticist movement, dramatists in the nineteenth century largely eschewed classical sources, and it is not until 1929 that another noteworthy adaptation of *Am.* appears with Giraudoux's delightful *Amphitryon 38*, which enjoyed a run of over two hundred performances at the Comédie des Champs Elysées. The title probably reflects Giraudoux's underestimated reckoning of the number of his dramatic predecessors and also purposefully calls attention to the hackneyed nature of the story, as if to suggest that *Amphitryon 38* will be yet another undifferentiated product to roll off the assembly line. But this richly poetic prose-play is anything but unoriginal. Giraudoux's earthy and wise Alcmène almost completely controls the action and Jupiter, who even more than Kleist's god is enamoured of human love, seems always to be at a nervous disadvantage in her presence; he at one point labels her *le vrai Prométhée*. Jupiter's vanity compels him to ask Alcmène to rate their love-making on the previous night: after some thought, and much to the god's consternation, she calmly concludes that *conjugale* most aptly describes it. Alcmène errs only in persuading Leda, whose sudden appearance is one of Giraudoux's many innovations, to sleep with Amphitryon, whom she mistakenly believes to be Jupiter in disguise. In the end, she manages to persuade Jupiter that the two of them should 'just be friends' and the god bestows upon her forgetfulness of the whole affair. Giraudoux's play is intelligent and richly ironic throughout, while sympathetically highlighting the enormous breach between the human and divine estates as human beings conceptualize them.[215]

Giraudoux's treatment was followed by Georg Kaiser's *Zweimal Amphitryon* in 1944, another highly innovative, albeit more heavy-handed adaptation. Unabashedly a product of its times, it features a war-obsessed Amphitryon and a Zeus so disgusted with the violence of the human world that he is contemplating its destruction; he is dissuaded from this extreme measure only through the enjoyment of love with Alkmene. A completely novel plot is played out, and in the end hope for the future of humankind is expressed through Jupiter's

---

[214] General discussion in Allan (1996) 106–38.
[215] Cf. Mankin (1971) 60–83.

closing revelation of the birth of the saviour god Herakles, who will establish the Olympic games to provide a forum for curbing human aggression. Other twentieth-century adaptations include: a Nazi-financed film (in French) entitled *Amphitryon*,[216] the Brazilian playwright Guilherme Figueirdo's *Un deus dormia la en casa*, Harold Pinter's *The lover* (1963), in which a husband impersonates his wife's paramour, and Peter Hacks' *Amphitryon* (1970) in Germany.

We have wandered far from Plautus' *Am.* in surveying just a few of the many adaptations to appear in European literature, but it should be stressed that all ultimately descend, if only indirectly in some cases, from this single play of the Roman playwright known to us only by a comic pseudonym. There can be no doubt that the tradition will continue, whether on stage or screen, or in some medium not yet fully developed or even invented. In Plautus, writers of vastly divergent cultures, epochs and sensibilities have repeatedly found material for treatments that range from the farcical to those which address fundamental questions of human fate. The number and variety of the adaptations attest to the inherent richness of Plautus' *tragicomoedia*.

7. TRANSMISSION OF THE TEXT

For some time after his death, the scripts of Plautus' plays existed in a highly fluid state in which they were no doubt altered by producers to meet the perceived demands of revival performances.[217] Disputes as to which plays were genuinely Plautine seem to have arisen already in the second century BC, when editors first begin to work on Roman texts after the Alexandrian fashion. The critical authority of Varro eventually prevailed: although Gellius (*NA* 3.1.11) knew of 130 plays circulating under Plautus' name in the second century AD, we presume that the twenty-one we possess today in differing states of completeness are those judged to be genuine by Varro. *Am.* is represented in only one of the two strands of the ancient recension, the Palatine, whose oldest minuscule MSS (B, C, D) are dated to the

---

[216] Closed down after only a week's run in New York because of anti-Nazi protest (review in *The New York Times*, 24 March, 1937, p. 29).

[217] Cf. *Cas.* 5–22; concise account of transmission in Tarrant (1983).

tenth/eleventh centuries (C does not include *Am.*). The most important MSS for establishing a text of *Am.* are:

B Palatinus Vaticanus (1615), tenth/eleventh century
D Vaticanus (3870), tenth/eleventh century
E Ambrosianus (I 257 inf.), twelfth century
J Londinensis (BL, Reg. 15 C XI), twelfth century

B has long been acknowledged to be the most reliable member of
the Palatine family, which is designated P (= the agreement of B, C,
D for most plays); in addition to its generally superior readings, it
provides important corrections in multiple hands, which are sometimes right against the entire tradition. J has been described as an
'enigma'[218] in that it sometimes presents readings that agree only
with B or, for some plays, A, the Ambrosian palimpsest (the other
main branch of the tradition). Besides the MSS, we receive extensive
testimony for Plautus' text from ancient grammarians, especially
Nonius Marcellus (fourth century AD); though much is quoted hastily
from memory, the grammarians sometimes give valuable readings.
This editor has most closely consulted the editions of Leo, Lindsay,
and Ernout; differences between the text printed here and those of
Leo and Lindsay are tabulated below. Entirely new proposals are
printed at 237 and fr. 5. Slight variations in orthography or differences in punctuation that have little effect on sense are not noted,
nor are the many instances where editors choose between similar
forms (e.g. *me* or *med*) out of (usually) metrical considerations. The
lack of a stable text for Plautus at an early date in the transmission
no doubt resulted in some modernization of the MSS; the result is a
jumble of contradictory spellings and forms (e.g. *quom* and *cum*). This
edition follows the general consensus of the MSS, even when this
presents seemingly irrational readings, such as assimilated and un-
assimilated forms in close proximity. Orthography was in a highly
fluid state in Plautus' day, and it is not unlikely that he is responsible
for some of these contradictions himself.[219] Like the MSS, the ancient grammarians and contemporary inscriptions give conflicting

---

[218] MacCary and Willcock (1976) 234.
[219] Cf. his fluidity in matters of syntax, where (e.g.) we find indirect questions with the indicative and subjunctive indifferently.

testimony as to archaic Latin orthography.[220] This edition takes a middle course regarding the systematic substitution of archaic or modernized spellings: always *seruos* and not *seruus*; *-o-* is universally adopted for *-e-* in *uester* and *uerto* (and its compounds and derivatives); and superlatives in *-imus* are written *-umus*.

Differences in the text[221]

locus	Christenson	Leo	Lindsay
Arg. II.9	†Alcumena†	(*corrupt*)	illa
5	bene expedire	bene ⟨me⟩ expedire	bene expedire
14	(*accepted*)	(*bracketed*)	(*accepted*)
32	fero	(*corrupt*)	fero
34	iustae	iusta	iustae
38	(*new section*)		
45	(*sound*)	regnator * architectus	(*sound*)
46	⟨ille⟩ illi	(*corrupt*)	⟨ille⟩ illi
54	faciam ex	faciam ex	faciam ⟨iam⟩ ex
56	fit an non? uoltis?	sit an non uoltis?	sit an non uoltis?
64	(*new section*)		
69	ambissent palmam his.	ambissint palmam his.	ambissent palmam ⟨his⟩ his.
71	ambisset	ambissit	ambisset
81	mandatis ⟨is⟩	mihi ⟨pater⟩	mandatis ⟨is⟩
93	(*bracketed*)	(*bracketed*)	(*accepted*)
125	abiuit	abiit	abiuit
143	usque in	usque in	usque ⟨hic⟩ in
146	nemo horum	nemo horum	nemo ⟨homo⟩ h.

[220] Sensible account of orthography in Ramsey's (1869) Intro. to *Mos.* pp. xvi–xlix.

[221] An asterisk marks a lacuna; an obelus is used to distinguish localized corruptions; entire verses suspected of being corrupt are so noted in parentheses.

locus	Christenson	Leo	Lindsay
149	nunc cum	nunc cum	nunc ⟨huc⟩ cum
152	facere histrioniam	facere histrioniam	facere hic hist.
158	nec ... me ⟨malo⟩	nec ... me ⟨malo⟩	siet, nec ... me om.
169	adest	adeost	adest
170	diues,	diues,	diues
173	(accepted)	(bracketed)	(accepted)
180	numero mihi	num numero mi	numero mihi
192	eri mei	eri mei	mei eri
193	praeda atque agro	praeda atque agro	praedaque agroque
198	mendacium –	mendacium,	mendacium,
207	reddere	redderent	reddere
217	contra Teloboae	Teloboae contra	contra Teloboae
234	uolnerum ui uiri	uolnerum ui uiri	uolneris ui et uirium
236	cadunt, ... ingruont,	cadunt, ... ingruont	cadunt, ... ingruont.
237	ui⟨n⟩cimus	[uicimus]	uicimus
238	fugam in	†fugam in	fugam in
240	amittunt	omittunt	amittunt
261	rex est solitus	solitus est rex	rex est solitus
264	hunc hominem hodie	huc hominem hodie	hunc hom. ⟨huc⟩ hod.
294	homo ⟨hodie⟩ h.	homo hoc	homo ⟨hodie⟩ h.
300	fab., ⟨ut⟩ h. aus.	fab., ⟨ut⟩ h. aus.	fab., aus. h.
301	modum ⟨in⟩ mai.	demum maiorem	modum maiorem
302	quod	quom	quod
329	hercle, naui	hercle, naui	hercle e naui
347	eri sum	eri ⟨iussu, eius⟩ sum	eri sum
355	familiaris,	familiaris	familiaris,
384	socium	†socium	socium
400	nobis praeter med	nobis praeter med	praesente nobis

locus	Christenson	Leo	Lindsay
401	*post* 403	*(bracketed)*	*post* 400
405	nonne me	nonne me	non me
408	nunc ⟨mihi⟩	nunc ⟨mihi⟩	⟨mi⟩ misero
418	Amphitruoni a	Amphitruoni a ⟨doni⟩	Amphitruoni a
423	quid? me	quid me	quid me
471	om. Amph. fam.	om. Amph. fam.	Amph. om. fam.
439	nolim Sosia	Sosia nolim	Sosia nolim
479	quod	quod	quo
481–2	*(bracketed)*	*(accepted)*	*(accepted)*
489–90	*(bracketed)*	*(bracketed)*	*(accepted)*
507	obseruatote ⟨eum⟩	obseruatote ⟨eum⟩	obseruatote, ⟨ut⟩
524	primo prima ⟨ut⟩	primo ⟨ut⟩ prima	primo ⟨ut⟩ prima
546, 548	Nox	nox	nox
549	disparet	disparet.	disparet
550	et dies	sed dies	et dies
555	facis	facis ⟨tu⟩	facis
572	si non id	*(corrupt)*	si id
595	mirum ⟨mirum⟩	mirum * magis	mirum ⟨mirum⟩
623	nunc ⟨te⟩	nunc ⟨te⟩	nunc ⟨ut⟩
629–31	*(bracketed)*	*(bracketed)*	*(accepted)*
632	*(accepted)*	*(bracketed)*	*(accepted)*
635	di⟨ui⟩s	diuis	dis
638	[mei] mihi	mei mihi	[mei] mi
670	d⟨u⟩ctare	putare	dictare
681	quom [te] grau.	†grauidam	quom [te] grau.
685	*(accepted)*	*(bracketed)*	*(accepted)*
726	uae [misero] mihi	ei misero mihi	uae [misero] mihi
770	fiat. ⟨i⟩	fiat. ⟨heus⟩	fiat ⟨i⟩
777	plenast. quid	plenast AL. quid	plenast AL. quid
785	⟨alium⟩, al. ego	ego alium	⟨alium⟩, ego. al.
838	⟨en⟩im u. proba's	†in u. probas	†in† uerbis probas

locus	Christenson	Leo	Lindsay
872	innocenti	innocenti	†innocenti†
875	frustrationem hodie	frustrationem hodie	hodie frus- trationem
884	infecta re esse	infecta ut reddat	†infectare est at†
897	qui me	qui me	qui ⟨modo⟩ me
899	⟨ingeni⟩ ing.	auortisti? * AL. ita	⟨ingeni⟩ ing.
952	⟨laute⟩ lud.	adeo * inpransus	(corrupt)
968	ut re	qui re	uti re
976	h. fac. ad. S.	h. fac. ad. S.	S., h. fac. ad.
978	fac Amph.	fac Amph.	face iam Amph.
985	quis. ⟨iam⟩ tam	quisquam tam	quis. tam au⟨i⟩dax
fr. 5	post., matula[m], u⟨r⟩nam ... aquai	post. matulam unam ... aquae	post. matulam unam ... aquai
fr. 12	eff. ⟨tu⟩ ... in dies	ecf. ⟨tu⟩ ... in die	ecf. ... in dies
fr. 13	pessumo	pessimo	pessumae
fr. 17	(IV.)	(AM.)	(AM.)
1038	opust med ad.	opust med ad.	med ad. opust
1040	ego ⟨faciam⟩,	ego ⟨faciam⟩,	ego * quem
1042	[nam]	(corrupt)	[nam]
1061	[sibi]	sibi	[sibi]
1062	prope	propere	prope
1108	iubatae	iubati	iubatae
1109	maxumae	maximi	maxumae
1111	conspicatae ... citae	conspicati ... citi	conspicatae ... citae
1116	alteram ... eas	alterum ... eos	alteram ... eas
1123	illas	illos	illas

T. MACCI PLAVTI

AMPHITRVO

PERSONAE

Speaking roles in order of appearance:

MERCVRIVS DEVS
SOSIA SERVOS
IVPPITER DEVS
ALCVMENA MATRONA
AMPHITRVO SENEX
BLEPHARO GVBERNATOR
BROMIA ANCILLA

Non-speaking roles:

slaves carrying Amphitryon's baggage, present 551–857 (854n.); Thessala, Alcmena's maid (770n.).

Scene 1: Thebes; a street in front of Amphitryon's palace (for the location of scene 4 see 551–632, 628nn.).

ARGVMENTVM I

In faciem uersus Amphitruonis Iuppiter,
dum bellum gereret cum Telobois hostibus,
Alcmenam uxorem cepit usurariam.
Mercurius formam Sosiae serui gerit
absentis: his Alcmena decipitur dolis.   5
postquam rediere ueri Amphitruo et Sosia,
uterque deluduntur [dolis] in mirum modum.
hinc iurgium, tumultus uxori et uiro,
donec cum tonitru uoce missa ex aethere
adulterum se Iuppiter confessus est.   10

ARGVMENTVM II

Amore captus Alcumenas Iuppiter
Mutauit sese in formam eius coniugis,
Pro patria Amphitruo dum decernit cum hostibus.
Habitu Mercurius ei subseruit Sosiae.
Is aduenientis seruum ac dominum frustra habet.   5
Turbas uxori ciet Amphitruo, atque inuicem
Raptant pro moechis. Blepharo captus arbiter
Vter sit non quit Amphitruo decernere.
Omnem rem noscunt. geminos †Alcumena† enititur.

T. MACCI PLAVTI

PROLOGVS

MERCVRIVS

ME. Vt uos in uostris uoltis mercimoniis
emundis uendundisque me laetum lucris
adficere atque adiuuare in rebus omnibus,
et ut res rationesque uostrorum omnium
bene expedire uoltis peregrique et domi,   5
bonoque atque amplo auctare perpetuo lucro
quasque incepistis res quasque inceptabitis,
et uti bonis uos uostrosque omnis nuntiis
me adficere uoltis, ea adferam, ea uti nuntiem
quae maxume in rem uostram communem sient   10
(nam uos quidem id iam scitis concessum et datum
mi esse ab dis aliis, nuntiis praesim et lucro):
haec ut me uoltis adprobare adnitier,
lucrum ut perenne uobis semper suppetat,
ita huic facietis fabulae silentium   15
itaque aequi et iusti hic eritis omnes arbitri.
　　Nunc cuius iussu uenio et quam ob rem uenerim
dicam simulque ipse eloquar nomen meum.
Iouis iussu uenio, nomen Mercuriost mihi.
pater huc me misit ad uos oratum meus,   20
tam etsi pro imperio uobis quod dictum foret
scibat facturos, quippe qui intellexerat
uereri uos se et metuere, ita ut aequom est Iouem;
uerum profecto hoc petere me precario
a uobis iussit leniter dictis bonis.   25
etenim ille, cuius huc iussu uenio, Iuppiter
non minus quam uostrum quiuis formidat malum:
humana matre natus, humano patre,
mirari non est aequom sibi si praetimet;
atque ego quoque etiam, qui Iouis sum filius,   30
contagione mei patris metuo malum.

propterea pace aduenio et pacem ad uos fero:
iustam rem et facilem esse oratam a uobis uolo,
nam iustae ab iustis iustus sum orator datus.
nam iniusta ab iustis impetrari non decet,   35
iusta autem ab iniustis petere insipientia est;
quippe illi iniqui ius ignorant neque tenent.
    Nunc iam huc animum omnes quae loquar aduortite.
debetis uelle quae uelimus: meruimus
et ego et pater de uobis et re publica;   40
nam quid ego memorem (ut alios in tragoediis
uidi, Neptunum Virtutem Victoriam
Martem Bellonam commemorare quae bona
uobis fecissent) quis benefactis meus pater,
deorum regnator, architectust omnibus?   45
sed mos numquam ⟨ille⟩ illi fuit patri meo
ut exprobraret quod bonis faceret boni;
gratum arbitratur esse id a uobis sibi
meritoque uobis bona se facere quae facit.
    Nunc quam rem oratum huc ueni primum proloquar;   50
post argumentum huius eloquar tragoediae.
quid? contraxistis frontem, quia tragoediam
dixi futuram hanc? deus sum, commutauero.
eandem hanc, si uoltis, faciam ex tragoedia
comoedia ut sit omnibus isdem uorsibus.   55
utrum fit an non? uoltis? sed ego stultior,
quasi nesciam uos uelle, qui diuos siem.
teneo quid animi uostri super hac re siet:
faciam ut commixta sit; ⟨sit⟩ tragicomoedia;
nam me perpetuo facere ut sit comoedia,   60
reges quo ueniant et di, non par arbitror.
quid igitur? quoniam hic seruos quoque partes habet,
faciam sit, proinde ut dixi, tragicomoedia.
    Nunc hoc me orare a uobis iussit Iuppiter
ut conquistores singula in subsellia   65
eant per totam caueam spectatoribus,

si cui fauitores delegatos uiderint,
ut is in cauea pignus capiantur togae;
siue qui ambissent palmam histrionibus
siue cuiquam artifici, seu per scriptas litteras   70
siue qui ipse ambisset seu per internuntium,
siue adeo aediles perfidiose cui duint,
sirempse legem iussit esse Iuppiter,
quasi magistratum sibi alteriue ambiuerit.
uirtute dixit uos uictores uiuere,   75
non ambitione neque perfidia: qui minus
eadem histrioni sit lex quae summo uiro?
uirtute ambire oportet, non fauitoribus.
sat habet fauitorum semper qui recte facit,
si illis fides est quibus est ea res in manu.   80
hoc quoque etiam mihi in mandatis ⟨is⟩ dedit
ut conquistores fierent histrionibus:
qui sibi mandasset delegati ut plauderent
quiue quo placeret alter fecisset minus,
eius ornamenta et corium uti conciderent.   85
mirari nolim uos, quapropter Iuppiter
nunc histriones curet; ne miremini:
ipse hanc acturust Iuppiter comoediam.
quid? admirati estis? quasi uero nouom
nunc proferatur, Iouem facere histrioniam;   90
etiam, histriones anno cum in proscaenio hic
Iouem inuocarunt, uenit, auxilio is fuit.
[praeterea certo prodit in tragoedia.]
hanc fabulam, inquam, hic Iuppiter hodie ipse aget
et ego una cum illo. nunc ⟨uos⟩ animum aduortite,   95
dum huius argumentum eloquar comoediae.
    Haec urbs est Thebae. in illisce habitat aedibus
Amphitruo, natus Argis ex Argo patre,
quicum Alcumena est nupta, Electri filia.
is nunc Amphitruo praefectust legionibus,   100
nam cum Telobois bellum est Thebano poplo.

is prius quam hinc abiit ipsemet in exercitum,
grauidam Alcumenam uxorem fecit suam.
nam ego uos nouisse credo iam ut sit pater meus,
quam liber harum rerum multarum siet   105
quantusque amator sit quod complacitum est semel.
is amare occepit Alcumenam clam uirum
usuramque eius corporis cepit sibi,
et grauidam fecit is eam compressu suo.
nunc de Alcumena ut rem teneatis rectius,   110
utrimque est grauida, et ex uiro et ex summo Ioue.
et meus pater nunc intus hic cum illa cubat,
et haec ob eam rem nox est facta longior,
dum ⟨cum⟩ illa quacum uolt uoluptatem capit;
sed ita adsimulauit se, quasi Amphitruo siet.   115
nunc ne hunc ornatum uos meum admiremini,
quod ego huc processi sic cum seruili schema:
ueterem atque antiquam rem nouam ad uos proferam;
propterea ornatus in nouom incessi modum.
nam meus pater intus nunc est eccum Iuppiter;   120
in Amphitruonis uertit sese imaginem
omnesque eum esse censent serui qui uident:
ita uorsipellem se facit quando lubet.
ego serui sumpsi Sosiae mi imaginem,
qui cum Amphitruone abiuit hinc in exercitum,   125
ut praeseruire amanti meo possem patri
atque ut ne qui essem familiares quaererent,
uorsari crebro hic cum uiderent me domi;
nunc, cum esse credent seruom et conseruom suom,
haud quisquam quaeret qui siem aut quid uenerim.   130
pater nunc intus suo animo morem gerit:
cubat complexus cuius cupiens maxume est;
quae illi ad legionem facta sunt memorat pater
meus Alcumenae: illa illum censet uirum
suom esse, quae cum moecho est. ibi nunc meus pater   135
memorat legiones hostium ut fugauerit,

quo pacto sit donis donatus plurimis.
ea dona, quae illic Amphitruoni sunt data,
abstulimus: facile meus pater quod uolt facit.
nunc hodie Amphitruo ueniet huc ab exercitu   140
et seruos, cuius ego hanc fero imaginem.
nunc internosse ut nos possitis facilius,
ego has habebo usque in petaso pinnulas;
tum meo patri autem torulus inerit aureus
sub petaso: id signum Amphitruoni non erit.   145
ea signa nemo horum familiarium
uidere poterit: uerum uos uidebitis.
sed Amphitruonis illi est seruos Sosia:
a portu illic nunc cum lanterna aduenit.
abigam iam ego illunc aduenientem ab aedibus.   150
adeste: erit operae pretium hic spectantibus
Iouem et Mercurium facere histrioniam. (*withdraws*)

Scene 1 (I 1)   S O S I A   M E R C V R I V S

(*Sosia enters, holding a lantern*)

SO. (*to audience*) Qui me alter est audacior homo aut qui
                                        confidentior,
iuuentutis mores qui sciam, qui hoc noctis solus ambulem?
quid faciam nunc si tresuiri me in carcerem compegerint?   155
inde cras quasi e promptaria cella depromar ad flagrum,
nec causam liceat dicere mihi, neque in ero quicquam auxili
nec quisquam sit quin me ⟨malo⟩ omnes esse dignum
                                        deputent.
   ita quasi incudem me miserum homines octo ualidi
                                        caedant:
      [nec aequom anne iniquom imperet cogitabit]   160
      ita peregre adueniens hospitio publicitus accipiar.   161-2
         haec eri immodestia
      coegit me, qui hoc noctis a portu ingratiis excitauit.

nonne idem hoc luci me mittere potuit? 165
   opulento homini hoc seruitus dura est,
   hoc magis miser est diuitis seruos:
noctesque diesque assiduo satis superque est
quod facto aut dicto adest opus, quietus ne sis.
ipse dominus diues, operis laboris expers, 170
quodcumque homini accidit libere, posse retur:
aequom esse putat, non reputat laboris quid sit,
   nec aequom anne iniquom imperet cogitabit.
   ergo in seruitute expetunt multa iniqua:
   habendum et ferundum hoc onust cum labore. 175
   ME. (*aside*) satiust me queri illo modo seruitutem:
      hodie qui fuerim liber, eum nunc
      potiuit pater seruitutis;
      hic qui uerna natust queritur.
SO. sum uero uerna uerbero: numero mihi in mentem fuit 180
dis aduenientem gratias pro meritis agere atque alloqui?
ne illi edepol si merito meo referre studeant gratiam,
aliquem hominem allegent, qui mihi aduenienti os occillet
                                      probe,
quoniam bene quae in me fecerunt ingrata ea habui atque
                                      inrita.
ME. (*aside*) facit ille quod uolgo haud solent, ut quid se sit
                                  dignum sciat. 185
SO. quod numquam opinatus fui neque alius quisquam
                                      ciuium
sibi euenturum, id contigit, ut salui poteremur domi.
uictores uictis hostibus legiones reueniunt domum,
duello exstincto maxumo atque internecatis hostibus.
quod multa Thebano poplo acerba obiecit funera, 190
id ui et uirtute militum uictum atque expugnatum oppidum
                                      est
imperio atque auspicio eri mei Amphitruonis maxume.
praeda atque agro adoriaque adfecit popularis suos
regique Thebano Creoni regnum stabiliuit suom.

me a portu praemisit domum, ut haec nuntiem uxori suae,   195
ut gesserit rem publicam ductu imperio auspicio suo.
ea nunc meditabor quo modo illi dicam, cum illo aduenero.
si dixero mendacium – solens meo more fecero.
nam cum pugnabant maxume, ego tum fugiebam maxume;
uerum quasi adfuerim tamen simulabo atque audita eloquar.   200
sed quo modo et uerbis quibus me deceat fabularier,
prius ipse mecum etiam uolo hic meditari. sic hoc proloquar.
    Principio ut illo aduenimus, ubi primum terram tetigimus,
continuo Amphitruo delegit uiros primorum principes;
eos legat, Telobois iubet sententiam ut dicant suam: 205
si sine ui et sine bello uelint rapta et raptores tradere,
si quae asportassent reddere, se exercitum extemplo domum
reducturum, abituros agro Argiuos, pacem atque otium
dare illis; sin aliter sient animati neque dent quae petat,
sese igitur summa ui uirisque eorum oppidum oppugnassere.   210
haec ubi Telobois ordine iterarunt quos praefecerat
Amphitruo, magnanimi uiri freti uirtute et uiribus
superbe nimis ferociter legatos nostros increpant,
respondent bello se et suos tutari posse, proinde uti
propere suis de finibus exercitus deducerent.   215
haec ubi legati pertulere, Amphitruo castris ilico
producit omnem exercitum; contra Teloboae ex oppido
legiones educunt suas nimis pulchris armis praeditas.
     postquam utrimque exitum est maxuma copia,
     dispertiti uiri, dispertiti ordines,   220
     nos nostras more nostro et modo instruximus
    legiones, item hostes contra legiones suas instruont.
      deinde utrique imperatores in medium exeunt,
     extra turbam ordinum conloquontur simul.
     conuenit, uicti utri sint eo proelio,   225
     urbem, agrum, aras, focos seque uti dederent.
     postquam id actum est, tubae contra utrimque occanunt,
     consonat terra, clamorem utrimque efferunt.
     imperator utrimque, hinc et illinc, Ioui

uota suscipere, ⟨utrimque⟩ hortari exercitum.   230
⟨tum⟩ pro se quisque id quod quisque potest et ualet
edit, ferro ferit, tela frangunt, boat
   caelum fremitu uirum, ex spiritu atque anhelitu
nebula constat, cadunt uolnerum ui uiri.
denique, ut uoluimus, nostra superat manus: 235
hostes crebri cadunt, nostri contra ingruont,
      ui⟨n⟩cimus ui feroces.
sed fugam in se tamen nemo conuortitur
nec recedit loco quin statim rem gerat;
animam amittunt prius quam loco demigrent: 240
quisque ut steterat iacet optinetque ordinem.
hoc ubi Amphitruo erus conspicatus est,
ilico equites iubet dextera inducere.
equites parent citi: ab dextera maxumo
      cum clamore inuolant impetu alacri,   245
foedant et proterunt hostium copias
      iure iniustas.
ME. (*aside*) numquam etiam quicquam adhuc uerborum est
                    prolocutus perperam:
namque ego fui illi in re praesenti et meus, cum pugnatum
                    est, pater.
SO. perduelles penetrant se in fugam; ibi nostris animus
                    additust: 250
uortentibus Telobois telis complebantur corpora,
ipsusque Amphitruo regem Pterelam sua obtruncauit manu.
haec illic est pugnata pugna usque a mani ad uesperum
(hoc adeo hoc commemini magis quia illo die inpransus fui),
sed proelium id tandem diremit nox interuentu suo.   255
postridie in castra ex urbe ad nos ueniunt flentes principes:
uelatis manibus orant ignoscamus peccatum suom,
deduntque se, diuina humanaque omnia, urbem et liberos
in dicionem atque in arbitratum cuncti Thebano poplo.
post ob uirtutem ero Amphitruoni patera donata aurea est, 260
qui Pterela potitare rex est solitus. haec sic dicam erae.

nunc pergam eri imperium exequi et me domum capessere.
ME. (*aside*) attat, illic huc iturust. ibo ego illic obuiam,
neque ego hunc hominem hodie ad aedis has sinam umquam
                                          accedere;
quando imago est huius in me, certum est hominem eludere.   265
et enim uero quoniam formam cepi huius in med et statum,
decet et facta moresque huius habere me similes item.
itaque me malum esse oportet, callidum, astutum admodum,
atque hunc telo suo sibi, malitia, a foribus pellere.
sed quid illuc est? caelum aspectat. obseruabo quam rem
                                          agat.   270
SO. certe edepol, si quicquamst aliud quod credam aut certo
                                          sciam,
credo ego hac noctu Nocturnum obdormiuisse ebrium.
nam neque se Septentriones quoquam in caelo commouent,
neque se Luna quoquam mutat atque uti exorta est semel,
nec Iugulae neque Vesperugo neque Vergiliae occidunt.   275
ita statim stant signa, neque nox quoquam concedit die.
ME. (*aside*) perge, Nox, ut occepisti; gere patri morem meo:
optumo optume optumam operam das, datam pulchre locas.
SO. neque ego hac nocte longiorem me uidisse censeo,
nisi item unam, uerberatus quam pependi perpetem;   280
eam quoque edepol etiam multo haec uicit longitudine.
credo edepol equidem dormire Solem atque adpotum probe;
mira sunt nisi inuitauit sese in cena plusculum.
ME. (*aside*) ain uero, uerbero? deos esse tui similis putas?
ego pol te istis tuis pro dictis et male factis, furcifer,   285
accipiam; modo sis ueni huc: inuenies infortunium.
SO. ubi sunt isti scortatores qui soli inuiti cubant?
haec nox scita est exercendo scorto conducto male.
ME. (*aside*) meus pater nunc pro huius uerbis recte et
                                          sapienter facit,
qui complexus cum Alcumena cubat amans, animo
                                          obsequens.   290
SO. ibo ut erus quod imperauit Alcumenae nuntiem.

sed quis hic est homo quem ante aedis uideo hoc noctis? non
placet.

ME. (*aside*) nullust hoc metuculosus aeque. SO. (*aside*) mi in
mentem uenit,

illic homo ⟨hodie⟩ hoc denuo uolt pallium detexere.

ME. (*aside*) timet homo: deludam ego illum. SO. (*aside*) perii,
dentes pruriunt; 295

certe aduenientem hic me hospitio pugneo accepturus est.

credo misericors est: nunc propterea quod me meus erus

fecit ut uigilarem, hic pugnis faciet hodie ut dormiam.

oppido interii. obsecro hercle, quantus et quam ualidus est!

ME. (*aside*) clare aduorsum fabulabor, ⟨ut⟩ hic auscultet
quae loquar; 300

igitur magis modum ⟨in⟩ maiorem in sese concipiet metum.

(*loudly*) agite, pugni, iam diu est quod uentri uictum non
datis:

iam pridem uidetur factum heri quod homines quattuor

in soporem collocastis nudos. SO. (*aside*) formido male

ne ego hic nomen meum commutem et Quintus fiam e Sosia; 305

quattuor uiros sopori se dedisse hic autumat:

metuo ne numerum augeam illum. ME. em nunciam ergo:
sic uolo.

SO. (*aside*) cingitur: certe expedit se. ME. non feret quin
uapulet.

SO. (*aside*) quis homo? ME quisquis homo huc profecto
uenerit, pugnos edet.

SO. (*aside*) apage, non placet me hoc noctis esse: cenaui
modo; 310

proin tu istam cenam largire, si sapis, essurientibus.

ME. haud malum huic est pondus pugno. SO. (*aside*) perii,
pugnos ponderat.

ME. quid si ego illum tractim tangam, ut dormiat? SO.
(*aside*) seruaueris,

nam continuas has tris noctes peruigilaui. ME. pessumest,

facimus nequiter, ferire malam male discit manus; 315

alia forma esse oportet quem tu pugno legeris.
SO. (*aside*) illic homo me interpolabit meumque os finget

                                   denuo.
ME. exossatum os esse oportet quem probe percusseris.
SO. (*aside*) mirum ni hic me quasi murenam exossare cogitat.
ultro istunc qui exossat homines! perii, si me aspexerit.   320
ME. olet homo quidam malo suo. SO. (*aside*) ei, numnam

                                ego obolui?
ME. atque haud longe abesse oportet, uerum longe hinc

                                  afuit.
SO. (*aside*) illic homo superstitiosust. ME. gestiunt pugni

                                  mihi.
SO. (*aside*) si in me exercituru's, quaeso in parietem ut

                            primum domes.
ME. uox mi ad aures aduolauit. SO. (*aside*) ne ego homo

                              infelix fui, 325
qui non alas interuelli: uolucrem uocem gestito.
ME. illic homo a me sibi malam rem arcessit iumento suo.
SO. (*aside*) non equidem ullum habeo iumentum. ME.

                         onerandus est pugnis probe.
SO. (*aside*) lassus sum hercle, naui ut uectus huc sum: etiam

                              nunc nauseo;
uix incedo inanis, ne ire posse cum onere existimes. 330
ME. certe enim hic nescioquis loquitur. SO. (*aside*) saluos

                          sum, non me uidet:
'nescioquem' loqui autumnat; mihi certo nomen Sosiaest.
ME. hinc enim mihi dextra uox auris, ut uidetur, uerberat.
SO. (*aside*) metuo, uocis ne uicem hodie hic uapulem, quae

                           hunc uerberat.
ME. (*aside*) optume eccum incedit ad me. SO. (*aside*) timeo,

                           totus torpeo. 335
non edepol nunc ubi terrarum sim scio, si quis roget,
neque miser me commouere possum prae formidine.
ilicet: mandata eri perierunt una et Sosia.

uerum certum est confidenter hominem contra conloqui,
qui possim uideri huic fortis, a me ut abstineat manum. (*faces*
Mercury) 340
ME. quo ambulas tu, qui Volcanum in cornu conclusum
geris?
SO. quid id exquiris tu qui pugnis os exossas hominibus?
ME. seruosne ⟨es⟩ an liber? SO. utcumque animo
conlibitum est meo.
ME. ain uero? SO. aio enim uero. ME. uerbero. SO.
mentire nunc.
ME. at iam faciam ut uerum dicas dicere. SO. quid eo est
opus? 345
ME. possum scire quo profectus, cuius sis aut quid ueneris?
SO. huc eo. eri sum seruos. numquid nunc es certior?
ME. ego tibi istam hodie, sceleste, comprimam linguam. SO.
haud potes:
bene pudiceque adseruatur. ME. pergin argutarier?
quid apud hasce aedis negoti est tibi? SO. immo quid tibi
est? 350
ME. rex Creo uigiles nocturnos singulos semper locat.
SO. bene facit: quia nos eramus peregri, tutatust domi;
at nunc abi sane, aduenisse familiares dicito.
ME. nescio quam tu familiaris sis: nisi actutum hinc abis,
familiaris, accipiere faxo haud familiariter. 355
SO. hic, inquam, habito ego atque horunc seruos sum. ME.
at scin quo modo?
faciam ego hodie te superbum, nisi hic abis. SO. quonam
modo?
ME. auferere, non abibis, si ego fustem sumpsero.
SO. quin me esse huius familiai familiarem praedico.
ME. uide sis quam mox uapulare uis, nisi actutum hinc abis. 360
SO. tun domo prohibere peregre me aduenientem postulas?
ME. haecine tua domust? SO. ita inquam. ME. quis erus est
igitur tibi?

SO. Amphitruo, qui nunc praefectust Thebanis legionibus,
quicum nupta est Alcumena. ME. quid ais? quid nomen tibi
                                                    est?
SO. Sosiam uocant Thebani, Dauo prognatum patre.   365
ME. ne tu istic hodie malo tuo compositis mendaciis
aduenisti, audaciai columen, consutis dolis.
SO. immo equidem tunicis consutis huc aduenio, non dolis.
ME. at mentiris etiam: certo pedibus, non tunicis uenis.
SO. ita profecto. ME. nunc profecto uapula ob mendacium.   370
SO. non edepol uolo profecto. ME. at pol profecto
                                            ingratiis.
hoc quidem 'profecto' certum est, non est arbitrarium.
SO. tuam fidem obsecro. ME. tun te audes Sosiam esse
                                                 dicere,
qui ego sum? SO. perii. ME. parum etiam, praeut futurum
                                            est, praedicas.
quoius nunc es? SO. tuos, nam pugnis usu fecisti tuom.   375
pro fidem, Thebani ciues! ME. etiam clamas, carnufex?
loquere, quid uenisti? SO. ut esset quem tu pugnis caederes.
ME. cuius es? SO. Amphitruonis, inquam, Sosia. ME. ergo
                                              istoc magis,
quia uaniloquo's, uapulabis: ego sum, non tu, Sosia.
SO. (aside) ita di faciant, ut tu potius sis atque ego te ut
                                            uerberem. 380
ME. etiam muttis? SO. iam tacebo. ME. quis tibi erust?
                              SO. quem tu uoles.
ME. quid igitur? qui nunc uocare? SO. nemo nisi quem
                                              iusseris.
ME. Amphitruonis te esse aiebas Sosiam. SO. peccaueram,
nam Amphitruonis socium ne me esse uolui dicere.
ME. scibam equidem nullum esse nobis nisi me seruom
                                       Sosiam. 385
fugit te ratio. SO. utinam istuc pugni fecissent tui.
ME. ego sum Sosia ille quem tu dudum esse aiebas mihi.
SO. obsecro ut per pacem liceat te alloqui, ut ne uapulem.

ME. immo indutiae parumper fiant, si quid uis loqui.
SO. non loquar nisi pace facta, quando pugnis plus uales.   390
ME. dic si quid uis, non nocebo. SO. tuae fide credo? ME.
                                     meae.
SO. quid si falles? ME. tum Mercurius Sosiae iratus siet.
SO. animum aduorte. nunc licet mi libere quiduis loqui.
Amphitruonis ego sum seruos Sosia. ME. etiam denuo?
SO. pacem feci, foedus feci, uera dico. ME. uapula.   395
SO. ut libet quid tibi libet fac, quoniam pugnis plus uales;
uerum, utut es facturus, hoc quidem hercle haud reticebo
                                   tamen.
ME. tu me uiuos hodie numquam facies quin sim Sosia.
SO. certe edepol tu me alienabis numquam quin noster
                                   siem;
nec nobis praeter med alius quisquam est seruos Sosia.   400
ME. hic homo sanus non est. SO. quod mihi praedicas
                          uitium, id tibi est. 402
quid, malum, non sum ego seruos Amphitruonis Sosia,   403
qui cum Amphitruone hinc una ieram in exercitum?   401
nonne hac noctu nostra nauis ⟨huc⟩ ex portu Persico   404
uenit, quae me aduexit? nonne me huc erus misit meus?   405
nonne ego nunc sto ante aedis nostras? non mi est lanterna in
                                 manu?
non loquor, non uigilo? nonne hic homo modo me pugnis
                               contudit?
fecit hercle, nam etiam misero nunc ⟨mihi⟩ malae dolent.
quid igitur ego dubito, aut cur non intro eo in nostram
                               domum?
ME. quid, domum uostram? SO. ita enim uero. ME. quin
                       quae dixisti modo 410
omnia ementitu's: equidem Sosia Amphitruonis sum.
nam noctu hac soluta est nauis nostra a portu Persico,
et ubi Pterela rex regnauit oppidum expugnauimus,
et legiones Teloboarum ui pugnando cepimus,
et ipsus Amphitruo optruncauit regem Pterelam in proelio.   415

SO. egomet mihi non credo, cum illaec autumare illum

                                           audio:

hic quidem certe quae illic sunt res gestae memorat

                                        memoriter.

sed quid ais? quid Amphitruoni a Telobois est datum?

ME. Pterela rex qui potitare solitus est patera aurea.

SO. (*aside*) elocutus est. (*to Mercury*) ubi patera nunc est? ME.

                                 ⟨est⟩ in cistula; 420

Amphitruonis obsignata signo est. SO. signi dic quid est?

ME. cum quadrigis Sol exoriens. quid? me captas, carnufex?

SO. (*aside*) argumentis uicit, aliud nomen quaerundum est

                                    mihi.

nescio unde haec hic spectauit. iam ego hunc decipiam

                                     probe;

nam quod egomet solus feci, nec quisquam alius affuit, 425

in tabernaclo, id quidem hodie numquam poterit dicere.

(*to Mercury*) si tu Sosia es, legiones cum pugnabant maxume,

quid in tabernaclo fecisti? uictus sum, si dixeris.

ME. cadus erat uini, inde impleui hirneam. SO. (*aside*)

                                 ingressust uiam.

ME. eam ego, ut matre fuerat natum, uini eduxi meri. 430

SO. (*aside*) factum est illud, ut ego illic uini hirneam

                                 ebiberim meri.

mira sunt nisi latuit intus illic in illac hirnea.

ME. quid nunc? uincon argumentis te non esse Sosiam?

SO. tu negas med esse? ME. quid ego ni negem, qui egomet

                                 siem?

SO. per Iouem iuro med esse neque me falsum dicere. 435

ME. at ego per Mercurium iuro tibi Iouem non credere;

nam iniurato scio plus credet mihi quam iurato tibi.

SO. quis ego sum saltem, si non sum Sosia? te interrogo.

ME. ubi ego nolim Sosia esse, tu esto sane Sosia;

nunc quando ego sum, uapulabis, ni hinc abis, ignobilis. 440

SO. (*aside*) certe edepol, quom illum contemplo et formam

                                 cognosco meam,

quem ad modum ego sum (saepe in speculum inspexi), nimis
similest mei;
itidem habet petasum ac uestitum: tam consimilest atque
ego;
sura, pes, statura, tonsus, oculi, nasum uel labra,
malae, mentum, barba, collus: totus. quid uerbis opust?   445
si tergum cicatricosum, nihil hoc similist similius.
sed quom cogito, equidem certo idem sum qui semper fui.
noui erum, noui aedis nostras; sane sapio et sentio.
non ego illi obtempero quod loquitur. pultabo fores. (*starts
toward palace*)
ME. quo agis te? SO. domum. ME. quadrigas si nunc
inscendas Iouis 450
atque hinc fugis, ita uix poteris effugere infortunium.
SO. nonne erae meae nuntiare quod erus meus iussit licet?
ME. tuae si quid uis nuntiare: hanc nostram adire non
sinam.
nam si me inritassis, hodie lumbifragium hinc auferes.
SO. (*retreats*) abeo potius. (*to audience*) di immortales, obsecro
uostram fidem, 455
ubi ego perii? ubi immutatus sum? ubi ego formam perdidi?
an egomet me illic reliqui, si forte oblitus fui?
nam hicquidem omnem imaginem meam, quae antehac
fuerat, possidet.
uiuo fit quod numquam quisquam mortuo faciet mihi.
ibo ad portum atque haec uti sunt facta ero dicam meo;   460
nisi etiam is quoque me ignorabit: quod ille faxit Iuppiter,
ut ego hodie raso capite caluos capiam pilleum. (*exits*)

Scene 2 (I 2)   MERCVRIVS

(*Mercury remains on stage and addresses the audience*)

ME. Bene prospere[que] hoc hodie operis processit mihi:
amoui a foribus maxumam molestiam,

patri ut liceret tuto illam amplexarier.   465
iam ille illuc ad erum cum Amphitruonem aduenerit,
narrabit seruom hinc sese a foribus Sosiam
amouisse; ille adeo illum mentiri sibi
credet, neque credet huc profectum, ut iusserat.
erroris ambo ego illos et dementiae   470
complebo atque omnem Amphitruonis familiam,
adeo usque satietatem dum capiet pater
illius quam amat. igitur demum omnes scient
quae facta. denique Alcumenam Iuppiter
rediget antiquam coniugi in concordiam.   475
nam Amphitruo actutum uxori turbas conciet
atque insimulabit eam probri; tum meus pater
eam seditionem illi in tranquillum conferet.
nunc de Alcumena dudum quod dixi minus,
hodie illa pariet filios geminos duos;   480
[alter decumo post mense nascetur puer
quam seminatust, alter mense septumo;]
eorum Amphitruonis alter est, alter Iouis:
uerum minori puero maior est pater,
minor maiori. iamne hoc scitis quid siet?   485
sed Alcumenae huius honoris gratia
pater curauit uno ut fetu fieret,
uno ut labore absoluat aerumnas duas.
[et ne in suspicione ponatur stupri
et clandestina ut celetur consuetio.]   490
quamquam, ut iam dudum dixi, resciscet tamen
Amphitruo rem omnem. quid igitur? nemo id probro
profecto ducet Alcumenae; nam deum
non par uidetur facere, delictum suom
suamque ut culpam expetere in mortalem ut sinat.   495
orationem comprimam: crepuit foris.
Amphitruo subditiuos eccum exit foras
cum Alcumena uxore usuraria.

Scene 3 (I 3)   IVPPITER   ALCVMENA   MERCVRIVS

(*Jupiter and Alcmena enter from the palace*)

IV. Bene uale, Alcumena, cura rem communem, quod facis,
atque inperce quaeso: menses iam tibi esse actos uides.   500
mihi necesse est ire hinc; uerum quod erit natum tollito.
AL. quid istuc est, mi uir, negoti, quod tu tam subito domo
abeas? IV. edepol haud quod tui me neque domi distaedeat;
sed ubi summus imperator non adest ad exercitum,
citius quod non facto est usus fit quam quod facto est opus.   505
ME. (*aside*) nimis hic scitust sycophanta, qui quidem meus sit
                                                         pater.
obseruatote ⟨eum⟩, quam blande mulieri palpabitur.
AL. ecastor te experior quanti facias uxorem tuam.
IV. satin habes, si feminarum nulla est quam aeque diligam?
ME. (*aside*) edepol ne illa si istis rebus te sciat operam dare,   510
ego faxim ted Amphitruonem esse malis quam Iouem.
AL. experiri istuc mauellem me quam mi memorarier.
prius abis quam lectus ubi cubuisti concaluit locus.
heri uenisti media nocte, nunc abis. hoccin placet?
ME. (*aside*) accedam atque hanc appellabo et subparasitabor
                                                         patri. 515
(*to Alcmena*) numquam edepol quemquam mortalem credo ego
                                                 uxorem suam
sic ecflictim amare, proinde ut hic te ecflictim deperit.
IV. carnufex, non ego te noui? abin e conspectu meo?
quid tibi hanc curatio est rem, uerbero, aut muttitio?
quoii ego iam hoc scipione – AL. ah noli. IV. muttito modo.   520
ME. (*aside*) nequiter paene expediuit prima parasitatio.
IV. uerum quod tu dicis, mea uxor, non te mi irasci decet.
clanculum abii: a legione operam hanc subrupui tibi,
ex me primo prima ⟨ut⟩ scires rem ut gessissem publicam.
ea tibi omnia enarraui. nisi te amarem plurumum,   525

non facerem. ME. (*aside*) facitne ut dixi? timidam palpo

                                     percutit.

IV. nunc, ne legio persentiscat, clam illuc redeundum est

                                        mihi,

ne me uxorem praeuertisse dicant prae re publica.

AL. lacrimantem ex abitu concinnas tu tuam uxorem. IV.

                                        tace,

ne corrumpe oculos, redibo actutum. AL. id 'actutum' diu

                                        est. 530

IV. non ego te hic lubens relinquo neque abeo abs te. AL.

                                      sentio,

nam qua nocte ad me uenisti, eadem abis. IV. cur me tenes?

tempus ⟨est⟩: exire ex urbe prius quam lucescat uolo.

nunc tibi hanc pateram, quae dono mi illi ob uirtutem data

                                        est,

Pterela rex qui potitauit, quem ego mea occidi manu,   535

Alcumena, tibi condono. AL. facis ut alias res soles.

ecastor condignum donum, qualest qui donum dedit.

ME. immo sic: condignum donum, qualest cui dono datumst.

IV. pergin autem? nonne ego possum, furcifer, te perdere?

AL. noli amabo, Amphitruo, irasci Sosiae causa mea.   540

IV. faciam ita ut uis. ME. (*aside*) ex amore hic admodum

                                   quam saeuos est.

IV. numquid uis? AL. ut quom absim me ames, me tuam te

                                   absenti tamen.

ME. eamus, Amphitruo; lucescit hoc iam. IV. abi prae,

                                   Sosia;

iam ego sequar. (*Mercury exits*) numquid uis? AL. etiam: ut

                                actutum aduenias. IV. licet,

prius tua opinione hic adero: bonum animum habe. (*Alcmena*

                                   enters palace) 545

nunc te, Nox, quae me mansisti, mitto ut ⟨con⟩cedas die,

ut mortalis inlucescat luce clara et candida.

atque quanto, Nox, fuisti longior hac proxuma,

tanto breuior dies ut fiat faciam, ut aeque disparet
et dies e nocte accedat. ibo et Mercurium subsequar. (*exits*)   550

Scene 4 (II 1)   AMPHITRVO   SOSIA

(*Amphitryon, Sosia, and slaves with baggage enter; they are somewhere
between the harbour and the palace*)

AM. Age i tu secundum. SO. sequor, subsequor te.
AM. scelestissumum te arbitror. SO. nam quamobrem?
AM. quia id quod neque est neque fuit neque futurum est
mihi praedicas. SO. eccere, iam tuatim
facis, ut tuis nulla apud te fides sit.   555
AM. quid est? quo modo? iam quidem hercle ego tibi istam
scelestam, scelus, linguam abscidam. SO. tuos sum,
proinde ut commodumst et lubet quidque facias;
tamen quin loquar haec uti facta sunt hic,
numquam ullo modo me potes deterrere.   560
AM. scelestissume, audes mihi praedicare id,
domi te esse nunc, qui hic ades? SO. uera dico.
AM. malum quod tibi di dabunt, atque ego hodie
dabo. SO. istuc tibist in manu, nam tuos sum.
AM. tun me, uerbero, audes erum ludificari?   565
tune id dicere audes, quod nemo umquam homo antehac
uidit nec potest fieri, tempore uno
homo idem duobus locis ut simul sit?
SO. profecto ut loquor res ita est. AM. Iuppiter te
perdat. SO. quid mali sum, ere, tua ex re promeritus?   570
AM. rogasne, improbe, etiam qui ludos facis me?
SO. merito maledicas mihi, si non id ita factum est.
uerum haud mentior, resque uti facta dico.
        AM. homo hic ebrius est, ut opinor.
           SO. utinam ita essem! AM. optas quae facta.   575
           SO. egone? AM. tu istic. ubi bibisti?

SO. nusquam equidem bibi. AM. quid hoc sit   576
hominis? SO. equidem deciens dixi:
domi ego sum, inquam, ecquid audis?   577
et apud te adsum Sosia idem.
satin hoc plane, satin diserte,   578
    ere, nunc uideor   578a
  tibi locutus esse? AM. uah,   579
apage te a me. SO. quid est negoti?   580
AM. pestis te tenet. SO. nam quor istuc
dicis? equidem ualeo et saluos
sum recte, Amphitruo. AM. at te ego faciam   583
  hodie proinde ac meritus es,
ut minus ualeas et miser sis,   584a
saluos domum si rediero: iam   584b
sequere sis, erum qui ludificas   585a
  dictis delirantibus,   585b
qui quoniam erus quod imperauit neglexisti persequi,
nunc uenis etiam ultro inrisum dominum: quae neque fieri
possunt neque fando umquam accepit quisquam profers,
                                 carnufex;
quoius ego hodie in tergum faxo ista expetant mendacia.
SO. Amphitruo, miserruma istaec miseria est seruo bono,   590
apud erum qui uera loquitur, si id ui uerum uincitur.
AM. quo id, malum, pacto potest nam (mecum argumentis
                                  puta)
fieri, nunc uti tu ⟨et⟩ hic sis et domi? id dici uolo.
SO. sum profecto et hic et illic. hoc cuiuis mirari licet.
neque tibi istuc mirum ⟨mirum⟩ magis uidetur quam mihi.   595
AM. quo modo? SO. nihilo, inquam, mirum magis tibi istuc
                                quam mihi;
neque, ita me di ament, credebam primo mihimet Sosiae,
donec Sosia illic egomet fecit sibi uti crederem.
ordine omne, uti quicque actum est, dum apud hostis
                                sedimus,
edissertauit. tum formam una abstulit cum nomine.   600

neque lac lactis magis est simile quam ille ego similest mei.
nam ut dudum ante lucem a portu me praemisisti domum –
AM. quid igitur? SO. prius multo ante aedis stabam quam
                                       illo adueneram.
AM. quas, malum, nugas? satin tu sanus es? SO. sic sum ut
                                              uides.
AM. huic homini nescioquid est mali mala obiectum manu,   605
postquam a me abiit. SO. fateor, nam sum obtusus pugnis
                                           pessume.
AM. quis te uerberauit? SO. egomet memet, qui nunc sum
                                             domi.
AM. caue quicquam, nisi quod rogabo te, mihi responderis.
omnium primum iste qui sit Sosia, hoc dici uolo.
SO. tuos est seruos. AM. mihi quidem uno te plus etiam est
                                    quam uolo, 610
neque, postquam sum natus, habui nisi te seruom Sosiam.
SO. at ego nunc, Amphitruo, dico: Sosiam seruom tuom
praeter me alterum, inquam, adueniens faciam ut offendas
                                       domi,
Dauo prognatum patre eodem quo ego sum, forma, aetate
                                               item
qua ego sum. quid opust uerbis? geminus Sosia hic factust
                                           tibi. 615
AM. nimia memoras mira. sed uidistin uxorem meam?
SO. quin intro ire in aedis numquam licitum est. AM. quis te
                                        prohibuit?
SO. Sosia ille quem iam dudum dico, is qui me contudit.
AM. quis istic Sosia est? SO. ego, inquam, quotiens
                                   dicendum est tibi?
AM. sed quid ais? num obdormiuisti dudum? SO. nusquam
                                     gentium. 620
AM. ibi forte istum si uidisses quendam in somnis Sosiam.
SO. non soleo ego somniculose eri imperia persequi.
uigilans uidi, uigilans nunc ⟨te⟩ uideo, uigilans fabulor,
uigilantem ille me iam dudum uigilans pugnis contudit.

AM. quis homo? SO. Sosia, inquam, ego ille. quaeso, nonne
                                                  intellegis?   625
AM. qui, malum, intellegere quisquam potis est? ita nugas
                                                      blatis.
SO. uerum actutum nosces, quom illum nosces seruom
                                                  Sosiam.
AM. sequere hac igitur me, nam mi istuc primum exquisito
                                                  est opus.
[sed uide ex naui efferantur quae imperaui iam omnia.
SO. et memor sum et diligens, ut quae imperes compareant;   630
non ego cum uino simitu ebibi imperium tuom.
AM.] utinam di faxint infecta dicta re eueniant tua.

Scene 5 (II 2)   ALCVMENA   AMPHITRVO   SOSIA

(*Alcmena enters from the palace; Amphitryon and Sosia perhaps
pantomime their journey*)

AL. Satin parua res est uoluptatum in uita atque in aetate
                                                  agunda
praequam quod molestum est? ita cuique comparatum est in
                                             aetate hominum;
ita di⟨ui⟩s est placitum, uoluptatem ut maeror comes
                                          consequatur: 635
quin incommodi plus malique ilico adsit, boni si optigit
                                             quid.
nam ego id nunc experior domo atque ipsa de me scio, cui
                                             uoluptas
parumper datast, dum uiri [mei] mihi potestas uidendi fuit
noctem unam modo; atque is repente abiit a med hinc ante
                                             lucem.
sola hic mi nunc uideor, quia ille hinc abest quem ego amo
                                          praeter omnis.   640
plus aegri ex abitu uiri, quam ex aduentu uoluptatis cepi.
                          sed hoc me beat   641a

saltem, quom perduellis uicit et domum laudis compos
reuenit:

id solacio est.

absit, dum modo laude parta

domum recipiat se; feram et perferam usque   645
abitum eius animo forti atque offirmato, id modo si mercedis
datur mi, ut meus uictor uir belli clueat.

satis mi esse ducam.   647a

uirtus praemium est optumum;

uirtus omnibus rebus anteit profecto:

libertas salus uita res et parentes, patria et prognati   650
tutantur, seruantur:

uirtus omnia in sese habet, omnia adsunt

bona quem penest uirtus.

AM. (to *Sosia*) edepol me uxori exoptatum credo aduenturum
domum,

quae me amat, quam contra amo, praesertim re gesta bene,   655
uictis hostibus: quos nemo posse superari ratust,
eos auspicio meo atque ductu primo coetu uicimus.
certe enim med illi expectatum optato uenturum scio.
SO. quid? me non rere expectatum amicae uenturum meae?
AL. (*aside*) meus uir hicquidem est. AM. (*to Sosia*) sequere
hac tu me. AL. (*aside*) nam quid ille reuortitur   660
qui dudum properare se aibat? an ille me temptat sciens
atque id se uolt experiri, suom abitum ut desiderem?
ecastor med haud inuita se domum recipit suam.
SO. (*notices Alcmena*) Amphitruo, redire ad nauem meliust
nos. AM. qua gratia?
SO. quia domi daturus nemo est prandium aduenientibus.   665
AM. qui tibi nunc istuc in mentemst? SO. quia enim sero
aduenimus.
AM. qui? SO. quia Alcumenam ante aedis stare saturam
intellego.
AM. grauidam ego illanc hic reliqui quom abeo. SO. ei perii
miser.

AM. quid tibi est? SO. ad aquam praebendam commodum
                                        adueni domum,
decumo post mense, ut rationem te d⟨u⟩ctare intellego.   670
AM. bono animo es. SO. scin quam bono animo sim? si
                                        situlam cepero,
numquam edepol tu mihi diuini [quicquam] creduis post
                                        hunc diem,
ni ego illi puteo, si occepso, animam omnem intertraxero.
AM. sequere hac me modo. alium ego isti rei allegabo, ne
                                        time.
AL. (*aside*) magis nunc ⟨me⟩ meum officium facere, si huic
                                eam aduorsum, arbitror. 675
AM. (*to Alcmena*) Amphitruo uxorem salutat laetus speratam
                                        suam,
quam omnium Thebis uir unam esse optumam diiudicat,
quamque adeo ciues Thebani uero rumiferant probam.
ualuistin usque? expectatun aduenio? SO. (*aside*) haud uidi
                                        magis.
expectatum eum salutat magis haud quicquam quam canem.   680
AM. et quom [te] grauidam et quom te pulchre plenam
                                        aspicio, gaudeo.
AL. obsecro ecastor, quid tu me deridiculi gratia
sic salutas atque appellas, quasi dudum non uideris,
quasi qui nunc primum recipias te domum huc ex hostibus,
atque me nunc proinde appellas quasi multo post uideris?   685
AM. immo equidem te nisi nunc hodie nusquam uidi
                                        gentium.
AL. cur negas? AM. quia uera didici dicere. AL. haud
                                        aequom facit
qui quod didicit id dediscit. an periclitamini
quid animi habeam? sed quid huc uos reuortimini tam cito?
an te auspicium commoratum est an tempestas continet   690
qui non abiisti ad legiones, ita uti dudum dixeras?
AM. dudum? quam dudum istuc factum est? AL. temptas.
                                        iam dudum, modo.

AM. qui istuc potis est fieri, quaeso, ut dicis: iam dudum,
                         modo?
AL. quid enim censes? te ut deludam contra lusorem meum,
qui nunc primum te aduenisse dicas, modo qui hinc abieris.   695
AM. (*to Sosia*) haec quidem deliramenta loquitur. SO.
                       paulisper mane,
dum edormiscat unum somnum. AM. quaene uigilans
                       somniat?
AL. equidem ecastor uigilo et uigilans id quod factum est
                       fabulor.
nam dudum ante lucem et istunc et te uidi. AM. quo in
                       loco?
AL. hic in aedibus ubi tu habitas. AM. numquam factum est.
             SO. (*to Amphitryon*) non taces?   700
quid si e portu nauis huc nos dormientis detulit?
AM. etiam tu quoque adsentaris huic? SO. quid uis fieri?
non tu scis? Bacchae bacchanti si uelis aduorsarier,
ex insana insaniorem facies, feriet saepius;
si obsequare, una resoluas plaga. AM. (*to himself*) at pol qui
                    certa res 705
hanc est obiurgare, quae me hodie aduenientem domum
noluerit salutare. SO. inritabis crabrones. AM. (*to Sosia*) tace.
(*to Alcmena*) Alcumena, unum rogare te uolo. AL. quid uis
                   roga.
AM. num tibi aut stultitia accessit aut superat superbia?
AL. qui istuc in mentemst tibi ex me, mi uir, percontarier?   710
AM. quia salutare aduenientem me solebas antidhac,
appellare itidem ut pudicae suos uiros quae sunt solent.
eo more expertem te factam adueniens offendi domi.
AL. ecastor equidem te certo heri aduenientem ilico
et salutaui et ualuissesne usque exquisiui simul,   715
mi uir, et manum prehendi et osculum tetuli tibi.
SO. tun heri hunc salutauisti? AL. et te quoque etiam, Sosia.
SO. Amphitruo, speraui ego istam tibi parituram filium;
uerum non est puero grauida. AM. quid igitur? SO. insania.

AL. equidem sana sum et deos quaeso, ut salua pariam

                                         filium. 720

uerum tu malum magnum habebis, si hic suom officium

                                         facit:

ob istuc omen, ominator, capies quod te condecet.

SO. (*aside*) enim uero praegnati oportet et malum et malum

                                         dari

ut quod obrodat sit, animo si male esse occeperit.

AM. tu me heri hic uidisti? AL. ego, inquam, si uis decies

                                      dicere. 725

AM. in somnis fortasse. AL. immo uigilans uigilantem. AM.

                                   uae [misero] mihi!

SO. quid tibi est? AM. delirat uxor. SO. atra bili percita

                                        est.

nulla res tam delirantis homines concinnat cito.

AM. ubi primum tibi sensisti, mulier, impliciscier?

AL. equidem ecastor sana et salua sum. AM. quor igitur

                                    praedicas 730

te heri me uidisse, qui hac noctu in portum aduecti sumus?

ibi cenaui atque ibi quieui in naui noctem perpetem,

neque meum pedem huc intuli etiam in aedis, ut cum

                                    exercitu

hinc profectus sum ad Teloboas hostis eosque ut uicimus.

AL. immo mecum cenauisti et mecum cubuisti. AM. quid

                                     est? 735

AL. uera dico. AM. non de hac quidem hercle re; de aliis

                                      nescio.

AL. primulo diluculo abiisti ad legiones. AM. quo modo?

SO. (*to Amphitryon*) recte dicit, ut commeminit: somnium

                                    narrat tibi.

(*to Alcmena*) sed, mulier, postquam experrecta es, te prodigiali

                                     Ioui

aut mola salsa hodie aut ture comprecatam oportuit.   740

AL. uae capiti tuo! SO. tua istuc refert – si curaueris.

AL. iterum iam hic in me inclementer dicit, atque id sine
                                                    malo.
AM. (*to Sosia*) tace tu. (*to Alcmena*) tu dic: egone abs te abii
                                hinc hodie cum diluculo?
AL. quis igitur nisi uos narrauit mi illi ut fuerit proelium?
AM. an etiam id tu scis? AL. quippe qui ex te audiui, ut
                                urbem maxumam 745
expugnauisses regemque Pterelam tute occideris.
AM. egone istuc dixi? AL. tute istic, etiam adstante hoc
                                                    Sosia.
AM. (*to Sosia*) audiuistin tu me narrare haec hodie? SO. ubi
                                ego audiuerim?
AM. hanc roga. SO. me quidem praesente numquam
                                factumst, quod sciam.
AL. mirum quin te aduorsus dicat. AM. (*pulls Sosia aside*)
                                Sosia, age me huc aspice. 750
SO. specto. AM. uera uolo loqui te, nolo adsentari mihi.
audiuistin tu hodie me illi dicere ea quae illa autumnat?
SO. quaeso edepol, num tu quoque etiam insanis, quom id
                                me interrogas,
qui ipsus equidem nunc primum istanc tecum conspicio
                                                    simul?
AM. quid nunc, mulier? audin illum? AL. ego uero, ac
                                falsum dicere. 755
AM. neque tu illi neque mihi uiro ipsi credis? AL. eo fit quia
                                                    mihi
plurimum credo et scio istaec facta proinde ut proloquor.
AM. tun me heri aduenisse dicis? AL. tun te abiisse hodie
                                hinc negas?
AM. nego enim uero, et me aduenire nunc primum aio ad te
                                domum.
AL. obsecro, etiamne hoc negabis, te auream pateram mihi 760
dedisse dono hodie, qua te illi donatum esse dixeras?
AM. neque edepol dedi neque dixi; uerum ita animatus fui

itaque nunc sum, ut ea te patera donem. sed quis istuc tibi
dixit? AL. ego equidem ex te audiui et ex tua accepi manu
pateram. AM. mane, mane obsecro te. (*turns to Sosia*) nimis
                                        demiror, Sosia, 765
qui illaec illic me donatum esse aurea patera sciat,
nisi tu dudum hanc conuenisti et narrauisti haec omnia.
SO. neque edepol ego dixi neque istam uidi nisi tecum simul.
AM. quid hoc sit hominis? AL. uin proferri pateram? AM.
                                        proferri uolo.
AL. fiat. (*calls toward palace*) ⟨i⟩ tu, Thessala, intus pateram
                                        proferto foras, 770
qua hodie meus uir donauit me. AM. (*withdraws*) secede huc
                                        tu, Sosia.
enim uero illud praeter alia mira miror maxume,
si haec habet pateram illam. SO. an etiam credis id, quae in
                                        hac cistellula
tuo signo obsignata fertur? AM. saluom signum est? SO.
                                        (*holds up the box*) inspice.
AM. recte, ita est ut obsignaui. SO. quaeso, quin tu istanc
                                        iubes 775
pro cerrita circumferri? AM. edepol qui facto est opus.
nam haec quidem edepol laruarum plenast. quid uerbis
                                        opust?

(*Thessala enters and gives the bowl to Alcmena*)

AL. (*to Amphitryon*) em tibi pateram, eccam. AM. cedo mi.
                    AL. age aspice huc sis nunciam
tu qui quae facta infitiare; quem ego iam hic conuincam
                                        palam.
estne haec patera qua donatu's illi? AM. (*takes the bowl*)
                                        summe Iuppiter, 780
quid ego uideo? haec ea est profecto patera. perii, Sosia.
SO. aut pol haec praestigiatrix mulier multo maxuma est
aut pateram hic inesse oportet. AM. agedum, exsolue
                                        cistulam.

SO. quid ego istam exsoluam? obsignatast recte, res gesta est
bene:
tu peperisti Amphitruonem ⟨alium⟩, alium ego peperi
Sosiam; 785
nunc si patera pateram peperit, omnes congeminauimus!
AM. certum est aperire atque inspicere. SO. uide sis signi
quid siet,
ne posterius in me culpam conferas. AM. aperi modo;
nam haec quidem nos delirantis facere dictis postulat.
AL. unde haec igitur est nisi abs te, quae mihi dono data est? 790
AM. opus mi est istuc exquisito. SO. (*opens the box*) Iuppiter,
pro Iuppiter!
AM. quid tibi est? SO. hic patera nulla in cistulast. AM.
quid ego audio?
SO. id quod uerumst. AM. at cum cruciatu iam, nisi
apparet, tuo.
AL. haec quidem apparet. AM. quis igitur tibi dedit? AL.
qui me rogat.
SO. (*to Amphitryon*) me captas, quia tute ab naui clanculum
huc alia uia 795
praecucurristi atque hinc pateram tute exemesti atque eam
huic dedisti, post hanc rursum obsignasti clanculum.
AM. (*to Sosia*) ei mihi! iam tu quoque huius adiuuas
insaniam?
(*to Alcmena*) ain heri nos aduenisse huc? AL. aio,
adueniensque ilico
me salutauisti, et ego te, et osculum tetuli tibi.   800
SO. iam illud non placet principium de osculo. AM. perge
exsequi.
AL. lauisti. AM. quid postquam laui? AL. accubuisti. SO.
euge optume!
nunc exquire. AM. ne interpella. perge porro dicere.
AL. cena adposita est; cenauisti mecum, ego accubui simul.
AM. in eodem lecto? AL. in eodem. SO. ei, non placet
conuiuium. 805

AM. sine modo argumenta dicat. quid postquam cenauimus?
AL. te dormitare aibas; mensa ablata est, cubitum hinc
abiimus.
AM. ubi tu cubuisti? AL. in eodem lecto tecum una in
cubiculo.
AM. perdidisti. SO. quid tibi est? AM. haec me modo ad
mortem dedit.
AL. quid iam, amabo? AM. ne me appella. SO. quid tibi
est? AM. perii miser, 810
quia pudicitiae huius uitium me hinc absente est additum.
AL. obsecro ecastor, cur istuc, mi uir, ex ted audio?
AM. uir ego tuos sim? ne me appella, falsa, falso nomine.
SO. (*aside*) haeret haec res, si quidem haec iam mulier facta
est ex uiro.
AL. quid ego feci, qua istaec propter dicta dicantur mihi?   815
AM. tute edictas facta tua, ex me quaeris quid delinqueris?
AL. quid ego tibi deliqui, si cui nupta sum tecum fui?
AM. tun mecum fueris? quid illac impudente audacius?
saltem, tute si pudoris egeas, sumas mutuom.
AL. istuc facinus, quod tu insimulas, nostro generi non
decet. 820
tu si me inpudicitiai captas, capere non potes.
AM. (*to Sosia*) pro di immortales, cognoscin tu me saltem,
Sosia?
SO. propemodum. AM. cenauin ego heri in naui in portu
Persico?
AL. mihi quoque adsunt testes, qui illud quod ego dicam
adsentiant.
SO. nescio quid istuc negoti dicam, nisi si quispiam est   825
Amphitruo alius, qui forte ted hinc absenti tamen
tuam rem curet teque absente hic munus fungatur tuom.
nam quom de illo subditiuo Sosia mirum nimist,
certe de istoc Amphitruone iam alterum mirum est magis.
AM. nescioquis praestigiator hanc frustratur mulierem.   830
AL. per supremi regis regnum iuro et matrem familias

Iunonem, quam me uereri et metuere est par maxume,
ut mi extra unum te mortalis nemo corpus corpore
contigit, quo me impudicam faceret. AM. uera istaec uelim.
AL. uero dico, sed nequiquam, quoniam non uis credere.   835
AM. mulier es, audacter iuras. AL. quae non deliquit, decet
audacem esse, confidenter pro se et proterue loqui.
AM. satis audacter. AL. ut pudicam decet. AM. ⟨en⟩im
                                             uerbis proba's.
AL. non ego illam mi dotem duco esse, quae dos dicitur,
sed pudicitiam et pudorem et sedatum cupidinem,   840
deum metum, parentum amorem et cognatum concordiam,
tibi morigera atque ut munifica sim bonis, prosim probis.
SO. (aside) ne ista edepol, si haec uera loquitur, examussim
                                             est optuma.
AM. delenitus sum profecto ita, ut me qui sim nesciam.
SO. Amphitruo es profecto, caue sis ne tu te usu perduis: 845
ita nunc homines immutantur, postquam peregre aduenimus.
AM. mulier, istam rem inquisitam certum est non amittere.
AL. edepol me libente facies. AM. quid ais? responde mihi,
quid si adduco tuom cognatum huc a naui Naucratem,
qui mecum una uectust una naui, atque is si denegat   850
facta quae tu facta dicis, quid tibi aequom est fieri?
numquid causam dicis, quin te hoc multem matrimonio?
AL. si deliqui, nulla causa est. AM. conuenit. tu, Sosia,
duc hos intro. ego huc ab naui mecum adducam Naucratem.
                                                        (exits)

SO. (to Alcmena) nunc quidem praeter nos nemo est. dic mihi
                                             uerum serio: 855
ecquis alius Sosia intust, qui mei similis siet?
AL. abin hinc a me, dignus domino seruos? SO abeo, si
                          iubes. (enters palace with slaves)
AL. nimis ecastor facinus mirum est, qui illi conlibitum siet
meo uiro, sic me insimulare falso facinus tam malum.
quidquid est, iam ex Naucrate cognato id cognoscam meo.
                          (enters palace with Thessala) 860

Scene 6 (III 1)   IVPPITER

(Jupiter enters and addresses the audience)

IV. Ego sum ille Amphitruo, cui est seruos Sosia,
idem Mercurius qui fit quando commodumst,
in superiore qui habito cenaculo,
qui interdum fio Iuppiter quando lubet;
huc autem quom extemplo aduentum adporto, ilico   865
Amphitruo fio et uestimentum immuto meum.
nunc huc honoris uostri uenio gratia,
ne hanc incohatam transigam comoediam.
simul Alcumenae, quam uir insontem probri
Amphitruo accusat, ueni ut auxilium feram: 870
nam mea sit culpa, quod egomet contraxerim,
si id Alcumenae innocenti expetat.
nunc Amphitruonem memet, ut occepi semel,
esse adsimulabo atque in horum familiam
frustrationem hodie iniciam maxumam;   875
post igitur demum faciam res fiat palam
atque Alcumenae in tempore auxilium feram
faciamque ut uno fetu et quod grauida est uiro
et me quod grauidast pariat sine doloribus.
Mercurium iussi me continuo consequi,   880
si quid uellem imperare. nunc hanc adloquar.

Scene 7 (III 2)   ALCVMENA   IVPPITER

(Alcmena enters from the palace without noticing Jupiter)

AL. *(to audience)* Durare nequeo in aedibus. ita me probri,
stupri, dedecoris a uiro argutam meo!
ea quae sunt facta infecta re esse clamitat,
quae neque sunt facta neque ego in me admisi arguit,   885
atque id me susque deque esse habituram putat.

non edepol faciam, neque me perpetiar probri
falso insimulatam, quin ego illum aut deseram
aut satis faciat mi ille atque adiuret insuper
nolle esse dicta quae in me insontem protulit. 890
IV. (*aside*) faciundum est mi illud fieri quod illaec postulat,
si me illam amantem ad sese studeam recipere:
quando ego quod feci id factum Amphitruoni offuit
atque illi dudum meus amor negotium
insonti exhibuit, nunc autem insonti mihi 895
illius ira in hanc et male dicta expetent.
AL. (*notices Jupiter*) sed eccum uideo qui me miseram arguit
stupri, dedecoris. IV. te uolo, uxor, conloqui. (*she turns away*)
quo te auortisti? AL. ita ⟨ingeni⟩ ingenium meumst:
inimicos semper osa sum optuerier. 900
IV. heia autem inimicos? AL. sic est, uera praedico;
nisi etiam hoc falso dici insimulaturus es.
IV. nimis iracunda es. (*touches her*) AL. potin ut abstineas
                                                    manum?
nam certo, si sis sanus aut sapias satis,
quam tu impudicam esse arbitrere et praedices, 905
cum ea tu sermonem nec ioco nec serio
tibi habeas, nisi sis stultior stultissimo.
IV. si dixi, nihilo magis es neque ego esse arbitror,
et id huc reuorti ut me purgarem tibi.
nam numquam quicquam meo animo fuit aegrius 910
quam postquam audiui ted esse iratam mihi.
cur dixisti? inquies. ego expediam tibi.
non edepol quo te esse impudicam crederem;
uerum periclitatus sum animum tuom
quid faceres et quo pacto id ferre induceres. 915
equidem ioco illa dixeram dudum tibi,
ridiculi causa. uel hunc rogato Sosiam.
AL. quin huc adducis meum cognatum Naucratem,
testem quem dudum te adducturum dixeras
te huc non uenisse? IV. si quid dictum est per iocum, 920

non aequom est id te serio praeuortier.

AL. ego illum scio quam doluerit cordi meo.

IV. per dextram tuam te, Alcumena, oro obsecro,

da mihi hanc ueniam, ignosce, irata ne sies.

AL. ego istaec feci uerba uirtute irrita; 925

nunc, quando factis me impudicis abstini,

ab impudicis dictis auorti uolo.

ualeas, tibi habeas res tuas, reddas meas.

iuben mi ire comites? IV. sanan es? AL. si non iubes,

ibo egomet; comitem mihi Pudicitiam duxero. (*starts to leave*) 930

IV. (*grabs her*) mane. arbitratu tuo ius iurandum dabo,

me meam pudicam esse uxorem arbitrarier.

id ego si fallo, tum te, summe Iuppiter,

quaeso Amphitruoni ut semper iratus sies.

AL. (*stops and turns around*) a, propitius sit potius! IV. confido

fore; 935

nam ius iurandum uerum te aduorsum dedi.

iam nunc irata non es? AL. non sum. IV. bene facis.

nam in hominum aetate multa eueniunt huius modi:

capiunt uoluptates, capiunt rursum miserias;

irae interueniunt, redeunt rursum in gratiam. 940

uerum irae si quae forte eueniunt huius modi

inter eos, rursum si reuentum in gratiam est,

bis tanto amici sunt inter se quam prius.

AL. primum cauisse oportuit ne diceres,

uerum eadem si isdem purgas mi, patiunda sunt. 945

IV. iube uero uasa pura adornari mihi,

ut quae apud legionem uota uoui, si domum

rediissem saluos, ea ego exsoluam omnia.

AL. ego istuc curabo. IV. (*to slaves in palace*) euocate huc

Sosiam;

gubernatorem qui in mea naui fuit 950

Blepharonem arcessat qui nobiscum prandeat.

is adeo inpransus ⟨laute⟩ ludificabitur,

cum ego Amphitruonem collo hinc obstricto traham.

AL. mirum quid solus secum secreto ille agat.
atque aperiuntur aedes. exit Sosia.   955

Scene 8 (III 3)   SOSIA   IVPPITER   ALCVMENA

(Sosia enters from the palace)

SO. Amphitruo, assum. si quid opus est, impera, imperium
                                                           exsequar.
IV. ⟨Sosia⟩, optume aduenis. SO. iam pax est inter uos
                                                             duos?
nam quia uos tranquillos uideo, gaudeo et uolup est mihi.
atque ita seruom par uidetur frugi sese instituere:
proinde eri ut sint, ipse item sit; uoltum e uoltu comparet: 960
tristis sit, si eri sint tristes; hilarus sit, si gaudeant.
sed age responde: iam uos rediistis in concordiam?
IV. derides qui scis haec dudum me dixisse per iocum.
SO. an id ioco dixisti? equidem serio ac uero ratus.
IV. habui expurigationem; facta pax est. SO. optume est.   965
IV. ego rem diuinam intus faciam, uota quae sunt. SO.
                                                           censeo.
IV. tu gubernatorem a naui huc euoca uerbis meis
Blepharonem, ut re diuina facta mecum prandeat.
SO. iam hic ero, cum illic censebis esse me. IV. actutum huc
                                      redi. *(Sosia exits)*
AL. numquid uis, quin abeam iam intro, ut apparentur
                                      quibus opust? 970
IV. i sane, et quantum potest parata fac sint omnia.
AL. quin uenis quando uis intro? faxo haud quicquam sit
                                                             morae.
IV. recte loquere et proinde diligentem ut uxorem decet.
                                      (Alcmena enters palace)
(to audience) iam hisce ambo, et seruos et era, frustra sunt duo,
qui me Amphitruonem rentur esse: errant probe.   975
nunc tu diuine huc fac adsis Sosia,

(audis quae dico, tam etsi praesens non ades),
fac Amphitruonem aduenientem ab aedibus
ut abigas; quouis pacto fac commentus sis.
uolo deludi illunc, dum cum hac usuraria   980
uxore nunc mihi morigero. haec curata sint
fac sis, proinde adeo ut uelle med intellegis,
atque ut ministres mihi, mihi cum sacruficem. (*enters palace*)

Scene 9 (III 4)   MERCVRIVS

(*Mercury enters and addresses the audience, perhaps passing through
them*)

ME. Concedite atque abscedite omnes, de uia decedite,
nec quisquam ⟨iam⟩ tam audax fuat homo qui obuiam
                          obsistat mihi.   985
nam mihi quidem hercle qui minus liceat deo minitarier
populo, ni decedat mihi, quam seruolo in comoediis?
ille nauem saluam nuntiat aut irati aduentum senis:
ego sum Ioui dicto audiens, eius iussu nunc huc me adfero.
quam ob rem mihi magis par est uia decedere et concedere.   990
pater uocat me, eum sequor, eius dicto imperio sum
                                audiens.
ut filium bonum patri esse oportet, itidem ego sum patri.
amanti subparasitor, hortor, adsto, admoneo, gaudeo.
si quid patri uolup est, uoluptas ea mihi multo maxumast.
amat: sapit; recte facit, animo quando obsequitur suo,   995
quod omnis homines facere oportet, dum id modo fiat bono.
nunc Amphitruonem uolt deludi meus pater; faxo probe
iam hic deludetur, spectatores, uobis inspectantibus.
capiam coronam mi in caput, adsimulabo me esse ebrium;
atque illuc susum escendero: inde optume aspellam uirum   1000
de supero, cum huc accesserit; faciam ut sit madidus sobrius.
deinde illi actutum sufferet suos seruos poenas Sosia:
eum fecisse ille hodie arguet quae ego fecero hic. quid mea?

meo me aequomst morigerum patri, eius studio seruire
addecet.

sed eccum Amphitruonem: aduenit; iam ille hic deludetur
probe,   1005

    siquidem uos uoltis auscultando operam dare.
    ibo intro, ornatum capiam qui potis decet;
    dein susum ascendam in tectum ut illum hinc prohibeam.
(enters palace)

Scene 10 (IV 1)   AMPHITRVO

    (Amphitryon enters and addresses the audience)

AM. Naucratem quem conuenire uolui in naui non erat,
neque domi neque in urbe inuenio quemquam qui illum
uiderit;   1010

nam omnis plateas perreptaui, gymnasia et myropolia;
apud emporium atque in macello, in palaestra atque in foro,
in medicinis, in tostrinis, apud omnis aedis sacras
sum defessus quaeritando: nusquam inuenio Naucratem.
nunc domum ibo atque ex uxore hanc rem pergam
exquirere,   1015

quis fuerit quem propter corpus suom stupri compleuerit.
nam me quam illam quaesitionem inquisitam hodie amittere
mortuom satiust. sed aedis occluserunt. eugepae!
pariter hoc fit atque ut alia facta sunt. feriam fores.
(approaches the palace)

aperite hoc; heus, ecquis hic est? ecquis hoc aperit ostium?   1020

Scene 11 (IV 2)   MERCVRIVS   AMPHITRVO

    (Mercury appears on the upper tier of the palace)

ME. Quis ad fores est? AM. ego sum. ME. quid 'ego sum'?
AM. ita loquor. ME. tibi Iuppiter

dique omnes irati certo sunt, qui sic frangas fores.
AM. quo modo? ME. eo modo, ut profecto uiuas aetatem

miser.
AM. Sosia. ME. ita, sum Sosia, nisi me esse oblitum

existimas.
quid nunc uis? AM. sceleste, at etiam quid uelim, id tu me

rogas? 1025
ME. ita, rogo. paene effregisti, fatue, foribus cardines.
an fores censebas nobis publicitus praeberier?
quid me aspectas, stolide? quid nunc uis tibi? aut quis tu es

homo?
AM. uerbero, etiam quis ego sim me rogitas, ulmorum

Accheruns?
quem pol ego hodie ob istaec dicta faciam feruentem flagris.   1030
ME. prodigum te fuisse oportet olim in adulescentia.
AM. quidum? ME. quia senecta aetate a me mendicas

malum.
AM. cum cruciatu tuo istaec hodie, uerna, uerba funditas.
ME. sacrufico ego tibi. AM. qui? ME. quia enim te macto

infortunio. 1034

(*lacuna*)

Fragmenta

Scene 11 (IV 2)   MERCVRIVS   AMPHITRVO

(AM.) at ego te cruce et cruciatu mactabo, mastigia.   1
(ME.) erus Amphitruo⟨st⟩ occupatus.   2
(ME.)   abiendi nunc tibi etiam occasiost.   3
(ME.) optumo iure infringatur aula cineris in caput.   4
(ME.) ne tu postules, matula[m], u⟨r⟩nam tibi aquai infundi

in caput. 5
(ME.) laruatu's. edepol hominem miserum! medicum

quaerita. 6

Scene 12 (IV 2a)   ALCVMENA   AMPHITRVO

> (*Alcmena has entered from the palace*)

(AL.) exiurauisti te mihi dixe per iocum.   7
(AL.) quaeso aduenienti morbo medicari iube: 8
tu certe aut laruatus aut cerritus es.
(AL.) nisi hoc ita factum est, proinde ut factum esse
                                                    autumo, 9
non causam dico quin uero insimules probri.
(AM.) cuius? quae me absente corpus uolgauit suom.   10

Scene 13 (IV 2b)   AMPHITRVO   BLEPHARO   SOSIA

> (*Sosia has returned from the harbor with Blepharo*)

(AM.) quid minitabas te facturum, si istas pepulissem fores?   11
(AM.) ibi scrobes effodito ⟨tu⟩ plus sexagenos in dies.   12
(AM.) noli pessumo precari   13
(BL.) animam comprime   14

Scene 14 (IV 3)   IVPPITER   AMPHITRVO   BLEPHARO

> (*Jupiter has entered from the palace*)

(IV.) manufestum hunc obtorto collo teneo furem flagiti.   15
(AM.) immo ego hunc, Thebani ciues, qui domi uxorem
                                                    meam 16
impudicitia impediuit, teneo, thensaurum stupri.
(AM. *siue* IV.) nilne te pudet, sceleste, populi in conspectum
                                                    ingredi? 17
(AM.) clandestino   18
(IV. *siue* AM.) qui nequeas nostrorum uter sit Amphitruo
                                                    decernere. 19

Scene 14 (IV 3)   IVPPITER   AMPHITRVO   BLEPHARO

(BL.) Vos inter uos partite; ego abeo, mihi negotium est;   1035
neque ego umquam usquam tanta mira me uidisse censeo.
AM. Blepharo, quaeso ut aduocatus mihi adsis neue abeas.
                                        BL. uale.
quid opust med aduocato qui utri sim aduocatus nescio?
                                                    (*exits*)
IV. intro ego hinc eo: Alcumena parturit. (*enters palace*) AM.
                                (*to audience*) perii miser.
quid ego ⟨faciam⟩, quem aduocati iam atque amici
                                        deserunt?   1040
numquam edepol me inultus istic ludificabit, quisquis est;
[nam] iam ad regem recta me ducam resque ut facta est
                                        eloquar.
ego pol illum ulciscar hodie Thessalum ueneficum,
qui peruorse perturbauit familiae mentem meae.
sed ubi illest? intro edepol abiit, credo, ad uxorem meam.   1045
qui me Thebis alter uiuit miserior? quid nunc agam,
quem omnes mortales ignorant et ludificant ut lubet?
certumst, intro rumpam in aedis: ubi quemque hominem
                                        aspexero,
si ancillam seu seruom siue uxorem siue adulterum
seu patrem siue auom uidebo, obtruncabo in aedibus.   1050
neque me Iuppiter neque di omnes id prohibebunt, si uolent,
quin sic faciam uti constitui; pergam in aedis nunciam. (*starts
            toward palace; clap of thunder; he collapses*)

Scene 15 (V 1)   BROMIA   AMPHITRVO

    (*Bromia enters from the palace without noticing Amphitryon*)

BR. (*to audience*) Spes atque opes uitae meae iacent sepultae
                                        in pectore,
neque ullast confidentia iam in corde, quin amiserim;

ita mihi uidentur omnia, mare terra caelum, consequi,   1055
iam ut opprimar, ut enicer. me miseram, quid agam nescio.
ita tanta mira in aedibus sunt facta. uae miserae mihi,
animo malest, aquam uelim. corrupta sum atque absumpta
                                              sum.
caput dolet, neque audio, nec oculis prospicio satis,
nec me miserior femina est neque ulla uideatur magis.   1060
ita erae meae hodie contigit. nam ubi parturit, deos [sibi]
                                        inuocat,
  strepitus, crepitus, sonitus, tonitrus: ut subito, ut prope, ut
                                      ualide tonuit!
ubi quisque institerat, concidit crepitu. ibi nescioquis
                                          maxuma
      uoce exclamat: 'Alcumena, adest auxilium, ne time;
      et tibi et tuis propitius caeli cultor aduenit.   1065
exsurgite' inquit 'qui terrore meo occidistis prae metu.'
ut iacui, exsurgo. ardere censui aedis, ita tum confulgebant.
ibi me inclamat Alcumena; iam ea res me horrore adficit.
erilis praeuertit metus: accurro, ut sciscam quid uelit.
atque illam geminos filios pueros peperisse conspicor;   1070
neque nostrum quisquam sensimus, quom peperit, neque
                          prouidimus. (*sees a collapsed figure*)
      sed quid hoc? quis hic est senex qui ante aedis nostras
                                      sic iacet?
            numnam hunc percussit Iuppiter?
credo edepol, nam pro Iuppiter, sepultust quasi sit mortuos.
ibo et cognoscam, quisquis est. (*moves closer*) Amphitruo hic
                          quidem ⟨est⟩ erus meus. 1075
Amphitruo. AM. perii. BR. surge. AM. interii. BR. cedo
            manum. (*helps him to his feet*) AM. quis me tenet?
BR. tua Bromia ancilla. AM. totus timeo, ita me increpuit
                                      Iuppiter.
nec secus est quasi si ab Accherunte ueniam. sed quid tu
                                          foras
egressa es? BR. eadem nos formido timidas terrore impulit

in aedibus, tu ubi habitas. nimia mira uidi. uae mihi,   1080
Amphitruo; ita mihi animus etiam nunc abest. AM. agedum
                                    expedi:
scin me tuom esse erum Ampitruonem? BR. scio. AM. uide
                              etiam nunc. BR. scio.
AM. haec sola sanam mentem gestat meorum familiarium!
BR. immo omnes sani sunt profecto. AM. at me uxor
                              insanum facit
suis foedis factis. BR. at ego faciam tu idem ut aliter
                              praedices,   1085
Amphitruo, piam et pudicam esse tuam uxorem ut scias,
de ea re signa atque argumenta paucis uerbis eloquar.
omnium primum: Alcumena geminos peperit filios.
AM. ain tu, geminos? BR. geminos. AM. di me seruant. BR.
                              sine me dicere,
ut scias tibi tuaeque uxori deos esse omnis propitios.   1090
AM. loquere. BR. postquam parturire hodie uxor occepit
                                    tua,
ubi utero exorti dolores, ut solent puerperae,
inuocat deos immortalis ut sibi auxilium ferant,
manibus puris, capite operto. ibi continuo contonat
sonitu maxumo: aedis primo ruere rebamur tuas.   1095
aedes totae confulgebant tuae, quasi essent aureae.
AM. quaeso, absoluito hinc me extemplo, quando satis
                              deluseris.
quid fit deinde? BR. dum haec aguntur, interea uxorem
                                    tuam
neque gementem neque plorantem nostrum quisquam
                              audiuimus;
ita profecto sine dolore peperit. AM. iam istuc gaudeo,   1100
utut me erga merita est. BR. mitte istaec atque haec quae
                              dicam accipe.
postquam peperit, pueros lauere iussit nos. occepimus.
sed puer ille quem ego laui, ut magnust et multum ualet!
neque eum quisquam colligare quiuit incunabulis.
AM. nimia mira memoras; si istaec uera sunt, diuinitus   1105

non metuo quin meae uxori latae suppetiae sient.
BR. magis iam faxo mira dices. postquam in cunas conditust,
deuolant angues iubatae deorsum in impluuium duo
maxumae: continuo extollunt ambo capita. AM. ei mihi!
BR. ne paue. sed angues oculis omnis circumuisere.   1110
postquam pueros conspicatae, pergunt ad cunas citae.
ego cunas recessim rursum uorsum trahere et ducere,
metuens pueris, mihi formidans; tantoque angues acrius
persequi. postquam conspexit angues ille alter puer,
citus e cunis exsilit, facit recta in anguis impetum: 1115
alteram altera prehendit eas manu perniciter.
AM. mira memoras, nimis formidolosum facinus praedicas;
nam mihi horror membra misero percipit dictis tuis.
quid fit deinde? porro loquere. BR. puer ambo angues
                                                    enicat.
dum haec aguntur, uoce clara exclamat uxorem tuam –   1120
AM. quis homo? BR. summus imperator diuom atque
                                        hominum Iuppiter.
is se dixit cum Alcumena clam consuetum cubitibus,
eumque filium suom esse qui illas anguis uicerit;
alterum tuom esse dixit puerum. AM. pol me haud paenitet,
si licet boni dimidium mihi diuidere cum Ioue.   1125
abi domum, iube uasa pura actutum adornari mihi,
ut Iouis supremi multis hostiis pacem expetam. (*Bromia enters
                                                    palace*)

ego Teresiam coniectorem aduocabo et consulam
quid faciendum censeat; simul hanc rem ut facta est eloquar.
(*thunderclap*) sed quid hoc? quam ualide tonuit. di, obsecro
                                        uostram fidem.   1130

Scene 16 (V 2)   IVPPITER   AMPHITRVO

    (*Jupiter appears, perhaps on the upper tier of the palace*)

IV. Bono animo es, adsum auxilio, Amphitruo, tibi et tuis:
nihil est quod timeas. hariolos, haruspices

mitte omnes: quae futura et quae facta eloquar
multo adeo melius quam illi, quom sum Iuppiter.
primum omnium Alcumenae usuram corporis   1135
cepi et concubitu grauidam feci filio.
tu grauidam item fecisti, cum in exercitum
profectu's: uno partu duos peperit simul.
eorum alter, nostro qui est susceptus semine,
suis factis te immortali adficiet gloria.   1140
tu cum Alcumena uxore antiquam in gratiam
redi: haud promeruit quam ob rem uitio uorteres;
mea ui subactast facere. ego in caelum migro. (*exits*)

Scene 17 (V 3)   AMPHITRVO

AM. faciam ita ut iubes et te oro, promissa ut serues tua.
ibo ad uxorem intro; missum facio Teresiam senem.   1145

nunc, spectatores, Iouis summi causa clare plaudite.

COMMENTARY

Argumentum I

Plot summaries in iambic senarii were added to P.'s plays in (probably) the second century AD. An acrostic version survives for most plays; some have in addition a non-acrostic summary of 15 verses (the 9-line non-acrostic of *Am.* is unique). The *argumenta* consciously archaize, and usually replicate the particulars of P.'s versification. For *Am.*, Arg. I is written more carefully than Arg. II, and demonstrates deeper understanding of the play's central themes. Acrostics were a mannerism of Hellenistic literature (cf. Virgil's reference to his own name at *G.* 1.429–33, with Thomas's (1988) note on 427–37), but their use in prophecy and the like suggests an origin in magical beliefs about the power of words.

1 faciem: the word does not occur in the play, where *forma* (266, 441, 456, 600, 614) and *imago* (121, 124, 141, 265, 458) are used in contexts describing the act of impersonation. The composer's appreciation of *uariatio* can be glimpsed in 4 (cf. Arg. I 7n.).

2 dum ... gereret: P. would probably have used the indicative in this purely temporal clause (Lindsay 133–4).

3 Alcmenam: the spelling *Alcu-* is universal in the play and is in fact the transmitted reading here and in 5, but it does not scan in either place. The composer perhaps thought the penult of *Alcumenam* was short. **uxorem cepit usurariam:** a conflation of the gods' favourite expressions, i.e. 108 *usuram corporis cepit* (cf. 1135–6) and 498 *uxor usuraria* (cf. 980–1), to describe the sexual ruse; cf. pp. 39–40.

5 decipitur: used only once in the play (424); the gods prefer *deludere* (cf. *deluduntur* Arg. I 7) when broadcasting their plans to the audience (295, 980, 997–8, 1005); the latter verb carries the additional metatheatrical connotation (cf. *ludus*) 'conduct a play-within-the-play (against)'.

7 deluduntur: *uariatio* again (cf. Arg. I 1n.). The MSS give *dolis* after *deluduntur*, which does not scan and was introduced because of *decipitur dolis* in 5. **in mirum modum:** for the pervasive theme of wonder see pp. 29–31.

129

10 adulterum: the composer alludes to the play's essential theme; cf. pp. 34–45.

Argumentum II

1 Alcumenas: the genitive is a deliberate archaism (cf. *pater, mater familias*), not found in the play.

2 formam eius: an instance of *c* / *D* hiatus that would be suspect in P. (p. 68); it does, however, coincide with word-end at the seventh element. Cf. 54n.

4 subseruit: an archaic verb, only at *Men.* 766 in P., perhaps suggested to the composer by *subparasitabor* (515).

5 frustra habet 'deceives'; P. has only *frustra esse* 'to be deceived', and for the active uses *frustrari* (cf. 830).

6 turbas uxori ciet Amphitruo: cf. 476.

6–7 inuicem | raptant pro moechis 'they mutually charge (*OLD rapto* 1b) each other as adulterers'. The change of subject to Amphitryon and Jupiter is awkward. The composer refers to the lacunose scene (fr. 15–1052) in which Amphitryon and Jupiter confront one another.

6 inuicem: found only here and at *Men.* Arg. 10 in P.'s MSS and first attested in the mid-first century BC

7 captus arbiter 'chosen as an arbiter'.

8 Vter sit non quit Amphitruo decernere: cf. fr. 19.

9 noscunt: another abrupt shift of subject (to Amphitryon and Alcmena?).

†Alcumena†: the line has one extra element if this is read (the composer of this *argumentum* knew that the penult was long: cf. 1); Bothe suggested *illa*.

Prologue

P.'s prologues show a variety of presentation that was already present in Greek New Comedy (cf. Hunter (1985) 24–34). The prologue may immediately precede the play or be delayed until an opening scene or two have taken place, or P. may dispense with a prologue altogether. In several plays, the prologist is an omniscient deity. In others, the prologue is delivered by a (human) character in the play or the unnamed *prologus* (probably the head of the troupe) who was apparently introduced into comedy by Roman playwrights. Mercury in *Am.* is unique in that he is both a divinity and character in the play. Certain elements recur, though they are not all simultaneously represented in every prologue or always strictly demarcated from each other, and give P.'s prologues a more or less uniform appearance (cf. Gratwick (1993) 30–3). These include (1) the *captatio beneuolentiae*, in which the prologist seeks to ingratiate the play and the players with the audience; (2) divulgence of the source play and/or playwright; (3) identification of the setting; (4) narration of the *argumentum* (i.e. background information and the current situation); (5) prediction of scenes to be enacted; and (6) a valediction to the audience. In Mercury's prologue, no source is revealed and a conventional valediction is lacking (75, 151–2nn.).

It is the *captatio* that puts a personal stamp on P.'s prologues. It is overwhelmingly the case in P. that the impetus to draw the audience into the world of the play and win their sympathies outstrips narration of the plot. The *captatio beneuolentiae* (the term belongs to formal rhetoric) properly refers to the prologist's opening effort to seize the audience's attention, but the techniques employed there usually permeate the entire prologue. Thus, the prologues as a whole are marked by familiar colloquy with the audience, jokes and elaborate word-play, overt recommendations of the play and playwright, and direct appeals for attentiveness. In this way the audience is immediately discouraged from imagining any barrier between themselves and the actors, and should instead embrace its participatory role in the spectacle. By contrast, Menander's prologists overwhelmingly keep to their appointed task and remain more distant from the audience; the strict communication of the *argumentum* is only rarely (and briefly) interrupted, e.g. *Dys.* 45–6, *Asp.* 97–100, *Sam.* 13. Among the fragments of Greek Middle and New Comedy, we do find prologists who converse more freely with the audience, and on topics that range outside the action of the play (e.g. Antiphanes 189 K–A, Heniochus 5 K–A), though nothing there suggests the prolixity and sportiveness of Mercury's opening. But the *parabases* and loosely defined prologues of Old Comedy do employ jests and strategies parallel to those in the Plautine prologues: see 1–16, 15, 16, 38, 42–4, 52, 64–96, 72, 118–19, 151nn.

The bloated proportions which the *captatio* often assumes in P., and the straightforward humour found there, have traditionally jarred with the sensibilities of classical scholars, who have dismissed these as necessary concessions to a vulgar Roman audience and seen in them an indication of raucous conditions in the Roman theatre. Although some critics (e.g. Chalmers (1965), Handley (1975)) have sought to vindicate the sophistication of Plautus' audience, the notion persists that Roman theatre-goers of this period were uncouth barbarians who had to be coaxed into watching a play (e.g. Gaiser (1972) 1035, Walton and Arnott (1996) 80). This perception is greatly exaggerated and apparently emerges from an overly literal reading of P.'s prologues, as well as of the rhetorically evasive ones of Terence. For example, the prologist's exchange with an audience member at *Capt.* 11–14 is usually taken to indicate an event spontaneously unfolding during delivery of the prologue. This overlooks the obvious fact that any event described in a dramatic script must be premeditated, and that the individual who putatively shouts from the back of the audience would have to be planted there by the troupe, as the prologist could not otherwise count on a perfectly timed outburst. Through jests like this one (cf. *Capt.* 15–16, 51–68) P. is striving to establish intimate contact with his audience, as they acknowledge (and even laugh at) their role as spectators. Perhaps the most telling piece of evidence that the Plautine prologist's appeals to the audience for their attentiveness and good will were established modes of induction and do not reflect chaotic conditions in the theatre is the opening of the delayed prologue at *Mil.* 79–83: *mihi ad enarrandum hoc argumentum est comitas, | si ad auscultandum uostra erit benignitas; | qui autem auscultare nolet exsurgat foras, | ut sit ubi sedeat ille qui auscultare uolt.* Surely, the audience has settled down during the opening exchange between Pyrgopolynices and Artotrogus. At least five of the extant plays of Plautus have no prologues at all, which is difficult to reconcile with the notion that the *captatio* exists to cajole an unsophisticated and roving audience into taking their seats. And the prologues of Terence, replete as they are with polemic, both against his critics and against his audiences, are of little relevance here; for their dubious value as historical documents see Gruen (1992) 210–22. Plautus was an indisputably popular playwright who routinely secured his audience's attention and won their approval by adapting and refashioning his Greek models in meaningful ways (cf. pp. 8–11).

Additionally, the *captatio* in P.'s prologues should be examined in light of the burgeoning interest in formal rhetoric at Rome in this period. The prologue of a play is a close structural analogue of the *prooemium* of a judicial speech, and Plautine prologists do refer to the audience as *arbitri* (*Am.* 16) or *iudices* (*Capt.* 67). In P. the desire to draw the audience into the performance takes on a bombastic quality and often exceeds the normal limits of courtroom decorum, but from the standpoint of rhetorical strategy, Mercury's remark 75–6 *uirtute dixit uos uictores uiuere,* | *non ambitione neque perfidia* is just the sort of tactful praise of the judge that Quintilian (*Inst.* 4.1.16–22) recommends to the speaker of the *prooemium*. Through aggressive strategies such as these, Mercury aims both to control the audience's perspective and to win their sympathies regarding the play (see 25, 33–37, 39–49, 41–2, 52–3, 62nn.); Caesar's assertion at Cic. *de Orat.* 2.236 that humour (*hilaritas*) is a sure means of gaining an audience's favour (*beneuolentia*), as well as of disarming an opponent, holds just as true for the comic prologist as for the orator.

Tragedies and comedies after the Greek fashion had been performed in Rome for several decades before P.'s *floruit*, and we should assume that his audience was versed in basic theatre etiquette. P. himself clearly assumed a considerable degree of sophistication and experience on their part regarding the practices of New Comedy; otherwise, he would not have flouted its conventions so liberally. In the earliest days of Roman theatre, perhaps conditions were as unruly as is suggested by a hyper-literal reading of the extant prologues, and this could have led to the establishment of a formal call for attention. In P., however, we are witnessing an innovative application of what was by now a fossilized convention.

Finally, P.'s prologues were no doubt subject to some revision in the course of revival performances (cf. *Cas.* 5–20). The older practice of imposing often arbitary rules of style or identifying every possible anachronism to sift out the post-Plautine from the Plautine is for the most part dispensed with here, and it is assumed, rightly or wrongly, that the prologue of *Am.* is essentially P.'s work.

1–16 Mercury offers the audience a playful *quid pro quo* that exploits

their typically Roman love of *lucrum*: if they will give the play a fair
hearing, they can be assured of his continued support, especially in
their financial affairs. The entire proposal takes the form of an in-
verted prayer of the *do ut des* type: the god with painstaking and
quasi-legalistic *abundantia* enumerates the benefactions the audience
can expect from him in return for their attentiveness. For the comically gentle threat of appropriate reward and punishment here cf.
Ar. *Av.* 1101–17, where the chorus seeks a favourable reception for
the play by the judges. The comic irony in putting this contract in
the mouth of a god known for lying and chicanery would not be lost
on at least some of the audience (cf. 1n.).

   This is the longest sentence in P., but not atypical of his style and
that of archaic Latin in general. Though far from artless, the sentence is informed by principles quite distinct from those that shape
the Ciceronian period. Grammatical structures accumulate in accordance with the natural flow of everyday speech and the speaker's
train of thought rather than the rigorous subordination of ideas.
Aural effects such as alliteration and assonance abound. The overall
structure here consists of three parallel subordinate *ut(i)* clauses ('in
the same way as ...' 1, 4, 8; *ut* in 9 and 14 introduces purpose
clauses), two lines of summation (13–14) again introduced by *ut*, followed by the climactic main clause (15–16) beginning with *ita*, which
finally provides a correlative. Mercury's presumptive opening (1–14)
is framed by ring composition: cf. 1–3 *ut ... uoltis ... me ... adficere
atque adiuuare* and 13 *ut me uoltis adprobare adnitier* (extended additions
to P.'s sources often seem to be marked by such repetitions, as is
most clear at 51 and 96: 50–96n.). The three sections marked by the
anaphora of *ut* (1–3, 4–7, 8–12) constitute a tricolon with crescendo:
these highly enjambed members are 3, 4, and 5 lines in length, respectively, with each being progressively expanded through subordination or a parenthesis. Sectional boundaries are also marked by a
somewhat imprecise species of ring composition (*in* + ablative in 1
and 3, *res* in 4 and 7, *nuntiis* in 8 and 12). Like a wheel, Mercury's
thoughts revolve in circles, but forward motion is nonetheless achieved. Alliterative pairs are common, e.g. 4 *res rationesque*, sometimes
in asyndeton, and especially when the words are of similar meaning,
e.g. 13 *adprobare adnitier*. Homoioteleuton is found both between con-
secutive line-ends, e.g. 1–2 *mercimoniis | lucris* and between the main

break (where, if there is elision, actual pronunciation probably did not entirely disguise the rhyme) and line-end, e.g. 6 *amplo* ... *lucro*; the latter type most often involves noun and adjective combinations. By contrast, classical writers, with notable exceptions such as Lucretius and Sallust, exercise considerable restraint with respect to all these types of sound effects. For a thorough investigation of Plautine style see Blänsdorf (1967).

1–3 uos ... | adficere atque adiuuare 'to endow and endorse you'.

1 mercimoniis: Mercury does not identify himself by name until 19, and if the audience had no (detailed) advance notice about the play, this would be their first verbal clue as to the prologist's identity; for the word-play cf. *St.* 404 (a prayer of thanks) *simul Mercurio, qui me in mercimoniis* ... (*Mercurius* and *merx* may in fact be cognate). Menander's Pan does not name himself until *Dys.* 12, but may offer a similar identifying pun (4 πάνυ), though the difference in vowel quantity is perhaps prohibitive). Cf. also the valediction of Auxilium at *Cist.* 200 *augete auxilia uostra iustis legibus*. Mercury's costume and mask will immediately suggest that he is a typical Plautine slave (116–19n.), but since he wears a traveller's hat (a *petasus*, part of his traditional iconography) and the distinguishing *pinnulae* (143), there are visual clues as to his identity as well. His immediate description of his own cult functions should make identification easy (as the parenthesis at 11–12 suggests).

2 emundis uendundisque me laetum lucris: scanned *A B C D A B c / D A B c D*, with word-end after the seventh and third elements (p. 60).   **laetum** 'propitiously' (adjective where English idiom prefers an adverb, as often in Latin: KS 1 236–7, GL §325 R.6), frequently with reference to a divinity's attitude, e.g. Virg. *A.* 1.415–16, Hor. *Carm.* 1.2.46. The god throughout his opening (3, 5, 6, 7, 13nn.) playfully casts back the language of his cult to the audience and in effect presupposes a hypothetical religious contract on their part: 'if you continue to benefit us, we will give the play a fair hearing'.   **lucris:** ablative with *adficere* (*OLD adficere* 3; cf. 193); the plural instead of the more usual singular (cf. 6, 12, 14) is logical here because of *mercimoniis* (1), with which it also rhymes. For the central theme of finance in the play see pp. 39–40.

3 adiuuare: frequently of divine assistance, as in the proverb of

Varro's proem, *R.* 1.1.4 *et quoniam, ut aiunt, dei facientes adiuuant, prius inuocabo eos* ...

4 res rationesque: for the semantic doubling see pp. 16–17.
uostrorum: either archaic genitive of *uos* or Mercury means 'the business affairs of all your family and friends'.

5 bene expedire 'to turn out well', the same (rare) intransitive use of the verb as in 521 (cf. *Trin.* 236). Sedgwick insists that *expedire* is transitive and understands *me*, as one must as subject of *auctare* in 6; Leo inserts *me* after *bene*. But absolute grammatical parallelism is not a priority for P. and Mercury is easily understood as subject of *auctare* because the word belongs to the language of cult (6n.). For the general religious character here cf. Cato, *Agr.* 141.1 (*suouetaurilia*) *cum diuis uolentibus quodque bene eueniat* ... and 141.2–3 *Mars pater, te precor quaesoque* ... *utique tu fruges, frumenta, uineta uirgultaque grandire beneque euenire siris* ... **peregrique:** properly 'abroad' (< **peregre-i*, where the ending is locative: *MHL* 15), originally distinct from *peregre*, 'from abroad', though in usage the words are often interchangeable. **-que et:** not in Cicero or Caesar, probably already an archaism in P. Cf. LHS II 515 and Ogilvie (1965) on Livy 1.43.2.

6 auctare 'bless', elsewhere found only in Lucretius' opening preface, 1.54–6 *nam tibi de summa caeli ratione deumque | disserere incipiam et rerum primordia pandam, | unde omnis natura creet res auctet alatque* ... and Cat. 67.2 (the *ianua* is addressed) *salue, teque bona Iuppiter auctet ope,* both of which suggest a solemn religious flavour for the verb.
perpetuo: adverb (as in 60).

7 quasque incepistis res quasque inceptabitis 'all your undertakings, present and future'. This type of polar expression or 'universalizing doublet' probably has its origin in colloquial speech (*LU* 99). It is an extremely common and (probably) native feature of Greek; cf. Barrett (1964) on E. *Hipp.* 441–2. **quasque ... quasque:** *-que ... -que* ('both ... and') is used sparingly in classical prose (once in Cicero (*Fin.* 1.51, an Ennian reminiscence), several times in the archaizing Sallust (usually with pronouns), and by Livy (to connect, as here, relative clauses: cf. *OLD* 3b), and seems not to have been colloquial. P. uses it less than twenty times in a fairly limited number of verse positions. Fraenkel (1960) 199–201 concluded that it was not a native idiom, but had been introduced into Latin by Ennius to translate τε ... τε, which he found in his epic and tragic

sources. This view is problematic, and not only because of the chronological difficulties (for which see Sedgwick *ad loc.* and Skutsch
(1985) on Enn. *Ann.* 170). The majority of Plautine examples fall
within just a few distinct contexts: prayer or (mock) religious language (*Cist.* 20, *Trin.* 825), paratragedy (*Rud.* 349, 369, 1145), passages
marked by moralizing and Roman conservatism (*Trin.* 645, 877, *Epid.*
220, *As.* 577), and one example (*Men.* 590) occurs within a description
of a thoroughly Roman legal situation; other cases (*Am.* 168, *Cas.* 51,
St. 103) defy obvious classification. *susque deque* in 886 (see n. *ad loc.*) is
a proverbial expression and therefore necessarily predates P., presumably by a considerable period of time. Plautine usage suggests,
then, that this use of correlative *-que ... -que* was an old Latin idiom
(perhaps an Indo-European inheritance: τε and *que* reflect different
treatments of the labiovelar **qw*) that had faded from informal
speech before P.'s time. Characters in Plautine comedy revive it to
evoke a more solemn, and perhaps even stilted tone, as Mercury
here in playing with the language of his cult (cf. 2n.). Later Latin
poets use *-que ... -que* more freely, often to recall Homer: cf. Wills
(1996) 372–7.

8 et uti: a permissible split (*aa*) resolution involving a conjunction (p. 62).   **bonis ... nuntiis:** i.e. they can expect favourable
reports from abroad regarding investments and military affairs.
Mercury of course superintends all messages and was identified with
the divine logos by the Stoics (Kenney (1990) on Apul. *Met.* 6.8.1).
He will himself shortly assume the role of Jupiter's *nuntius* (19–
20n.).   **nuntiis:** here (as in 9 *nuntiem*) Feeney (1998) 27 sees a
bilingual pun on ἑρμηνεύς, 'interpreter', commonly offered as an
etymology of 'Hermes'. Cf. 1n.

9 me adficere uoltis, ea adferam, ea uti nuntiem: scan
A bb c D a / B c dd A B c D; the first *ea* is a monosyllable subject to elision, the second is disyllabic and splits a resolution (*dd*) with the following conjunction.   **uti:** construed with both verbs (for the word
order cf. 842).

10 sient = *sint*. Though these older forms (cf. *MHL* 178) tend to
occur at verse-end in P. (out of metrical convenience), they may not
be obsolete archaisms, as they are found in Cato's prose: see Sblendorio Cugusi (1982) on *orat.* 51, p. 221.

11–12 Parenthesis is a common feature in colloquial speech (*LU*

114–16). Mercury explicitly reveals his identity (cf. 1n.) by stating that he is the god presiding over profiteering and messages. **concessum et datum | ... praesim:** for the passive + noun clause cf. Ter. *Eun.* 395 *est istuc datum | profecto, ut grata mihi sint quae facio omnia*, and *Poen.* 501 *profestos festos habeam decretum est mihi*. The subjunctive may be termed 'paratactic' here in the sense that it is not 'introduced' by a subordinating conjunction, i.e. it is not independent of *concessum et datum*, but only dimly reflects original parataxis. The use of *ut* (originally an adverb meaning 'in some way') with jussives and optatives to mark subordination is not standardized in early Latin. Cf. Bennett 1 208–9, 234–5, 244.

11 quidem 'most certainly' (emphasizing *uos*).   **iam scitis** 'you've long been aware'.

13–14 'As you want me to bless these things, (and) work for them on your behalf, so that you may be perpetually loaded with limitless lucre.'

13 adprobare adnitier: for the asyndeton see 1–16n. and Lindsay 127.   **adprobare:** regularly of divine approval of human affairs, e.g. *Poen.* 1254–5 *eas dis est aequom gratias nos agere sempiternas, | quom nostram pietatem adprobant decorantque di immortales*. Cf. the ironic *di approbent* (*OLD approbo* 1c).   **adnitier:** not part of the vocabulary of ritual, and here only in P. (to achieve alliteration with *adprobare*). The infinitive in *-ier* is archaic (cf. Skutsch (1985) on Enn. *Ann.* 574), and in P. it overwhelmingly occurs at verse-end, where archaisms regularly become relegated (cf. 10n.). There are three instances in Cato's prose (*hist.* 83, *Agr.* 154, *orat.* 152 Sblendorio Cugusi), though context suggests each of these may be a conscious archaism.

15–16 facietis ... eritis: the future indicative is used as an equivalent of an imperative primarily in early Latin (Bennett 1 39).

15 huic ... fabulae 'for the sake of this play'. *huic* is a long monosyllable here (p. 61).   **silentium:** for the prologist's call for silence in Greek comedy cf. Ar. *Vesp.* 86 and Cratinus 151 K–A.

16 aequi et iusti ... arbitri: the awarding of prizes to actors was apparently the responsibility of the presiding *aediles* (72), but the audience's applause no doubt influenced their decision (cf. 65–85). Evidence for the awarding of prizes to playwrights is lacking, though it is not improbable that there was some sort of competition to identify the best play at a festival; cf. p. 40 and *Capt.* 67 *iudices iustissumi*, where the audience is addressed. There are no references to prizes or judges in the extant prologues of Greek New Comedy. The hope or flattering assumption that the audience and/or judges will be intelligent enough to reward the poet for his efforts is a *topos* in the *parabases* of Aristophanes, e.g. *Nub.* 518–62, *Av.* 1101–17.

17–96 These lines constitute a major structural unit of the prologue (as do 97–152). The unifying thread is Mercury's promise to announce a *res* (17, 33, 50; cf. 64) on Jupiter's behalf; no longer jocundly proposing a contractual agreement with his worshippers, Mercury assumes the role of emissary of Jupiter and, in effect, the play and playwright. After a series of false starts and playful but important digressions (esp. 52–63), the long-awaited announcement proves to be the parodic decree on histrionic *ambitio* (64–85). This in turn leads to a final digression on Jupiter's appearance as a character in the play (86–95). If P. used a Greek source for *Am.* (pp. 50–5), he must himself have introduced this entire section to his model, as it is so squarely focused on issues relevant to Roman theatre. In a hypothetical Greek play, we can imagine an opening address by Hermes roughly corresponding to *Am.* 1–14, followed closely by the *argumentum* (cf. *Am.* 97–152), which would probably have been dispatched with greater economy than it is by Mercury.

17–18 Nunc cuius iussu uenio et quam ob rem uenerim | dicam ... : the use of the subjunctive to distinguish indirect questions from direct ones is not yet generalized in P. (KS II 488–90, Woodcock §179, GL §467 N). Here P.'s choice of *uenerim* over a parallel indicative was motivated by aural as well as metrical considerations (*quam ... rem uenerim | dicam simul ... nomen meum*).

17 Nunc 'Now then ...'; here and at 17, 38, 50, 64, 95, 116, 140, and 142 *nunc* marks a transition (*OLD* 9c) and is without temporal significance.   **cuius:** disyllabic; more often a monosyllable in P. (as in 26).

18 eloquar 'state'; its more common meaning in P. (where it is always transitive) is 'divulge'.

19–20 Iouis iussu uenio ... | pater huc me misit ad uos oratum meus: taking this with Mercury's description of himself as an *orator* in 34, the audience will recognize that the god is assuming the persona of an envoy on official business: the original meaning of *orator* is 'ambassador', not 'orator' (cf. *OLD* 1). This older meaning of it is foremost at *Mos.* 1126, *Poen.* 358, *St.* 291, 615, and Ter. *Hec.* 1, where Ambivius Turpio speaks as the poet's representative. That at P.'s time both senses were current is demonstrated by the word play at *St.* 490–5 (with Petersmann's (1973) note on 494ff.); the two meanings also exist side by side in Ennius' *Annales* (202, 304 Skutsch). The spheres of diplomacy and judicial speaking overlap, as in each a spokesman for another seeks to persuade a third party. In that Mercury stresses that he is present at Jupiter's request, a Roman audience would understand an additional reference to judicial advocacy. The unusual nature of the play calls for special pleading, and Mercury's casting as Jupiter's (and the play's) advocate would clearly constitute a Plautine innovation, as in Athens advocacy was frowned upon and permitted only under special circumstances (though speechwriters were always in demand: Kennedy (1968)).

19 Iouis iussu uenio, nomen Mercuriost mihi: scan *aa B C dd A B C D aa B c D*.   **Iouis:** for the scansion see p. 62. **Mercuriost:** in accordance with a convention of New Comedy, Mercury identifies himself by name, as do all the other divine prologists in P., though usually with greater dispatch (cf. *Aul.* 2, *Cist.* 154, *Rud.* 5, *Trin.* 8). Menander's divine prologists could be quite casual about naming themselves; *Tyche* in *Aspis* waits until the very end of her prologue (148). Such flexibility was seen already in the prologues of Euripides.

20 oratum: the supine expressing purpose (cf. 587).

21–2 'Even though he knew that if something should be said to you, you, by virtue of his power, would do it.'

21 tam etsi introduces a concessive clause (sometimes written as one word).   **pro imperio** could be construed 'in accordance with his bidding' (cf. 956), but the emphasis is on Jupiter's awe-inspiring power (cf. 23).   **dictum foret** = *dictum esset* (conditional relative clause: KS ii 309).

22 quippe qui 'as is natural for one who …'; *quippe* is an interrogative in origin (< *quid-pe, 'why then?') used to introduce an explanation. *qui* here is the nominative of the relative, joined with *quippe* as often in Cicero, though there usually with the subjunctive (in P. the subjunctive only at *Per.* 699).   **quippe:** the ultima here uncharacteristically retains its metrical value (p. 62).   **intellexerat** 'knew'; the pluperfect often approaches the meaning of the perfect in P. (Lindsay 62).

23 uereri ... et metuere 'venerate and fear', conventional Roman attitudes toward divinity (cf. 832 and *Poen.* 281–2). **Iouem:** sc. *uereri et metuere.*

24–5 uerum profecto ... iussit 'be that as it may, he actually did instruct me ...'

25 leniter: Mercury's stated approach would please Quintilian: *prooemio frequentissime lenis conuenit pronuntiatio. nihil enim est ad conciliandum gratius uerecundia ... (Inst.* 11.3.161).

26 etenim 'The fact of the matter is ...' (only here in P.).

26–7 Iuppiter | non minus quam uostrum quiuis formidat malum. . . : the jest turns on the fact that *malum* frequently indicates a 'beating' or 'flogging' in P. (e.g. *Pers.* 816–17 *ne tibi hoc scipione | malum magnum dem*; cf. Amphitryon's threat to Sosia at 563), and that Roman actors in P.'s time, in contrast to their Greek counterparts, were primarily slaves and therefore subject to corporal punishment for poor performances, if *Cist.* 784–5 can be trusted (cf. *As.* 946 and *Trin.* 989–90, with Muecke (1986) 227; summary of evidence for actors' status in Abel (1955) 9). The joke is swift and generic: 'Jupiter [like all actors] fears a flogging just as much as any one of you does, seeing that he's not actually a god.' *Pace* Oniga (n. *ad* 26), the audience would probably not reflect on the (possibly) higher social status of the actor–impresario who might have played Jupiter. Nor is testimony that a *lex Porcia* prohibiting the flogging of Roman citizens was passed in the first decade of the second century BC of use in dating the play. For the sake of a metatheatrical joke, Mercury steps out of his role as divine prologist to identify himself and the actor playing Jupiter as persons of low status in real life. Cf. *A midsummer night's dream* III.1 'Write me a prologue; and let that prologue say, we will do no harm with our swords and that Pyramus is not killed indeed; and, for the more better assurance, tell them that I Pyramus am not Pyramus, but Bottom the weaver: this will put them out of fear.' Cf. 1146n.

27 minus: -*s* does not 'make position' here (p. 62), whereas it does in 986 (the rarer practice); see further Wallace (1984).

28 humana matre natus, humano patre: the joke is probably bipartite. The actor playing Jupiter obviously lacks the god's omnipotence and cannot escape a flogging. And if he is a slave, he has no legal claim to ancestry: cf. *Capt.* 574 *quem patrem, qui seruos est?* and Caecilius 245 R = 251–2 W *st! tacete! quid hoc clamoris? quibus nec*

mater nec pater | tanta confidentia estis? In the carnivalesque world of
Plautine comedy, however, slaves frequently claim otherwise (*Mil.*
372–3, *St.* 303–5, *Ps.* 581, *Cas.* 418). Cf. p. 2 and 365n.

29 praetimet: the prefix of this extremely rare verb has its usual
temporal force, as the actor fears what may happen after the play.

30 quoque etiam: this pleonastic combination lends special emphasis to the word it follows in P. (Lindsay 113); the actor's tone is
mock-indignant ('And yes, I too, I who am the son of Jupiter ...').
Cf. 81 and 717; the emphasized word is sometimes enclosed by *etiam
... quoque* (461).

31 contagione: a comic absurdity in that the son of Jupiter is
made to fear pollution through association with the chief god.
mei: synizesis (p. 61); scan $A B c D a / B c D a a B c D$.

32 propterea pace aduenio et pacem ad uos fero: after the
series of associative jests (21–31), Mercury reassumes the persona of
the *orator* (19–20n.). An envoy's basic function is to obtain a peaceful
settlement from a potentially hostile body; cf. Ennius' description of
Cineas' failed mission on behalf of King Pyrrhus, *Ann.* 202 Skutsch
orator sine pace redit regique refert rem. In the mouth of a god there is the
additional sense 'I come without resentment and offer you my blessing' (cf. 1127 and *OLD pax* 2).   **propterea:** sc. 'because the possibility of a drubbing exists [if I don't win your applause], I come
peacefully ...'   **pace:** ablative of manner.

33–7 The connection between 32 and 33ff. similarly lies in Mercury's re-establishment of his role as an *orator* (32n.). His return to his
central message (33 *rem*; cf. 17–96n.) proves to be another false start,
and instead a playful excursus on justice and pleading ensues. For
the jingly style cf. *Capt.* 255–6 *qui cauet ne decipiatur, uix cauet, cum etiam
cauet; | etiam cum cauisse ratus est, saepe is cautor captus est*; Ennius takes
this to the point of incomprehensibility in his *Satires*: 59–62 V = 28–
31 W *nam qui lepide postulat alterum frustrari | quem frustratur frustra eum
dicit frustra esse; | nam qui sese frustrari quem frustra sentit, | qui frustratur
frustra est si non ille est frustra.* Perhaps both writers are parodying the
(over)fondness for antithesis and hair-splitting generally associated
with Greek rhetoric, which was being introduced contempora-
neously at Rome. For the complex love–hate relationship between
Romans and Greeks (and their cultures) in P. cf. the tirade against
isti Graeci palliati (*Cur.* 288–95), primarily directed at Greek philoso-

phers in Rome, among whom P.'s audience might indiscriminately lump teachers of rhetoric.

See 16n. for the emphasis on the audience's justness.

33 iustam rem et facilem esse oratam a uobis uolo 'It's a just and simple matter I want asked of you'; cf. 64, where the idea is turned in the active.

34 nam iustae ab iustis iustus sum orator datus: lit., 'for I have been appointed a just pleader for a just cause from just people'. **nam:** explicative here and in 35, but often asseverative ('yes', 'surely') in P. **iustae ... iustis iustus:** polyptoton of three or more elements occurs chiefly in early Latin (LHS II 708); cf. 221, 278 and *Cas.* 826 *mala malae male monstrat.* **iustae:** with Lindsay's emendation of the senseless *iuste* in the MSS understand the genitive *rei* (cf. 33 *rem*). **ab iustis:** construed with *orator* on the analogy of verbs of asking, etc. (cf. 36 *ab iniustis petere*). **orator:** both 'envoy' and 'pleader' (19–20n.).

35 iniusta ... iustis: a proverbial opposition; cf. 36 *iusta ... iniustis*, Otto (1890) 180, and 173n.

36 iniustis: word-end very rarely (cf. *Men.* 750, *Per.* 410, *Ps.* 39) falls precisely in the middle of the senarius, i.e. after the sixth element rather than the fifth or seventh (cf. p. 60). Here the unusual rhythm enhances the jingle.

37 quippe 'for naturally ...', with a confident tone (cf. 22n.).

38 Nunc iam ... animum ... aduortite: the formal call for attentiveness is a regular feature of the *captatio* and often marks a transition to a new thought (cf. 95, 151, *Men.* 5, *Mer.* 15, Ter. *Ph.* 25, *Hec.* 55, *An.* 24). The chorus of Old Comedy similarly exhorts the audience to pay attention (Ar. *Eq.* 503, *Nub.* 575, *Vesp.* 1015, *Av.* 688); such admonitions are altogether lacking in Menander (the supplement at *Asp.* 100 is not quite parallel). **Nunc iam:** written as two words to distinguish it from the trisyllabic *nunciam* (see *OLD*); more often separated (*nunc ... iam*), it (unlike *nunciam*) implies a contrast with the past ('pay attention, as you haven't up to now'). Cf. *iam nunc*, which may look to the future. **loquar:** an iamb (p. 58).

39–49 A new rhetorical stategy ('you ought to accede to the wishes of my father and me, given our history of beneficence toward you and the state') and another false start (17–96n.). The *Rhet. Her.* 1.5 recommends the same approach at the opening of a speech: *ab* *nostra persona beniuolentiam contrahemus si nostrum officium sine adrogantia laudabimus, atque in rem publicam quales fuerimus, aut in parentes, aut in amicos, aut in eos qui audiunt* ... This reflects a Roman inclination: 'a Greek orator tends to argue his audience into believing something; a Roman by his authority convinces the audience that something should be believed because he says so' (Kennedy (1972) 42). Cf. Quintilian, *Inst.* 4.1.7.

39 The line scans *A B C D a / B c D A bb c D*.   **debetis:** the verb is used only here and at *Per.* 160 in the sense 'ought' + infinitive (elsewhere in P. it means 'owe').   **uelimus:** generalizing subjunctive.

41–4 'Yes, why should I mention (as I've seen other gods in tragic theatre – Neptune, Courage, Victory, Mars, Bellona – recall their benefactions to you) the good deeds of which my father, the ruler of the gods, was the instigator, for the benefit of all?'

41 nam quid ego memorem ...: Mercury employs the rhetorical technique (*praeteritio* or *occultatio*) whereby special emphasis is lent to what the speaker claims to be reluctant to mention: cf. *Rhet. Her.* 4.37 and for a complex use of this device in early Latin Cato, *orat.* 169 Sblendorio Cugusi.   **nam:** 34n.

41–2 ut alios in tragoediis | uidi: the claim to novelty is another commonplace in *prooemia*: *Rhet. Her.* 1.10 (cf. 1.8) *promiserimus aliter ac parati fuerimus nos esse dicturos; nos non eodem modo ut ceteri soleant uerba facturos.* Cf. Charinus' opening monologue in *Mer.*, where he claims that he will not relate his woes 3 *ut alios in comoediis,* 118–19n., and for Aristophanes' dissociation of his comedy from that of his rivals see Muecke (1977) 61.

41 in tragoediis: overt critique and/or ridicule of tragedy were stock features of Old Comedy and seem to have persisted in Greek Middle and New Comedy prologues as well (Antiphanes 189 K–A, Diphilus 29 K–A), though they are not found in Menander. Cf. 987n.

42–4 No trace survives among the fragments of Roman tragedy of any such patriotic appeal by these deities. Presumably, these divine prologists implored the audience to rally in times of (esp. military) crisis out of gratitude for their past benefactions; for the possibility of such prologues in Ennius' tragedies see Skutsch (1968) 174–81. Along with the fact that the *praeteritio* here only highlights Jupiter's beneficence (41n.; cf. 46–9), there is ironic humour in Mercury's eschewal of precisely what he had done in his opening (1–16n.).

42 uidi, Neptunum Virtutem Victoriam: an unusually 'heavy' line, with every element long except the obligatory short in eleventh position. The ponderous rhythm perhaps reflects Mercury's mock-indignation as he pretends to scorn the self-aggrandizement of the tragic prologists; cf. the comparatively 'light' (i.e. highly re-solved) lines with which this jocund sequence of thought begins (41 *A bb c dd a bb C D a B c D*) and ends (49 *aa B c D A bb C dd a B c D*). The expressive possibilities of iambo-trochaic verse are explored by Gratwick and Lightly (1982).   **Virtutem:** a very old stratum of Roman religion was steeped in 'personified' abstractions or powers (e.g. Ops, Salus, Robigus), but Virtus belongs to the 'wave of Hel-lenising religious innovation' (Feeney (1998) 86) that spans the third century. In 205 BC, a temple was dedicated to Honos and Virtus in honour of Marcus Claudius Marcellus' conquest of Syracuse (212 BC). For P.'s play with such deities see *Bac.* 115–20 *Amor, Voluptas, Venus, Venustas, Gaudium, | Iocus, Ludus, Sermo, Suauisauiatio ... :: an deus est ullus Suauisauiatio?* Cf. 75n.   **Victoriam** = the Greek Nike. A temple was dedicated to her during the Samnite War (294 BC). Her cult was especially important for Roman soldiers and she is often as-sociated with Mars (cf. 43) as well as Jupiter: Axtell (1907) 15–18. See further Fears (1981).

43 Bellonam: a very ancient goddess of war (= Duellona) with a temple on the Campus Martius, where military business was some-times conducted. She is frequently coupled with Virtus (cf. 42) in in-scriptions: Axtell (1907) 25–6.   **commemorare:** cf. 41 *memorem.* There are many examples in P. of the simple verb being followed by one of its compounds in a corrective sense; the stronger compound 'suggests that the preceding simplex has understated or inadequately emphasized the realities of the situation' (Renehan (1977) 246). There is a suggestion here that the divine prologists do not simply list their benefactions but boast of them. Cf. 86–9n.

44 fecissent: the subjunctive is perhaps generalizing ('whatever good deeds they had done for you').   **quis benefactis:** no pre-cise parallel for *architectus* + the dative instead of the genitive has been adduced; Palmer *ad loc.* compares Hor. *S.* 1.6.71 *causa fuit pater his.* Cf. the use of the dative of 'sympathy' with nouns (LHS II 95–6).

meus pater: as 'Jupiter' has just been 'unmasked' as a humble actor (26–7n.), Mercury's mention of his father's past benefactions may on another level refer to theatrical performances (cf. 45n.).

45 deorum: *A B* here (synizesis: p. 61). **architectust** = *architectus est* (prodelision: p. 62). The reference is somewhat obscure: to Jupiter as master of the universe (Oniga *ad loc.*) or is a metatheatrical joke intended (p. 1 n. 5)? For the indicative in indirect questions see 17–18n. **omnibus** 'for all [gods and human beings?]'.

46–7 'But it's never been the practice of that father of mine to cast in the teeth of good people whatever good he did them'; *exprobrare* with an object such as *quod . . . boni* is an oxymoron.

46 patri meo: *a B / c D* ; a breach of Luchs' law (p. 64), if the line is sound as printed here with Ussing's simple supplement ⟨*ille*⟩ (*patrem meum* is found at line-end at *Men.* 750, where see Gratwick's (1993) n.).

48 gratum ... a uobis sibi 'he is of the opinion that you are grateful to him for this' (lit. 'received with thanks for himself from you'); for the construction see Williams (1959) 158–9.

49 meritoque uobis bona se facere quae facit 'and that as you deserve he does the good deeds for you which he does'. Such flattery is typical in the *captatio* (cf. 47 *bonis* and 75–6).

50–96 Mercury continues his rhetorical striptease: a fourth start (50) at divulging the *res* (cf. 17–18, 33, 38) is arrested when the god casually 'drops a bomb' (51 *tragoediae*), and a digression on the play's unusual genre follows (52–63). After a fifth announcement of Jupiter's request (64), Mercury's promise is finally and surprisingly fulfilled (64–96n.). On the basis of content alone, this entire section of the prologue must be of purely Plautine origin (cf. 17–96n.), as is also suggested by the verbal repetition at 51 and 96 (cf. 1–16n.). In prologues, departure from narration of the *argumentum* in favour of the jests and blandishments associated with the *captatio* is often so framed, e.g. *Poen.* 46–58.

50 proloquar: *proloqui* is frequent in comedy but generally avoided in classical prose.

51–63 The audience is prepared for a mythological travesty in a manner suggesting that this type of drama is a novelty for them. Mercury's chatty excursus here playfully mimics the process of composing such a travesty (cf. p. 54): the playwright takes a tragedy (51) and not unlike an omnipotent god (53) transforms it into a special type of comedy (55). The resulting admixture can be termed a 'tragicomedy' (59, 63) in that it retains figures of both tragedy (61n.) and comedy (62n.). Mercury does not mean that serious and comic elements will be confused; the gods subsequently always refer to the play as a *comoedia* (88, 96, 868; cf. 987).

51 huius: monosyllabic.

52–3 Prologs of Old and Middle Comedy freely employ the rhetorical strategy of forestalling dissent by creating an imaginary objector (e.g. Ar. *Pax* 44–5, Heniochus *incert.* 5 K–A, Pherecrates 163 K–A, Cratinus 342 K–A); in Menander it is (possibly) found in more indirect form at *Phasma* 18–19. That P. was versed in this technique is best illustrated by *Cas.* 67 *sunt hic inter se quos nunc credo dicere* ... Here Mercury dispenses with a formula such as 'someone may say ...' and assumes the entire audience's objection to tragedy (52n.). Cf. the similar anticipation of objections at 86–94, 116–19 and *Capt.* 58–66.

52 quid: exclamatory *quid* is regularly followed by a question in rhetoric, e.g. *Rhet. Her.* 4. 13 *quaeret aliquis: 'quid? Fregellani non sua sponte conati sunt?'*, where likewise it is combined with an imaginary objection. Cf. 89.   **contraxistis frontem:** at Ar. *Eq.* 37–9 a character similarly pretends to take the audience's facial expressions into account. Tragedy is conventionally treated as a cause for ennui or distress in Aristophanes, e.g. *Av.* 785–9; cf. Lucil. 875 M = 879 W *uerum tristis contorto aliquo ex Pacuuiano exordio.*   **quia:** more common in P. after verbs of feeling (*contraxistis frontem* = 'you're disturbed') than *quod*, which is preferred in classical Latin.

53 deus sum: divine prologists in New Comedy commonly jest about their divine status: cf. Men. *Asp.* 97–8, *Cist.* 152–3.   **commutauero** 'I'll have it completely changed immediately.' Though the future perfect can be used very precisely in P., it is often indistinguishable from the simple future (e.g. 930: Bennett 1 54–7) and can be used in place of the latter for metrical convenience. Here it stresses the instantaneous completion of the god's magical transformation of the play.

54–5 eandem hanc ... faciam ex tragoedia | comoedia ut

sit 'I'll make this same play into a comedy instead of a tragedy', a very common form of prolepsis (cf. οἶδά σε τίς εἶ, lit., 'I know you who you are') in P. Cf. Lindsay 27–8.

54 faciam ex: an instance where C / D hiatus (p. 68) should be tolerated, as it falls after the seventh element, the second most common place for word-end in the senarius (cf. Petersmann (1973) on *St.* 171). The line scans *A B C D A / bb c D a B c D* (with synizesis in the initial syllable of *eandem*).

55 omnibus isdem uorsibus: since the characterization of the play as a *tragoedia* (51–4) was only a disingenuous ploy to introduce the notion of mythical burlesque, the comic script remains the same. **omnibus:** scanned *B cc*, an apparent exception to the rules of resolution (p. 62), as the text is not otherwise suspect here.

56 fit: editors generally read *sit* (E) for *fit* here and punctuate to indicate an indirect disjunctive question. But the *lectio difficilior* is defensible (so Sedgwick *ad loc.*): 'Is it to be made into comedy or not? You want me to?' The deliberative (present) indicative, while common in the first person (e.g. *Capt.* 479 *quo imus . . . ?*, 481 *ubi cenamus?*), is found in the third person in P. in a few instances: *Cist.* 768 *quid fit, Lampadio?*, *Ps.* 1159 *quid nunc fit, Simo?*, *Rud.* 687 *nam, obsecro, unde iste animus mi inuenitur?* Each of these examples occurs within animated dialogue and is virtually equivalent to the more common first person deliberative (Mercury in effect says 'Do I do it?'). For third person examples in Juvenal see Courtney (1980) *ad* 4.130. The use of the indicative instead of the subjunctive calls for, as Sedgwick observes, immediate action. Cf. KS I 120, LHS II 308.   **sed ego stultior** 'But I am a bit foolish.'

57 quasi nesciam 'as though I didn't know . . .', a lively colloquialism (*LU* 52).   **uelle:** the eighth occurrence of the uerb with reference to the audience (cf. 1, 5, 9, 13, 39, 54, 56); intense concern for the audience's wishes is naturally a mark of the *captatio*.   **qui diuos siem** 'since I'm a god'. P. has both the subjunctive (e.g. 506) and the indicative (e.g. 326) in causal relative clauses.   **siem:** Ion.

58–9 Lit., 'I understand what your opinion is in this matter. I'll make it mixed: let it be a "tragicomedy".'

58 quid animi: for the genitive (one of respect or 'sphere'?) cf. 689, 105, LHS II 74, *LL* 293–4, and Lindsay 12.

59 ⟨sit⟩: easily lost (by haplography) after *commixta sit* (cf. 63n.). **tragicomoedia:** Mercury coins a new term to denote what is probably an unfamiliar genre for his audience. We find notices of Middle Comedy plays titled *Komoidotragoidia* (see Alcaeus 21 K–A) and Rhinthon's *hilarotragoidia* (pp. 52–3), but never this precise formation, which reverses the constituent elements of the corresponding Greek words (other Plautine neologisms of the type adjective + unaltered noun include *perenniserue, semihomines,* and *semisenem*: Stein (1971) 599). Vigorous word coinage is similarly a trait of Aristophanic language; Mercury's here has enjoyed enduring influence in European drama and undergone various transformations of meaning (cf. Herrick (1962), Hirst (1984)) and we must guard against these colouring our perception of P.'s play. P. was no Shakespeare: 'In comedy, the distance of the audience from the characters' plights is central to the effect; in tragedy, the closeness of the audience to the characters' crises is an ultimate factor in the achievement of its catharsis. In Shakespeare's tragicomedies, however, there is a simultaneous emphasis on both engagement and detachment producing a state of wonderment which holds these apparently opposite responses in equilibrium' (Hartwig (1972) 18). P. by contrast maintains the sense of comic detachment throughout *Am.* that farce demands: cf. pp. 37–45.

60–3 Mercury echoes the Aristotelian distinction between comedy and tragedy as mimesis of 'those worse and those better than people are today' (*Poet.* 1448a), respectively, but we need not assume that P. had read Aristotle. Renaissance theorists continued the emphasis on social status in distinguishing tragedy and comedy (Hartwig (1972) 13–14).

61 reges 'regal personages' (*OLD* 6); translators generally overlook the fact that no kings appear in *Am.* (Creon, not Amphitryon, is king of Thebes: 194, 351).   **quo** 'to which' (brachylogy for *comoedia ⟨ea⟩ in quam*).   **ueniant:** generalizing subjunctive, as Mercury is stating a principle.   **non par:** sc. *esse*; the omission of the copulative is common in colloquial expressions (e.g. *mirum quin, pote*: LHS II 420–1, GL §209 N.2).

62 quid igitur? 'What to do then?', an elliptical formula also used by orators to highlight a conclusion (cf. *OLD quis, quid* 14a). Here it creates a sense of conversational naturalness ('You know, it really wouldn't be right to make it a comedy all the way through, since it features gods and regal personages. What to do then? I'll make it a "tragicomedy" (as I just said), since it's got a slave's part in it'). **hic** 'in the play' (adverb). **seruos:** slaves do play significant roles in Greek tragedy (e.g. the Paedagogus of S. *El.*, the slave in *OT*, and the nurses of various heroines); Mercury is thinking of the typically cunning slave of New Comedy.

63 tragicomoedia: the critical point of the digression (52–63) is repeated and given special emphasis through *ut dixi* and the final position. The MSS offer *tragicocomoedia* here, which does not scan and is an obvious slip, and at 59, where it should similarly be emended (cf. n. *ad loc.*).

64–96 Mercury at last divulges the message first promised at 17. With all subterfuge finally put aside, and with a view to ensuring fairness in the awarding of prizes to the actors, the god energetically delivers a legalistic proclamation against the planting of claques in the theatre. Once again, the theatrical milieu here is suggestive of Old Comedy, where the agonistic element and the attendant notion of judicial fairness figure prominently in *parabases*. Legalistic parody is exceedingly common in P., as it is in Aristophanes (e.g. *Av.* 1071–87). The absence of a specific point of reference for the parody here – i.e. record of a contemporary *lex de ambitu* – has led some critics to declare all or part of Mercury's proclamation to be the work of a later interpolator (cf. McDonnell (1986)). In addition to being an argument *ex silentio*, this view assumes that P. was incapable of composing a comic law on histrionic *ambitio* by himself. Legal and other types of public proclamation were a ubiquitous feature of Roman society, and were rendered in a formal, stereotypical style that could be easily mimicked; no one would assume a specific model for the mock edicts on theatre etiquette delivered by the prologist of *Poen.* (11–43). Political corruption had been a perennial issue since the earliest days of Republican politics, and furnished P. with a ready analogy for the planting of claques.

This section of the prologue falls into distinct structural units: (1) formal announcement of the proclamation (64); (2) the appointment of *conquistores* to search for guilty parties among the audience, whether planted spectators or the aediles themselves (65–74); (3) Jupiter's opinion on the issue and a gnomic summation (75–80); (4)

announcement of a second corollary proclamation (81); (5) the appointment of *conquistores* to search for guilty actors (82–5); (6) an associative digression on Jupiter's appearance as an actor on stage (86–95); (7) a new call for attention pending narration of the *argumentum* (95–6). 1 and 4 obviously mirror each other, as do 2 and 5, and, less perfectly, 3 and 6; 7 marks a transition. The roundabout manner of composition is typically Plautine, and the overall structural integrity seems unassailable.

Obviously, little in 64–96 could have stood in a Greek source play.

64 Nunc hoc me orare a uobis iussit Iuppiter: the long-anticipated proclamation is announced with a rhythmically heavy line (42n.).

65 conquistores: generally read by editors for the unmetrical *conquisitores* in the MSS (*conquestores* Leo; cf. Var. *L.* 6.79), this is P.'s term for low-ranking police officers or 'inspectors' (cf. *Mer.* 665). **subsellia** 'benches'. References to seating in P. formerly were regarded as sure signs of later interpolation, but there now is a consensus that P.'s theatre had temporary seating (cf. Beare (1964) 171–2). For the primary evidence see *Poen.* 5, 17–20, 1224, *Capt.* 12, *Mil.* 81–3, *Aul.* 718, and *Truc.* 968. Tradition held that seats of honour were reserved for senators first in 194 BC (cf. pp. 20–1).

66 caueam: the area for the spectators (though at *Truc.* 931 it stands, by synecdoche, for the theatre in general), distinct from that for the actors, the *proscaenium* (cf. 91). The physical structure of the theatre is frequently referred to in the plays (see Knapp (1919), but little is known of the precise arrangement (pp. 19–21). Sedgwick (n. *ad* 66) seems to be thinking of much later permanent structures when he writes of 'the sloping semicircular rows of seats, the auditorium'; most scholars imagine parallel wooden benches or grandstands, e.g. Sandbach (1977) 108.   **spectatoribus** 'as concerns the spectators', a vague dative of reference.

67 si cui fauitores delegatos uiderint '(and) if they should see supporters assigned to anyone'; the string of conditional clauses initiated here is typical of legal language, which strives for all-inclusiveness (70–1n.).   **fauitores** = classical *fautores*, the placement of whom was a perennial concern in the Roman theatre (cf. Tac. *Ann.* 13.28). It is unclear whether the *fauitores* here are planted on behalf of individual actors or competing troupes performing in different plays: cf. the singular *cui* here against 69 *histrionibus*. The performance of an individual actor, Chrysalus in *Bac.* reminds the audience (213–15), could make or break a play. Cf. 69n.

68 is ... pignus capiantur togae 'that their togas be seized from them for security', a humorous application of the legal process (*pignoris capio*) whereby property is impounded to insure payment of a debt or is to be sold to make restitution. According to the conceit here, male citizens found guilty of histrionic partisanship are to be left sitting in their undergarments; by contrast, the primarily servile actors guilty of self-promotion will have their costumes shredded and be beaten (85).   **is** = *eis* (dative of disadvantage, as with verbs of taking away *et sim.*: cf. Woodcock §61, GL §345 R.1). **pignus:** the use of the predicate nominative instead of the more common *pignori* is chiefly poetic (Woodcock §68 N.3). Cf. *Poen.* 145 *si tibi lubido est aut uoluptati, sino*.   **togae:** although the *toga* originally was worn by men and women of all estates (Serv. *A.* 1.282), by P.'s day it had probably become the badge of free-born males. Cf. Moore (1994) 120–2.

69 qui: sc. *fauitores*; similarly in 71, *qui ipse* should be a *fauitor*, not a *histrio* (cf. 69 *histrionibus*). The malfeasance of the *histriones* is to be taken up in 81–5. *qui* is the second short of a *bb* resolution (prosodic hiatus: pp. 63–4).   **ambissent:** the pluperfect subjunctive should be read here and in 71 despite attempts by some editors to introduce uniformity into the sequence of tenses; P.'s colloquial Latin defies such rigidity (cf. 745–6 and Lindsay 56–7).   **palmam histrionibus:** the hiatus here is perhaps tolerable (i.e. after the seventh element: 54n.); Lindsay supplies ⟨*his*⟩ before *histrionibus*. *palma* is used with reference to the victory of an *artifex* at *Poen.* 37, but to that of a *comoedia* at *Trin.* 705.   **histrionibus:** according to Livy 7.2.6, *histrio* is from the Etruscan word for actor (*ister*); for the Etruscan tradition of music and dance see Bieber (1961) 147–8.

70–1 Mercury's parody echoes typically legal *abundantia*, which aims at covering every possible contingency; cf. *sacra in oquolted ne quisquam fecise uelet, neue in poplicod neue in preiuatod neue exstrad urbem sacra quisquam fecise uelet, nisei ...* (*senatus consultum de Bacchanalibus* = *CIL* 1 2.581). The three methods of canvassing here – by letter, in person, and through an intermediary – are ludicrously applied to a

fauitor acting on behalf of an actor.   **seu per scriptas litteras |
siue qui ipse ambisset seu per internuntium** = *seu qui per
scriptas litteras siue ipse seu per internuntium ambisset.*

70 artifici: a vague term that could refer to someone involved in
just about any aspect of theatrical production (cf. pp. 1–2). The
tibicen and the playwright are likely participants in a competition,
though *siue cuiquam artifici* may simply be an emphatic repetition of
69 *siue … histrionibus*; cf. *Poen.* 36–8 *quodque ad ludorum curatores attinet,
| ne palma detur quoiquam artifici iniuria | neue ambitionis causa extrudantur
foras.* That Mercury has actors foremost in mind is also strongly suggested by 77.

71 ambisset: 69n.

72 Aristophanes' choruses often complain that the judges have
awarded prizes unjustly in the past, e.g. *Vesp.* 1015–50. No such
complaint is found in extant Greek New Comedy. Cf. 16n.   **siue
adeo** 'or if for that matter …'; *adeo* marks a climax. Cf. *Men.* 296 *ego
te non noui neque nouisse adeo uolo.*   **aediles:** Abel (1955) 31 maintains that these *aediles* must be *curules* rather than *plebeii* because only
the former had the right to exercise *pignoris capio*; thus *Am.* would
have been performed at either the *ludi Romani* in September or the
Megalensia in April, as only *curules* could superintend these particular
festivals. We should perhaps not press such a fine distinction within a
parody.   **duint** = *dent* (sc. *palmam*; cf. 69). *duint* is an optative in
origin, formed with *-i*, as also the subjunctive *uelim*, etc. (*LL* 278); its
position at line-end reflects its status as an archaism for P.

73 sirempse: probably 'the very same' rather than 'in the very
same way' (an archaic legal term of uncertain formation). The *OLD*
fails to recognize the adjectival use, as in the formula *lex siremps(e)
esto.*

74 magistratum: with iambic shortening in the ante-penult
(p. 63).   **ambiuerit:** the understood subject is 'the guilty party'.

75–7 Extremely ironic in the mouth of Mercury, as Oniga notes
on 75: in the play, the gods use deceit and trickery against Amphitryon and Alcmena, both of whom champion the cause of *uirtus*
(cf. pp. 41–2).

75 uirtute dixit uos uictores uiuere: a remarkable line, with
its alliteration and relatively heavy rhythm (*A B c D A / B C D A B c D*;
cf. 42n.).   **uirtute:** a (cf. ἀρετή) predominant theme of the Sci-

pionic *elogia* which captures the essence of Roman aristrocratic aspirations: '*uirtus* ... does not mean courage simply, but stands rather for the whole aristocratic ideal with its emphasis on *gloria* won by the commission of great deeds in the service of the *respublica* according to certain standards of conduct' (Earl (1960) 238). This is clearly illustrated here by its combination with *uiuere*, which looks beyond the military sphere, and the direct contrast with 76 *ambitio* and *perfidia*. The concept could be extended to legionaries of the lower classes as well, in its general promotion of patriotism and proper performance of duty; cf. Enn. *Ann.* 326-8 Skutsch. Thus, Mercury's flattering statement is relevant to a significant portion of the male members of the audience in addition to the aediles. Similar imputation of *uirtus* to the audience is found in valedictions at *Cas.* 87-8 and *Cist.* 197-8. Cf. 42n.

76 ambitione: within a few years of the début of *Am.*, a *lex de ambitu* (Livy 40.19, 181 BC) may have prescribed death for those found guilty of illegal canvassing (Scullard (1950) 172).   **qui minus** 'why shouldn't ...'; *qui* is an old ablative or instrumental in origin.

77 eadem: with synizesis.   **summo uiro:** i.e., a member of the oligarchy that dominated republican politics, and thus diametrically opposite to the *histrio* in the social hierarchy. Mercury presumably underscored the comic absurdity of a theatrical *lex de ambitu* through pompous delivery of his lines.

78 uirtute ambire oportet, non fauitoribus 'It's proper to canvass on the strength of one's *uirtus*, not one's partisans.'

79–80 'He who behaves rightly never lacks for supporters, provided those who judge the matter are honest'; more mock-righteousness by the arch-trickster (75–7n.), who in the play twice asserts that Jupiter 'behaves properly' (289, 995 *recte facit*) in deceitfully pursuing his affair with Alcmena. For the obsession with judicial fairness in the theatre see 16, 72nn.

81–5 These lines do not repeat 64–80, and (*pace* Sedgwick on 81) there are no firm grounds for suspecting interpolation. Their purpose is to articulate the *lex de ambitu* as it applies to actors; nor, conversely, are 64–80 likely to be interpolated (*pace* McDonnell (1986) 574). Mercury offers a second legal 'angle' here and also brings his pompous parody to an appropriately bathetic conclusion (85). Cf. 64–85n.

81 hoc quoque etiam: 30n.   **mihi in:** B / C hiatus is doubtful here (p. 68); Palmer's suggestion of ⟨*is*⟩ after *mandatis* is adopted. **in mandatis ⟨is⟩ dedit:** *uariatio* on 64 *iussit*; similarly, with 82 *ut conquistores fierent histrionibus* cf. 65–6, and with the relative clauses of 83–4 cf. the conditionals of 67–72.

83 sibi: monosyllabic. The line is 'heavy' (42n.).   **delegati:** with *ut plauderent*; *OLD delego* 1 classifies the participle as substantive here, but *fauitores* can be understood from 67–71.

84 quiue quo placeret alter fecisset minus 'or who had taken steps to see that another would be received less favourably' (*quiue* is subject of *fecisset* and *quo ... minus* introduces the negative purpose clause; native speakers construing sentences as a whole presumably were not troubled by such word-order). This suggests that prizes were awarded to individual actors: cf. 67n.

85 ornamenta 'costumes', a theatrical technical term for which in general see Duckworth (1952) 88–94 and Bieber (1961) 91ff. **corium uti conciderent:** P.'s vigorous comic language frequently expands the semantic capacities of verbs; here *conciderent* has its literal meaning ('tear up') in reference to *ornamenta*, but a metaphorical sense ('thrash') with *corium* (zeugma or syllepsis: cf. LHS II 831–2, GL §690). P. is especially innovative in the figurative use of verbs of 'cutting' (Corbett (1964) 61).

86–95 The preceding report of Jupiter's commands regarding actors leads to an associative digression on Jupiter as an actor.

86–9 mirari nolim ... ne miremini: | ... | quid? admirati estis? 'I'd prefer that you not wonder ... don't wonder ... What? You're absolutely astonished?'; the pretence of self-correction (43n.) promotes the sense of intimacy Mercury seeks to establish with his audience as he inducts them into the world of the play. For the theme of wonder see pp. 29–31.

87 ne miremini: the use of the subjunctive in commands and prohibitions is widespread in early (and colloquial) Latin, whereas in classical Latin prose the imperative or *noli* + the infinitive is preferred except in generalizing precepts in the second person (Woodcock §126–30, GL §263).

88 ipse 'in person' (as in 94) strongly suggests that Jupiter's appearance as a character in a comedy is a novelty for the Roman audience; *nunc* (87, 90), *hodie* (94), and the various forms of *hic* (88,

91, 94) similarly stress this point.   **acturust** 'is going to act' (the future participle is only used in the periphrastic conjugation in early Latin). For the prodelision see p. 62   **comoediam:** the playful digression on mythical travesty long since passed (51–63n.), Mercury applies the appropriate tag to the play.

89 admirati estis: the perfect in an imaginary objection (as 52 *contraxistis*: cf. n. *ad loc.*). The *A / B* hiatus at the main break in the senarius here is unquestionably legitimate.

89–90 'As if something new really were being presented now, having Jupiter be an actor.' To ease the audience into acceptance of a novelty, Mercury blurs the very real distinction between Jupiter's playing an extended role in a play and merely appearing as a *deus ex machina*. Cf. 91–2n.

89 uero: ironic, as often in combination with *quasi*.

90 Iouem facere histrioniam: with *histrioniam* (a rare word) understand *artem*; the association of the king of the gods with the humble art of acting is patently absurd and will be repeated at the end of the prologue (152).   **Iouem:** with iambic shortening (p. 63); the resulting proceleusmatic (*Iouem facere*) is rare but attested (Questa (1967) 64). The line scans *A B c D A / bb cc D a B c D*.

91–2 These lines refer to an (apparently rare) appearance of Jupiter as a *deus ex machina* in an adaptation of a Greek tragedy performed in Rome a year before *Am.*; for the possibility of a performance of Euripides' *Alkmene* see p. 3.

91 anno 'last year'.   **proscaenio:** 66n.

92 Iouem inuocarunt, uenit: i.e. as when in this play Alcmena calls for assistance in childbirth (1069 *deos sibi inuocat*, as narrated by Bromia) and Jupiter appears as *deus ex machina*. In extant Greek tragedy a character does not invoke a god, or the gods in general, and have his or her prayer immediately answered; closest to the denouement of *Am.* is S. *Ph.* 1406, where Philoctetes obliquely mentions the 'arrows of Herakles' (1409) before the god appears. For tragic epiphany in general see Barrett (1964) on E. *Hipp.* 1283. Zeus in fact does not appear as a *deus ex machina* in extant tragedy (an accident of transmission?), though the revelations of other deities sometimes are said to be in accordance with his will (cf. Dodds (1960) on Eur. *Bacc.* 1348–9).   **auxilio is fuit:** cf. Jupiter's words to Alcmena in 1064 *adest auxilium*, and similarly when he appears for a second time as *deus ex machina* before Amphitryon, 1131 *adsum auxilio*.

93 The line is rightly bracketed by Ussing and Leo, as having the ring of a clumsy marginal gloss ('moreover (?) he did in fact appear in a tragedy'; the combination *praeterea certo* is found nowhere else in P.) that crept into P.'s text, written by someone who did not fully understand 91–2.

94 Scan *A B c D A / B c d + aa B c D* (see p. 64 for the *locus Jacobsohnianus*). **inquam** 'I tell you'; for special emphasis (88n.). In the absence of periodic structure, P. often uses *inquam et sim.* to resume the main thought after a digression (cf. 89–92).

95 nunc ⟨uos⟩ animum aduortite: 38n.

96 dum huius = *a / B*, a legitimate hiatus (*huius* is monosyllabic). **argumentum eloquar:** formulaic in P. (cf. *Mer.* 2, *Mil.* 85), though more often *argumentum dicere*. Mercury will at last fulfil his promise (cf. 51) to relate the plot.   **comoediae:** 51–63, 88nn.

97–109 The necessary background to the play. Mercury swiftly moves toward the core of the comic situation – the adultery plot (cf. 100–14n.) – and ignores Amphitryon's and Alcmena's extensive background in myth (cf. pp. 45–7). His style becomes more terse and formal as he turns to the plot, but his jocund manner resurfaces once Alcmena's pregnancy is mentioned (103).

97 Haec urbs est Thebae: P. follows the usual convention (observed in Attic theatre) of naming the setting in the prologue only if it is not Athens.   **Haec:** Mercury extends his hands to define the theatrical space around him.

97–8 in illisce habitat aedibus | Amphitruo: at *Rud.* 33 Arcturus similarly gestures to the stage-house and identifies the owner at the beginning of his *argumentum*; cf. *Cas.* 35–6 and *Mil.* 88. The deferral of Amphitryon's name to initial position in the verse following the naming of the setting is similar to E. *Bacc.* 1–2 (cf. pp. 54–5) and E. *HF* 1–3.

98 Argo: according to Non. p. 782 and Serv. *A.* 1.268, *Argus* is a biform of *Argiuus*; the shorter form was more attractive to P. because of the jingle with *Argis*.

99 quicum: cf. 76n.   **est nupta:** *nubere* (lit., 'to put the veil on') in P. and Latin in general is more commonly construed with a dative (cf. 817).   **Electri:** Electryon, slain by Amphitryon.

100–14 Mercury intentionally titillates the audience, some of whom might not have been well-versed in Greek myth, by underscoring the carnal nature (107–9, 112–14: pp. 39–45) of the adulterous affair without mentioning Jupiter's impersonation of Amphitryon until 115. At the same time he emphasizes Alcmena's dual pregnancy (103, 109, 111).

100 legionibus 'army' or 'host' (*OLD* 2), a sense found in both the singular and plural.

101 cum Telobois bellum est Thebano poplo: Mercury shows no interest in the mythic background (98–9, 100–14nn.) and the campaign is briefly mentioned as if it were a typical war between states.   **poplo:** a metrically convenient form (cf. 190, 259), probably felt as archaic, though it is found in a contemporary inscription (*CIL* I 2.614, 189 BC). Ennius has only *popul-* in *Ann.*

102 is prius quam hinc abiit ipsemet in exercitum: scan *A bb C dd A / B c d + A B c D*.   **ipsemet:** the emphatic enclitic (most common with *ego*) is attached to *ipse* only here in P.   **in exercitum** 'on campaign' (as in 125 and *ad legionem* 133); *in* is set *d +* (a *locus Jacobsohnianus*: p. 64).

103 Alcumenam uxorem: see 89n. for the hiatus. *uxorem* underscores the adulterous nature of Jupiter's relationship with Amphitryon's wife (100–14nn.).

104–6 A playfully euphemistic (cf. esp. 106 *liber harum rerum multarum, quod complacitum est*) description of Jupiter's penchant for dalliance to introduce the central theme of adultery. Much of the Roman audience would have some knowledge of Jupiter's multifarious affairs through tragedy (e.g. Naevius' *Danae*) and comedy, as well as epic or oral accounts of Greek myths.

104 nam ego uos nouisse credo iam ut sit pater meus: scan *aa B C D a B C D A bb cD*.   **nam** 'now then' (transitional: *OLD* 4). **iam** 'already' (with *nouisse*).   **ut sit** 'what he's like'.   **pater:** *bb* by iambic shortening, which is rare but attested (e.g. 1131) in the last *B* of senarii (Questa (1967) 66).

105 liber harum rerum multarum 'unrestrained in these matters, numerous as they are'; a loose genitive of respect or 'sphere'. Cf. 58n.   **siet:** 1on.

106 amator 'lover' in a purely sexual sense (*OLD* 1). Cf. 126n. **quod** = *eius quod*; in colloquial Latin, the omission of the antecedent is common in (esp.) the oblique cases (LHS II 555–6, GL §619). The neuter is generalizing; cf. *Poen.* 820 *quod amat* and *Mer.* 744 (the use is especially common in love-elegy).

107–9 This suggests at least one earlier visitation, which would conflict with the single long night of conception in the mythological tradition; cf. 481–2 (with n.), 489–90, 1122. P. may be broadening the sexual farce (p. 47 n. 146).

107 clam uirum 'without her husband's knowledge', suggestive of a milieu closer to Ovid's *Amores* than heroic myth. *clam* as a preposition in archaic Latin always takes the accusative (on the analogy of its cognate *celare*).

108 usuramque: see pp. 39–40.

109 is: hardly necessary after *is* in 107, but it is purposefully juxtaposed with *eam*, with which it splits a *bb* resolution, to reinforce the idea of *compressu* (cf. 134 *illa illum*).   **compressu suo** 'by his embrace'; like *comprimere*, a common sexual euphemism (Adams (1982) 182).

110–47 The current situation (cf. 98–109n.), along with a prediction (140–1).

110 ut rem teneatis rectius: a formulaic expression in P.'s prologues that reflects the prologist's desire to control the audience's reception of the play: cf. 142, *Capt.* 10, 14, *Men.* 47, *Trin.* 4, *Poen.* 116.

111 utrimque est grauida, et ex uiro et ex summo Ioue: a playful reiteration of an essential point (100–14n.).   **utrimque est grauida:** the ancient scientific tradition considered *superfetatio* to be possible when only a small period of time separated the two acts of conception (Plin. *Nat.* 7.9), but P. would not expect his audience to reflect deeply on these matters. Cf. 481–2n.   **utrimque:** adverbs formed with the suffix *-im* are widespread in archaic Latin, but rare in classical (they resurface in later writers such as Apuleius). **et ex ... et ex:** for linguistic doubling, esp. where Alcmena's pregnancy is concerned, see pp. 15–17. The second *et ex* is set *dd* (*ex* undergoes iambic shortening).

112 cum illa cubat: *cubare* + *cum* (or just the ablative) to describe sexual intercourse euphemistically can have the man (290, 735, *Bac.* 1009) or the woman (807–8, *Cas.* 671, *Mil.* 65) as subject. Cf. 132–5n.

113 nox: the play of course is staged outdoors in the daylight. The setting is night-time up until the 'darkness' is magically dispelled by Jupiter midway through the play (546–50), but beyond Sosia's lantern (149), no effort is made to create an illusion of night. The nocturnal setting primarily serves to furnish Sosia and Mercury with material for (often risqué) humour (153–74, 271–98).

114 dum ⟨cum⟩ illa quacum uolt uoluptatem capit: an

appropriately playful jumble of alliteration and assonance to describe Jupiter's dalliance.

115 Mercury has made the affair seem all the more salacious by delaying any mention of the impersonation up to this point (cf. 100–14n.). **sed** 'yes, and what's more ...' (*OLD* 3).

116–30 After explaining Jupiter's role in the farce, Mercury turns to his own.

116–19 Mercury explains why he is not wearing his usual Olympian garb (as he would in a tragedy). Plautine slaves were grotesquely outfitted: Pseudolus is described (*Ps.* 1218–20) as having 'red hair, a pot belly, thick calves, a dark complexion, angular eyes, a flushed face, and big feet', and at *As.* 399–400 a slave is said to be 'thin-cheeked, reddish-haired, pot-bellied, with savage eyes, of average height, and with a stern brow'. From Sosia we learn additionally that the doubles have beards (445). The slave wore a cloak and tunic, and a *pallium*, a mantle that could be tossed over the shoulder to create a sense of energetic motion (cf. *Capt.* 778–9).

116 ne ... admiremini: for anticipation of an objection see 52–3n. **ornatum:** his costume is not only unexpected from a theatrical perspective (cf. 85, 116–19nn.), but it would also clash with his image in cult: Cic. *ND* 1.81 *a paruis enim Iouem Iunonem Mineruam Neptunum Vulcanum Apollinem reliquos deos ea facie nouimus qua pictores fictoresque uoluerunt, neque solum facie sed etiam ornatu aetate uestitu.*

117 seruili: the choice between an adjective and a genitive (cf. 124 *serui*, 261 *erae* and 1069 *erilis*) is a matter of metrical convenience rather than style in P. **schema** 'get-up', less concrete than 116 *ornatum* ('costume').

118–19 nouam ... nouom: the play's (and the playwright's) novelty is frequently vouched for by the chorus of Old Comedy (*Nub.* 546–62, *Vesp.* 1044, 1051–5). Cf. *Capt.* 53–8 and 41–2n.

118 ueterem atque antiquam rem nouam ad uos proferam 'I'll present to you anew an old and hackneyed story' (cf. *OLD antiquus* 9b), i.e. the ancient myth, probably most familiar to the audience from Roman adaptations of Greek tragedy, is to be travestied. For the possibility that this is P.'s own doing see pp. 53–5. **ueterem atque antiquam:** this particular combination occurs eight times in P. (*Bac.* 711, *Cas.* 7, *Mil.* 751, *Mos.* 476, *Per.* 53, *Poen.* 978, *Trin.* 381).

120–30 After telling the audience that he as well as Jupiter will appear in the play, Mercury describes the situation again for the sake of clarity. Repetition, false starts and restarts, and circular sequences of thought are characteristic of P.'s vigorously colloquial style, especially in prologues (cf. 1–16n.), and we should not automatically see the hand of an interpolator where these occur. 116–19 had been introduced by way of digression, and 120 picks up where Mercury had left off in 115.

120 nam 'Yes, then ...', to mark a transition (*OLD* 4).   **eccum** 'right here' (Mercury gestures toward the stage-house), < *ec* + *-ce* (deictic particle in *cedo, hic* etc.) + *hom* (= *hunc*); cf. *LU* 33–4.

121 imaginem 'likeness'.

122 eum esse: sc. *Amphitruonem*.

123 uorsipellem: with its literal meaning here, 'changed in outward appearance'; the word properly does not mean 'werewolf' (*pace* Sedgwick *ad loc.*), but can be used to describe one (Petr. 62.13, Plin. *NH* 8.80). Amphitryon is not far off the mark when he claims that a Thessalian *ueneficus* (1043) has bewitched the household (cf. 830n.). *uorsipellis* is found elsewhere in P. only at *Bac.* 658 (*Pers.* 230 is doubtful), where it is used figuratively of the ideally adaptable slave ('chameleon'); cf. Lucil. 670 M = 653 W *quicum uersipellis fio et quicum conmuto omnia.*   **quando lubet** 'when it suits his fancy', a kind of festive refrain in P.'s carnivalesque comedy, frequently voiced by triumphant slaves: cf. Leadbeater (1987). Cf. 558n.

124 ego 'But as for myself ...' (adversative asyndeton).   **serui:** 117n.   **Sosiae:** one of the stock names for slaves in all types of ancient comedy; cf Schol. on Ar. *Ach.* 243 and Schmidt (1902) 207. The casting of Mercury in the role of Sosia is appropriate insofar as the god is traditionally the 'servant' (λάτρις) of the gods; cf. E. *Ion* 4.

125 in exercitum: the initial syllable of *exercitum* undergoes iambic shortening and the resulting *aa* resolution is split between the preposition and its noun. Scan *A B cc D a B c D aa B c D.* Cf. 102n. for the meaning of *exercitus* here.

126 praeseruire amanti ... patri 'play the slave for my love-sick father'. The rare compound (first attested here) conveys a higher degree of subservience than the simplex: cf. Lucil. 1004 M = 1106 W *praeseruit, labra linguit, delenit amore.* Mercury is innovative in this semantic field: cf. 521 *parasitatio* and 515 *subparasitabor*, which make explicit the role (cf. p. 26) hinted at here.　　**amanti:** Jupiter's interest in Alcmena is portrayed as purely carnal throughout the farce, and no distinction between *amans* and *amator* as drawn by Don. Ter. *And.* 76 (*amator fingi potest, amans uere amat*) is made here. Cf. 892 and 106n.　　**meo:** with synizesis.

127 ut ne: common in negative purpose clauses in P., and found in Cicero's speeches (cf. LHS ii 643, GL §545 R.1). Cf. 388. **qui** = *quis*, the interrogative pronoun, as often (cf. 130) in P. (*MHL* 86).

128 uorsari crebro hic cum uiderent me domi 'when they see me bustling about the house here all the time' (the infinitive is passive with a middle sense: *OLD uerto* 10).

129 cum ... credent: tending toward pure causal; for the indicative (regular in P.) see Lindsay 120–1.　　**seruom et conseruom:** a clear instance of semantic doubling, but the prefix of the latter may also be corrective (as happens in compound verbs: 43n.): 'since they will think that I am a slave, and one of their lot ...' (*et* is epexegetic = 'i.e.').

130 siem: not in its more usual position at line-end (10n.).

131–9 Not simple repetition (cf. 112, 120), but important new information is given: (1) Jupiter is telling Alcmena about her husband's campaign and (2) the gods have stolen his spoils of victory. The gods' omniscience regarding the activities of Amphitryon and Sosia on campaign will sustain much of the plot. And there is further emphasis here on the carnality of the adulterous relationship (132, 135: cf. 100–14n.).

131 suo animo morem gerit 'indulges his desire', a colloquial idiom that is extremely common in P. Jupiter's carefree indulgence is stressed throughout; cf. 104–6, 114, 132, 139, 290, 472–3, 980–1, 995.

132–5 cubat ... cuius cupiens ... Alcumenae ... cum moecho: given the play's sharp focus on adultery, Hough's (1970) suggestion that the repetition of *cu* here and elsewhere (112, 290, 735, 807–8, 1122) is meant to evoke *cuculus* and the notion of cuckoldry is attractive, but the desired connotation is not attested in classical Latin. Alternatively, E. J. Kenney suggests a possible pun on *cunnus*, which in Latin slang may (by synecdoche) refer to a woman (e.g. Hor. *S.* 1.2.36, 70); for Roman sensitivity regarding this word cf. Cic.

Orat. 154 *quid, illud non olet unde sit, quod dicitur cum illis, cum autem nobis non dicitur, sed nobiscum? quia si ita diceretur, obscenius concurrerent litterae, ut etiam modo, nisi autem interposuissem, concurrissent.*

132 complexus: a sexual euphemism much like 109 *compressu.* **cuius cupiens maxume est:** 106, 131nn. The participle is used as an adjective with a genitive as at Enn. *Ann.* 72–3 Skutsch; classical Latin prefers *cupidus* + genitive. The colloquial use of the present participle with *esse* reflects the preference of the Italic linguistic family for periphrastic conjugations (Lindsay 78–9). For the alliteration of four words (*cubat complexus cuius cupiens*) cf. 75.

133 illi 'there in battle' (= *illic*, as at 249; cf. 138).   **ad legionem:** 100n.

134 Alcumenae: illa: for the hiatus see 89n.   **illa illum:** Catullus similarly juxtaposes lovers in verse: 92.1–2 *Lesbia mi ... de me: Lesbia me ...* Cf. 109n.

135 moecho: Jupiter is the only successful *moechus* in Plautine comedy (pp. 34–45). Whereas in this special play adultery is a badge of honour in the gods' eyes, *moechus* is scornfully applied to (e.g.) Pyrgopolynices in *Mil.* (924, 1398; cf. 1436), as generally in P. P. (and Terence) uses this Greek loan-word rather than *adulter* (but see 1049n.) of men who have illicit sex with *matronae*; cf. Scafuro (1997) 216–17.   **meus:** *B* here (synizesis).

135–7 Because he is a victorious general, P. endows Amphitryon with some of the characteristics of the *miles gloriosus* (cf. 654–8n.), and so Jupiter must exhibit these as well (cf. 504–5n.): 'Plautus simplifies ethos drastically according to the doctrines of a comic catechism, an absurd catalogue of appropriate behaviour' (*CHCL* II 106).

137 donis donatus: *figura etymologica* (as often in P.).

138 dona: most important among these for the plot is the *patera aurea* of King Pterelas, which becomes a token of confusion rather than recognition (cf. 260–1, 418–20, 534–6, 760ff.).

139 facile meus pater quod uolt facit 'what my father deems desirable is easily done'; for this proverbial power of the gods see Otto (1890) 108. Cf. 123n.

140–1 Prediction (see 'prologue' above) of scenes 1 and 3.

140 ab exercitu: iambic shortening as in 125 (see n.).

141 fero imaginem: *D* / *a* hiatus.

142–7 A final important consideration: Jupiter and Mercury will bear distinguishing tokens for the audience's benefit. These are helpful, but unnecessary, as P. goes to great lengths to identify (through words) the double(s) on stage or about to enter. This communication also allows for some time to pass between the prediction (141) of Sosia's approach and announcement of his arrival (148), though P. is little concerned with verisimilitude in such matters. Cf. 143n.

142 nunc ... ut ... possitis facilius: 110n.

143 habebo usque: see 89n. for the hiatus (similarly 145 *signum Amphitruoni* and 146 *nemo horum*).   **petaso:** 1n.   **pinnulas:** these, like Jupiter's *torulus* (144), are not referred to in the play, whereas we might expect a metatheatrical jest from P. But apart from the unusually high number of (legitimate) hiatuses in 142–7, there is no certain indication of interpolation.

144 torulus: a strand of rope at Cat. *Agr.* 135.4 and so perhaps a sort of tassel hanging from Jupiter's hat (Oniga *ad loc.* suggests an encircling ribbon).

146–7 ea signa nemo horum familiarium | uidere poterit: uerum uos uidebitis: by establishing this convention to which the human characters remain oblivious, Mercury draws the audience deeper into the gods' conspiratorial net (cf. pp. 25–6).

148–50 Announcement of and transition to scene 1. No further information about the play, save for the fact that Ampitryon will arrive (140), has been divulged in the prologue. This is reserved for the gods' various addresses to the audience (scenes 2, 6, 9). Prologues in New Comedy, like those of Euripides, often end with some intimation of the outcome, e.g. *Cas.* 79–83, Men. *Asp.* 141–6.

149 a portu: the regular stage convention is probably invoked automatically. Alternatively, Anthedon, the natural harbour of Thebes, fifteen miles away from the city, was well within 'theatrical' walking distance: cf. Blackman (1969) 12–17.   **lanterna aduenit:** legitimate *A* / *B* hiatus. See 113n. for the function of the prop.

151–2 A unique form of valediction in P., where the prologist usually wishes the audience well and offers patriotic words of encouragement, e.g. *Capt.* 67–8, *Cist.* 197–202, *Rud.* 82. Here instead, as an indicator of the play's self-conscious theatricality, the final emphasis is on the audience's prospective pleasure in watching an unusual play with gods as characters. In New Comedy, divine prologists do not act in the play; in scenes of mythological travesty in Old Comedy gods of course did, e.g. Dionysus in Ar. *Ran.* But in extant drama, only in Euripides' *Bacchae* does a god in human disguise, as here, deliver the prologue and then continue to act in the play: pp. 54–5.

151 adeste 'Pay attention'; the injunction is regularly combined with valedictions, e.g. *Poen.* 126, *Trin.* 22.   **erit operae pretium** 'It'll be worth your while ...', a variation on a common expression, *operae pretium est audire aut sim.*, aimed at grabbing an audience's attention, and probably rooted in forensic oratory (cf. Fraenkel (1957) 81). Cf. Enn. *Ann.* 494–5 Skutsch, *Cas.* 879, Ter. *And.* 217, and Ar. *Eq.* 624. For overt recommendation of the play in general cf. *As.* 13–14, *Capt.* 53–8, Ar. *Vesp.* 56–66.

152 facere histrioniam: hiatus after the seventh element (54n.).

153–462 (Scene 1) The longest scene in P. and one of the most entertaining, skilfully paced, and richly varied in comic technique and music. Sosia enters and communicates directly with the audience as if to secure their sympathy. The convention of the monologue (or monody as may be the case in P.), like the aside, acknowledges the central role of the audience in the performance: '... the aside and soliloquy are conventions inseparable from role-playing in non-illusory theatre ... these devices imply a complicity between actor and audience in the pleasure of putting on a play. The view that their apparent purpose was merely to inform the spectator of what was passing in the character's mind, like an interior monologue in the modern novel, is the mistake of superficial, anachronistic, and literary thinking' (Styan (1975) 153; cf. Slater (1985) 155–65). The situation here is complicated by the presence of Mercury, who has just won the audience over to the gods' side in the prologue. As an eavesdropper, he continues to communicate with the audience through asides, thereby foiling any attempt by Sosia to gain their favour. Sosia does not become aware of Mercury's presence until 292, which creates abundant opportunities for (esp.) ironic humour in the meantime.

In the mirroring structure of *Am.*, the scene corresponds to the one in which the second set of doubles confront one another (pp. 13–15).

METRICAL STRUCTURE of 153–262 (for specific units see pp. 70–1):

153–8	iambic octonarii	(recitative)
159	trochaic octonarius	(recitative)
161–2	five anapaests + ?	(song until 180)
163	trochaic dimeter catalectic	
164	three bacchiacs + ?	
165	two cola reiziana	
166–7	anapaestic dimeters	
168–72	sotadeans	
173–6	bacchiac tetrameters	
177	three bacchiacs	
178	three bacchiacs	
179	three bacchiacs with syncopation	
180–218	iambic octonarii	(recitative)
219–21	cretic tetrameters	(song until 248)
222	trochaic septenarius	
223	two cretics + trochaic dimeter catalectic	
224–32	cretic tetrameters	
233	two cretics + trochaic dimeter catalectic	
234–6	cretic tetrameters	
237	cretic + trochaic monometer	
238–41	cretic tetrameters	
242	cretic tetrameter with syncopation	
243–4	cretic tetrameters	
245	two cretics + trochaic monometer	
246	cretic tetrameter	
247	trochaic monometer	
248–62	iambic octonarii	(recitative)

153–74 P.'s clever slaves typically make blustery entrances, sometimes claiming that their (mis)deeds surpass those of mythic figures, e.g. *Bac.* 925ff.; with Sosia's boastful question (153–4), the audience will expect him to serve up the usual bombast. But his attitude quickly changes, and he soon reveals an essential aspect of his character: he is a coward and a slacker. Though Sosia is endowed with the very attributes that usually lead the Plautine slave to comic heroism, the divinely directed sex-farce forces him to assume an atypically passive role, and he will pose no formidable challenge to Mercury. He does, however, manage to 'compose' a brilliant literary parody after the manner of a comic playwright (186–26n.).

Fraenkel (1960) 172–5 saw sure signs of Plautine originality here.

153 Qui me alter est audacior homo aut qui confidentior 'Who else can match my daring and determination ...?' Comparison (*similitudo*) and hyperbole (*exsuperatio*) are two of the methods suggested at *Rhet. Her.* 1.10 to grab an audience's attention at the opening of a speech; comparatives (and superlatives) similarly are a trademark of the Plautine slave's entrance. Tobias (1979) 15 observes that iambic octonarii often occur in contexts of 'comic or heroic exaggeration'. **Qui ... alter:** a formula in this type of opening (e.g. *Mil.* 313). **audacior:** with the original long quantity in the ultima.

154 iuuentutis mores: for a palpable and perhaps only slightly exaggerated later picture of the manifold dangers on the streets of Rome at night see Juv. 3.268–314. Like the poor citizen (Umbricius) who speaks there, the unaccompanied Sosia would be an easy target for thugs (*grassatores*), not to mention the *tresuiri* (155n.). **hoc noctis** 'at this time of night', a favourite phrase of Sosia (cf. 164, 292, 310), elsewhere in P. only at *Cur.* 1. It is analogous to such chiefly unclassical adverbial accusatives as *id temporis*, *id aetatis*, etc. (LHS II 47, GL §336 N.2, §369).

155 tresuiri: the *tresuiri capitales* were minor magistrates in charge of maintaining order in the city. Also called *tresuiri nocturni*, they supervised prisons and executions, and one of their special functions seems to have been the punishisment of *fures* and *serui nequam* (a solitary slave wandering the streets at night would cause suspicion). Here they lend a distinctly Roman shading to the imagined scene; for Romanization in P. see *CHCL* II 112–14. **carcerem:** incarceration in a public Roman prison was not a form of punishment, but mainly a short-term measure to ensure appearances at proceedings or executions. In the comic conceit here, Sosia, as a slave with no rights and no master present to defend him, imagines that he will be summarily flogged the next day (156).

156 quasi e promptaria cella depromar ad flagrum 'I

would, as it were, be uncorked for a beating.' Imaginative and often bizarre imagery that distorts and defamiliarizes conventional usage, here combined with *figura etymologica* (*promptaria ... depromar*), is a feature of P.'s verbal comedy. Slaves in fear of punishment are especially creative, e.g. *Epid.* 310–11 *quod pol ego metuo si senex resciuerit | ne ulmos parasitos faciat quae usque attondeant* (cf. *Epid.* 125, *Trin.* 1010–11), as are starved parasites, e.g. *St.* 155–70. In employing such humour, often at their own expense, even the most unsympathetic characters may win the audience's approval.   **ad flagrum:** in real life, Sosia would be flogged by the assistants to the *tresuiri capitales*, probably the *homines octo ualidi* mentioned at 160. It remains a point of controversy whether or not the *tresuiri* administered a kind of summary justice to the lowest classes (as is suggested here); cf. Scafuro (1997) 454–7.

157 nec causam liceat dicere mihi: as a slave he could not defend himself before a magistrate (only his master could do this).

158 quin me ... deputent: lit., 'who wouldn't classify me as ...' (the verb is not found in Classical Latin).   ⟨**malo**⟩: cf. 26–7n. Leo's text is adopted, with the excision of the unnecessary *siet* in the MSS and Mueller's supplement (to provide *dignum* with an ablative).

159 incudem ... caedant: more bizarre imagery (156n.). **homines octo ualidi:** probably the *uiatores* among the various attendants (*apparitores*) of the *tresuiri capitales*.

161–2 ita peregre adueniens hospitio publicitus accipiar 'This is how when I arrive from abroad I'll be treated to "hospitality" at public expense'; a sarcastic jest on the public entertainment bestowed upon foreign dignitaries in Rome.   **peregre:** 5n. **publicitus:** the adverb (cf. *publice*) instead of the more usual *hospitium publicum* (cf. *OLD hospitium* 2b and 296n.).   **accipiar:** *accipere* is formulaic with the ablative (of means) in P. to describe the boons aspired to by the more bombastic slaves, e.g. *Ps.* 946–9, *Pers.* 30–1.

163–4 haec ... | coegit me 'forced me into this situation'. P. and Terence freely employ the double accusative (accusative of person affected + accusative of the inner object, usually a neuter pronoun): Lindsay 31.

163 immodestia 'unreasonableness'.

164 hoc noctis: 154n.   **a portu:** 149n.   **ingratiis** 'against my will'; for its use in connection with the direct object (here sc. *me*) cf. *Mil.* 449–50.

165 idem hoc ... me mittere 'send me for this same purpose' (for the double accusative see 163–4n., *Mos.* 747, *Ps.* 639.   **luci:** locative (*MHL* 15).   **potuit** 'could have'; in Latin potentiality is regularly expressed by the indicative of *possum* + infinitive rather than by the subjunctive (Woodcock §125, GL §254).

166–75 The revelation that his master's *immodestia* (163) is the cause of Sosia's current distress leads to a digression on the hardship of service to a rich man. Criticism of one's master is a conventional means of opening a comic monologue: cf. *Ar. Plut.* 1ff., *Poen.* 823ff., *Ps.* 767ff.

166 homini: dative with *seruitus* on the analogy of *seruire*. **hoc:** a loose ablative of specification with *dura*, which seems to look both backward and forward (so *hoc* in 167). After raising the issue that his master's will is arbitrary (165), Sosia generalizes that it is in this respect that enslavement to a rich man is difficult, a point which he then abundantly elaborates (168–73).   **seruitus dura:** the ultima of *seruitus* undergoes iambic shortening.

168 noctesque diesque: this came to be used in hexameter poetry for the unmetrical *noctes diesque* and *noctes et dies*, e.g. Enn. *Ann.* 336 Skutsch, Cic. *Arat.* 3.2, Virg. *A.* 6.556; in prose it is found only at Cic. *Fin.* 1.51, which seems to recall the Ennian passage. Cf. 7n. **assiduo** 'without pause', adverbial with *noctesque diesque* rather than 'for a rich man' (cf. *OLD* 1) as Sedgwick suggests.

169 quod facto aut dicto adest opus 'whatever need for a thing said or done presents itself': cf. 504–5. *quod* is nominative, and *opus adest* is construed with the neuter ablative singular of the perfect passive participle; in this chiefly archaic construction, the speaker's will to have happen what he deems necessary is presumptively represented as a completed act (KS I 764–5; cf. GL §406).   **sis:** generalizing ('one', 'a person').

170 ipse dominus: cf. *St.* 296 *uix ipsa domina ... audeat* and *Capt.* 810 *ex ipsis dominis*; from expressions such as these evolved the colloquial use of *ipse* and *ipsa* to indicate master and mistress (already in P., e.g. *Cas.* 790, *Aul.* 356).   **operis laboris expers** 'free of work and toil' (asyndeton: *et* of the MSS is expunged *metri causa*); some editors construe *operis* with *diues* ('rich in tasks' = 'having an abundance of tasks to assign'), which seems strained.

171 quodcumque homini accidit libere, posse retur 'considers possible whatever happens to strike a person's fancy' (for *posse* = 'be possible' see *OLD* 6). Cf. also 123n.   **accidit:** ancient grammarians note that *accidere* is more often associated with *mala*, and *contingere* with *bona* (Ernout–Meillet *s.v. cado*); here *accidit* has a neutral sense (= *euenire*).

172–3 'He deems it fair, doesn't give a second thought to what work is involved, and won't even consider whether his command is fair or unfair.' Leo brackets 173 as being logically inconsistent with 172 *aequom esse putat*. But in typically colloquial fashion, 173 is an expansion of the idea introduced in 172 for clarification and emphasis; the three consecutive clauses constitute a tricolon with crescendo (cf. 1–16n.).

172 putat ... reputat: 43n.   **laboris quid:** 58, 105nn.

173 The line is also transmitted at 160, where it is obviously out of place.   **aequom ... iniquom:** a proverbial pairing, usually plural, as *iusta/iniusta* (35n.); cf. Otto (1890) 5.   **cogitabit:** the 'prospective' future in gnomic expressions (*LL* 307).

174 expetunt 'occur' (*OLD* 4); the intransitive use reflects the Indo-European root **pet-* 'to rush', 'fly' (Watkins (1985) 50), with various grades (cf. *penna, pinna*, etc.); cf. 495, 589, 872, 896.

175 habendum et ferundum hoc onust cum labore: two synonymous nouns balance the two synonymous verbs.

176–9 Mercury in his first aside (153–462n.) draws attention to the irony in Sosia's complaint about his servile duties in light of his own drastic descent from god to slave. There is further irony in that the actor actually is a slave, as he had jested in the prologue (26–7n.).

176 satiust 'there is better ground ...' (= *potius est*).

177–8 'I who was a free citizen this very day, his own father now has placed in slavery.' Such a statement has special relevance to an audience in Rome, where children were considered to be the property of the *paterfamilias* and could in fact be sold into slavery. Cf. 991–6n.

177 fuerim: subjunctive because Mercury is generalizing about his personal situation (cf. 178 *eum* and 61n.).   **eum:** a long monosyllable (synizesis).

178 potiuit: *potire* (lit., 'to put someone [accusative] into possession of something' [genitive]) is attested here only in the active, but *compotire* occurs (*Rud.* 911; cf. Apul. *Met.* 2.22).

179 uerna: a slave born in the master's house and granted a relatively higher status than those acquired from abroad. **queritur:** the end of the aside is marked by ring composition (cf. 175 *queri*).

180–218 Virtually all the octonarii have the regular word-end at mid-line (p. 60).

180–4 As if taking up Mercury's designation of him as a *uerna* (179) in the aside, Sosia admits that, despite all his high-minded criticisms (165–75), he is a poor specimen of a household slave (180 *uerbero*), who has failed to give thanks to the gods for his safe arrival (which he in fact never does). Multiple ironies are operative: (1) Sosia is about to become Mercury's 'whipping-post' (the literal meaning of *uerbero*: 370n.); (2) he unknowingly communicates to a god his failure to give thanksgiving; (3) someone has been commissioned to thrash him upon his arrival but, far from being a *homo* as he supposes (183), it is one of the gods themselves.

180 uerna uerbero 'a rascal of a household slave'. As if correcting Mercury's aside (180–4n.), Sosia places *uerbero* in apposition to *uerna* (combined here only in P.); for the lack of realism here see p. 29 n. 95.   **numero mi in mentem fuit** 'Did it instantly pop into my head to ...' (sarcastically self-deprecatory). This notion is regularly expressed in P. without a verb of motion (a colloquialism: *LU* 166). Cf. 666, 710 and 293 *mi in mentem uenit*.   **numero:** from the ablative singular of *numerus* ('precisely', 'in time'), used adverbially in early Latin with the sense 'quickly' or 'too quickly'.

181 Travellers in P. regularly offer a prayer of thanks upon their arrival, e.g. *St.* 402–5, *Trin.* 820–38: see further Wright (1974) 141ff. **aduenientem:** sc. *me*; for the accusative after a dative (180 *mihi*) cf. KS I 679–80.   **pro meritis** 'in return for their benefactions'; for the fundamentally contractual nature of Roman religion cf. 1–16, 39–49.   **alloqui** 'invoke' (*sc. eos*), a formal religious term.

182 ne 'For sure ...'; the affirmative particle (cf. νή, ναί), regularly in initial position and followed by a personal pronoun, and often in combination with interjections such as *edepol*.   **edepol:** chiefly in comedy; used by both sexes, whereas only women swear by Castor (*ecastor, mecastor*). Cf. 299n.   **merito meo** 'as I deserve' (ablative; more explicitly with *pro*, e.g. *As.* 560).

183 qui ... os occillet 'to furrow my face' (*occillet* is the diminutive of *occare*, probably coined here). For the irony see 180–4n.

probe 'absolutely' (i.e., he will do a 'proper' job of it), a lively colloquialism; cf. 975, *Capt.* 635.

184 bene quae in me fecerunt: yet another way of designating the gods' benefactions: cf. 47, 49, 181.   **ingrata ea habui atque inrita:** lit., 'these I have treated without appreciation and regarded as invalid' (i.e. non-binding), an instance of syllepsis (85n.). **ingrata:** with a passive sense, as *gratum* in 48.

185 quod uolgo haud solent 'what human beings generally don't do'.   **uolgo:** the adverb is common with the third person plural in gnomic statements (*OLD* 2b).   **quid se sit dignum** 'what he deserves'; for the unusual passive use cf. *Rud.* 640 *te digna ut eueniant precor*, Lucil. 173 M = 166 W *cumque hic tam formosus homo ac te dignus puellus*.

186–261 Sosia's battle narrative has made a strong impression on critics, some of whom have even regarded it as a very solemn piece of poetry, written by P. to display his literary virtuosity: 'We find P. at his best, a splendidly vigorous piece of writing, unsurpassed in Roman literature, with complete mastery of language and versification: with a congenial subject (as again with Alcumena's loyalty and tenderness), P. forgets his buffoonery, and, we may well believe, his original' (Sedgwick, n. *ad* 203ff.). Though Sosia's account displays linguistic brilliance, context is crucial for interpretation. The report of Amphitryon's glorious exploits is delivered by a slave who has just proclaimed his cowardice to the audience (153–74n.). Sosia manifests a Falstaffian dedication to survival and the gratification of his visceral desires, and has no appetite for danger or heroism. He did not participate in the battle which he will describe (199 *nam cum pugnabant maxume, ego tum fugiebam maxume*), though this does not prevent him from narrating in the first person (235–6) at the height of the fray. He brashly admits that his account may be fallacious (198), and he can only vouch for his claim that the battle continued into the evening by noting that the loss of his midday meal fixed this fact in his memory (254). The battle narrative is closed with the awarding of the defeated king's golden bowl to Amphitryon; reflecting his own preoccupations, Sosia characterizes it as the one 'with which King Pterelas was in the habit of getting drunk' (261).

The humour arising from the incongruity of speaker and speech, often overlooked by readers impressed by the archaic grandeur and vigour of Sosia's language, would be obvious to a live audience. By his gestures and intonation the actor playing Sosia would make the parodic aspects of his narrative most explicit: the *canticum* was clearly meant to be performed with full bravado. Nor should we forget that the slave appears grotesquely costumed (116–19n.). Critics have long seen parody of tragic messenger speeches here (e.g. Leo (1912) 134). Some stress points of contact with official government parlance (e.g. Cèbe (1966) 85), while others emphasize the connections with Roman historiography (e.g. Pascucci (1961–2)); the best and most complete treatment (Oniga (1985)) argues primarily for epic parody. Successful parody is both an act of homage and one of satire with respect to its models, and it is a tribute to the richness of P.'s narrative that a strong case can be made for each of these views. Sosia appropriates various modes of discourse in effecting an unusual comic triumph through poetry rather than trickery (cf. 153–74n.). As the notes demonstrate, Sosia's battle narrative is formally rooted in the tradition of messenger speeches inherited from Greek drama. To this structural core are added elements from contemporary Roman epic poetry, according to demands of both style and content (already in Greek tragedy, messenger speeches, as narrative set-pieces, drew inspiration from epic: cf. Page (1938) on Eur. *Med.* 1141). And given that early Roman epic is chiefly historical (cf. Naev. *Bel. Pun.* and Enn. *Ann.*), much of Sosia's narrative naturally bears a relationship with the later-attested Roman historiographical tradition. The result is a brilliant pastiche strongly suggestive of Plautine originality.

In Greek New Comedy, a general parallel for a battle narrative combining serious and comic elements is found at the beginning of Men. *Asp.*, though there the fusion of genres (and the humour) is more subtle: cf. Goldberg (1980) 29–43.

186–96 Sosia associatively explains why he should be especially indebted to the gods (cf. 180–4n.) by providing a summary of the events of the war with the Teleboans. A fully detailed account is to be given shortly (203–62). We also learn that he has been dispatched at such an unseasonable hour so that he may convey advance notice of the successful campaign to his master's wife (195). Herein lies the cause for his dissatisfaction with his master's *immodestia* (163), and the connection with his previous complaint is marked by the repetition of *a portu* in 164 and 195.

186–7 Cf. Amphitryon's similar assertion at 656 and Cato, *orat.* 15 Sblendorio Cugusi *laudant me maximis laudibus, tantum nauium, tantum exercitum, tantum ⟨com⟩meatum non opinatum esse quemque hominem comparare potuisse; ide me tam matur⟨r⟩ime comparauisse.* In the era of the Second Punic War, extravagant self-praise was already a hallmark of the victorious Roman generals reporting their successes, e.g. Livy 22.24.14 (cf. 193n.). **quod ... euenturum:** resumed by *id contigit* and defined by the noun clause 187 *ut salui poteremur domi.*

186 opinatus fui: the auxiliary *fui,* etc., as opposed to *sum,* etc. makes the aorist sense ('what I at no point expected. . .') of passive or deponent verbs explicit (*MHL* 228). **ciuium** loosely denotes 'countrymen' rather than 'citizens' in the mouth of a *uerna.*

187 sibi euenturum 'would happen to himself', i.e. 'would experience'. **salui** 'safely': adjective, where English prefers an adverb (2n.). For the commonplace thought cf. Livy 29.27.3 *saluos incolumesque* (Scipio's prayer for a successful outcome to the war against Hannibal and a safe homecoming). **domi:** genitive with *poteremur* ('get possession of', i.e. 'reach').

188–96 Sosia's summary of the battle here corresponds in general with the conventions of messenger speeches in Attic drama, which report events which would be difficult to stage. The messenger typically enters and divulges the essence of his report to a character already on stage (or the chorus), so as to seize the audience's attention. A brief dialogue between the messenger and the character ensues, in which the latter typically asks for more detailed information, and the narrative piece follows; cf. Fraenkel (1912) 5–53. Sosia's summation in 188–96 is more expansive than is usual in the tragic examples and is thoroughly Romanized (e.g. 192n.). With no other character to engage him, Sosia innovatively acts as his own interlocutor, and in effect questions himself for further details (cf. 197, 201).

188 uictis hostibus: ablative absolutes (cf. 189) were a stock feature of the official military reports of victorious generals, as is evidenced by their extensive use in the *commentarii* of Caesar. They are well represented in *tabulae triumphales* and other dedicatory inscriptions, e.g. *CIL* I 541 *Corinto deleto* in the *titulus Mummianus*; cf. I 2.626, VIII 8324 and Livy 29.27.3 *uictis perduellibus* (Scipio's prayer). Cf. the scurrilous boasts of P.'s slaves who have carried off their deceptions successfully, e.g. *Pers.* 753–4 *hostibus uictis, ciuibus saluis, re*

placida, pacibus perfectis, | *bello extincto, re bene gesta integro exercitu et prae-*
sidiis ... (cf. *Bac.* 1070–1). Part of the burlesque in Sosia's speech
derives from his echoing the claims made by victorious Roman generals solicitous of celebrating a full triumph. The senate generally
acknowledged a set of requirements (i.e. established precedents)
which had to be met before it could award a triumph, though in the
highly competitive climate of P.'s day their decisions must often
have been controversial (Gruen (1990) 129–33). The general, through
a written report, a tablet, or a high-ranking envoy, would openly
campaign to show that his victory met these criteria. Sosia's assumption of this important public function here is highly farcical.
legiones reueniunt domum: the victorious general's army had to
be sent home, to mark completion of the campaign, before application for a triumph could be made (cf. Livy 26.21.1–6). For *legiones* cf.
100n.

189 duello exstincto maxumo atque internecatis hosti-
bus: the enemy had to be formidable and combat must have actually taken place to recommend the general for the triumph (the
death of at least 5,000 of the enemy may have been required). For
the language here cf. the *triumphalis tabula* commemorating the victory of Lucius Aemilius Regillus over the prefects of King Anti-
ochus, Livy 29.27.3 *duello magno dirimendo, regibus subigendis* ...
duello: an archaism already in P.'s day (elsewhere only at *Capt.* 68,
As. 559 and *Truc.* 483), against many instances of *bellum. duello* is
either trisyllabic here or, if disyllabic, the *B* / *C* hiatus is perhaps
obviated by a reminiscence of the original *-d* of the ablative termi-
nation (so Clausen (1971)).   **internecatis** 'exterminated'; here
only in extant Latin. This use of *inter* as an intensifying prefix (cf.
intermorior) is colloquial.

190 quod multa Thebano poplo acerba obiecit funera:
this sounds a note of high poetry, as Virg. *A.* 6.428–9 (cf. 11.28) *quos*
... *abstulit atra dies et funere mersit acerbo* (perhaps Ennian). The other
instance of this expression in P., *As.* 595 *acerbum funus filiae faciet, si te*
carendum est, is paratragic.   **quod:** resumed by *id* ... *oppidum* in
191.   **poplo acerba:** *D* / *a* hiatus at the main break of the octonarius. Cf. 101n.

191 ui et uirtute militum: cf. 212 and Livy 1.28.4, where Tullus
Hostilius echoes 'the formal language in which a general reported his

victory' (Ogilvie (1965) *ad loc.*).   **uictum atque expugnatum:**
this type of semantic doubling was especially prevalent in the prologue (pp. 15–17), where it served to introduce the theme of gemination. In the *canticum* cf. 208 *pacem atque otium*, 221 *more … et modo*,
231 *potest et ualet*, 233 *spiritu atque anhelitu*, 246 *foedant et proterunt*, 259 *in
dicionem atque in arbitratum*.   **atque** from the earliest period belongs to a higher stylistic level than *et* and *-que*, especially in rhetoric
(LHS II 476–9), and when it is used to link synonyms.

192 imperio atque auspicio: the general can claim a triumph
only if he holds *imperium* and *auspicium*; cf. 196 and *CIL* I 541 *ductu
auspicio imperioque eius Achaia capta*. *imperium* indicates that the victorious general was not subordinate to another commander. As for all
important public activity in Rome, auspices had to be consulted (e.g.
through observation of the flight of birds or the sacred chickens as
they ate) before launching a military campaign, and favourable signs
were taken to indicate divine approval of the proposed action.
auspicio eri: with *B* / *c* hiatus, but perhaps tolerable after a 'solemn formula' such as *imperio atque auspicio* (so Ernout).   **maxume**
'especially', prominently emphasizing (by its position) Amphitryon's
agency.

193 praeda atque agro adoriaque adfecit popularis suos
'he has bestowed loot, land and *adoria* [?] upon his compatriots'. It
was not necessary for a general to extend Roman territory to qualify
for a triumph (*RE* VII A1.498–9), but this information would naturally be included in the accounts of victory. Land distribution did
not occur until 201 BC (it was not normally a custom in post-classical
Greece); the line itself, then, perhaps demonstrates that the play was
performed after this date (Harvey (1981) 485–9). Cf. also Livy 29.27.2
and *CIL* VIII 8324 *uictores, spoliis decoratos, praeda onustos, secunda praeda
facta*. For the topicality of the Roman general's distribution of
booty see Gruen (1990) 133–40.   **agro adoria:** *D* / *a* hiatus.
adoria: a rare word of uncertain etymology; the *OLD* lists only
'glory' and 'distinction' as meanings, but it may properly refer to
wheat (cf. Plin. *NH* 18.14), which later was commonly distributed by
victorious generals. Its combination with *praeda* and *agro* here suggests the more concrete meaning.   **popularis:** probably 'compatriots' (for the thesis that it may in the archaic period mean *milites*,
and that *populus* is used for *exercitus* see Harvey (1981) 486 n. 28).

suos: a form of *suus* falls at line-end in each of 193–6. Three of the four instances refer to Amphitryon. Sosia is mocking the pronounced self-glorification of the Roman generals' solicitations; it is clear why the figure of the *miles gloriosus* inherited from Greek comedy had special appeal for Roman audiences.

194 regique Thebano Creoni regnum stabiliuit suom: lit., 'and for Creon, the king of Thebes, he steadied his [i.e. Creon's] kingship'. For the language cf. Enn. *Ann.* 91 Skutsch *auspicio regni stabilita scamna solumque* and Acc. *praet.* 40 R = 40 W *Tullius qui libertatem ciuibus stabiliuerat. rem publicam stabilire (vel sim.)* becomes a slogan in pro-Republican ideology, e.g. Cic. *Sest.* 143, *Leg.* 1.37.   **suom:** for *suus* not referring to the subject see KS 1 603–4, GL §309.

195 a portu: 186–96n.   **ut haec nuntiem uxori suae:** the real reason for Sosia's being commissioned at this time of night is finally given: *uxori suae* is unexpected (παρὰ προσδοκίαν) for *populo (vel sim.)*, to whom a Roman audience would expect such a report to be given. The Roman custom whereby a husband returning from a journey sends a messenger to his wife to announce his arrival (Ter. *Hec.* 314, Plut. *Quaest. Rom.* 9 266b) would in actual practice be much less elaborate than Sosia's *canticum*.

196 ut gesserit rem publicam ductu imperio auspicio suo: lit., 'how he conducted an affair of state under his own leadership, command, and auspices', anticipated by *haec* in 195. Cf. 657 and Livy 29.27.2 *uos precor quaesoque uti quae in meo imperio gesta sunt, geruntur, postque gerentur, ea mihi, populo plebique Romanae . . .* (cf. 2.54.5). For the chiefly archaic asyndeton of three elements see LHS II 830.

197–202 Sosia prepares to rehearse the full version of the battle narrative which he has just given in summary (186–96); since Mercury will be successful in driving him from the house, this proves to be the only opportunity for the audience to hear the full account. A comic fragment of Epicharmus (99 Kaibel) has been adduced as a parallel, but its interpretation and relevance to Sosia's speech are dubious (Stanford (1950) 167–9). Sosia's pretext for delivering his battle narrative should be related to P.'s fascination with metatheatre. Plautine characters regularly rehearse their schemes together, with a clever slave most often fulfilling the function of stage director: cf. *Mil.* 874ff., *Ps.* 905ff., *Pers.* 462ff., *Poen.* 578ff. The fact that Sosia is alone (or at least believes himself to be) gives his rehearsal an improvisatory air. His battle narrative is deceptive in that he intends to give the impression that he was a participant in the battle. P.'s hypothetical Greek source would presumably have introduced the battle-narrative in a more conventional fashion (188–96n.). That 197–202 should be of Plautine origin is also suggested by the ring composition: cf. 197 *meditabor* and 202 *meditari*, 197 *quo modo . . . dicam* and 202 *sic . . . proloquar*.

197 ea nunc meditabor quo modo illi dicam 'as for these matters, I'll now think out / rehearse how I am to report them to her'. Because he fled immediately from the battle (199), Sosia lacks first-hand knowledge of the details and must rely on what he has heard (200 *audita*) to formulate an account. Oniga (1985) 205–6 compares Sosia's predicament to that of the Homeric poet who calls upon the Muses when faced with the special challenges of enumerating a long list or describing a scene of great import, e.g. *Il.* 2.484–96, where the bard who has only heard rumour (κλέος) requires the further assistance of the omniscient Muses. By contrast, Sosia in his 'programmatic opening' here playfully invokes his own inventiveness and conventional capacity for deceit as a comic slave (198n.). His ultimate solution to his predicament is to draw on the traditions of early Roman poetry, especially historical epic (186–261n.), and he manages to produce an account that Mercury concedes is accurate (248–9). The correlation between poetic composition and a clever slave's scheming is made explicitly in P.: in both endeavours, as Pseudolus (one of P.'s most talented improvisers) says (*Ps.* 401–5), a lie (*mendacium*) is made to sound plausible (*ueri simile*). For the lengthy history of the notion that poetry, as a species of rhetoric, can 'lie' (already in Hes. *Th.* 27–8) see Kroll (1924) 44–63.　**meditabor:** here both in its technical theatrical sense (cf. *Pers.* 466 *tragici et comici | numquam aeque sunt meditati*) and to emphasize Sosia's improvisatory skills.　**illo** 'there', adverb (as *quo, eo*); cf. 203.

198 si dixero mendacium – solens meo more fecero 'If I do end up telling a lie – I'll only be following my usual practice.' The apodosis here is παρὰ προσδοκίαν (195n.) for the expected calling down of bad fortune upon the speaker should his words be shown to be false (Kassel (1966) 1–2; cf. *Mer.* 308 *decide collum stanti, si falsum loquor*). Punctuating with a dash marks the unexpected twist after the main break of the octonarius. By *solens meo more fecero*, Sosia means that he will be acting in accordance with the stock ethos of the clever slave in New Comedy.   **si dixero ... fecero:** the future perfect as a rule in P. is used in threats with *si*, whereas in the case of those with *nisi/ni*, the present indicative is preferred (Lindsay 125–6).   **mendacium:** 197n.   **solens** 'as is usual for me' (the participle functions like an adverb; cf. *Cas.* 870), reinforced by *meo more*.   **meo:** with synizesis.

199 'For the moment they started to fight – I started from sight.' **cum ... maxume** 'just as' (*OLD maxime* 6), correlative with *tum ... maxume* ('at that very moment').   **ego tum fugiebam maxume:** unexpected after *cum pugnabant maxume*. The surprise twist is underscored by the repetition of *maxume* and the verse rhythm, with hiatus at the main break (*maxume, ego*) between the half-lines.

200 uerum quasi adfuerim tamen simulabo: this admission may have had special relevance to a Roman audience. According to Gellius (*NA* 17.21.45), who cites Varro as his authority, Naevius had served in the war which was the subject of his epic and said so himself in the *Bellum Punicum*. This information would most likely have been conveyed by Naevius in his programmatic opening, along with his invocation of *nouem Iouis concordes filiae sorores* (cf. 197n.). Cicero says (*Sen.* 50) that Naevius wrote *Bel. Pun.* in his old age, that is, some time near the end of the third century BC. If this is correct, the epic was published before the probable date of *Am.* (pp. 2–4), and had already become canonical in Roman education.   **audita** 'what I heard' (neuter plural accusative). Sosia, because he fled, is reliant on the reports of others. Messengers in the dramatic tradition tend to distinguish carefully their personal observation ('autopsy') of the events they describe and the inferior evidence they have only heard from others: cf. Oniga (1985) 123–4 and de Jong (1991) 9–12. Cf. also 197n.

201–2 Sedgwick (n. *ad loc.*) regards these lines as an 'alternative to 197–200, from another performance'. But the composition of 197–202 is typically Plautine. Lines 201–2 resume (and elaborate) the idea of rehearsal introduced in 197, but interrupted by the digression of 198–200, where Sosia informed the audience that he was not actually present at the battle he is about to describe and that his narrative therefore may contain fictive elements.

201 quo modo et uerbis quibus ...: the indirect question is governed by *meditari* in 202 (cf. 197).   **fabularier:** *fabula* is already the standard word for a play (cf. 94, Naev. *com.* 1 R = *com.* 1 W, *Bac.* 214, *Capt.* 52), and thus the verb here contains a further suggestion of theatrical role-playing (197–202n.). For the infinitive in -*ier* see 13n. Cf. also 300n.

202 ipse mecum: highly ironic. As the audience knows, Sosia's other 'self' is in fact present (and will soon set about divesting him of his identity).   **hic:** adverb.

203–18 The preliminaries to the battle between the Thebans and Teleboans are described. Virtually all the iambic octonarii in this section have word-end at the middle of the line (p. 60). The recitative octonarii give way to lyric song at 219, after the respective armies have been led out of camp and on to the battlefield. The octonarii are resumed at 248. The structural units of the octonarii on either side of the song mirror each other, as noted by Braun (1970) 36. On the outer limits, the embassy of the Thebans to the Teleboans (203–15) corresponds to the surrender and plea for clemency of the Teleboans to the Thebans (256–61); framed within these, the movement of the armies into battle (216–18) corresponds to the flight of the Teleboans from the battlefield (250–2). Lines 248–9 and 253–5 contain the extraneous remarks of Mercury and Sosia. See further 219–47, 248–62nn.

203 Principio ut ... ubi primum: messenger speeches typically begin with an ecphrasis or with one or two temporal conjunctions. The audience is thus immediately transported to a temporal and spatial realm outside the drama, and invited to enjoy the narrative set-piece. Bromia's messenger speech begins similarly with the two temporal conjunctions at 1091–2; cf. also Enn. *incert.* 333 Jocelyn *ubi fortuna Hectoris nostram acrem aciem inclinatam* (probably the opening of a messenger's speech).   **Principio:** the adverbial use of *principium* (with or without *in*) is common in early Latin (Bennett II 382).   **illo:** 197n.   **aduenimus ... tetigimus:** rhyme at the main break and line-end. The first-person perspective (singular or plural) mostly gives way to third-person narrative at this point of the speech, and resurfaces with Sosia's quip about missing lunch (253–4) and his formal closure (261); many Euripidean messenger speeches are similarly patterned (de Jong (1991) 5). Cf. 186–261, 200, 221, 235, 254nn.   **ubi primum** 'as soon as' = *simulac*.

204–15 The settlement proposed by the Thebans here, along with its rejection by the Teleboans, is thoroughly Romanized and reflects the very ancient institution of *ius fetiale*, so called after the *fetiales* (Haffter (1967) 48–61). In the earliest period these priestly officials were dispatched to seek restitution from Rome's neighbours in the event of some offence, which was stereotypically attributed to the *superbia* (213n.) of foreigners. Fetial procedure originally required the performance of various rituals (cf. Livy 1.32, Naev. *Bel. Pun.* 27 W), whose purpose was to demonstrate that any war to be undertaken by Rome was just in the eyes of the gods. By P.'s day fetial law had been secularized, owing to the scope and complexity of Roman military endeavours, and *legati* such as those Amphitryon sends (205) were now commissioned by the senate to seek restitution from the alleged offenders. P.'s casting of the mythic dispute in terms of Roman political ideology is all the more striking when we consider what he might have found in a Greek source. In the Greek mythical tradition (cf. pp. 45–7), Amphitryon undertook the expedition at Alkmene's insistence, as she refused to consummate their marriage until he avenged the death of her brothers at the hands of the Teleboans. P. has removed the factor of personal revenge and politicized the campaign against the Teleboans by portraying them as aggressive raiders. Amphitryon, in accordance with standard Roman ideology, is portrayed as being forced into a war with foreigners (cf. 213, 247nn.). It was also probably necessary for a victorious general hoping to win the right to celebrate a triumph to demonstrate that the war won was taken up from a just cause; according to Gellius (*NA* 5.6.21), failure to meet this stipulation entitled the general to a mere *ouatio*.

204 delegit uiros primorum principes 'he selects men who are the *crème de la crème*'. 'Hyper-superlative' expressions such as *primorum principes* are common in early Latin, e.g. *Cas.* 793 *pessumarum pessuma* (cf. Naev. *incert.* 20 W), *Men.* 817 *miserorum miserrumus*, Enn. *Alex.* 34 Jocelyn *mater optumatum multo mulier melior mulierum*, and *CIL* 1 292 *duonoro optumo fuise uiro*. Cf. also Enn. *Med. ex.* 212 Jocelyn *Argiui ... delecti uiri*, and Lucretius 1.86 *ductores Danaum delecti, prima uirorum*.
delegit = *deligit*; Sosia skilfully draws the audience (and Mercury) into his narrative by using the historic present throughout (a common technique in messenger's speeches).

205 eos: *A* here (with synizesis); the line scans *A B C D aa B c D /
A B c D A B c D.*   **legat** 'he commissions' (as *legati*: cf. 213 *legatos*), a
more technical term than *delegit* (204).   **suam:** i.e. Amphitryon's.

206–10 The message which Amphitryon orders the legates to
convey is reported in indirect discourse (another early example in
Naev. *Bel. Pun.* 61–2 W). The ultimatum to the Teleboans is articulated with legalistic *abundantia* (cf. 70–1n.), with the protasis of 206–7
being repeated from a negative point of view (209), and the apodoses
stating the possible consequences of the Teleboans' decision with
similar precision.

206 si sine ui et sine bello: 70–1, 206–10nn.   **rapta et
raptores tradere:** the embassy seeks both restitution of the items
seized and apprehension of the perpetrators. P. does not bother to
identify what is alleged to have been seized. Though *rapta et raptores*
suggests the plundering raids of a more antique mode of warfare
than that of P.'s day, P. evokes an ideological situation (cf. 204–15n.)
familiar to his audience: 'Prior to the war itself, all that the Romans
thought was required was the proper procedure, the formally correct
actions and words. This religious obligation was treated in the apparently pedantic and formalistic manner in which the Romans
(among others) commonly treated such obligations ...' (Harris (1979)
170). For the *figura etymologica* cf. 253 *pugnata pugna.*

207 si quae asportassent reddere: sc. *uelint*; for the implied
notion of *rem repetere* cf. 206, 209nn.   **exercitum extemplo:** for
the alliteration cf. Naev. *Bel. Pun.* 29–30 W *exerciti | in expeditionem.*
extemplo 'immediately', a chiefly archaic adverb.

208 reducturum: *sc. esse*, as with *abituros. reducere exercitum (vel
sim.)* is a technical term in historiography (*OLD reduco* 2).   **agro
Argiuos:** hiatus at the mid-line break.   **Argiuos:** the Thebans,
as forces commanded by Amphitryon, who is of Argive descent (98),
can be designated thus; the desire for alliteration with *abituros agro* no
doubt influenced the choice here.   **pacem atque otium:** cf.
191n. and Cic. *Pis.* 73 (Cicero sardonically responds to Piso's criticism of *cedant arma togae*) *sed quia pacis est insigne et otii toga, contra autem
arma tumultus atque belli, poetarum more cum locutus, hoc intellegi uolui, bellum ac tumultum paci atque otio concessurum.*

209 dare: after *reducturum* and *abituros* (208), we might expect another future infinitive. But early Latin freely employs a present in-

finitive for a future after verbs of saying, promising, and hoping; *dare* is common in such cases, e.g., *As.* 366, *Mos.* 633. LHS II 357–8 report 144 instances of the future infinitive in Plautus against 50 of the present for the future (the ratio is 218 : 15 in Terence).   **sin aliter animati neque dent quae petat:** lit., 'but if they were inclined otherwise and would not give (back) what he sought ...' The latter periphrasis reflects the Roman idea of seeking due restitution (*rem repetere, rerum repetitio*) as a pretext for undertaking war against foreigners, as is fundamental to fetial law: cf. the description of the Latins' response to the Roman *fetiales*, Livy 1.32.3 *et cum incursionem in agrum Romanum fecissent repetentibus res Romanis superbe responsum reddunt* (cf. 1.22.4), and Enn. *Ann.* 253 Skutsch *rem repetunt regnumque petunt.* **dent** = *reddant.* The iteration of a compound verb (cf. *redderent* 207) through the corresponding simplex is an Indo-European phenomenon (Renehan (1977) 243); *petat* similarly seems to be equivalent to *repetat* here. Cf. 43n.

210 igitur 'then', the archaic (and original) temporal meaning (cf. Ernout–Meillet *s.v.*).   **summa ui uirisque** 'with the utmost manpower', a kind of hendiadys.   **eorum:** with synizesis. **oppidum oppugnassere:** *oppidum oppugnare* is a favourite expression of Caesar's, e.g. *Gal.* 3.21.2, 7.12.2, *Civ.* 3.9.2, 3.80.7. **oppugnassere** = *oppugnaturum esse* (*sese* should still refer to Amphitryon); for future forms in *-so* (originally a sigmatic aorist) see *MHL* 162–6. The infinitive in *-assere* occurs only 6 times in P. and always at verse-end, where it seems to be an elevated archaism.

212 magnanimi: an epic-sounding compound (cf. Virg. *A.* 6.649 *magnanimi heroes*) of the type apparently avoided by Livius Andronicus, but favoured by Naevius and Ennius, who may have used this very word (see Oniga (1985) 182–4).   **freti uirtute et uiribus:** cf. Enn. *Ann.* 547 Skutsch *inuictus ca⟨nis nare sagax et ui⟩ribus fretus,* which may be modelled on a similar Homeric formula (Skutsch (1985) *ad loc.*). Both *fretus uirtute* (e.g. *Bel. Hisp.* 16.3, Curt. 5.8.10, Tac. *Hist.* 4.34.3) and *fretus uiribus* (e.g. Livy 7.14.6) are stock phrases in the historiographical tradition. P.'s precise combination here is not found again; the choice of vocabulary is in part motivated by the alliteration (cf. *uiri*). A variation of the phrase is put to scurrilous use at *Ps.* 581 *maiorum meum fretus uirtute* (Pseudolus speaks).

213 superbe nimis ferociter legatos nostros increpant

'they chide our representatives with utter arrogance and insolence'. Cf. the less animated response attributed to the Latins at Livy 1.32.3 *superbe responsum reddunt* (cf. 209n.). According to the ideology of *iustum bellum*, the Roman enemy is typically portrayed as being possessed of *superbia*, which is meant to suggest depravity and barbarism that erupt in violations of international law and threaten Roman security; cf. Naev. *Bel. Pun.* 39 W *superbiter contentim conterit legiones*, Hor. *Saec.* 55–6, Caes. *Gal.* 1.31.12, 1.34.2, and Anchises' famous injunction to Aeneas, Virg. *A.* 6.853 *parcere subiectis et debellare superbos*. **nimis ferociter:** the use of *nimis* with an adverb or adjective to form a kind of superlative is chiefly archaic and colloquial.

214 respondent bello se et suos tutari posse: lit., 'they respond that they can protect themselves and their own in battle'; cf. Sal. *Iug.* 110.6 *at finis meos aduorsum armatos armis tutatus sum* (King Bocchus speaks).   **proinde uti** '(and) that accordingly....'; for this use with the subjunctive in exhortations see *OLD proinde* 3; with *uti*, a verb of bidding is easily understood in this context.

215 propere suis de finibus exercitus deducerent: cf. the similarly arrogant response attributed to Ariovistus at Caes. *Gal.* 1.44.11 and 213n.   **exercitus:** accusative plural; according to Apollod. *Bibl.* 2.4.6–7, Amphitryon was accompanied by several allies on his campaign.

216 For the *topos* of the return of an unsuccessful embassy cf. Enn. *Ann.* 202 Skutsch (cited at 32n.).   **pertulere:** this older inflexion of the perfect (*LL* 275) apparently was already archaic, and in early comedy is retained primarily in solemn formulas and various types of mock-serious passages.

217–23 The marshalling of the opposing forces of the Thebans and Teleboans is painstakingly described through a series of verbal correspondences, i.e. 217 *producit* and 218 *educunt*; 219 *exitum* and 223 *exeunt*; 220 *dispertiti ... dispertiti*; 221 *instruximus* and 222 *instruont*. Though repetition is characteristic of Plautine (and archaic) composition, the pronounced parallelism here suggests the simultaneous preparations of massive forces (another instance of linguistic mirroring: pp. 15–17).

217 contra Teloboae: the final vowel of *contra* appears to be short elsewhere in early Latin (cf. Skutsch (1985) on Enn. *Ann.* 576), but it is rash to transpose here with Sedgwick (after Leo), as this destroys the effect of having *contra* introduce the drawing-up of the opposing army immediately after the central break. *supra* with long ultima seems certain at *Cur.* 477.

218 legiones educunt suas nimis pulchris armis praeditas 'they lead out their legions furnished with exceedingly fine weaponry'. *legiones educunt* is prosaic, but the line as a whole affects high poetry: cf. Enn. *Hect. lyt.* 153 Jocelyn *Hector ui summa armatos educit foras* (perhaps within a messenger's speech). **legiones:** 100n. **pulchris:** *pulcher* (cf. καλός) occurs frequently in the fragments of early epic (8 instances among the fragments of Ennius' *Ann.*), to mark out persons or things as belonging to a superior dimension (cf. Oniga (1985) 195); with *nimis* here it forms a superlative (213n.).

219–47 With the inevitability of battle now established (cf. 203–18n.), the armies take the field. The heightened intensity of imminent battle is reflected in the switch to song. The song divides into three sections. The first (219–26), a description of the final placement of troops and the colloquy of the commanders, forms a unit marked by the three consecutive cretic tetrameters at its limits (219–21, 224–6). The latter two sections, 227–37, the actual joining of battle, and 238–47, the increased resistance and cavalry attack of the Thebans, correspond closely but not precisely to each other in metre. P. in general avoids absolute strophic responsion.

219 postquam utrimque exitum est maxuma copia 'after there was a forward march in full array from both sides' (the impersonal passive is common in early Latin: Bennett II 7–9). Cf. 249.

220 dispertiti uiri, dispertiti ordines: *Rhet. Her.* 4.19 recommends this type of *repetitio* at the beginnings of phrases: *cum multum uenustatis habet tum grauitatis et acrimoniae plurimum; quare uidetur esse adhibenda et ad ornandam et ad exaugendam orationem.* This, like the brief asyndetic clauses, is both rhetorical and poetic (it is a Lucretian mannerism: see Bailey (1947) Proleg. I 156).

221–2 instruximus | ... instruont: the repetition of the last word of successive phrases is another stylistic nicety (termed *conuersio* at *Rhet. Her.* 4.19; cf. 220n.), as is the variation of tense. Cf. Livy 8.38.8 *instruit aciem ... instruunt contra et hostes ...* (within a highly poetic and archaizing account of the Samnite war of 322 BC).

221 nos nostros ... nostro: see 34n. for the polyptoton.

instruximus: though the narration has been in the third person since 203, the verb is not inapt here, as Sosia claims to have fled only after the fighting commenced (198). Cf. 186–261, 200, 235nn.

222 suas: with synizesis.

223 utrique imperatores: cf. Sal. *Cat.* 30.4 *ei utrique ad urbem imperatores erant.*

224 extra: it is possible that the ultima scans long here; cf. 217n.

225 conuenit: according to Spengel-Meyer's law (Questa (1967) 224–6: cf. pp. 64–5), word-end is avoided in cretic tetrameters at the third and ninth element in the case of polysyllabic words whose immediately preceding syllable is long. Thus *conuenit* is historic present, and the sequence of tenses mixed (225 *sint*, but 226 *dederent*). Cf. Naev. *Bel. Pun.* 37 W *conuenit regnum simul atque locos ut haberent*, and, for negotiations in general in early epic, *Bel. Pun.* 41–3 W.

226 urbem, agrum, aras, focos seque uti dederent 'that they would surrender their city, territory, hearths, homes and persons'. Cf. 258–9, where Sosia similarly invokes a very old Roman formula for surrender (*deditio*). The Teleboans and Thebans agree that the defeated party will unconditionally surrender itself to the *fides* of the victor. Cf. Livy 1.38.1–2 *deditosque Collatinos ita accipio eamque deditionis formulam esse: rex interrogauit: ... 'deditisne uos populumque Collatinum, urbem, agros, aquam, terminos, delubra, utensilia, diuina humanaque omnia, in meam populique Romani dicionem?'* Cf. also Livy 7.31.4 and, in poetry of the early period, Enn. *Cres.* 137 Jocelyn *an inter se sortiunt urbem atque agros?*   **aras, focos:** a combination with special emotive significance, often found in patriotic contexts, e.g. Sal. *Cat.* 52.3 *qui patriae, parentibus, aris atque focis suis bellum parauere* (Cato recommends the death penalty for the conspirators). Cf. *OLD ara* 1d.

227 tubae contra utrimque occanunt: the sounding of the trumpet is a *topos* of battle narratives in tragedy, e.g. Aesch. *Pers.* 395, E. *Heracl.* 830–1, and epic, e.g. Enn. *Ann.* 451 Skutsch, with Virg. *A.* 9.503.

228 consonat terra: cf. Virg. *A.* 5.148–9, 8.305, before which the verb occurs only here and at Var. *R.* 3.16.30.   **clamorem utrimque efferunt:** cf. Enn. *Ann.* 428 Skutsch *tollitur in caelum clamor exortus utrimque* and Sal. *Cat.* 45.3 *simul utrimque clamor exortus est.* For the commonplace of the din of battle cf. 232–3n. and, e.g., Eur. *Supp.* 700–1.

229–30 'The general on each side, on this one and that [Sosia gestures], offered his vows to Jupiter, and on each side exhorted his army.'

229 imperator: with the original long quantity in the ultima.

230 uota suscipere: reflecting the contractual nature of Roman religion, the general would promise to honour the deity (with a sacrifice, construction of a temple, etc.) for bestowing victory upon himself and his army.   ⟨**utrimque**⟩: supplied (cf. 228) to preserve the series of cretic tetrameters (so also 231 ⟨*tum*⟩, which easily could have dropped out after 230 *exercitum*).   **hortari exercitum:** cf. Livy 8.39.4 *tum adhortari milites*, where the historic infinitive similarly marks a climax (cf. LHS II 367–8, Woodcock §21, GL §647); it is often found in paratragic contexts in P., e.g. 1110–14, *Trin.* 835–6. The exhortation of the troops by their generals is likewise a stock motif of battle narratives, e.g. Eur. *Heracl.* 824ff.

231 ⟨tum⟩ pro se quisque 'then each individual according to his own capability ...'; cf. Virg. *A.* 12.552 *pro se quisque uiri summa nituntur opum ui* (the second hemistich is Ennian: see Skutsch (1985) on *Ann.* 151).   **potest et ualet:** cf. Livy 1.24.8 *potes pollesque* (part of the fetial formula), trag. *inc.* 175 R, Afran. 226 R, and *As.* 636 *uidetne uiginti minae quid pollent quidue possunt?*

232–3 The sound effects and short asyndetic clauses with shifting subjects create a powerful description of battle whose vigour brings to mind several tragic and epic fragments of Ennius. Cf. *Hect. lyt.* 165 Jocelyn *aes sonit, franguntur hastae, terra sudat sanguine,* and 166 Jocelyn *saeuiter fortuna ferro cernunt de uictoria* (probably a messenger's speech), *Ann.* 266 Skutsch *hastati spargunt hastas, fit ferreus imber, Ann.* 391–8 Skutsch, and Virg. *G.* 4.77–80.

232 edit, ferro ferit, tela frangunt, boat: a carefully balanced chiasmus, with the disyllabic verbs (*edit, boat*) framing two isosyllabic clauses. With *ferro ferit* cf. Virg. *A.* 4.580, and with *tela frangunt* cf. Virg. *A.* 11.484, 12.8.   **edit** 'gives forth', 'displays', perhaps with pregnant connotations, as in the euphemism for death *animam edere.*   **frangunt:** the apparently intransitive usage is unparalleled.   **boat:** the verb belongs to the elevated diction of archaic poetry and occurs only here in comedy; cf. Enn. *Ann.* 594 Skutsch *clamore bouantes,* and Pacuvius 223 R = 264 W *clamore et sonitu colles resonantes bount.*

233 caelum fremitu uirum: the scale of battle in epic is traditionally portrayed as being so enormous as to have an effect in the
heavens (hyperbole; cf. 233-4, 251nn.). Cf. *Il.* 2.153 and 19.363,
where the effects of battle extend from earth to sky, Enn. *Ann.* 545
Skutsch *clamor ad caelum uoluendus per aethera uagit* (cf. 428 Skutsch), and
Virg. *A.* 9.504 *sequitur clamor caelumque remugit* (cf. 5. 451, 2.488).

233-4 ex spiritu atque anhelitu | nebula constat 'a fog
forms from their panting breath', a marvellous parody of epic
hyperbole; cf. Oniga (1985) 186.

233 spiritu atque anhelitu: a hendiadys. Cf. 191n.

234 uolnerum ui uiri: Luchs' correction of the meaningless *uol-
neris ui et uirium* yields a cretic tetrameter.

235 ut uoluimus: somewhat weak and prosaic in this context;
E. J. Kenney suggests *uouimus* 'prayed' (a sense not otherwise attested
before Horace: *OLD uoueo* 2). Sosia's inclusion of himself in the
heavy fighting comically contradicts his earlier admission of flight
(198).   **nostra superat manus** 'our army gets the upper hand':
see 237n.

236 hostes crebri cadunt, nostri contra ingruont: a neatly
balanced cretic tetrameter, with rhyme at the main break and line-
end (cf. 203n.).   **ingruont:** a poetic word not found again until
Virg. A. 2.301, etc.

237 ui⟨n⟩cimus ui feroces 'fierce as we are, we prevail forc-
ibly'. The impulse to delete *uicimus* (Leo, after Spengel) to get responsion with 247 seems misguided (cf. 219-47n.), but the perfect
does give deficient sense, in that absolute victory cannot yet be
claimed (cf. 238-41). Better to punctuate with a comma after *ingruont*,
thus continuing the asyndetic, three-word cola of 236, and read the
present with a sense similar to *superat* in 235. Cf. 246n.

238-41 Though a Theban victory is imminent, the Teleboans
are described as heroically holding their ground, much as Roman
soldiers would be expected to do. For the widespread *topos* of the
warrior's stout resistance to death, and avoidance of the shame of
flight, cf. (closest to P.) Naev. *Bel. Pun.* 59-60 W *sese ei perire mauolunt
ibidem | quam cum stupro redire ad suos popularis.* In P. here these con-
ventional ideas are articulated emphatically through a series of negative and positive clauses (see the analysis of Oniga (1985) 199),
which reach a hyperbolic (and oxymoronic) climax in 241.

238 fugam in: apart from cases involving the relative (cf. 653, 1016), anastrophe of true prepositions is doubted in early Latin, but *gratiam per* seems secure at *St.* 71 (with Petersmann's (1973) n. *ad loc.*); cf. LHS II 216, GL §413 R.1.   **se ... conuortitur** 'directs himself'. The use of a reflexive pronoun in the accusative with a medial-passive verb is also questioned, but cf. *St.* 306 *simulque ad cursuram meditabor me ad ludos Olympios*, and Var. *Men.* 439 *nemo se excalceatur*. Petersmann (1973) *ad St.* 306 regards this use as a colloquial pleonasm. The speaker there is a slave who has just mock-heroically declared that his delivery of good news will surpass the efforts of Talthybius and all other messengers (cf. 153–74n.), and so, alternatively, the construction may convey a kind of hyper-elegance (as in stilted English 'betakes himself'). Cf. also Enn. *Alex.* 50–1 Jocelyn *parere se ardentem facem | uisa est in somnis*.

239 nec recedit loco quin statim rem gerat 'nor does (anyone) withdraw from his position so that he does not perform his duty relentlessly'.   **recedit loco:** *loco* (with the pregnant sense 'position taken up in battle') *recedere* (*vel sim.*) is a technical term in Caesar, e.g. *Gal.* 5.34.1, 5.43.6.   **statim** < *stare* (cf. 277) has its original local meaning 'in place', i.e. 'unyieldingly', as also in Enn. *Aiax* 15 Jocelyn *qui rem cum Achiuis gesserunt statim*. Cf. *ibidem* in Naev. *Bel. Pun.* 59–60 W (quoted on 238–41n.). Cf. 241n.

240 animam amittunt 'they forfeit their lives'; again the Teleboans are said to perform up to the highest Roman standards (cf. 238–41n.).   **demigrent:** subjunctive because connoting intention.

241 ut steterat: *stare* in the quasi-technical sense 'hold one's position in battle' (cf. 239n.) is found also in Enn. *Ann.* 143, 583 Skutsch. Cf. *Mil.* 1389.   **iacet:** for the pregnant sense 'lie dead' cf. Enn. *scen.* 399 Jocelyn *ferro foedati iacent*, Virg. *A.* 1.99 *saeuus ubi ... iacet Hector* (cf. 5.871).   **optinetque ordinem** 'keeps rank', a variation on the more usual technical phrase *seruare ordinem/es* (e.g. Caes. *Gal.* 4.26.1), chosen out of aural considerations. The sharp antithesis of *steterat* and *iacet*, both in pregnant senses, and the image of the slain warriors dutifully preserving the battle line has a horrific, almost Lucanesque quality; cf. also Sal. *Cat.* 61.2 *nam fere quem quisque uiuos pugnando locum ceperat, eum amissa anima corpore tegebat*. For epic hyperbole cf. 233, 234–5, 251nn. Palmer compares 'Even as they fell in files they lay' from Byron's *Siege of Corinth*.

242-7 Wilamowitz (*ad* E. *HF* (repr. 1969) III 226) thought that the cavalry attack reflected a Greek style of warfare in the period of P.'s original. Others have argued that Sosia is describing an actual battle of recent Roman history. But as the range of these interpretations alone suggests, there is nothing precise enough in the description to link it with any specific battle or war; cf. Harvey (1981) 485.

242-3 conspicatus est, | ilico ... iubet: *conspicari*, 'to perceive', is common in military contexts, e.g. Caes. *Gal.* 1.25.6, Sal. *Iug.* 49.4, Livy 25.16.23.

243 equites iubet dextera inducere 'he gives the order to bring on the cavalry from the right', with ellipsis of the accusative of the recipient of the order (cf. *OLD iubeo* 1).

244 equites parent citi: for this quasi-adverbial use of *citus*, chiefly in poetry, see 2n. In early poetry cf. Andr. *Ody.* 34 W *topper citi ad aedis uenimus Circai*, and Enn. *Ann.* 18 Skutsch *transnauit cita per teneras caliginis auras*.

244-5 maxumo | cum clamore: cf. Sis. *hist.* 26 *proelium magno cum clamore uirorum commissum est*, Sall. *Iurg.* 53.2, and Hirt. *Gal.* 8.42.4.

245 inuolant 'fly at', 'swoop down on', a colloquialism; cf. *Mil.* 1400 (Pyrgopolynices is threatened with castration). The verb is avoided by classical but common in post-Augustan writers.

246 foedant et proterunt hostium copias 'they mutilate the enemy ranks by trampling them underfoot', a powerful hendiadys. The final rout is described in the most vivid terms: cf. the colourless *superat* (235) and *ui⟨n⟩cimus* (237) at the battle's turn. For *foedare* cf. Enn. *scen.* 399 Jocelyn, Lucr. 4.844, and Virg. *A.* 2.55.

247 iure iniustas: at the violent climax of the battle, Sosia underscores the justness of the Thebans' war against the Teleboans, as in accordance with *ius fetiale* (204-15, 213nn.). As is the case for many peoples in the ancient and modern worlds, victory in battle was taken by the Romans as confirmation that their entry into the conflict was just. In this quasi-legalistic view, the gods serve as the ultimate *iudices* in international disputes. The idea is given special prominence through the polyptoton (cf. 35n.) of the trochaic clausula.

248-62 The description reaches a climax with the successful cavalry attack, and with Mercury's aside in 248-9 the metre reverts to iambic octonarii; these, in contrast to the octonarii at 203-18 (cf.

n. *ad loc.*), predominantly have word-break after the ninth element rather than at mid-line (p. 60).

248–9 Sosia's fiction (186–261, 197nn.) wins the approval of the god of mendacity!

248 'In absolutely no instance up to this point has he uttered a jot of fiction.'   **numquam etiam quicquam:** for the special (colloquial) emphasis on the negative here cf. *Ps.* 134 *quorum numquam quicquam quoiquam uenit in mentem …*   **quicquam … uerborum est prolocutus:** a variation on the expression *uerba dare* ('to deceive', e.g. *Mos.* 925, *Trin.* 60, one of the stock capabilities of the clever slave in P.). Mercury mockingly picks up Sosia's *proloquar* at the beginning of his narrative (204).   **perperam** 'inaccurately', a colloquial adverb (of the same type as *clam*) < *perperus* ('wrong'), added here, with the *abundantia* that is typical of early Latin, to clarify the meaning of the verbal idiom.

249 illi: 133n.   **in re praesenti** 'at the scene of the action' (cf. the *ab urbe condita* construction).   **cum pugnatum est:** 219n.

250 perduelles penetrant se in fugam 'the enemy warriors plunge themselves into flight', an unusual use of *penetrare*, partly conditioned by the desire for alliteration with *perduelles*. Cf. *Men.* 400 *intra portam penetraui pedem, Truc.* 44 *intra pectus se penetrauit potio.* **perduelles:** trisyllabic and probably archaic-sounding; it is almost completely supplanted by *hostis* (originally 'foreigner') in the classical period, and preserved only in formal or archaizing documents, although *perduellio* remained in use. The word is appropriated by grandiloquent Plautine slaves on their 'campaigns' of trickery, e.g. *Ps.* 583 *facile ut uincam, facile ut spoliem meos perduellis meis perfidiis* (cf. *hostibus* in 580).   **nostris animus additust** 'the fighting spirit was enhanced in our men', a stock phrase in descriptions of battle, e.g. Virg. *A.* 9.717–18, *Bel. Afr.* 52.3.

251 uortentibus: intransitive or reflexive (cf. 238n. and Petersmann (1973) on *St.* 414); *in fugam* (250) is probably to be understood with it. The Teleboans finally cease to fight as idealized Roman soldiers (238–41, 240nn.): P. wants to treat every possible battle *topos*, including the flight of the vanquished.   **Telobois:** dative of reference, i.e. 'disadvantage'(!).   **telis complebantur corpora** 'bodies were being thronged with spears'. The hyperbole is epic: cf. Enn. *Ann.* 573 Skutsch *decretum est stare ⟨et fossari⟩ corpora telis*, and, for

the rain of spears more generally, *Ann.* 266 Skutsch (quoted at 232–
3n.), Virg. *A.* 12.284. To be struck down in the back while fleeing is
of course a supreme disgrace in Greek and Roman warfare, e.g.
Tyrtaeus 11.19–20 West.   **telis:** for the ablative with verbs of filling see GL §405. Cf. 470–1n.

**252 ipsusque Amphitruo regem Pterelam sua obtrun-
cauit manu:** single combat between the leaders of armies can be
paralleled in the messenger-speech tradition (e.g. Eteocles and Poly-
nices in Eur. *Phoen.* 1356ff.), but the manner of Amphitryon's slaying
of his rival held special significance for a Roman audience. Through
ipsusque ... sua ... manu here Sosia emphasizes that Amphitryon
would be eligible to dedicate the *spolia opima*, which Roman tradition
maintained was won only three times (first by Romulus). By contrast,
in the Greek mythical tradition, Pterelas is said to die after his
daughter Comaetho falls in love with Amphitryon and plucks the
golden hair of immortality from her father's head (Apollod. *Bibl.*
2.4.7); the single combat presumably is a Plautine innovation. Naevius within memory (222 BC) had put on his *Clastidium*, a *fabula prae-
texta* (undoubtedly a tragedy) which treated the slaying and de-
spoiling of the Gaul Virdomarus by Marcus Claudius Marcellus.
sua: *bb* (prosodic hiatus).   **obtruncauit:** this evocative verb is
used by Livy to describe the successful single combat of Romulus
against the king of the Caeninenses, 1.10.4 *regem in proelio obtruncat et
spoliat* and that of the tribune Marcus Valerius against an enormous
Gaul (7.26.5). Cf. also Virg. *A.* 3.55, 3.332 and 1050n.

253 pugnata pugna: this *figura etymologica* is also found in Lucil.
1323 M = 1181 W *uicimus o socii et magnam pugnauimus pugnam* (presumably within a parody). Cf. Livy 6.42.5, Nep. *Hann.* 5.1.   **pugna
usque:** *d+/A* hiatus (at mid-line; for the *locus Jacobsohnianus* see
p. 64).

254 Sosia breaks the battle narrative here, and quips from his
archetypically comic and unheroic perspective: the duration of the
battle is fixed in his memory by the loss of a meal! This line should
serve to reorientate readers who, deprived of the performance spectacle, may have forgotten that the *canticum* is delivered by a grotesquely attired and gluttonous coward. Cf. 186–261, 197–202nn.
hoc adeo hoc: the first *hoc* is accusative, the second ablative of
cause (correlative with *quia*).

255 sed proelium id tandem diremit nox interuentu suo:
the interruption of battle by nightfall is already a commonplace in
Homer (*Il.* 7.279–82, 8.485–8, 18.241–2). Cf. Enn. *Ann.* 160 Skutsch
bellum aequis manibus nox intempesta diremit. nox is semi-personified in
these phrases (cf. *Il.* 7.293, 9.65, 8.502). Cf. *Bel. Alex.* 11.5, Livy
7.33.15 and Pliny's play with the motif, *Ep.* 4.9.9 *actionem meam, ut
proelia solet, nox diremit.*   **nox interuentu suo:** cf. Caes. *Gal.*
3.15.4 *noctis interuentu.*

256–9 Though *uelatis manibus* (257) suggests a Greek custom, the
supplication and surrender are thoroughly Romanized (for such
scenes in general see Gould (1973)). Cf. Enn. *Ann.* 498 Skutsch *flentes
plorantes lacrumantes obtestantes*, 162 Skutsch *cogebant hostes lacrumantes ut
misererent.* Cf. 257, 258–9nn.

256 principes: cf. 204 *principes*, where the diplomatic situation is
inverse (cf. 203–18n.).

257 uelatis manibus orant ignoscamus peccatum suom:
scan $A\,B\,C\,dd\,a\,B\,C\,D\,A\,B\,C\,D\,A\,B\,c\,D$ (an exceptional octonarius, with
word-end after neither the eighth nor ninth element: cf. Questa
(1967) 176).   **uelatis manibus:** typically, olive branches are en-
twined with wool for this purpose.   **orant ignoscamus peccatum suom:** P. does not bother to tell us explicitly that the Teleboans' plea for *clementia* is answered, as the ideological situation is so
formulaic that the Romanized Thebans' merciful response can be
tacitly assumed (cf. 206n.). The notion of *clementia*, which is given
such prominence in Augustan ideology (cf. Aug. *Anc.* 3.1–2), was
already a part of Roman political consciousness; Cato had appealed
to *clementia* and *mansuetudo maiorum* in asking his fellow senators to
pardon the Rhodians for their perceived *superbia* (*orat.* 125 Sblendorio
Cugusi: cf. 213n.). *peccare* is regular in such contexts, as in Livy's
account of the Rhodian affair (45.22.1).   **orant:** the ellipsis of *ut*
is common after *orare* (*OLD* 1b).

258–9 The Teleboans surrender according to Roman formula
and in keeping with the agreement made before the battle (226n.).

259 in dicionem atque in arbitratum: cf. *CIL* 1 2.583 1 (*lex
repetund.*) *in arbitratu, dicione, potestate.*   **poplo:** 101n.

**260 post ob uirtutem ero Amphitruoni patera donata
aurea est:** having subdued and spared the once haughty forces of
the Teleboans, Amphitryon is awarded the defeated king's golden

libation bowl. Cf. the honour bestowed upon Octavian when he was formally proclaimed 'Augustus': *Anc.* 34.2 ... *et clupeus aureus* ... *quem mihi senatum populumque Romanum dare uirtutis clementiaeque et iustitiae et pietatis caussa* ...   **ob uirtutem:** 75n.   **ero:** a cue that the exotic narrative (203n.) is coming to an end, and that the audience is about to be transported back to 'Plautinopolis' (for the term see *CHCL* II 113).   **patera ... aurea:** according to Theoc. *Id.* 24.4, Amphitryon received a bronze shield. P. follows the tradition as represented in Anaximander of Miletus (*FGrH* 9 F1 J), who speaks of a cup (σκύφος), which had been given to the Teleboans by Poseidon. A *patera* was regularly used for libations to the gods: cf. 261n. and DS IV/I *s.v.*

261 qui Pterela potitare rex est solitus 'with which King Pterelas was in the habit of getting drunk', a bathetic conclusion reflecting Sosia's preoccupations (cf. 186–261, 254nn.). Sosia's characterization of the *patera aurea* here becomes a leitmotiv: cf. 419 (spoken by Mercury) and 535 (spoken by Jupiter).   **qui:** 76n. **Pterela:** the nominative scans as a tribrach.   **haec sic dicam erae:** Sosia marks the end of his narrative by restating (cf. 195) the reason for his appearance.

262 eri: 117n.   **me domum capessere** 'get myself home' (colloquial).

263–462 Following Mercury's rhetorically deft prologue and Sosia's brilliant parody, the doubles move toward direct confrontation. Mercury has secured a position of superiority (153–452n.), and the audience anticipates that he will best his human counterpart in this scene of confused identity; the only suspense lies in how the encounter will be played out. This lengthy portion of the first scene is characterized by a variety of jests and playful verbal duelling. It culminates in Sosia's complete loss of identity.   METRE: recitative trochaic septenarii (pp. 60–1, 67–8).

263–92 P. wrings as much as he can from the eavesdropping framework before Sosia finally observes Mercury. The god immediately elaborates on his plan to delude Sosia (263–70; cf. 150) in an aside that confidently assumes the audience's role as co-conspirators. Sosia's comments about the long night here, together with Mercury's responses, focus attention on the carnality of Jupiter's and Alcmena's affair (esp. 271–90) and broaden the sexual farce.

263 attat, illic huc iturust 'Ah yes, the fellow is right on his way here'; the colloquial particle *attat* (shortened form of *attatae*) marks Mercury's excitement at the prospect of engaging Sosia. **illic:** nominative (set *D a*), whereas *illic* in the second half of the line is dative (*DA*); scan *B c D a B c D A* / *B c D A B c D*.

264 hominem hodie: *a* / *b* hiatus. **aedis has:** cf. 97 *illisce ... aedibus.* The demonstrative suggests that when Sosia arrived (153) Mercury had receded from a position at the forefront of the stage that he probably held during the prologue and now stands closer to the backdrop, perhaps within a vestibule (cf. Beacham (1992) 71–85) in front of Amphitryon's palace.

265–9 To play the role of Sosia, Mercury acknowledges that he must adopt the conventional behaviour that comes with the costume of the clever slave: pp. 26–7.

265 certum est hominem eludere 'I'm sure to trick the fellow' (cf. *OLD certus* 6).

266 enim uero quoniam 'and, since of course ...', an emphatic and colloquial combination. *enim* seems to be used only as an asseverative particle in P. (Lindsay 97); cf. 34n. **formam ... statum** 'appearance' and 'bearing', for which see 116–19n.

267 et facta moresque: this form of polysyndeton is widespread in Latin (LHS II 516).

268 malum ... callidum, astutum: these adjectives point to the conventional behaviour of the clever slave; cf. Pseudolus' call for a servile assistant who is (*Ps.* 724–5) *malum,* | *callidum, doctum.* Hunter (1987) 293 observes that these are also the traditional attributes of Hermes. **admodum** 'utterly'; the usage with adjectives is colloquial (*LU* 72).

269 telo suo ... malitia ... pellere: the *modus operandi* of the clever slave in P. is regularly described in terms of military imagery. The use of *telum* is proverbial in such expressions (Otto (1890) 342). **suo sibi:** a colloquial and chiefly archaic type of pleonasm; *sibi* usually has no clear grammatical function in such phrases (Lindsay 41), though here it could be possessive. **suo:** with synizesis. **malitia** 'roguery'. The *malitia* of P.'s slaves is, like the πονηρία of Aristophanic protagonists, 'an unscrupulous, but thoroughly enjoyable exercise of craft' (Whitman (1964) 30); through it, the Plautine slave may aspire to win his freedom: *Epid.* 732 *hic is homo qui libertatem* *malitia inuenit sua.* Sosia's capacity for *malitia* and *calliditas* is largely neutralized in this unusual play (cf. 153–74n.)

270 illuc = *illud*, set *cD*, with iambic shortening. The line scans *BccDABCDA / BCDABcD*.   **aspectat:** a chiefly archaic verb; cf. Serv. *ad A.* 12.136 *aspectabat: amat usurpare antiquitatem. nam potuit spectabat dicere.*

271 certe edepol 'By god, there can be no doubt ...'; cf. 182n. **si ... sciam:** cf. English 'if there's one thing I know for sure ...'

272 hac noctu 'tonight', but the more usual meaning is 'last night'; *hac noctu* is a conflation of *hac nocte* and *noctu* (adv.). Cf. 404, 412.   **Nocturnum:** the reference has not been convincingly explained. Stewart (1960) argues that it is an epithet of Dionysus here, García-Hernández (1984) that it (cf. 275 *Vesperugo*) refers to Venus, *alii aliter.* Oniga *ad loc.* plausibly suggests that it is a typical personification ('God of Night') of Roman religion: cf. 42n. There is an *a / B* hiatus after *Nocturnum.*   **obdormuisse ebrium:** by attributing the unusually long night to Nocturnus' intoxication, Sosia again betrays his typical perspective (186–261, 261nn.). For the theme of intoxication in the play see p. 31.

273 Septentriones: the seven stars of Ursa Major.   **quoquam** '(to) anywhere' (adverb, as in 274 and 276).

274 neque se Luna quoquam mutat atque uti exorta est semel: lit., 'nor does the Moon change her position to anywhere different from when she initially rose'.

275 Iugulae: either the stars marking Orion's shoulders (cognate with *iugulum* 'clavicle'), or loosely describing the entire constellation. **Vesperugo:** the Evening Star (= *Hesperus, Vesper*), actually the planet Venus, which reflects sunlight (as the morning star, Venus is called *Lucifer*).   **Vergiliae:** the Pleiades (< *uergere* 'to decline', 'to sink'); *Vergiliae occidunt* with *A / B* hiatus.

276 ita statim stant signa, neque nox quoquam concedit die: a typically Plautine summary of 271–5.   **statim stant** 'stay fixed in position' (239n.).   **neque ... quoquam:** Sosia's repeated insistence on the absence of motion is not so much meant to conjure up an image of such a night as to suggest the long, languishing sexual activity of the couple inside the house, as becomes explicit shortly (287–90).   **die:** dative (*MHL* 70–1).

277 Nox: personified, probably = *Nocturnus* (272n.). **gere patri morem meo:** 131n.

278 optumo optume optumam operam das, datam pulchre locas 'you're doing the finest work in the finest fashion for the finest god, and your work is a fine investment'. The use of an adjective with an adverb of the same root in close proximity is a Plautine mannerism, e.g. *Bac.* 207 *unice unum*, *Cur.* 462 *lepidum lepide*. For the polyptoton of three elements see 34n. **optumo** playfully refers to Jupiter's cult-title *Iuppiter optimus maximus*. **das, datam:** the repetition (epanalepsis, here a mark of Mercury's colloquial style) of the participle directly after the finite verb is found only here and at *Truc.* 490 *quid audiunt audita dicunt* in P. Cf. *Aul.* 365–6 *coquant | inde coctam*, and for the figure in general (curiously frequent in Ovid) see further Wills (1996) 311–25. **datam:** sc. *operam* (a kind of cognate accusative with *locas*, lit., 'you invest your labour'). **pulchre** 'splendidly'; adverbs such as *pulchre*, *belle*, and *lepide* are used extensively in colloquial language for *bene, prospere, et sim.* (*LU* 70–1).

279 neque: Mercury's aside of course has no effect on Sosia's syntax (cf. 276).

280 nisi item unam 'except for the one spent in a similar way'. Editors generally accept the *bb / c* hiatus at the beginning of the line. **quam pependi perpetem:** sc. *noctem*; the use of the accusative to express duration of time is not fully established in early Latin; P. uses adjectives such as *perpes*, *totus*, etc. to make the idea clear (LHS II 41). *perpes* was replaced in classical Latin by *perpetuus*, perhaps by analogy with its synonyms *assiduus* and *continuus* (cf. GL §84). For the Roman practice of punishing slaves by tying their hands to a beam and leaving them to hang see MacCary and Willcock (1976) on *Cas.* 390.

281 quoque ... etiam: 30n.

282 edepol: the last syllable is *d +* (a *locus Jacobsohnianus*). The line scans *B cc d + aa B C D a / B C D A B c D.* **dormire Solem ... adpotum:** Sosia considers the strange phenomenon from the opposite point of view (cf. 272), but with the same comic perspective. **adpotum probe** 'totally tanked'; the use of *probe* to intensify an adjective is colloquial (*LU* 75); cf. *Mos.* 342 *homo ebrius probe* and 183n.

283 mira sunt 'it's a wonder ...' = *mirum est*, as often in Latin.
nisi inuitauit sese in cena plusculum 'if he didn't treat himself
a bit too much at dinner'; cf. Turpilius 71 R *non inuitat plusculum sese
ut solet*, and 132 R *inuitauit plusculum hic se in prandio*.   **inuitauit:**
regularly used of overindulgence, especially in drinking (*OLD* 1).

284 ain uero 'Oh, indeed!'; cf. *OLD aio* 2.   **deos esse tui
similis putas?:** it is remarkable enough that Sosia should depict
the gods in his own bibulous image (186–261, 261, 272nn.), but Mercury is made to appear oblivious to the irony of his words. The pretext for the gods' performances in this play is Jupiter's uncontrolla-
ble sexual passion, and, in respect of appearance, Mercury is, as
Sosia quips (601), as similar to the slave as 'milk is to milk'. Cf. pp.
32–3.

**285–6 ego pol te istis pro dictis et male factis, furcifer, |
accipiam** 'I most certainly will entertain you in a style befitting
your ill-advised words and deeds, you jailbird'; cf. 161–2 (with n.),
which Mercury here sardonically picks up.

285 tuis: with synizesis.   **furcifer:** i.e. *furcae supplicio digne*, a
favourite term of reproach in comedy whose literal meaning was
probably lost. A yoke was placed on the neck of a slave guilty of
minor offences, and his hands were tied to it; this relatively mild
punishment was intended to humiliate the bearer and serve as a de-
terrent to others (Don. Ter. *And.* 618).

286 sis = *si uis*, often ironic ('Oh, please do come here') rather
than polite (cf. *LU* 7).   **infortunium:** another comic euphemism
for 'beating' (cf. 26–7n.).

287–8 'Where are those horny fellows who can't stand sleeping
alone? This night is perfect for a tumble with an expensive tart.'

287 ubi sunt isti scortatores, qui soli inuiti cubant?: cf. *Ps.*
203 *ubi sunt, ubi latent, quibus aetas integra est, qui amant a lenone?*, *Men.*
128 *ubi sunt amatores mariti?*, and *Most.* 356–8. Fraenkel (1960) 134,
who had a keen eye for performance, understood that this type
of appeal was made directly to the audience. Here presumably
the self-styled *scortatores* are to identify themselves vociferously.
scortatores 'whoremongers', i.e. men interested in short-term sexual liaisons with *scorta*; cf. *scortari* and 288n.   **inuiti:** 2n.

288 haec nox scita est exercendo scorto conducto male: a
rhythmically heavy line (42n.).   **scita:** properly 'knowing', but in

colloquial usage it may more generally describe anything positive (*OLD* 4). **exercendo scorto:** cf. the pun at *Cist.* 379–80 *pol ad cubituram, mater, magis sum exercita | fere quam ad cursuram* (the speaker is a *meretrix*); for sex as a kind of 'exercise' see Adams (1982) 157–9. **scorto:** *scortum* ('whore') is much more pejorative than *meretrix* ('prostitute'), which, by contrast, in P. often refers to a man's long-term love-interest: Adams (1983) 324–5. **conducto male** 'hired at great expense'; cf. *male* and *bene emere*, 'to buy dearly/cheaply'. The Roman moral tradition generally attached no stigma to men using prostitutes, provided they did not jeopardize their finances in doing so; cf. p. 44.

289–90 Mercury's approving aside in effect equates the love-making of Jupiter and Alcmena with that of *scortator* and *scortum*; for the farcical emphasis on sexuality in the play see pp. 34–45.

289 recte et sapienter facit: cf. 995–6.

290 cum Alcumena cubat: for the possible obscene pun see 132–5n. **complexus:** 132n. **amans:** 106n. **animo obsequens** 'obeying his heart's desire'. Cf. 131n.

291 The excursus on the night comes to an end, and Sosia restates his mission (cf. 261–2). **imperauit Alcumenae:** *a / B* hiatus at the main break of the septenarius.

292 homo: 180–4n. **ante aedis:** Hunter (1987) 294 notes that statues of Hermes (owing to his association with boundaries and prosperity) were thought to protect the doors of Athenian houses, whereas here the god ironically 'keeps out those who rightly belong'. **hoc noctis:** 154n. **non placet** 'I don't like this.'

293 hoc: ablative of comparison with *aeque* ('as much as this fellow'), a colloquial idiom (cf. LHS ii 110, GL §296, n.1).

293–4 mi in mentem uenit, | illic homo ... uolt: a typically colloquial form of parataxis (*LU* 107). Cf. 180n.

294 denuo ... pallium detexere: lit., 'to weave this cloak of mine completely over again', i.e. 'thrash me to pieces'. The repetitive, piston-like motion of the shuttle accounts for the metaphor here. Cf. *OLD pecto* 1b, and 317 for the image of 'pugilistic refashioning'.

295 deludam ego illum: Mercury will befuddle Sosia by assuming a new role as a thug; for *deludere* (cf. *ludus*) in this metatheatrical sense cf. 980, 997–8, 1005 and Arg. 1 5n. **perii** 'I'm done for'; *perii* becomes a kind of refrain for Sosia (cf. 312, 320, 374, 456 and 299 *interii*). By the end of the scene, the figurative exclamation becomes a literal truth in his mind: 455–62n.   **dentes pruriunt** 'my teeth are tingling'; various body parts are said to 'itch' in P., either out of fear (as here: cf. *Poen.* 1315–16, *Mil.* 397) or from excitement (*Bac.* 1193).

296 certe aduenientem hic me hospitio pugneo accepturus est 'I'm sure this fellow's going to shower my arrival with blows.' Sosia picks up his earlier jest and pun on *hospitium publicum* (161–2n.). Mercury has presumably begun to shadow-box, as the frequent references to his fists from here on suggest. Cf. 285–6n. **pugneo:** a Plautine coinage, only here and at *Rud.* 763.

297 credo misericors est 'he's compassionate, I do believe' (sarcastic; explained by *nunc ... dormiam*). For the colloquial use of *credo* in paratactic phrases see *LU* 106.

297–8 me ... | fecit ut uigilarem: for the prolepsis see 54–5n.

298 uigilarem ... dormiam: for the theme of sleep (or dreaming) and wakefulness see p. 31. **hic pugnis faciet hodie ut dormiam** 'his fists will make sure that I rest in peace today' (*dormire* is used euphemistically of the dead, e.g. *CIL* 1 1202. 6 *dormias sine qura*).

299 oppido 'utterly'; a colloquial adverb (= *ualde*) of uncertain etymology. **interii:** 295n. **obsecro hercle, quantus et quam ualidus est!** 'Oh my goodness, he's so huge and so strong!' Sosia's cowardice is taken to farcical extremes: Mercury is his precise physical double (cf. 441–6). **hercle:** this interjection (a vocative) in extant Latin is used only by men, with the exception of *Cist.* 52, where a *meretrix* speaks. Cf. 182n.

300 clare aduorsum fabulabor 'I'll speak out aloud in his direction.' *fabulabor* also suggests role-playing (cf. *fabula*) and deceit; Mercury will turn one of Sosia's own weapons against him (cf. 201 *fabularier*, with n., and 197–202n.). **aduorsum:** adverb. ⟨**ut**⟩ **hic auscultet quae loquar:** a variation on a typical eavesdropping frame (cf. 153–462n.), frequent in P. (e.g. *Per.* 83ff.), whereby a character with deceitful intentions allows himself to be overheard. **hic:** the nominative singular is always short in P., and so ⟨*ut*⟩ is added by some editors to save the metre, and the subjunctive is taken as one of purpose rather than exhortation.

301 magis ... maiorem: this particular pleonasm is common in

P. and attested in later colloquial usage (LHS II 166–7).   **modum** ⟨**in**⟩ **maiorem** 'to a greater extent'; Camerarius' supplement produces a phrase unattested elsewhere in P., but straightforward Latin, very common in Cicero (*OLD maior* 4c); cf. the alliteration with *magis ... metum*.

302 agite, pugni: mock-grandiose (cf. the conventional address to one's own heart in tragedy, e.g. E. *Med.* 1056, with Page's (1938) n.).   **iam diu est quod uentri uictum non datis** 'it's been a long time since you provided ...' (lit., 'it's been a long time that you've not provided your stomach with nourishment'); some editors question *quod* in this quasi-temporal sense, but for this colloquial idiom after temporal adverbs or substantives denoting time see LHS II 580.   **uentri:** practically = 'appetite' (vividly attributed to the personified fists; see 156n. for exotic imagery in P.).

303 quod: 302n.

304 in soporem: 298n.   **nudos:** Mercury pretends to have stolen his victims' clothes in addition to beating them into a state of unconsciousness; he thus casts himself in the mould of the Aristophanic highway-robber (λωποδύτης), sometimes called Orestes (*Av.* 1491ff.). In a society generally without mass production, an everyday cloak has considerable value (Solon is said to have set the death penalty for the theft of clothing in the Athenian gymnasia). **formido male** 'I'm terribly afraid', a colloquial use of *male* (*LU* 74).

305 Quintus: the pun on the Roman *praenomen* and the ordinal is of indisputably Plautine origin. Cf. *Bac.* 361–2 *credo hercle adueniens nomen mutabit mihi | facietque extemplo Crucisialum me ex Chrysalo*.

306–7 The simple pun on *Quintus* is explained explicitly, as is typical of P.'s style.

307 em nunciam ergo: sic uolo 'There now, all right – just the way I want it.' What has Mercury done? Sosia's subsequent description ('he's girded himself, I know he's preparing himself for action' (308)) is vague. Perhaps Mercury merely hitches up his garment. Alternatively, he may have put on the *caestus* (placed somewhere on the stage before the performance), the leather strips worn by Roman boxers, which could be weighted with lead or iron, and were designed (cf. 'brass knuckles') to mutilate an opponent's face (cf. 312, 317–18, 324).   **em:** for its use in colloquial Latin in general see Luck (1964) 47–68.

308 se: monosyllables are normally avoided at the main break of the trochaic septenarius, but *se* is really part of the preceding verb.   **non feret quin uapulet** 'he will not escape without a beating'; cf. *impune ferre*, etc. (*OLD fero* 37).

309 quisquis homo: though he still pretends to be unaware of Sosia's presence, Mercury in effect answers Sosia's question *quis homo?* For this playful treatment of the convention of eavesdropping cf. *Mil.* 1227-8, and for P.'s general disdain for realism pp. 27-31. *quisque homo* introduces the equivalent of a threat with *si* and the future perfect (198n.).   **quisquis** is pyrrhic here (enclisis: p. 64); scan *bb C dd a B c D A / B c D A B c D.*   **pugnos edet** 'he's going to get a knuckle sandwich'.

310 apage, non placet me hoc noctis esse: cenaui modo 'Forget it! I don't like eating at this time of night. I've just had dinner.'   **apage:** a colloquialism borrowed from Greek (*LU* 39), often in combination with *non places/placet*.   **hoc noctis:** cf. 154n.   **esse** < *edo*.

311 largire: imperative.   **si sapis:** the idiomatic use ('if you have any sense'), but also with a pun on the literal sense 'taste'.

312 haud malum 'pretty good' (the litotes puts special emphasis on the 'pack' of Mercury's punch).   **pondus pugno:** cf. 307n. and Virg. *A.* 5.401 *immani pondere caestus.*   **perii, pugnos ponderat:** the succession of labial stops emphasizes Sosia's fear. For *perii* see 295n.

313 quid si ego illum tractim tangam, ut dormiat? 'What if I give him a nice long handling, so that he falls asleep?', i.e. the repeated blows will eventually render Sosia unconscious. Palmer *ad loc.* compares *Od.* 18.90-4, where the disguised Odysseus deliberates strategies for his boxing match against Iros. The Homeric scene would be familiar to some of P.'s audience through Livius Andronicus' translation. Cf. 331-2n.   **tractim:** lit., 'in a drawn-out manner' (< *traho*); not in classical prose.   **dormiat:** Hermes can magically dispense sleep (cf. Hom. *Il.* 24.343-4 and Hunter (1987) 295).   **seruaueris** 'you'd save my life' (potential subjunctive, apodosis to *quid si ... tangam*). For the extreme flexibility of conditions in P. see Lindsay 123-7.

314 nam continuas has tris noctes peruigilaui: elsewhere in the play we hear nothing of Sosia's last few nights, but such a joke in a slave's mouth (186-261n.) is straightforward enough.

**314–15 pessumest, | facimus nequiter, ferire malam male
discit manus** 'How awful! I've got it all wrong: I'm training my
hand to strike a jaw weakly!' (cf. 313).

314 pessumest: the impersonal and personal use of the adverb
with *esse* is common in colloquial Latin (Lindsay 79–80).

315 nequiter 'disastrously', 'all wrong' (< *nequam*).   **male:** the
adverb can be construed with either *ferire* or *discit* ('is receiving im-
proper instruction') or with both (ἀπὸ κοινοῦ).

316 alia forma esse oportet quem tu pugno legeris 'The
person whom you've grazed with your fist should take on a new
appearance.'   **forma esse:** *A / B* hiatus.   **legeris:** apparently
'graze'; commentators cite Virg. *A.* 2.207–8 *pars cetera pontum | pone
legit* (description of the *angues* pursuing Laocoön). Cf. *OLD* 7b.

317 illic homo: apparently *B cc D* (see further Questa (1967)
105).   **interpolabit** 'will wipe me out'; in origin a term from
fulling.   **meumque os finget denuo** 'and he's going to re-
arrange my face' (cf. 294n.).

318 exossatum os esse oportet quem probe percusseris
'The face of the person you've pummelled properly should end up
filleted'; Mercury threatens to fulfil Sosia's earlier fear (183; cf. 180–
4n.).   **exossatum os:** typically Plautine word-play.   **probe:**
183n.

319 mirum ni 'it's a wonder if he isn't ...', i.e. 'I'm afraid
he's ...'   **me quasi murenam exossare:** as the simile shows,
exossare is a culinary term to describe the filleting of seafood: cf. *Aul.*
399, Ter. *Ad.* 376–8. At *Ps.* 382 *exossabo ego illum simulter itidem ut
murenam coquos*, by contrast, it is metaphorical ('deceive'). There is a
hiatus at the main break here (*murenam exossare*); scan *B CD A bb C
D A B C D a B c D*.

320 ultro istunc 'To hell with this fellow' (with ellipsis of an
imperative).   **perii, si me aspexerit** 'I'm dead if he sees me.'
Cf. 295n.

321 olet homo quidam malo suo. :: **ei, numnam ego obo-
lui?:** Mercury uses *olet* figuratively ('I detect someone's presence'),
but Sosia takes him literally ('Oh, no! Have I given off a stink?'), a
reference to farting (with sound effect?) or, more likely, Sosia buries
his face in his armpit (cf. 326n.). There is a similar play on *olere* at
Mil. 1255–8, where Acroteleutium likewise wants to be overheard by
the duped *miles*. The odours produced by the human body are one

of the staples of popular comedy.   **malo suo** 'at his own peril',
very common in P. (cf. 366), with or without *cum* (the ablative is one
of attendant circumstances).   **ei:** a monosyllabic interjection of
despair, etc. (often with *mihi*), also found in serious poetry. It is
used almost exclusively by men (*LU* 13).   **numnam ego:** $d + / a$
hiatus. The line scans $bb\,c\,D\,A\,B\,c\,D\,a\,B\,C\,d + a\,bb\,c\,D$.

**322 atque haud longe abesse oportet, uerum longe hinc
afuit** 'And he ought to be close at hand, though he has been far
away from here', a mock-oracular pronouncement intended to baffle
and frighten Sosia further. Cf. *Rud.* 266-7 *ilico hinc imus, haud longule
ex loco;* | *uerum longe hinc abest unde aduectae huc sumus*, to which a para-
tragic response is given, *nempe equo ligneo per uias caerulas* | *estis uectae.*
haud longe 'very close' (312n.).   **oportet:** cf. 315, 318.

323 illic homo superstitiosust: Sosia is unaware of how inappropriate his repeated designation of Mercury as a *homo* (cf. 292, 316,
339) is. Cf. 180-4n.   **gestiunt pugni mihi** 'my fists are out of
control' (for the likelihood that Mercury is shadow-boxing here see
296); *gestire* often refers to unrestrained or irrational behaviour (cf.
Fordyce (1961) on Catul. 51.14), befitting beasts rather than human
beings (cf. 324n.).

**324 si in me exercituru's, quaeso in parietem ut primum
domes** 'If you intend to put 'em through their paces on me, for
heaven's sake break 'em in first on the wall' (Nixon).

325 uox mi ad aures aduolauit: a poetic cliché, as old as
Homer's 'winged words' (e.g. *Il.* 1.201); cf. Aesch. *PV* 115, *Mer.* 864,
Rud. 332.   **ne ego:** B / c hiatus (*ne* adheres closely to the pronoun
following: 182n.).

326 qui non alas interuelli 'since I neglected to pluck my *alae*';
Sosia plays on two different meanings of *alae* ('wings' and 'armpits'),
and the joke on body odour is rounded off here, probably with an
appropriate gesture (cf. 321n.). Failure to depilate is said to produce
uolucres hirquinae at *Poen.* 871-3. Cf. also *Ps.* 738, where Pseudolus'
clever assistant Simia is said to have a *hircus* in his *alae* (cf. Catul.
69).   **uolucrem uocem gestito:** 325n.

**327 illic homo a me sibi malam rem arcessit iumento
suo:** lit., 'This fellow comes begging me for a beating, with his own
mule to boot.' The general sense is that Sosia voluntarily makes
himself available for a beating ('he brings the noose to his own

hanging'). Otto (1890) 154 compares expressions such as Ter. *Ad.* 958 *suo sibi gladio hunc iugulo*, but a precise parallel for this proverbial expression is lacking. Cf. also *Most.* 778–82 *uehit hic clitellas, uehit hic autem alter senex.* | *nouicium mihi quaestum institui non malum:* | *nam muliones mulos clitellarios* | *habent, et ego habeo homines clitellarios.* | *magni sunt oneris: quidquid imponas uehunt.*   **malam rem:** 26–7n.

328 non equidem ullum habeo iumentum 'What mule?' Sosia again literally interprets a figurative expression: cf. 321, 324, 326, 329–30, 368–9.   **probe:** 183n.

329 lassus sum hercle, naui ut uectus huc sum: lit., 'My goodness, I'm tired, seeing that I travelled here by ship.' **hercle:** 299n.   **etiam nunc nauseo:** as he stumbles (perhaps like a surging ship: cf. 330n.), Sosia feigns illness; for the threat of vomiting in P. cf. *Cas.* 732; in Old Comedy, Ar. *Ach.* 585ff.

330 A second (cf. 329) joke based on seafaring; picking up Mercury's figurative *onerandus est pugnis* (328), Sosia absurdly identifies himself with an *oneraria* that has spilled its contents (Clark (1980)). For such imagery see 156n.   **inanis:** used to describe both an empty stomach (*OLD* 1b) and ships carrying no load (*OLD* 5).   **ne ... existumes:** 87n.

331–2 The joke on *nescioquis* is probably modelled on Odysseus' verbal trick in the Polyphemus episode (*Od.* 9.366ff.); the Homeric scene is also parodied at Ar. *Vesp.* 175–89). Cf. 313n. Ironically, Sosia is about to be divested of his name and identity (295n.).

331 certe enim 'Yes, I'm sure.'

332 'nescioquem' loqui autumnat; mihi certo nomen Sosiaest 'He says that "Somebody" is talking, and, no doubt about it, my name is Sosia.'   **certo:** cf. *certe* 331; both forms are common in P. and the choice of *certo* here (cf. *nomen* following) may be for euphony.

333 hinc ... dextra: Sosia had entered from the audience's left (from the harbour = stage right). This and the corresponding convention that places the forum exit to the audience's right accords with several other passages in P. and Ter. *An.* 734, though this arrangement may not have been an absolute rule in a temporary Roman theatre: see Gratwick (1993) on *Men.* 555. Cf. 264n.   **uox auris, ut uidetur, uerberat** 'A sound does strike my ears, methinks'; again (325n.) Mercury affects grandiloquent diction. Cf. *Il.*

10.535, Ap. Rhod. *Argon.* 2.555–6, Soph. *Ant.* 1187–8 and *Phil.* 205–7, Enn. *Thy.* 305 Jocelyn, *Truc.* 112, *Poen.* 434.

334 metuo, uocis ne uicem hodie hic uapulem, quae hunc uerberat 'I'm afraid that I'll take the fall for my voice on this one.'

335 optume eccum incedit ad me 'Excellent! Look, he's coming my way' (Mercury expresses his joy at Sosia's approach in an aside).   **eccum:** cf. 120n.   **timeo, totus torpeo** 'I'm terrified, totally stopped in my tracks' (the dental stops might be delivered with a slight stutter). Cf. *Mil.* 1273–4 *ut tremit! atque extimuit, | postquam te aspexit.*

336 ubi terrarum 'where in the world' (elsewhere only at *As.* 32); in early Latin, 'the inhabited world' is usually expressed by *gentes* (cf. in P. *ubi gentium, quo gentium, nusquam gentium*).

337 neque ... me commouere possum: cf. 274.

338 ilicet 'that's it', an exclamation of dismissal or dismay = *ire licet*. Cf. *Capt.* 469 *ilicet parasiticae arti maximam malam crucem.* **mandata eri perierunt una et Sosia:** ironically true: 295, 455–62nn.

339–40 Sosia's mustering of his resolve here (accentuated by the alliteration of *c* in 339) is obviously doomed to fail (cf. 153–462n.).

339 certum est 'I'm resolved' (*OLD certus* 10). Cf. 265n. **hominem:** for the irony see 180–4n.   **contra** 'face to face'.

340 qui = *quo* ('whereby'); cf. 76n.

341–87 Mercury aggressively interrogates Sosia. Through the repetition of particular questions ('what is your business here?', 'who is your master?', 'what is your name?'), in conjunction with curt rejoinders and threats of violence, Mercury launches his assault on Sosia's sense of personal identity. Here, as in the entire scene from 292 on, Martin (1970) sees a prefiguration of twentieth-century 'brainwashing' techniques in totalitarian regimes (we may also compare the interrogation techniques of some police agencies in democratic states); the modern parallels are valid, as long as we do not forget that for P.'s audience the scene is one of uproarious farce.

341 tu, qui Volcanum in cornu conclusum geris: Mercury adopts a grandiloquently menacing tone (cf. 325, 333nn.). The metonymy (*Volcanus* = 'fire') belongs to serious poetry: cf. Enn. *Ann.* 509 Skutsch *cum magno strepitu Volcanum uentus uegebat*, Virg. *A.* 7.77, and the use of *Hephaistos* in Greek epic and tragedy, e.g. Soph. *Ant.* 123. Such metonymies would be known to P.'s audience through Roman tragedy, and had already been parodied by Naevius, *incert. com.* 30a–c W *cocus edit Neptunum Cererem | et Venerem expertam Vulcanom Liberumque absorbuit | pariter*. Cf. *Rud.* 761, *Aul.* 359, and *Men.* 330.   **in cornu:** i.e. in a lantern with sides made of strips of horn, as attested in Greece and Rome from the fifth century BC on. In the absence of street lighting, Roman slaves (*lanternarii*) lit their masters' way at night.

342 quid id exquiris tu qui pugnis os exossas hominibus? 'Why do you inquire into this, you who with your fists fillet men's faces?' Sosia casts Mercury's grandiloquence back in his teeth. Cf. 318, 319nn.

343 utcumque animo conlibitum est meo 'whichever strikes my fancy'. Sosia assumes the saucy posture of the clever slave (cf. 123n.).

344 ain uero? :: aio enim uero 'Is that so?' 'Yes, it most certainly is so' (cf. 362n.).   **ain ... aio:** the former is disyllabic (set *Bc*), the latter with synizesis (*B*). The line scans *B C D A B cc D A / B c D A B c D*, with *A / B* hiatus (*uero aio*).   **enim:** pyrrhic (iambic shortening).   **uerbero. :: mentire nunc:** Sosia puns on *uerbero* ('I'm thrashing you'), knowing that Mercury intended the vocative of the noun (cf. 180, 284).   **mentire:** the original form of the second person singular (< *-se*) predominates in P.; there are fewer than ten examples of the later formation (by analogy with the active ending) in *-ris* (*MHL* 122, *LL* 264). Cf. 369 *mentiris*.

345 at iam faciam ut uerum dicas dicere 'But I shall soon make you say that I'm telling the truth' (sc. *me* as subject of *dicere*, a frequent omission in colloquial Latin: LHS II 362).   **quid eo est opus?** 'No need for that.' Presumably Mercury's preceding assertion was accompanied by a threatening gesture (cf. 344 *uerbero*, with n.).

346 cuius sis 'who owns you'. Sosia's conventional sauciness has made the answer to Mercury's question about his status (343) obvious. As slaves are viewed as property, such a question is paramount in determining identity: cf. 399n.

347 Sosia gives intentionally vague (*huc eo*) and tautological (*eri sum seruos*) responses to Mercury's first two questions, and ignores the

third (346 *quid ueneris?*), which Mercury will shortly ask again (350).
eo. eri: *D / a* hiatus at the opening of the line (*eo* is disyllabic).

348–9 By *comprimam linguam* (348) Mercury means he will restrain
Sosia's saucy tongue, but Sosia puns on the sexual sense of the verb
(109n.): 'You can't have your way with her: she's kept proper and
chaste.' Adams (1982) 126 sees a more specific reference to *irrumatio*.
This particular pun is a Plautine favourite: cf. *Rud.* 1072–5, *Truc.*
262–3, *As.* 290–3, *Cas.* 362.

349 bene pudiceque adseruatur: sc. *lingua*; the adverbs
suggest the preservation of (esp.) a young girl's virginity: cf. *Cist.*
172–3 *eaque educauit eam sibi pro filia | bene et pudice*, *Cur.* 518, 698.
argutarier: 13n.

350 hasce aedis: both actors now probably occupy the centre of
the stage in front of the palace: cf. 264n.   **negoti est:** hiatus at
the main break.   **immo quid tibi est?** 'The question is, what's
your business here?'

352 peregri: cf. 5n.   **tutatust domi** 'he's kept watch at our
house'; a rare instance of the intransitive.

353 at nunc abi sane 'but will you please go away now and ...'
abi: pyrrhic (iambic shortening).   **sane:** untranslatable in a per-
emptory command (*OLD* 3), as at 439.   **dicito:** the future imperative is used with precision by P. (Sosia tells Mercury to go off
and then announce the arrival of the *familiares*). Cf. *Mer.* 770 *cras petito;
dabitur. nunc abi.*

354–5 'I don't understand how you are a *familiaris*. If you do not
leave immediately, my "friend", I'll have you welcomed in a very
unfriendly fashion.' By *familiares* in 353, Sosia of course meant 'members of the household'; cf. the similar pun at *Epid.* 2.

354 nisi ... abis: 198n.

355 familiaris ... familiter: the polyptoton of juxtaposed
adjective and adverb is very common in P., e.g. *Rud.* 977 *impudenter
impudens*, *As.* 676 *bella belle*, *As.* 208 *unice unum*; the hyperbaton
here underscores the pun (354–5n.).   **accipiere:** 296, 344nn.
faxo: *faxo* (for the future in *-so* see *MHL* 162–3) is often used para-
tactically by P. with the subjunctive or the future, whereas he uses
faciam only with *ut* (cf. Lindsay 61). The broad distribution of *faxo* in
Plautus (30 instances in senarii and 41 in all other measures) suggests
that the form was still used in everday speech (cf. Happ (1967) 90–1).

356 inquam: 94n.   **horunc** 'of the people here' < *horum* +
-ce.   **sum :: at:** a questionable *c / D* hiatus (though at change of
speaker: see pp. 63, 68–9).   **at scin quo modo?** 'But do you
know what . . . ?'; a formula in P. that prefaces a threat without necessarily referring to what has just been said (as here). Its elliptical
origin is seen in such instances as *Rud.* 797 *tangam hercle uero.* :: *tanges,*
at scin quo modo?

357 faciam ego hodie te superbum 'I'll see that you stand
proud today.' Sosia will be 'exalted' when he is carried off unconscious (358 *auferere*); the joke depends on confusion of the literal
('aloft') and figurative ('lofty') senses of the adjective. Palmer (n. *ad*
loc.) compares the sinister exchange between Dionysus and Pentheus
at E. *Bac.* 968–9 (cf. pp. 54–5).   **nisi ... abis:** 198n.   **quo-**
nam modo: Sosia's naïve response prepares the way for the
'punch-line'. For this (common) type of humour in P. see Fraenkel
(1960) 35–54.

358 auferere: the primary meaning is 'you will be carried off',
but the word (in the active) is later attested in the sense 'kill' (*OLD*
8). Cf. 344n.

359 quin 'Why . . .' (the use in emphatic objections).   **fami-**
liai: the disyllabic ending, which is replaced by the diphthong *-ae* in
classical Latin, is apparently already archaic in P.: see further
Skutsch (1985) on Enn. *Ann.* p. 61 and *MHL* 19–21. Cf. *Mil.* 103 *mag-*
nai rei publicai gratia, which, as does Sosia here (cf. *praedico*), affects a
grand tone.

360 uide sis quam mox uapulare uis 'Do kindly consider
how soon you want your walloping.' Cf. 286n.   **uis:** 17–18n.
nisi actutum hinc abis: this has become a kind of refrain (354,
357 and 198n.).

362 haecine tua domust? 'This is *your* house?' Mercury expresses further indignation at Sosia's failure to designate *domo* (361)
with the plural pronoun, in accordance with the usual idiom of
slaves (cf. 385, 400, 406, 409, 410, 453).   **ita inquam** 'That's so,
yes.' For ways of saying 'yes' and 'no' in Latin see Woodcock §171,
GL §471.

364 quicum nupta est Alcumena: 99n.   **quid ais?** 'What
do you mean?', a colloquial formula that prepares the listener for
further questioning (*LU* 43).

365 Sosiam uocant Thebani, Dauo prognatum patre: pure bombast in a slave's mouth; the Romanized Thebans would generally call him *puer* (or worse). Legally, the slave can claim no father (28n.). Cf. 614.   **Dauo:** Daos is one of the stock names of Greek comic slaves (cf. 124n.), and perhaps the name of Amphitryon's slave in P.'s hypothetical source, from whom Sosia thus could be said to 'descend'. That P. was fond of such metatheatrical jests with character names is proved by the *Dis exapaton* papyrus: P. renamed Menander's Syros Chrysalus, a change to which the Plautine slave cleverly alludes in the play, *Bac.* 649–50 *non mihi isti placent Parmenones, Syri,* | *qui duas aut tris minas auferunt eris.* In Menander Daos typically functions as both 'schemer' and 'victim' (Wiles (1991) 95–7), and traces of this duality can be seen in Sosia: 153–74, 186–261nn.   **prognatum:** *prognatus* is much more solemn and grandiose-sounding than *natus*; cf. Naev. *trag.* 55–6 W *proinde huc Dryante regem prognatum patre* | *Lycurgum cette*, Enn. *Ann.* 36 Skutsch *Eurydica prognata* and Enn. *Thy.* 291 Jocelyn (with (1967) n. *ad loc.*) *Tantalo prognatus Pelope*, and CIL 1 2.7 *prognatum Publio* (the epitaph of Scipio Barbatus).

366–7 'Well now, with your arrival today comes your undoing, that's for sure, what with your concoction of lies and web of tricks, you peak of audacity.' Through his vocabulary (*mendaciis, audaciai, dolis*), Mercury in effect accuses Sosia of playing the *seruus callidus* of New Comedy, a role he himself has usurped (265–9n.).

366 ne tu istic hodie malo tuo compositis mendaciis: scan *B C D aa B c D A* / *B cc D A B c D* (*tuo* with synizesis; for the monosyllable at the main break see 308n.).   **ne:** 182n.   **istic:** the adverb.   **malo tuo:** 321n.   **compositis mendaciis:** Mercury refers to Sosia's claim to be a member of the *familia*, but the phrase also aptly describes his messenger's speech (197, 198nn.).

367 audaciai columen: for the development of such phrases see Fantham (1972) 45–6; for the genitive in *-ai* 359n.   **consutis dolis:** the same expression is used at *Ps.* 540. The metaphor of 'sewing together' a plan, an act of trickery, etc. is found in many languages (present already in Homer: Greek and Latin examples collected by Siewert (1894) 44–5).

368 immo equidem tunicis consutis huc aduenio, non dolis: more humour derived from literal reinterpretation of the figurative (328n.).   **tunicis consutis:** the plural probably by assimilation to 367 *consutis dolis*, though the Romans did wear both an inner (*subucula*) and outer (*indusium*) tunic. See further DS v *s.v. tunica*.

369 at mentiris etiam 'Ah you lie yet again.' Cf. 344n. **certo pedibus, non tunicis uenis:** Mercury gives Sosia a taste of his own medicine with this grammatical joke, in which he deliberately misconstrues the ablatives expressing accompaniment (368) as instrumental. As evidence of his increasing control over Sosia, Mercury is fast stealing all the slave's capabilities, including his brand of verbal humour. Cf. *Men.* 3 *apporto uobis Plautum, lingua non manu.* **uenis** = *aduenis*; cf. 368 *aduenio* and 209n.

370–2 The comic repetition of a single word, as *profecto* here, in a lively exchange is a common Plautine technique that is difficult to reproduce in translation (Carrier renders 369–72 'You came with your tunic, liar? You came with your feet.' 'Of course.' 'And of course you're going to be thrashed for lying.' 'Well, I object, of course.' 'As a matter of course, that's useless. My course is a solid fact, not a mere opinion.'). Cf. the playful repetition of *censeo* at *Rud.* 1268–79 and *aio* at *Mos.* 975–9.

370 ita profecto: in effect, almost 'Touché!' or 'How droll!' **nunc profecto uapula ob mendacium:** Mercury physically assaults Sosia (*uapula* = 'take that') and continues to do so throughout the scene (cf. 379, 395, 440). Though threats of punishment are ubiquitous in P., clever slaves are never beaten in the course of the play, despite their many machinations: the festival context of Plautine comedy provides the triumphant slave with a kind of general amnesty (Segal (1987) 137–69). In this unusual scene (and play), Sosia, who would normally be expected to enjoy this licence, is beaten for telling the truth: p. 31.

371 at pol profecto ingratiis 'Well then, of course [you decline it] against my will.'

372 hoc quidem 'profecto' certum est, non est arbitrarium 'This "of course" is in fact already decided on, and is not subject to your wishes.' Another grammatical joke (cf. 369n.): Mercury distortingly treats Sosia's *profecto* (371) as the object of *uolo*, as though he had meant 'I don't want the "of course" attached to that word' instead of 'Of course I don't want a beating.' Mercury presumably strikes Sosia again (cf. 373 *tuam fidem obsecro*).

373 tuam fidem obsecro: Sosia attempts to surrender himself unconditionally to the *fides* of Mercury (cf. 226n.); the irony in making such a plea that, according to an ancient formula, usually is addressed to the gods is even more explicit at 455.

374 perii :: parum etiam, praeut futurum est, praedicas 'I'm done for!' 'What you declare is a mere trifle indeed, in comparison with what's to come' (i.e. 'You may think you're "done for" now, but soon you'll believe you're "dead"': cf. 295, 456nn.).

375 tuos, nam pugnis usu fecisti tuom 'Yours because, thanks to your fists, you have claimed me by right of occupation.' According to the Roman legal notion of *usucapio*, continuous possession of another's property results in transfer of ownership (usually after one year in the case of portable items, two years for land and immovable structures; cf. 'squatter's right' and the similar jest at 845). Sosia jokes that Mercury has taken control of him physically, and that the beatings have been of sufficent duration to justify a transfer of title. Again, there is deeper irony in that Sosia is about to surrender his entire identity to Mercury (455–62n.).

376 pro fidem, Thebani ciues: Sosia bombastically pleads for protection that normally would be afforded only to free citizens. Cf. 161–2, 365nn.   **pro:** the colloquial interjection. The accusative *fidem* was originally the object of *obsecro* (*vel sim.*); cf. the exaggerated comic version of the formula, Caec. *com.* 211–12 R = 201–2 W *pro deum popularium omnium, omnium adulescentium | clamo postulo obsecro oro ploro atque imploro fidem.*   **etiam clamas ...?** 'Crying out, are you?' (i.e. 'You have the audacity to cry for help'); for this colloquial use of *etiam* in indignant questions see *OLD etiam* 4c. Cf. 381n.   **carnufex:** technically an executioner, but used as a general pejorative ('scum') in comedy.

377 ut esset quem tu pugnis caederes 'to be your punching-bag'.

378 istoc: ablative of cause, anticipating 379 *quia uaniloquo's.*

379 uaniloquo's: one of several Plautine coinages of this type, e.g. *Capt.* 264 (cf. *Mil.* 191) *falsiloquos, Per.* 514 *stultiloquos, Bac.* 1174 *blandiloquos*; P. is similarly innovative with compounds in *-dicus*, e.g. *Trin.* 275 *uanidicus, Capt.* 56 *spurcidicus*, and *Poen.* 138 *blandidicus.*

380 'I wish the gods would make *you* Sosia rather than me, so that I could pound you'; an aside, as Mercury's response shows (381).

ita di faciant: extremely ironic in that Mercury has made precisely the transformation Sosia prays for.

381 etiam muttis? 'Muttering away, are you?' Mercury follows up on his earlier indignant question (376n.); together these form a kind of universalizing doublet (7n.), in effect forbidding Sosia to make any sound whatsoever. Plautine characters often acknowledge each other's asides, e.g. 954 *mirum quid solus secum secreto ille agat, Aul.* 52 *at ut scelesta sola secum murmurat, Mos.* 512 *quid tute tecum loquere.*

381–7 With *quem tu uoles* (381) Sosia makes a full retreat, to be followed by the proposal for a truce (388ff.).

382 qui = *quis.*

383 peccaueram 'I made a mistake': 22n.

384 Amphitruonis socium ' "Amphitryon's associate" ' (Nixon). P.'s puns can be derived from the most minimal of linguistic correspondences (cf. examples in Duckworth (1952) 354). Some commentators assume that Sosia lapses into the Osco-Umbrian dialect here and pronounces *socium* with a 'soft' *c.* This seemingly recherché view presupposes that P. was Umbrian (cf. p. 1) and that characters in Roman comedy readily introduced dialectical pronunciations. **uolui dicere** 'I meant to say', a formula of self-correction in P., as nervously employed by Lysidamus to correct his 'Freudian slips' at *Cas.* 365–7, 672–4. Rhetoricians frequently employ this figure of speech (*reprehensio*), as in the notorious example at Cic. *Cael.* 32 *quod quidem facerem uehementius, nisi intercederent mihi inimicitiae cum istius mulieris uiro – fratrem uolui dicere; semper hic erro.*

385 scibam: the imperfect of fourth-conjugation verbs is variously -*ibam* or -*iebam* in the early dramatists (*MHL* 158). **nobis:** dative of possession ('we have no slave Sosia except me'); with the plural, Mercury slips into the vernacular of domestic slaves (cf. 362n.).

386 fugit te ratio 'you've made a mistake', a colloquial expression (e.g. Catul. 10.29). *fugit* is perfect here. **ratio utinam:** *B / c* hiatus, at change of speaker (pp. 63, 68). **utinam istuc pugni fecissent tui:** i.e. *utinam tui pugni fugissent.*

387 ego sum Sosia ille quem tu dudum esse aiebas mihi 'I'm the very Sosia you told me that you were a while back' (understand *te* with *esse*; cf. 345n.).

388–95 Sosia's attempt to strike a truce will only end in renewal of the beating (395n.).

388 obsecro: 373n.   **per pacem liceat te alloqui, ut ne uapulem:** in the prologue, the actor playing Mercury, in fear of a beating (26–7n.) himself, similarly addressed the audience 'in peace' (32); the parallelism underscores how they, no less than an *architectus doli* such as Mercury, are essential to Plautine performance. The application of formal international parlance to relations between individuals is widespread in comedy (cf. *OLD pax* 1b and 390 *pace facta*).   **ut ne:** 127n.

389 immo indutiae parumper fiant 'No, but we can strike a truce instead, for a short while.'

390 pugnis: ablative of respect.

391 dic si quid uis, non nocebo 'Say whatever you want, you won't be harmed.' Sosia takes this as Mercury's agreement to a full-fledged *pax* (cf. 390, 395) rather than the more narrow *indutiae* proposed in 389   **fide:** 276n.   **credo:** deliberative indicative, as often in the first person (56n.).   **meae** 'yes' (assimilated to *tuae*), the usual means of assent in Latin, but ironic here, not only because one entrusts oneself to the *fides* of a patron in the religious as well as the political sphere (cf. Fordyce (1961) on Catul. 34.1), but also because of the god's deceptive nature (cf. 268n.).

392 quid si falles?: cf. 75–7, 391nn.   **tum Mercurius Sosiae iratus siet:** for this kind of irony see p. 32.

393 animum aduorte: the prologist's formulaic appeal for attention (38n.) is also common in Plautine dialogue, where it similarly signals that something important is about to be said.

394 etiam denuo? 'Still at it? Again?'

395 pacem feci, foedus feci, uera dico. :: uapula: a delightful line. Sosia protests in three brief but syntactically parallel clauses, each made up of a pair of disyllabic words, and thick with alliteration and assonance; Oniga (n. *ad loc.*) characterizes the style as that of a nursery rhyme. But Sosia's innocent protest swiftly meets with violent blows.   **uapula:** the ironic conclusion to the exchange; Mercury has in fact deceived Sosia and is now angry with him (391, 392nn.). Cf. 370n.

396–462 Following their mutual claims to Sosia's identity (396–401), the doubles enter into a sort of loosely structured ἀγών (i.e. the competitive debate best known from Aristophanic comedy and Euripidean tragedy) that spans the rest of the scene. Here the focus of the dispute shifts from mere assertion to consideration of the evidence (402–49 *passim*). Sosia, to his own astonishment, is gradually forced to acknowledge that neither his experiences nor his appearance are unique. Ultimately he must conclude that Mercury has stolen his *imago* (458) and that effectively he is dead (456). The weighing of the evidence is permeated with farcical humour (e.g. 406–7, 436–7, 445–6), and the scene is appropriately rounded off with a joke (462n.).

396 ut libet quid tibi libet fac 'Do what you like, however you like it' (cf. 123n.). **quoniam pugnis plus uales:** cf. 390.

397 uerum ... tamen 'but even so' (cf. *OLD uerumtamen*). **utut:** such geminated forms, colloquial in origin, are generally avoided in later literature (*LU* 59–60). For their thematic significance in *Am.* see pp. 15–17. **reticebo** 'keep from saying'.

398 tu me uiuos hodie numquam facies quin sim Sosia 'As long as *you* are alive you will never cause *me* not to be Sosia.' **me:** proleptic accusative (54–5n.), here in sharp contrast with *tu.* **uiuos:** for the irony see 295, 396–462, 455–62nn. **quin** 'so that ... not' (cf. 399, 559 and *OLD* 4a).

399 certe edepol: 271n. **tu me:** Sosia casts Mercury's *tu me* (398) back in his face. **alienabis:** the literal sense 'you will never make me belong to someone else' is apropos. Sosia is property and his identity is intimately connected with the household: 346, 448nn. (*OLD* 2a unnecessarily postulates a distinct sense 'to change the nature or identity of').

400 nobis: cf. 362n.

402 sanus non est: 386n.

403–7 *nonne* is used before vowels and *non* before consonants in this series of indignant questions expecting a positive answer (cf. Lindsay 129).

403 quid, malum, non sum ego seruos Amphitruonis Sosia ...? 'What, damn it, I'm not Amphitryon's slave Sosia?' (*malum* is always in 2nd or 3rd position in such questions: *LU* 32). The original expression is perhaps *malum habebis* (cf. 721).

401 If the line is to be read, it fits the context better after 403, but the two hiatuses (*cum Amphitruone, una ieram*), of which only the latter

(*A* / *B* at the main break) is legitimate, make it suspect (cf. also 125), as does the fact that Mercury omits this information in 410–15 (see n. *ad loc.*).

404–8 Sosia desperately grasps for something on which he can securely base his unique identity. He courses through his experiences during the night leading up to the present moment, where (with appropriate gestures) he insists that he is now standing before the house with lantern in hand. The sequence of vehement questions is concluded, as typically, with a joke: the beating he has endured is the best proof of his existence, and he starts toward the house (409).

404 hac noctu: 272n.   **ex portu Persico:** an obscure reference to the Thebans' last port of call on their lengthy return voyage from the land of the Teleboans at the north entrance to the Corinthian Gulf. Festus' explanation (p. 217) that a harbour on the Gulf of Euboea (so named because the Persian fleet put in there) not far from Thebes is meant has been doubted; at any rate, to place Amphitryon at such a port would pose a glaring anachronism. Blackman (1969) 21–2 attributes the port to P.'s source and argues that *Persicus* is derived fom *Perseus*, a city with a harbour in Attica (cf. St. Byz. 519.8–9).

406 aedis nostras: cf. 362n.   **lanterna:** referred to only at 149 and 341, but held by Sosia for the entire scene (as readers may easily forget).

407 loquor: pyrrhic here (iambic shortening). The line scans *B cc D aa B C dd A / bb C D A B c D.*   **uigilo:** 298n.   **homo:** 180–4n.

408 etiam ... nunc 'still' (*OLD etiamnum* 1).

410–15 Mercury counters with a messenger's speech in miniature. Though Sosia prefaced his earlier speech with the caveat that he might utter a *mendacium* (198n.), the account turned out to be accurate. Reflecting the topsy-turvidom of the doubles-comedy, Mercury prefaces his fallacious appropriation of Sosia's experiences here with the assertion that Sosia is a liar (411 *omnia ementitu's*). Cf. 418, 419nn.

410 quid, domum uostram? :: ita enim uero. :: quin quae dixisti modo: scan *B cc D A bb c D A / B C D A B c D* (with iambic shortening of the ultima of *domum* and *enim*; there is an apparent hiatus at change of speaker that results in an unusual split *bb* resolution).   **domum uostram:** 362n.   **ita enim uero** 'Yes, absolutely!' (cf. 362n).

411 Sosia Amphitruonis: Mercury reverses the usual word order in this expression (cf. 148, 378, 394, 403), which normally puts master before slave.

412 nam noctu hac soluta est nauis nostra a portu Persico: Mercury deliberately inverts Sosia's word order in his corresponding assertion at 404: *hac noctu > noctu hac, nostra nauis > nauis nostra.* Cf. 410–15n.

413–15 The revelation of these details will further mystify Sosia (cf. 416–17).

413 rex regnauit: *figura etymologica.*   **oppidum expugnauimus:** cf. 191, 210.

414 ui pugnando cepimus: technical military language (cf. Cic. *Ad fam.* 5.10b *sex oppida ui oppugnando cepi*) to emphasize that a victory was achieved through combat rather than immediate capitulation (cf. 189n.).

415 ipsus Amphitruo optruncauit regem Pterelam: cf. 252. **ipsus:** pyrrhic (iambic shortening).

416 egomet mihi non credo, cum ... audio: cf. English 'I can't believe my own ears.'   **egomet** 'I myself' (the emphatic particle is very common in colloquial Latin).   **mihi:** Sosia or Mercury? For the breakdown of language here see p. 17.

417 hic quidem certe quae illic sunt res gestae memorat memoriter: scan *B cc D A B C D A / B C dd A bb c D* (*quidem* is pyrrhic by iambic shortening).   **illic:** adverb (i.e. 'on the campaign'; cf. 138).   **memorat memoriter:** the use of adverb and verb of the same root in close proximity is a mannerism of early Latin (LHS ii 791).

418 sed quid ais? 'But what about this?' (cf. 364n.). As is typical in messenger's speeches, Sosia asks for more detailed information (cf. 188–96, 410–5nn.).

419 Pterela rex qui potitare solitus est patera aurea: Mercury mimics the close of Sosia's battle narrative (260–1).

420 elocutus est 'He's hit the nail on the head.'   **cistula:** for the object see DS 1/2 *s.v. cista.*

421 signi dic quid est? 'Tell me, what's his seal?' (cf. 58n.): cf. *Vid.* fr. 11 *at ego signi dicam quid siet.*

422 cum quadrigis Sol exoriens: no doubt a popular motif on *signa*, but also with thematic significance, as Sosia had earlier (282) quipped that the long night was the result of Sol's intoxication. The image likewise looks ahead to the imminent daylight: 546–50. **quid? me captas, carnufex?** 'What? Trying to catch me out, are you, you scum?'

423–8 Sosia is on the verge of defeat (423 *argumentis uicit*), but decides to take a new approach by turning to his own private experience; if Mercury can accurately recount this, he will have to admit defeat in the ἀγών (428: cf. 396–462n.).

423–6 Sosia speaks directly to the audience.

424 hunc decipiam: Sosia vainly attempts to draw the audience into his conspiratorial net (cf. 153–462n.); the proposal to deceive the arch-deceiver among the gods is obviously ill-fated.

425 egomet: extremely emphatic with *solus* here ('what *I* did all on my lonesome'). Cf. 416n.

427 legiones cum pugnabant maxume: cf. 199 (the audience will fondly recall Sosia's humorous correlative clause) and 429n.

428 uictus sum, si dixeris 'I'm beat if you say it.' For the conditional type here cf. 320.

429 cadus erat: instead of giving the expected response *ego tum fugiebam maxume* (427n.), Mercury heightens Sosia's suspense by beginning with a formula (cf. *locus erat*, etc.) used to introduce an ecphrasis in serious literature (so Oniga *ad loc.*). **cadus:** a large vessel regularly used to store wine. **hirneam:** the precise size of this earthenware vessel is unknown, but given the stress on Sosia's bibulousness (186–261n.), it was no doubt large. **ingressust uiam** 'he's on the right track' (Nixon).

430 ut matre fuerat natum 'as it had been poured forth from its own mother' (i.e., he drank it in its originally undiluted state). The image of the grapevine as mother of the wine is commonplace, e.g. Pind. *N.* 9.52, Aesch. *Pers.* 614–15, E. *Alc.* 757. Cf. *OLD mater* 6. **uini ... meri:** there was a consensus in Graeco-Roman antiquity that the drinking of undiluted wine was uncivilized. The audience will not be surprised to learn of Sosia's preference (cf. 429n.). See generally the *OCD* entries 'alcoholism' and 'wine' (with further references). The genitive here apparently is on the analogy of that with verbs of filling (LHS II 82–3; cf. GL §383). The *C / D* hiatus (*uini* *eduxi*) is suspect, but the text otherwise seems sound. **eduxi** 'I emptied it of its unmixed wine.' Perhaps a pun on *educere* = 'nurture' (children, etc.: *OLD* 10), suggested by *ut matre fuerat natum*, is also intended (cf. English 'nurse a beer').

431 factum est illud, ut ... ebiberim 'That's what happened, that's how I drank off...' (indirect question with the subjunctive: 17–18n.). **illic:** adverb.

432 mira sunt nisi: 283n. **illic:** nominative.

433 quid nunc? 'Well?' (a rhetorical formula: *OLD nunc* 10). **uincon argumentis te non esse Sosiam?** 'Based on the evidence, don't I carry my point that you are not Sosia?'; Mercury unrealistically takes up Sosia's aside in 423 (*argumentis uicit* ...). Cf. 180, 309, 423–8nn. **uincon:** *-ne* in P. often has the force of *nonne*; cf. 485, 526 and Lindsay 128–9.

434 tu negas med esse?: *sc. Sosiam.* **quid ego ni negem** 'Of course I do' (cf. *OLD quidni*). **qui ... siem:** causal subjunctive (cf. the indicative at 326).

435–7 See pp. 32–3.

437 nam iniurato scio plus credet mihi quam iurato tibi 'For I know he will give more credence to me unsworn than to you sworn.' **iniurato:** *bb CD* (with iambic shortening in the antepenult). **scio ... credet:** parataxis with *scio* is very common in early and colloquial Latin (LHS ii 528–9).

438 quis ego sum saltem, si non sum Sosia? te interrogo: a natural arrangement of ideas in animated colloquial speech; cf. *Aul.* 321 *sed uter uestrorum est celerior? memora mihi.* The later literary language tends to invert the clauses and subordinate the direct question: cf. *LU* 107. **Sosia:** *B c d+*.

439 ubi ego nolim Sosia esse, tu esto sane Sosia: a metatheatrical joke; Sosia can have his unique identity back when the gods' ruse (i.e. the play-within-the-play) is over. **ubi ... nolim:** *ubi* can have a quasi-conditional force in early Latin, with the indicative or subjunctive (Bennett 1 90). A cretic scansion of *Sosia* (nominative) is doubtful, and *Sosia nolim* of the MSS is transposed here. **esto:** 353n.

440 uapulabis, ni hinc abis: 198n. **ignobilis:** generally taken as a vocative with the literal sense 'you unknown' (cf. *Ps.* 591), but perhaps proleptic with *uapulabis* ('you'll be beaten to oblivion').

441–9 Sosia presumably holds his lantern up to inspect Mercury more closely. Popular comedy revels in the most palpable deformations of the body, and Sosia's inspection is typical in that it invites the audience to scrutinize in detail the distorted features of the two comic slaves (cf. 116–19n.). Despite being confronted with his mirror image, Sosia perseveres in his conviction that he is the same person he has always been (cf. 447–9n.).

441–2 General inspection of Mercury's *forma*. Conclusion: 442 *nimis similest mei.*

442 quem ad modum ego sum: lit., 'how I am', i.e. 'what I look like'.   **speculum:** in antiquity, mirrors most commonly were polished pieces of bronze and silver: see further DS iv/2 *s.v.* **nimis similest:** 213n.

443 Inspection of Mercury's clothing. Conclusion: *tam consimilest atque ego*, 'he's as like myself as I am' (a strictly illogical but emphatic colloquialism).

444–6 Detailed inspection of Mercury's body. Conclusion: 446 *nihil hoc similist similius.*

444 sura: the comic slave's calves were probably made exaggeratedly thick (cf. *Ps.* 1218) through the use of padded tights. **pes:** apparently very large, as a clown's feet (*Ps.* 1220).   **tonsus:** possibly a red wig (*Ps.* 1218).   **oculi:** *acuti* at *Ps.* 1219.   **nasum uel labra** 'nose, or, if you like, lips' (*uel* here shows its origin from *uolo* (*OLD uel* 1), as commonly in lists, e.g. *As.* 693–4). These features were greatly distorted on the slave's mask.

445 quid uerbis opust?: a very common formula in P. (cf. 615, 777 and English 'What can I say?').

446 The evaluation of Mercury's clothing, limbs and features is comically concluded: a scarred back would constitute the decisive token of recognition. Though P.'s slaves generally elude punishment on stage (cf. 370n.), they frequently jest about the harsh realities of slavery: 'In a comic way, the purple stripes on his back distinguish the Plautine slave much as the purple border on his toga distinguished the Roman senator' (Segal (1987) 139). Slave-beating is one of the oldest comic motifs; cf. Ar. *Pax* 743–8.   **si tergum cicatricosum:** *sc. habet* (cf. 443).   **nihil hoc similist similius:** lit., 'nothing is more alike than this like(ness)'; the emphatic doubling of the adjective (and demonstrative) in the ablative after a comparison is a chiefly Plautine colloquialism. Cf. *Capt.* 644 *nihil, inquam, inuenies magis hoc certo certius*, *Most.* 279 *nihil hac docta doctius*, *LU* 95–6, English 'bigger than big', and Wills (1996) 232.

447 sed quom cogito … sum: as Barnes (1957) 20 notes, Sosia 'comes very close to asserting the Cartesian *"Cogito, ergo sum"*'. Sosia's cogitations, however, are very concrete in nature ('when I consider my appearance, prior experiences, etc., I'm the same person I've always been'; cf. 448n.).

448 noui erum, noui aedis nostras; sane sapio et sentio: a tricolon with crescendo, with anaphora, alliteration, and assonance, to mark Sosia's new-found resolve. For the importance of the household for Sosia cf. 399n.   **sane sapio** 'I'm soundly in my senses' (*sane* with its literal meaning, as *Men.* 790 *sane sapit*).

449 non ego illi obtempero quod loquitur 'I'm not giving in to him whatever he says'. In early Latin, the present indicative with *non* is often used (instead of the future) to express refusal to comply with a command (Bennett I 21).   **pultabo fores:** cf. pp. 14, 20.

450 quo agis te? 'Where are you going?' (*OLD ago* 3a). Scan *bb C D* (*quo*: with prosodic hiatus).   **quadrigas … Iouis:** this image would be familiar to the audience from the *fastigium* of the Capitolium (for the irony see pp. 32–3).

451 ita 'even so'.   **infortunium:** 286n.

452 nonne: 403–7n.

453 tuae si quid uis nuntiare: *sc. licet* (cf. 452).

454 inritassis: for the (archaic) future form in *-so* see 355n. **lumbifragium** 'a shipwreck of a man' (Nixon), probably a Plautine coinage (elsewhere only at *Cas.* 968) formed on the analogy of *naufragium*. Cf. *Poen.* 886 *Crurifragius* (a comic name proposed by a slave).   **auferes:** 358n.

455–62 Sosia, after being physically prevented by his double from entering the house, fears that Mercury has stolen his *imago* (458), and that he himself in effect is 'dead' (456). One final test to determine his identity remains: recognition by his master (460–1). By a kind of ring composition, the lengthy scene is concluded when the topic of the master's control over the slave's life (cf. 161–75) is renewed, and Sosia appoints Amphitryon as the ultimate arbiter of his identity. His reflections, as usual, are capped with a joke (462n.).

For further analysis of Sosia's 'identity crisis' in terms of Roman popular thought see Bettini (1991*c*).

455 abeo potius 'I'm going away instead.' The present of the verb 'to go' easily lapses into the future (*LL* 306), as in many Indo-European languages.   **di immortales, obsecro uostram fidem:** the standard formula of appeal (e.g. *Cist.* 663, *Mos.* 77, *Poen.* 967) for divine assistance, ridiculously inapt here. Cf. 373n.

456 ubi ego perii?: 295n.   **ubi ego formam perdidi?:** cf. *Mil.* 429–30 *quid metuis? :: enim me nos nosmet perdiderimus uspiam; | nam nec te neque me nouisse ait haec.*

457 illic: reflecting Sosia's confusion, the adverb is somewhat vague. Does he mean 'on the campaign' (417n.) or 'at the harbour' (cf. 460)?   **si forte oblitus fui** 'if I happened to forget myself'; Sosia is thinking aloud in a disjointed manner.

458 hicquidem omnem imaginem meam ... possidet 'Why, this fellow has got hold of my entire likeness.' There is a meta-theatrical dimension to Sosia's claim as well, given that Mercury wears his slave's mask and costume.   **quae antehac fuerat:** *sc. mea.*

459 uiuo fit quod numquam quisquam mortuo faciet mihi 'What's being done for me when I'm alive no one will ever do when I'm dead.' A punning jest on Roman aristocratic funerary ritual, in which professional actors wore the wax portrait-masks (*imagines*) of distinguished citizens at family funerals (see Polyb. 6.53, Suet. *Ves.* 19). The joke here turns not only on Sosia's lowly social position, but also on the visual disparities between the aristocratic portraits and the grotesque masks of Roman comedy (cf. Wiles (1991) 130–1). Cf. *Mos.* 427–8 *ludos ego hodie uiuo praesenti hic seni | faciam, quod credo mortuo numquam fore.*

460 haec ... ero dicam meo: Sosia is utterly confused, and now must perform the inverse of his original mission: cf. 195, 261.

461 nisi etiam is quoque me ignorabit 'unless *he* likewise won't know me'.   **quod ille faxit Iuppiter** 'and may almighty Jupiter bring this about'; *ille* is formulaic with Jupiter (*OLD ille* 4b).   **faxit:** for the archaic subjunctive in *-im* see *MHL* 165–6.

462 ut ego hodie raso capite caluos capiam pilleum 'I'll shave my head and once I'm bald I'll put on the cap of freedom.' Newly manumitted slaves shaved their heads, as did sailors after escaping a shipwreck. In both cases, the cutting of hair is symbolic of new life (cf. Ferguson (1979) on Juv. 12.81), in that the human head continuously grows a 'crop' of hair that can be periodically 'harvested'.   **ego hodie:** a questionable *c* / *d* hiatus, but the text is sound.   **pilleum:** a *pilleus* was worn by the manumitted slave until his hair grew out again and the transition to a life of freedom was effected. Sosia makes the best of a confusing situation by finding a new identity in 'death'.

463–98 (Scene 2) Left alone on stage at the conclusion of the lengthy first scene, Mercury reassumes his persona as a prologist and continues his opening address, so as to maintain his firm hold over the audience's reception of the play. He begins by summarizing (463–5) the action immediately preceding, and then forecasts (466–9) the scene of confusion (i.e. 551ff.) that will be the direct result of this, as well as the general confusion in store for the entire household (470–3). And to forestall any anxiety about the adulterous tryst, he announces that the truth will ultimately be revealed and matrimonial harmony restored (473–8). Alcmena for her trouble will deliver two sons in a single parturition, despite their differences in age (479–90). Before effecting the transition (496–8) to the next scene, he adds that adultery in a situation such as Alcmena's should be excused (491–5). There is continued emphasis on the carnality of the affair throughout (465 *amplexarier*, 472 *satietatem ... capiet*, 472 *amat*, 498 *uxore usuraria*), and he explicitly states that Amphitryon will learn of his cuckolding (491–2).

Like the prologue proper (cf. 'Prologue') Mercury's address here has been suspected of interpolation: see esp. 481–2, 486–90nn. METRE: iambic senarii.

463 Bene prospere[que] hoc hodie operis processit mihi: a celebratory formula uttered by the clever slave or his accomplices as their trickery unfolds: cf. *Ps.* 574 *lepide omnia prospereque eueniunt*, *Mos.* 734, *Per.* 455–6.   **Bene prospere[que] hoc:** *-que* is deleted to avoid an unlikely case of iambic shortening in the penult of *prospereque*.   **hoc ... operis** 'this piece of work' (cf. 154n.).

464 amoui a ... maxumam molestiam: a pronounced example of alliteration and assonance; cf. 467 *seruom ... sese ... foribus Sosiam.*   **molestiam** 'pest'; the use of abstract nouns as pejoratives is a feature of colloquial Latin (cf. *LU* 87).

465 tuto: adverb.   **amplexarier:** a common euphemism for sexual intercourse: Adams (1982) 181.

466 illuc: i.e. at the harbour (cf. 457n.).   **aduenerit:** the precise use of the future perfect (cf. 467 *narrabit*).

468 ille adeo illum: *ille* = Amphitryon, *illum* somewhat awkwardly refers to Sosia.

469 profectum: sc. *esse.*

470–1 Mercury will personally delude Amphitryon in scene 11 (1021–fr. 6), and in doing so manufacture further trouble for Sosia (cf. 1002–3 and frs. 11–14); the entire *familia* naturally can be presumed to fall victim to the gods' ruse throughout the play. Mercury here betrays a sense of *Schadenfreude*, as does Jupiter at 874–5. Typically, Plautine tricksters broadcast their duplicitous intentions, as is symptomatic of the conspiratorial relationship entered into by actor and audience in non-illusory theatre. But as Petrone (1983) 156–8 points out, *error* and *dementia* are unusual in this context, where *fallacia* (e.g. *Cas.* 860) and *fabrica* (e.g. *Bac.* 366, *Cist.* 540), along with the ubiquitous *lud-* family of expressions, are regular. Mercury's seeming delight in spreading 'madness' and 'folly', though not inconsistent with the tone of the sex farce (cf. 472–3), possibly betrays a tragic source: cf. (e.g.) Athena's delusion of Ajax at Soph. *Ai.* 51–4 and pp. 53–5.

470–1 erroris ... | complebo: verbs of filling in early Latin indifferently take genitive or ablative constructions; cf. 251 and LHS I 82–3.

470 dementiae: here only in P.

471 atque: < *ad + que* ('and the whole household of Amphitryon to boot').   **omnem Amphitruonis:** *a / B* hiatus at the main break of the senarius.

472 adeo usque ... dum 'right up to the point when ...' (*adeo* is frequently strengthened by *usque* in P.).   **satietatem:** sexual satisfaction typically is considered only from the male's perspective (e.g. *Mos.* 196, Ter. *Ph.* 834), but is about to become a farcical motif with regard to Alcmena: see pp. 40–4.

473–92 This entire section either clarifies or adds to information given in the *argumentum* (97–152); the link with the prologue is made explicit at 479 *dudum quod dixi minus.*

473 quam amat 'whom he is making love to'. For the sexual euphemism cf. Adams (1982) 188 and 465 *amplexarier. quam amat* is *ddA* here (prodosic hiatus).   **igitur demum** 'then and not till then' (cf. Sonnenschein (repr. 1979) on *Rud.* 930). Cf. 876.

473–4 omnes scient | quae facta: i.e. through Jupiter's revelations as *deus ex machina* (1131–43).

474 facta: sc. *sunt*.

474–5 denique Alcumenam Iuppiter | rediget antiquam coniugi in concordiam: for the arbitrary manner in which this harmony is achieved see pp. 17–18, 44–5.

476 actutum uxori turbas conciet 'will start by raising a commotion with his wife', i.e. in the first encounter of the spouses at 676ff. The *turbae* are renewed in scene 12 (fr. 7–10).

477 insimulabit eam probri: the charge of adultery is first made explicitly at 810ff.   **probri:** for general terms of moral disapproval that took on the specialized meaning 'sexual disgrace' in Latin see Adams (1982) 200–1.

478 seditionem: etymologically 'a sitting apart' ($<$ *sedeo* + *eo*), applied to situations outside politics and the military first in P.; cf. *Mer.* 124 *seditionem facit lien.* Sedgwick compares Cic. *Att.* 2.15 *ea est enim seditiosa, ea cum uiro bellum gerit* (by contrast, Alcmena only unwittingly 'rebels' against her husband).   **illi:** i.e. for Amphitryon's benefit. Adultery was viewed primarily as an offence against the husband and Alcmena's feelings are never considered by the gods.

479 nunc de Alcumena dudum quod dixi minus 'Now, what I neglected to say fully about Alcumena a while back ...'; cf. *Mer.* 24 *sed amori accedunt etiam haec quae dixi minus.*   **nunc:** 17n.   **dudum:** cf. esp. 110–11.   **minus:** for *minus* 'incompletely' cf. *Mer.* 24 (quoted above), Ter. *Eun.* 737 *correxit miles quod intellexi minus*, and *OLD* 4a.

480–4 In addition to continuing the *argumentum* (472–92n.), Mercury is piquing the audience's curiosity about the prospect of an (extremely) pregnant Alcmena appearing on stage.

480 hodie: i.e. within the time-frame of the play, a standard usage in the prologues (e.g. 94, 140, *Men.* 70, *Cap.* 40); cf. *cras* to indicate loosely 'after the play' (e.g. *Poen.* 1364, 1417).

[481–2] These problematic lines that have spawned much commentary are probably the work of an interpolator (cf. 93n.) rather than P. For purposes of this mythical travesty, P. or his hypothetical

source (cf. Leo (1911), with the critique of Prescott (1913)) has con-
flated the long night of Herakles' conception with the day of his
birth (cf. p. 47 n. 146), a remarkable telescoping of events, though
not inappropriate in the miraculous world of this play (see pp. 29–
31). P. would not expect his audience to reckon the months of gesta-
tion. Moreover, the three-month gap between the conception of
the boys presupposes an earlier visit by Jupiter, of which we hear
nothing in the play. The audience is told only that Amphitryon's son
was conceived before the start of the campaign (102–3, 1137–8; nine
months before by Sosia's reckoning: 670). Expressions such as 498
uxor usuraria and 1122 *is se dixit cum Alcumena clam consuetum cubitibus*
are not decisive, as Alcmena may be said to 'be on loan' only within
the dramatic time of the play, where in fact more than one instance
of *cubitus* (cf. 980–1) is mentioned, and *consuesco* (cf. 490 *consuetio*) is
a euphemism for sexual intercourse that need not imply a long-
standing affair. Cf. 107–9n. and Reinhardt (1974) 107–10. If P. really
did write 481–2, we must either chalk these up to careless blundering
(like Shakespeare, he seems to have worked quickly, as Horace asserted), or accept the lines as a somewhat clumsy attempt to broaden
the farce.

For the *superfetatio* see 111n.

[482] seminatust: the word occurs only here in P. and generally seems to be used of animal and plant production (cf. *OLD
semino*) rather than human procreation.

483 eorum Amphitruonis alter est, alter Iouis: a neat
chiasmus to describe the dual paternity. If 481–2 are in fact interpolated, 483 follows smoothly after 480 ('Alcmena will give birth to two
twin boys; one of these . . .').

**484–5 uerum minori puero maior est pater, | minor
maiori** 'but the younger boy has the greater father, the older boy
the lesser one', a clever play on the double meanings of *minor* and
maior (for linguistic doubling see pp. 15–17). 481–2 need not precede
the statement of this paradox, as Mercury has already suggested
(102–11) that Alcmena is impregnated first by Amphitryon.

484 uerum: the contrast with the preceding clause (483) is slight
and elliptical, as though to counter any sense of equality suggested
by the chiasmus there: 'one is Amphitryon's, one is Jupiter's, but
there are differences between them . . .'

485 iamne hoc scitis quid siet? 'You get how this is now, don't you?' For the Plautine prologist's tendency to guide the audience through the use of such formulas see 110n.   **iamne:** 433n. **hoc:** for the prolepsis cf. 54–5n. and Duckworth (1940) on *Epid.* 575.

486–90 Multiple motivations seem to be attributed to Jupiter in arranging for Alcmena to give birth *uno fetu*. Lines 486–8 offer a rationalization for the birth of Hercules the day after his conception, and the audience will readily accept that Jupiter has the ability to effect such a miracle. Lines 489–90 point to a different plot from P.'s, as Amphitryon will shortly suspect Alcmena of adultery (477n.), and Jupiter, as Mercury has just suggested (473–4n.), will reveal the entire affair (cf. 491–2) immediately after the birth of the twins. Leo similarly brackets 489–90.

486 Alcumenae huius: *A / B* hiatus at the main break (*huius* is a monosyllable). The demonstrative suggests that Mercury points to the backdrop from which Alcmena is to emerge shortly. **honoris gratia** 'out of respect for . . .'

487 uno ut fetu fieret 'that it be done in a single parturition', with vague subject (i.e. the birth of the twins). Cf. 878 *faciamque ut uno fetu* . . . , where Jupiter in his similar address adds that the birth will be painless (879).

488 uno ut labore absoluat aerumnas duas: an even more studied chiasmus than 483. To accomplish two goals by one action is proverbial in Latin: cf. *Cas.* 476 *iam ego uno in saltu lepide apros capiam duos*, Otto (1890) 122 and English 'kill two birds with one stone'.

[489–90] In addition to being nonsensical (486–90n.), these lines follow awkwardly from the purpose clause in 488.

[490] consuetio: the MSS have *suspicio* (cf. 489), but on the basis of Don. Ter. *Ad.* 666 and Festus p. 61 (*consuetionem Plautus pro consuetudine dixit*), Bentley reasonably proposed the otherwise unattested form *consuetio*. But neither Festus nor Donatus gives the name of the play and it is probable that this line belongs elsewhere in P. (cf. 486–90n.).

491 quamquam . . . tamen: with 489–90 deleted, the elliptical train of thought is 'Alcmena will give birth to twins in a single parturition; though Amphityron naturally will believe both sons are his, he nevertheless will find out the whole truth.' The line has a heavy rhythm (cf. 42n.).   **ut iam dudum dixi:** he refers back to 473–4.

492 quid igitur?: 62n.

492–3 probro | ... Alcumenae: predicate and referential datives, respectively ('no one will really consider this as an offence so far as Alcmena is concerned').

493–5 'for it doesn't seem a fair thing for a god to do, allowing his own offence and wrongdoing to fall on a human being' (the substantive clause *delictum ... ut sinat* is dependent on *non par uidetur facere*). Jupiter reiterates this 'chivalrous' sentiment at 871–2.

494–5 delictum suom | suamque ... culpam: Tolliver (1952) 55 argues that this open admission of moral culpability must have 'decreased regard for Jupiter and Mercury' among audience members. But such a moralizing view, in addition to being inconsonant with the festive spirit of the sex farce, overlooks the Romans' ability to distinguish between the anthropomorphic conceptions of deity introduced to them through Greek myth and the more animistic gods of state cult (cf. Segal (1987) 186–8). P. was no religious reformer; the plays generally uphold conventional Roman religious values (cf. Hanson (1959)).

495 ut ... ut: the repetition is common in P.'s colloquial Latin (Lindsay 10).   **expetere:** 174n.

496 orationem comprimam: crepuit foris: a typical formula to announce the arrival of other characters (e.g. *Mil.* 270, *Ps.* 409–11, 787–8, *Cur.* 486), probably accompanied by a sound effect. For door noise in Greek drama see Frost (1988) 6–7.   **foris:** either one wing of a double door is meant (so Sedgwick *ad loc.*) or the singular is used collectively.

497 Amphitruo subditiuos: the adjective is also used at *Ps.* 752 to describe one of the participants in a play-within-the-play; all actors are in fact supposititious. Cf. 828.   **eccum** 'there he is'; cf. 120n.

498 cum Alcumena uxore usuraria: the striking and thematically significant (pp. 39–40) phrase *uxore usuraria* is highlighted by the *A / B* hiatus at the main break here, which enhances the παρὰ προσδοκίαν.   **cum Alcumena:** *a / B* prosodic hiatus.

499–550 (Scene 3) The second 'Act' opens with the much anticipated appearance of the supreme god (88, 90nn.) and a *very* pregnant Alcmena (100–14, 480–4nn.). The grossly padded male actor playing her will elicit instantaneous laughter (pp. 38–9), and by the time Jupiter remarks on her condition (500), the audience should be guffawing uncontrollably. As Perelli (1983) 386–8 argues, Alcmena's demeanour in this scene is more like that of the caricatured shrewish wife of bourgeois comedy or even the Plautine *meretrix* (cf. 529, 530, 536–7, 544nn.) than that of the misplaced tragic heroine critics have envisioned. The scene as a whole can be viewed as a parody of epic departure scenes, the *locus classicus* being that of Hector and Andromache (*Il.* 6.390ff.; cf. 503–5n.). And just as the gods throughout the play emphasize the carnal nature of her relationship with Jupiter, Alcmena herself here displays an active interest in sexuality that hardly befits the idealized Roman *matrona* (cf. 513–14n. and Luc. 4.1274–7). We also should consider how the audience's awareness that the two lovers are played by male actors might have influenced their reception of the scene. All of this indelibly colours the audience's reception of Alcmena's subsequent appearances.

In the mirroring structure of the doubles comedy (pp. 13–15), this scene corresponds both with 882–955, where Jupiter and Alcmena likewise appear, and 633–860, the arrival scene of her real husband. METRE: trochaic septenarii.

499 Bene uale, Alcumena, cura rem communem, quod facis 'Goodbye, Alcmena, keep looking after our shared interest, as you are.' It is easy to imagine the actor playing Alcmena proudly patting his belly as Jupiter speaks. For Jupiter's 'paternalism' here cf. Antipho's words to his daughters, *St.* 145 *curate igitur familiarem rem, ut potestis.*   **quod facis** = *ut facis*, a common idiom (cf. Lucke (1982) on Ov. *Rem.* 704).

500 atque inperce quaeso 'and please be easy on yourself'; cf. *Cas.* 833 (with reference to the 'virgin' Chalinus) *integrae atque imperitae huic inpercito.* The more usual, colloquial phrase is *sibi parcere.* **esse actos** 'are completed'; for *ago* in expressions of time see *OLD* 31.   **uides:** Jupiter focuses all attention on her distended belly.

501 quod erit natum tollito: Jupiter as counterfeit husband instructs Alcmena not to expose the offspring. A Roman father, whose *potestas* allowed him the privilege of deciding such cases (but probably not without some restrictions: cf. Dion. Hal. *Ant. Rom.* 2.15.1), formally recognized a new-born as his own by lifting it up. Here the false Amphitryon transfers his authority to his 'wife', as would normally happen in the case of a husband's absence. The application of such a mundane (and Roman) formula to the birth of a great mythic hero is comically incongruous.   **quod:** appropriate here, as the real Amphitryon would not have foreknowledge of the gender. Cf. Ter. *And.* 219 *quidquid peperisset decreuerunt tollere,* Cic. *Att.* 10.18 *quod quidem est natum perimbecillum est,* and the English use of 'it' with reference to infants.

502–3 quid istuc est ... negoti, quod ... | abeas? 'What reason do you have to go off?', much more animated than a simple *quid* or *cur.* Alcmena's solicitousness is apparent in her first words, as *quid istuc* carries a tone of contempt and/or suspicion.

502 istuc: with iambic shortening of the penult.   **quod:** lit., 'as regards which'; the pronoun is on its way to becoming a conjunction ('that': cf. 302n., *Cas.* 460, *Capt.* 541, and Lindsay 111–12).

503–5 In an epic scene of departure between spouses, the warrior typically must leave to engage the enemy in (often protracted) battle, like the ill-fated Hector (*Il.* 6.440ff.). Jupiter's pretext for departing, by contrast, is that he must briefly (cf. 530) serve in a supervisory role as the army returns to Thebes. Cf. 499–550n.

503 haud quod ... distaedeat: the subjunctive is one of 'reason rejected' (Sedgwick *ad loc.*; *quod* = 'because'). The blandiloquent Jupiter is pooh-poohing Alcmena's suggestion (502–3) that he has had enough of her.   **domi:** genitive (cf. *MHL* 66–7).   **distaedeat:** colloquial Latin tends to intensify with *dis-* simple verbs expressing strong emotions, as *dispereo* (a frequent exclamation in the perfect) and *discrucior.* Cf. *Trin.* 932 *discupio,* *Mos.* 1166 *dispudet* (cf. *pudet* in 1165), *Cas.* 248 *disperdo.*

504–5 Jupiter conveniently assumes the ethos of the *miles gloriosus* in this scene (cf. 524, 531, 534, 534–5nn.). Given the traditional Roman antithesis between *amor* and *bellum,* personal indulgence and public service, etc., this pompous declaration on military duty is delightfully incongruous in the mouth of the philandering Jupiter (cf. Mercury's aside in 506–7). The ideologically incorrect preference he seeks to conceal is explicitly brought out at 527–8.

504 summus imperator: ironic; Jupiter is elsewhere referred to not only as *summus,* but also 1121 *imperator diuom atque hominum* (cf. *Rud.* 9).   **exercitum:** with iambic shortening in the initial syllable.

505 citius quod non facto est usus fit quam quod facto est opus: lit., 'what should not be done happens more readily than

what should be done'.   **est usus ... est opus:** there is no distinction in meaning. Cf. 169n.

**506 nimis hic scitust sycophanta, qui quidem meus sit
pater** 'He is a really excellent flimflam man – naturally, since he's
my father.' Mercury alludes to his (and Hermes') traditional role as a
trickster. Mercury's saucy asides in this scene (cf. esp. 510–11, 515,
521, 526, 541) show how eagerly he has taken up the role of the
clever slave (cf. pp. 25–7). For the conspiratorial nature of asides in
P. see 153–462n.   **nimis ... scitust:** cf. 213, 288nn.   **sycophanta:** a 'swindler' in New Comedy; cf. Duckworth (1952) 261 for
the type.   **qui ... sit:** 57n.

507 opseruatote ⟨eum⟩ ... palpabitur: for the prolepsis see
54–5n.   **quam blande mulieri palpabitur** 'how smoothly
he'll charm the woman'; cf. *Mer.* 169 (likewise figurative) *hoc sis uide,
ut palpatur. nullust quando occepit blandior,* and *Poen.* 357 *exora, blandire,
expalpa* (where the young master Agorastocles enjoins his slave Mil-
phio to assist him in his amorous quest).   **mulieri:** her actual
status *vis-à-vis* Jupiter, though she believes she is his *uxor* (508).

508 ecastor te experior quanti facias uxorem tuam 'Oh,
I'm beginning to find out for myself how much you think of your
wife'; a fine piece of comic irony, as Mercury shortly (510–11) points
out, in the light of Jupiter's current and prior philandering.
ecastor: 182n.   **te experior ... facias:** 54–5n.

509 satin habes '*Aren't* you satisfied ...?' For the positive question suggesting the speaker's annoyance see 433n. It seems that
Jupiter, unlike Alcmena (513–14n.), is for now sated after the long
night of lovemaking.   **si feminarum nulla est quam aeque
diligam:** another stroke of irony (508n.) that the audience cannot
miss: the class of *feminae* includes only mortal women, and *quam aeque
diligam* is true for the moment, at least.   **diligam:** the use of *dili-
gere* here does not suggest a passion of any less intensity than *amare*
does (cf. *OLD diligo* 1). Such protestations of love are usually reserved
for the *meretrix* in New Comedy, but Jupiter in fact is an adulterer
only playing the role of husband here (cf. 515, 516, 517, 518–20,
523nn.)

510 edepol ne illa: 182n.   **illa** of course is Juno (cf. 508n.);
Mercury points to the sky. Cf. 182n.   **istis rebus te ... operam dare:** the common phrase *operam dare* ('to give one's atten-

tion', 'apply one's efforts') is frequently by itself employed as a euphemism for sex, e.g. *Trin.* 651 *in foro operam amicis da, ne in lecto amicae, ut solitus es.* Mercury's use of it here in combination with the further euphemism *istis rebus* is mock-genteel. Cf. Adams (1982) 157, 203.

511 faxim 'I'd guarantee that ...', a colloquial and archaic usage
(for the subjunctive see 461n.; for the folksy tone of *ego faxim* cf. *Mer.*
824–9).   **ted Amphitruonem esse malis quam Iouem:** cf.
Sosia's similar jest at 380 and 369n.   **Amphitruonem esse:**
a / B hiatus at the main break.   **malis:** subjunctive in noun
object clause after *faxim* (cf. 355n.).

512 experiri istuc mauellem me quam mi memorarier 'I
would prefer to get first-hand experience of that, rather than having
it told to me' (in response to 509); that she is thinking primarily of
sex is shown by 513–14. The contrast between direct experience
(*factum*) and mere word (*dictum*) is commonplace in the plays, e.g.
Capt. 429, *Men.* 334, *Mer.* 771, *Mil.* 633.   **mauellem:** the original
form without crasis (*mauolo* < **mag(i)s uolo*), to be replaced by the
analogical formation *mallem* in later writers (cf. 511 *malis*). In P. the
imperfect subjunctive in wishes can refer to the present (as here) or
past (Bennett 1 196). Cf. 575n.

513–14 prius abis ... nunc abis 'You're leaving before the
part of the couch where you lay warmed up. You arrived in the
middle of this past night, now you're going off' (cf. 532). P.'s Alcmena is an unabashed sensualist. The audience has repeatedly been
reminded of the lovers' activities inside, and that the night has been
lengthened specifically for their amours. In P.'s sex farce, not even
Alcmena's obviously forthcoming parturition is allowed to curb her
sexual appetite.

513 prius abis quam lectus ubi cubuisti concaluit locus:
the rhythm of the entire line is markedly light (*bb c D A B C dd aa B C
D aa B c D*; cf. 42n.); its farcical quality is also enhanced by the alliteration and assonance of *c*, *u*, and *l*. Cf. pp. 40–4.   **lectus ubi
cubuisti concaluit locus:** the warmth of a bed shared by lovers
is a *topos* of erotic poetry, e.g. *Anth. Pal.* 5.172 (where Meleager also
refers to the long night of Alkmene and Zeus); similarly, a cold bed
is cause for the lover's consternation, e.g. Prop. 4.7.6 *et quererer lecti
frigida regna mei.*   **lectus:** this form of the genitive (as in the fourth

declension) occurs here only.   **ubi cubuisti:** set *dd aa B C*; proce-
leusmatics are rare in trochaics (cf. 718 and Lindsay (1922) 103–5).

514 hoccin placet? 'You think this is all right, do you?' (cf. *OLD placeo* 4a). *hoccine* is composed of *hoc* and *-ne*, here with syncope of final *-e*.

515 accedam ... appellabo ... subparasitabor: a boister-ous tricolon with crescendo to announce to the audience that he will assume a new role. For the pronounced metatheatricality of Mer-cury's playing see pp. 24–7.   **subparasitabor:** the word is also found at 993 and *Mil.* 348. The prefix *sub-* intensifies the idea of fawning ingratiation in *parasitor* (cf. *Mil.* 106 *suppalparier*), but there is also a suggestion that Jupiter himself is a kind of 'parasite' who has wheedled his way into Alcmena's good graces (cf. 506–7), and that Mercury is only mirroring his father's actions on a subordinate level. For the latter usage cf. the impostor Pseudolus' characterization of himself as *Subbalio* (*Ps.* 607), and the designation of the saucy cook's assistant as *sublingulo* (*Ps.* 893).

For the figure of the Plautine parasite in general see Damon (1997) 37–79.

516–17 More obvious irony: no 'mortal man' could love 'his own wife' exactly as Jupiter does.

516 numquam edepol quemquam: for the colloquial colloca-tion (stressing the negative) cf. Mercury's aside at 248 (*numquam etiam quicquam...*).   **uxorem suam:** in the world of New Comedy, passionate love or lust for a spouse, as opposed to a prostitute, is ex-ceptional (cf. 517n.). But in this unusual play, P. even has the real Amphitryon match Jupiter's affection for Alcmena (655).

517 ecflictim amare 'to love to distraction/death' (*ecflictim* < *effligo*, 'to strike dead'), a cliché in Roman comedy (cf. Naev. 37 R = 37–8 W *nolo ego | hanc adeo efflictim amare*, Pompon. 42 R, Laber. 12 R), as evidenced by its use in prologues (*Cas.* 49) to describe the conventional relationship of *adulescens* and *meretrix*. With typically self-conscious theatricality, Mercury manipulates stock motifs of New Comedy in the service of this unconventional love affair (cf. 515, 516nn.).   **ecflictim deperit:** an even stronger colloquialism than *ecflictim amare*. Cf. *Mer.* 444 *ecflictim perit*, *Poen.* 96 and 1095. *deper-ire* by itself in this metaphorical sense is widespread (*OLD* 3). Mercury is ironically playing on his father's immortality (cf. 516 *mortalem*) here.

518–20 Jupiter's ire is provoked by Mercury's ironic hint (cf. 516–17n.) at his true identity. His anger is also consonant with the conventional rancour of the comic master (*iratus senex*; cf. Ter. *Hau.* 37), who easily becomes enraged at his slaves for intervening in his affairs, and often threatens physical violence (cf. the relations of the real master and slave at 551–632). Jupiter, like his co-conspirator Mercury, possesses a ready ability to assume stereotypical comic roles (cf. 515n.).

518 carnufex: 376n. The tendency to string together (cf. 519 *uerbero*) such terms of abuse is one index of the considerable stylistic differences between P. and Terence.   **non ego te noui?** 'I know you, don't I?' (for *non* = *nonne* see 433n.), referring to Mercury's true identity (i.e. 'I can spoil your fun too': cf. 518–20n.), or, perhaps, more generally, 'I know what you're like.' For this latter pregnant sense cf. *Mos.* 894, *Epid.* 153, and *OLD nosco* 10b.   **noui? abin:** *A / b* hiatus at the main break.   **abin e conspectu meo?** 'Get out of my sight.' The use of a question to express a vehement order is widespread in colloquial Latin (*LU* 68–9).

519 quid tibi hanc curatio est rem ... aut muttitio? 'What's this matter got to do with you, why the muttering?' The verbal substantive in *-io* (derived from a transitive verb) + accusative is virtually restricted to P., where it is found mostly in questions with *quid* (LHS II 34; cf. GL §330 N.3).

520 scipione: carried by old men in comedy (cf. *As.* 124, *Cas.* 1009), it can conveniently be used for beating (e.g. *Per.* 816, *Men.* 856). For Jupiter's stereotypical behaviour here see 518–20n.; for his costume and mask p. 37 and 1072n.   **ah noli:** *ah* can be used to express a wide variety of emotions in Latin (see *OLD a, ah*); here, as often, it indicates a strong objection. It is doubtful that the variation between *a* and *ah* in the MSS of P. reflects any real difference in pronunciation. The aspirated pronunciation was probably still current in P.'s time, but, as happened to *h* in other positions, was gradually lost by the classical period. Thereafter the pronunciation of *h* became a matter of dispute, and the variation in P. presumably reflects the general confusion at an early stage of transmission: cf. Allen (1978) 43–5. Thus, *ah* is printed in Alcmena's similar objection at 935. **muttito modo** 'just make a single sound' (Jupiter speaks with the *scipio* menacingly poised over Mercury); *mu*, after the Greek letter, in Latin represents the slightest human utterance (cf. English 'let out a peep'). Cf. Var. *L.* 7.101, Lucil. 426 M = 454 W *non laudare hominem quemquam neque mu facere umquam.*

521 nequiter paene expediuit prima parasitatio 'My first stab at playing the parasite was almost a total flop.' **nequiter:** 315n. **expediuit:** 5n. **parasitatio** 'parasitehood', probably coined here by P., with the formation being suggested by 519 *curatio ... muttitio.* The alliteration of *paene expediuit prima parasitatio* reflects Mercury's animation.

522 uerum quod tu dicis, mea uxor, non te mi irasci decet 'But as to what you're saying, my dear, you shouldn't be mad at me', referring to 512–14 (before Mercury's interruption). **quod tu dicis:** *OLD quod* 6.

523 clanculum: a colloquial diminutive of *clam.* **abii: a:** *A / B* hiatus. **a legione operam hanc subrupui tibi** 'I have snatched this service from the troops for you...' Construing *a legione* with *abii* (as Leo and Ernout) destroys this vivid phrase and masks the antithesis between *militia* and *amor* (504–5n.). **operam:** see 510n. for the sexual connotations.

524 rem ut gessissem publicam: cf. Sosia's full-blown version at 196. Jupiter, in contrast to Amphitryon (195n.), delivered this news himself.

525 ea tibi omnia enarraui: this fact prepares the way for the extreme confusion at 744ff.

525–6 amarem ... facerem 'if I did not love you the most, I would not have done this', a 'mixed' unreal condition (the interchangeability of imperfect and pluperfect subjunctive in such conditions persists in classical Latin, despite the evolution of general 'rules').

526 facitne ut dixi? 'Isn't he doing just what I said he would?' Mercury refers back to his similarly cynical aside at 507. For *-ne* here see 433n. **timidam palpo percutit:** Casson's rendering, 'A little buttering up, and he has the poor girl eating out of his hand', captures the spirit of the aside. The figurative phrase *palpo percutere,* lit., 'to strike with the palm of the hand' (cf. *Mer.* 153), is a kind of oxymoron, as *percutere* suggests a violent blow or assault (Corbett

(1964) 60). The sense 'strike an emotional chord' (cf. *OLD percutio* 8a) may also be felt. Cf. Caecilius 193–4 R = 183–4 W *tum inter laudandum hunc timidum tremulis palpebris | percutere nictu; hic gaudere et mirarier.* **timidam** she is more 'apprehensive' about her husband's affections than 'fearful'.

527 persentiscat: an archaic and colloquial word resurrected by Lucretius at 3.249 (with Kenney's (1971) n. *ad loc.* and at 179–80). **illuc:** i.e. to where the army is encamped, the precise location of which is unimportant for purposes of the play (cf. 188n.).

528 ne me uxorem praeuertisse dicant prae re publica 'so they [= the army] don't say that I put my wife in front of an affair of state'; for the 'un-Romanness' of such a preference cf. 504–5, 523nn.

529 lacrimantem ex abitu concinnas tu tuam uxorem 'You make your own wife weepy by your departure.' There is a suggestion of maudlin sententiousness in Alcmena's objectification of herself.   **lacrimantem:** cf. Andromache's tears in the vastly different departure scene in Homer (*Il.* 6.405, 484).   **concinnas:** *concinnare* in colloquial Latin can be used like *facere* or *reddere* with two accusatives in the sense 'render', 'make'.

529–30 tace, | ne corrumpe oculos, redibo actutum 'Hush now, don't spoil your eyes, I'll be back soon.' Similarly condescending admonitions are made by the lecherous *senex* Lysimachus to the unwilling courtesan he has purchased for his friend at *Mer.* 501 and by the river Anio to Ilia at Ov. *Am.* 3.6.57 as he prepares to rape her.

530 ne corrumpe: 87n.   **redibo actutum:** highly ironic, in that it is the real Amphitryon who will return shortly.   **id 'actutum' diu est:** cf. the similarly melodramatic complaint of the prostitute Philamatium to the lovesick *adulescens* Philolaches as the latter leaves her, *Mos.* 338 *iam reuertar :: diu est 'iam' id mihi.*

531 non ego te hic lubens relinquo neque abeo abs te: Jupiter's claim of being reluctant to leave calls to mind Aeneas' parting words to Dido (Virg. *A.* 4.360–1, 6.460). Here of course Jupiter is neither a warrior nor founder of a new civilization, but much more like an elegiac *miles amoris*, who in this case is comically trying to escape his sexually insatiable mistress.   **sentio** 'I can see that' (extremely sarcastic).

532 qua nocte ... eadem: *idem* etc. properly means, as here, 'that very' (Lindsay 49).   **nocte ad me uenisti:** the use of *uerbs* of coming and going to refer euphemistically to sexual activity is widespread in all periods of Latin (Adams (1982) 175–6). *uenire* is frequently used of men visiting prostitutes; cf. Catul. 32.1–3 *amabo, mea dulcis Ipsithilla | … | iube ad te ueniam meridiatum,* Ter. *Hec.* 67–9. In P. a customer at a brothel can be referred to as an *aduentor* (cf. *Truc.* 616).   **cur me tenes?:** either figurative ('detain') or a literal stage direction.

533 tempus ⟨est⟩ 'it's high time for me to go' (*OLD tempus* 8). **exire ex urbe:** i.e. he will go back toward the harbour, which, as the scenic antithesis of the city, need not be explicitly designated. **prius quam lucescat:** the subjunctive is used after *ante-* and *priusquam* in early Latin when the main clause expresses an order or wish (LHS II 600).

534–5 Jupiter gives his account (cf. 261, 415, 419) of the bowl; in the play this token of recognition only causes further confusion (cf. 760ff.).

534 tibi: resumed after the three subordinate clauses in 534–5 (as typically in colloquial language: *LU* 96–7).   **dono:** dative of purpose, common in P. and Terence (Bennett II 171–7), as in all periods.   **illi** 'there' (= *illic*), i.e. on the battlefield.   **uirtutem:** 75, 260nn.

535 qui potitauit: 261n.   **ego mea occidi manu:** Jupiter again plays the *miles gloriosus*: cf. 186–7, 193, 504–5, 534–5nn. The disjunction *mea … manu* lends special emphasis to the pronoun.

536 tibi: 534n.   **condono** 'I present', more ceremonious than the simple verb in this sense; cf. 534–5n.

536–7 facis ut alias res soles. | ecastor condignum donum, qualest qui donum dedit: a good example of P.'s preference for delineating character in broad strokes. Here the immediacy with which Alcmena casts aside her reservations and tearful protestations when presented with a valuable and visually impressive gift evokes the ethos of the conventionally mercantile comic courtesan: cf. Perelli (1983) 387 and 544n.

537 ecastor: 182n.   **condignum donum:** most likely the accusative of exclamation (closely with *ecastor*), a construction with colloquial origins (Lindsay 29–30, LHS II 48–9; cf. GL §343). **qualest** = *qualis est* (cf. 443 *consimilest*); 'my god, a worthy gift –

worthy as he who gave it'. *condignum* functions like the correlative (*talis*) to *qualest* here.

538 immo sic: condignum donum, qualest cui dono da-tumst 'No, no, it's as worthy as its recipient.' As Jupiter's parasite (515n.), Mercury takes it upon himself to flatter his patron's beloved. As at 515–20, his efforts are met with rancour from Jupiter, which Alcmena would again understand in conventional terms (518–20n.). There is a further irony in that *condignus* is often used of what a person 'deserves' (in a negative sense) and so Mercury is hinting that the stolen *patera* is the perfect gift for the stolen wife.

539 pergin autem? 'So, you're at it again?' For *autem* in indignant questions see *OLD* 6. **furcifer:** 285n. **perdere:** for the wide range of verbs of killing *et sim.* used in the lively colloquial exchanges of Roman comedy see Corbett (1964) 52–69.

540 noli ... irasci: the normal classical usage (cf. 87n.). **amabo** 'please'; a colloquial abreviation of a formula originally of the type (e.g.) 'If you do what I want, I will love you.' In early Latin it is used with questions and imperatives, in 84 out of 91 instances in P. (always so in Terence) by women (reflecting their relative social status: cf. MacCary and Willcock (1976) *ad Cas.* 917–18). Later it, or *amabo te*, is used more freely by men, e.g. Cic. *Att.* 2.2.1, Catul. 32.1, Mart. 8.76.1.

541 ex amore hic admodum quam saeuos est 'How very savage he is because of his passion.' Mercury sarcastically invokes conventional notions of love as a kind of cruel madness or sickness; cf. *Bac.* fr. 14 *Cupidon tecum saeuust anne Amor?* and Enn. *Med. ex.* 216 Jocelyn *Medea animo aegro amore saevo saucia*. Cf. the related *topos* on the difficulty of serving a smitten master, e.g. *Poen.* 820 *seruire amanti miseria est, praesertim qui quod amat caret*. **admodum quam:** cf. *nimis quam*, *perquam*, and *sane quam*.

542 numquid uis? 'Anything else?' (*sc. aliud*), 'Is that all?' *numquid uis* is 'a polite formula of departure whereby one might gracefully indicate a desire to terminate a conversation and withdraw' (Hough (1945) 282; cf. Horace's attempt to take leave of a pest at *S.* 1.9.6). Jupiter clearly wants to depart (cf. 531n.), and expects a brief and equally formulaic answer such as *uale, ut ualeas, vel sim.* But P. often has a character humorously pretend to understand the formula literally, as Alcmena here. The melodramatic expostulation of love by the sexually insatiable and pregnant *uxor usuraria* will only further annoy Jupiter, who, without acknowledging her request, repeats the formula (544). Mercury is similarly anxious to leave (543 *eamus, Amphitruo*).   **ut quom absim me ames, me tuam te absenti tamen** 'That, when I am not with you, you love me, I who am still yours though you are away.' P. turns an amatory commonplace (cf. Ter. *Eun.* 191–6) to humorous effect in this context by having the *matrona* profess her undying love for someone with whom she unknowingly commits adultery. The fact that this is uttered by a male actor in exaggerated maternity garb will evoke further belly laughs, as will any physical gestures of affection 'she' might make here.   **me ... me tuam te:** cf. 134n. and for the anaphora of the pronoun in the comic *Liebessprache, Mil.* 1386 *te uolt, te quaerit, teque expectans expetit*.   **tamen:** the emphatic final position is not unusual in P.'s colloquial Latin (cf. Duckworth (1940) on *Epid.* 426); syntactically it goes with *tuam* and the participle (*absenti*) represents a concessive clause, as often in later poetry (cf. Clausen (1994) on Virg. *Ecl.* 1.27).

543 eamus, Amphitruo; lucescit hoc iam: *hoc* (i.e. 'the sky', 'the day') is accompanied by a gesture. The transition to a scene of daylight in the open-air theatre is effected through mere words: cf. 533 *tempus est, lucescat*, and the formal dismissal of the night to follow (546–50).   **eamus:** set *B c* (with synizesis).   **lucescit:** cf. the impersonal use in 533. The verb is chiefly archaic.   **abi prae, Sosia** 'Go on ahead, Sosia' (Mercury exits by the harbour wing), a comic formula for dismissing a subordinate (cf. *Cist.* 773, *Ps.* 170, Ter. *Eun.* 499).

544 iam 'soon' (cf. 345, 969).   **numquid uis?:** Jupiter delivers the formula of dismissal with increasing irritation (542n.).   **etiam** 'Yes', a colloquialism (*OLD* 5). Cf. 362n.   **ut actutum aduenias:** she again gives a literal response to Jupiter's *numquid uis?* (542n.); the gift of the bowl has achieved its intended effect (536–7n.) and *actutum* is now satisfactory (cf. 530n.) to Alcmena.   **licet** 'All right', 'OK', a colloquial form of reply (*OLD* 2).

545 prius tua opinione hic adero: bonum animum habe: a metrically complicated line as it stands: the penult of *prius* is apparently long, *tua* is a monosyllable (synizesis), there are two hiatuses (*tua opinione* is *D / a* and *bonum animum* is *a / b*), and the eleventh

element (*bo-*) is *d +* (*locus Jacobsohnianus*). Scan *B C D a B c D A /
bb C d+ a bb c D*.   **prius tua opinione hic adero** 'I'll be here
sooner than you expect', ironically pointed at the imminent arrival
of the real Amphitryon.   **bonum animum habe** 'cheer up', like
1131 *bono animo es* (cf. 671), 'a bare, colourless formula of reassurance'
(Ogilvie (1965) on Livy 1.41.5). This colloquialism is not found in
Terence.

546–50 After Alcmena's exit into the stage-house (545), Jupiter
alone on stage dismisses the night and effects the change to a day-
time setting (cf. 543n.). Characters in tragedy often convey their
travails to the night or the *aether* above (e.g. E. *El.* 54ff., Enn. *Hec.* 171
Jocelyn; cf. *Mer.* 3–5), but the tone and situation are far different
here. The night of Heracles' conception was usually tripled in myth,
a motif reflecting the uniquely superhuman capabilities of the hero;
cf. Diod. 4.9.2, Apollod. *Biblio.* 2.4.8, Sen. *Ag.* 808–28. In P. this
magical belief has been comically rationalized, with the night instead being prolonged to maximize Jupiter's sexual pleasure (cf. 112–
14). With the deft power of a sorcerer, Jupiter brings this traditional
fantasy of lovers (cf. Ovid *Am.* 1.13.40 *'lente currite, noctis equi'* and
Segal (1987) 179) to an end so that the comedy of errors may
continue.

546 nunc te ... mitto ut ⟨con⟩cedas die 'Now I dismiss you,
so that you may make way for day.' For the conventional poetic
image cf. Virg. *A.* 10.215 *iamque dies caelo concesserat.*   **Nox:** Night
figures prominently in Greek cosmogonies; as a personified goddess
she regularly drives a chariot, and may herself have wings; cf. Aesch.
Cho. 660–2, where she rides forth to supplant the day, and thereby
change the setting of the play to night-time.   **die:** dative (276n.).

547 mortalis inlucescat: the accusative is governed by the prefix of the verb (cf. Lindsay 28), whose understood subject is *dies. mortalis* (for *homines*) affects a tone of high poetry, as does the verb (cf.
Virg. *G.* 2.337).

548–9 'And, Night, I'll make the day shorter by the amount you
were prolonged last night.'

548 atque: *atque* here, as often in a series, marks an intensification of the main thought (KS II 21).   **Nox:** from a formal dramaturgical standpoint, the invocation of *Nox* at the close of Jupiter's
monologue here is like that of *Fides* in Euclio's exit at *Aul.* 580–6.

hac proxuma 'last night' (ablative of time rather than comparison, whose use is restricted to a few formal types in early Latin: cf. LHS II 108 and Löfstedt I (1956) 312).

549 tanto breuior: according to the mythic tradition (cf. 546–50n.), the day would have to be reduced by 2/3 to compensate for the tripling of the night.   **dies:** *bb* (iambic shortening).   **fiat faciam:** for the jingle cf. the less emphatically positioned *faciam ... fit* in 54–5, with 56n.).   **aeque disparet** 'differ in like proportion' (*OLD disparo* 2b).

551–632 (Scene 4) Sosia has reported the strange events that happened in front of the house to his master, and the two perform a lively duet as they proceed toward the house. They enter from the harbour wing, accompanied by a train of mute baggage-carriers (cf. 854) attending the returning general. They are apparently supposed to be somewhere near the harbour, but their precise location is unimportant in P.'s stylized theatre (pp. 19–21). They are simply imagined to be on a street, designated as 'here' (which is opposed to being 'at home': 561–2n., cf. 593), though there is some confusion, perhaps intentional (559, 577nn.).

Amphitryon immediately establishes himself as the irascible comic master (cf. 518–20n.) who lords it over his somewhat saucy slave, and also begins to assume the function of a 'blocking character', i.e. the humourless and inflexible figure who resists the prevailing climate of misrule, and is destined to be defeated by the comic hero(es). The blustery entrance of the angry *paterfamilias* is a stock scene of Roman comedy. Much of the humour in Sosia's treatment here turns on the manipulation of comic stereotypes (p. 31).

In the overall structure of the play, the scene corresponds to frs. 11–14, where Sosia must again bear his master's indignation. There are also cross-references to the lengthy opening scene, where the slave likewise was accused of prevaricating when he was telling the truth (cf. 558, 562nn.).   METRE: with the exception of 574, the duet is in bacchiac and trochaic measures (p. 70).

551–73	bacchiac tetrameters	(song until 586)
574	anapaestic dimeter catalectic	
575–8	trochaic dimeters	
578a	trochaic monometer	

579	trochaic dimeter catalectic	
580-3	trochaic dimeters	
584	trochaic dimeter catalectic	
584a-85a	trochaic dimeters	
585b	trochaic dimeter catalectic	
586-632	trochaic septenarii	(recitative)

551-73 The bacchiacs constitute a sense-unit in which Amphitryon vigorously denies Sosia's claims on the grounds that they defy the logic of everyday experience. The master wrongly concludes that his slave must be scheming against him (565, 571; cf. 470-1n.). Word-end most commonly occurs at the fifth element of the bacchiac tetrameter (often at change of speaker), in which case the element immediately preceding must be a single short (so too when word-end falls at the eleventh element); cf. Questa (1967) 215-17, 224-6. Cf. also n. on 574-85b.

551 secundum. :: sequor, subsequor: Sosia playfully chooses verbs that are cognate with the adverb. For the self-correction ('I'm following you, I'm right on your heels') see 43n. The entire *canticum* is marked off by ring-composition: cf. 585a *sequere* and 1-16n. **subsequor te:** *te* adheres closely with the verb, and so the line strictly does not end with a monosyllable. Cf. 308n.

552 scelestissumum: cf. 557n.   **nam quamobrem?** 'Come now, why?' (cf. *OLD nam* 7).

553-4 For Amphitryon's inflexibility see pp. 30-1; in a play where the miraculous and mysterious prevail, he easily becomes the 'butt of the joke'. For the polar expression (7n.) cf. *Mil.* 775-6 *erus meus ita magnus moechus mulierum est, ut neminem | fuisse aeque neque futurum credo.*

554-5 eccere, iam tuatim | facis 'Hah! Now you're acting in your usual manner.'   **eccere:** here with long ultima. **tuatim:** < *tuus* + adverbial suffix (cf. *paullatim*, etc.).   **facis:** for the long *-i-* here see Questa (1967) 9 n. 1 and Lindsay (1922) 183-4.

555 tuis: Sosia has himself and his fellow slaves in mind, but Amphitryon's lack of trust will shortly extend to Alcmena as well. *tuis* is disyllabic here.

556 quid est? quo modo? 'What? How can it be?' Both interrogatives express extreme indignation (cf. 596, 735, 737, 1023, all spoken by Amphitryon, and Enk (repr. 1979) *ad Mer.* 758 and 813).

quidem hercle 'By God indeed ...' (cf. 397, 736).   **ego tibi istam:** very strong; *iste* can have a contemptuous force already in archaic Latin.

557 scelus 'jailbird', much stronger than the cognate adjective *scelestus* (cf. 552, 561) when applied to a person (*LU* 87).   **linguam abscidam:** a common threat in Latin; cf. *Aul.* 189, 250, *Mil.* 318, Catul. 108.4, Cic. *Clu.* 187.   **tuos sum** 'I'm your property' (a reminder of how natural the condition of slavery was in this culture); the saucy remark is repeated at 564. *tuos* is monosyllabic here (synizesis), but disyllabic in 564.

558 proinde ut commodumst et lubet quidque facias 'So you may do whatever serves your interest and suits your fancy' (cf. 396). As the play progresses, Amphitryon is gradually stripped of the prerogatives of the master ascribed to him by Sosia here, and at the height of his confusion imagines himself to be subject to the will of all *mortales* (with the usual irony), who mock him *ut lubet* (1047). Ultimate power in *Am.* rests with the gods and their ability to play their theatrical roles, *quando lubet* (cf. 123, 864). Cf. 123n.

559 quin loquar haec uti facta sunt hic 'from saying how these things happened here' or 'from saying right here how ...' (?); if the former, P. demonstrates his typical disregard for verisimilitude by having Sosia point (*hic*) to the stage-house behind them (cf. 551–632n. and p. 29 n. 95).

561–2 audes mihi praedicare id, | domi te esse nunc, qui hic ades?: cf. 559n.

562 uera dico: cf. 395, where Sosia used the same words to assert the uniqueness of his identity. Here he tries to convince Amphitryon of his duality. As appearances and realities are confuted in the play, truth becomes an increasingly elusive concept.

563–4 malum quod tibi di dabunt, atque ego hodie | dabo 'For this the gods will punish you, as I also will today.' The conventional imprecation is ironic: one god already has beaten Sosia, and an even greater *malum* lies in store for Amphitryon.   **malum:** 26–7n.   **quod:** lit., 'as to which' (accusative of respect; it refers to the idea of Sosia 'telling the truth' (562)).

564 istuc tibist in manu, nam tuos sum 'That's within your power, since I'm your property' Cf. 557, 558nn.

565–8: cf. 553–4n.

565 uerbero: 180n.   **audes erum ludificari:** the perennial pursuit of the Plautine slave (e.g. *Bac.* 642, *Epid.* 671, *Mil.* 906), one of whose stock attributes is *audacia*.

566–7 quod … fieri: *quod* is direct object of *uidit*, but subject of the parallel *potest*. For such changes of subject, natural in colloquial Latin, see Lindsay 8–9.

566 nemo umquam homo antehac 'absolutely no one ever before this time'. For the colloquial *abundantia* cf. *Cas.* 294 *homini nato nemini* and *LU* 92.   **antehac:** this suffers internal elision (in the penult) in P. and scans as a spondee (Lindsay (1922) 149).

567 fieri: the antepenult is long here; cf. Lindsay (1922) 200.

568 ut: the delayed position (answering 566 *id*) is not unusual in P.

569–70 Iuppiter te | perdat: cf. 563n. Jupiter's 'curse' will redound more directly upon himself than Sosia (cf. 1051n.).

570 tua ex re: apparently 'of relevance to you' rather than the usual meaning 'in your interest' (cf. *OLD res* 13).

571 rogasne, improbe, etiam qui ludos facis me? 'You dare ask me that, scoundrel, and mock me in the same breath?' *ludos facere* = *ludificari*; cf. 565n.

572 merito maledicas mihi, si non id ita factum est 'You'd have every right to call me names if this did not happen just so' (i.e. 'as I say it happened'). *non*, found only in J (cf. p. 76), preserves the tetrameter and the sense.

573 resque uti facta dico: with *facta* understand *est* or *sit* (cf. 17–18n.).

574–85b In this (chiefly) trochaic section, the master levels new and untrue charges against the slave: Sosia must either be drunk (574–5) or mad (581). Amphitryon again (cf. 551–73n.) concludes that the slave is deluding him (585a).

574 homo hic ebrius est, ut opinor: a new and reasonable (given Sosia's proclivities: 186–261n.) explanation is offered to account for the strange story; for the theme of intoxication see p. 31.

575 utinam ita essem: either 'I wish I had been drunk' (i.e. when encountering his double) or (better?) 'I wish I were drunk right now.' Cf. 512n.   **optas quae facta** 'You're wishing for what's already been done' (sc. *sunt* with *facta*).   **tu istic:** 366n.

576 quid hoc sit hominis 'What sort of person can this be?', extremely contemptuous (cf. 769, where Amphitryon refers to Alcmena); elsewhere in P. only at *Poen.* 92, where the pimp Lycus' very humanity is called into question. As Sedgwick suggests, the genitive is probably conditioned by an assumed answer such as *monstrum hominis, flagitium hominis*, etc.   **decies dixi** 'I've told you ten times' (cf. 725). The adverb by convention can denote frequency (cf. *OLD decie(n)s* 1b).

577 domi ego sum ... apud te adsum: a paradox brought about by the strange circumstances, but perhaps also a metatheatrical joke that would be visually immediate to an audience; while he is presumed to be with Amphitryon somewhere near the harbour, the stage-house stands immediately behind him. Cf. 551–632, 559nn. **inquam, ecquid:** *a / B* hiatus.

580 apage: 310n.   **quid est negoti?** 'What's the matter?' (*OLD negotium* 11b); *quid est* is set *bb* (with iambic shortening).

581 pestis te tenet: another possible explanation for Sosia's irrational account (cf. 574n.): he has contracted plague and his mental faculties are affected (cf. note on 584a). For the theme of (in)sanity see p. 31.   **tenet:** pyrrhic (iambic shortening).

583 recte 'thoroughly' (*OLD* 8).

583–4 at te ego faciam | hodie proinde ac meritus es 'Oh I'll treat you just as you deserve' (cf. *OLD facio* 28c).

584a miser 'sick' (in a medical sense); in response to Sosia's contention that he is 582 *saluos* ('healthy').

584b saluos domum si rediero 'once I've returned home safe', continuing the jejune play on *saluos* in 582; blocking characters (551–632n.) are typically less verbally dexterous than slaves, parasites, *et sim.* in P.

584b–85a iam | sequere sis 'now I'd kindly appreciate your following me' (continuing the alliteration with 584b *saluos*). Cf. 286n.

585a erum qui ludificas: cf. 565n. *erum* is pyrrhic here (iambic shortening).

585b dictis delirantibus: cf. 581n.

586–632 The presumed transition between sung and recitative trochaics is abrupt, taking place in mid-sentence. If P. is adapting a Greek comedy, then the preceding *canticum*, as a purely Plautine invention, most likely anticipates the material P. found in the tetrameters of his source; cf. (e.g.) 553–4 and 587–8.

586 quoniam erus quod imperauit neglexisti persequi:
Amphitryon again can only interpret the situation in the most conventional terms (551–632, 565nn.).   **persequi** 'carry out', the same sense as 262 *exsequi*.

587 nunc uenis etiam ultro inrisum dominum 'on top of everything else now you even come to mock your master'. **inrisum:** supine (cf. 20n.).

588 neque fando umquam accepit quisquam 'and what no person ever has heard told' (*fando*: lit., 'in speaking', 'hearsay'), an exaggeration, as stories such as Sosia's would be familiar from myths and folktales.   **profers:** with a legalistic tone (*OLD* 5c). **carnufex:** 376n.

589 tergum: 446n.   **faxo:** 355n.   **expetant** 'come home to' (cf. 495).   **mendacia:** cf. 198, 562nn.

590–1 The 'good slave' is a topic for moralizing reflection in P. (e.g. *Men.* 966ff., *Ps.* 1103–12; cf. Chrysalus' variations at *Bac.* 648–60), but such passages are usually laced with humorous irony (Hunter (1985) 145–7). Sosia has already demonstrated that he is a slacker and a liar (153–74n.). He affects a dignified tone, as is regular in such contexts; cf. *si id ui uerum uincitur* and the exalted *figura etymologica, miserruma ... miseria.* The deeper irony is that he actually is telling the truth (562n.). Cf. 958–61n.

590 miserruma ... miseria: the repetition of cognate noun and adjective is common in P.; cf. Wills (1996) 240.   **istaec** 'caused by you'.

592–3: cf. 553–4n.

592 malum: 403n.   **mecum argumentis puta** 'think it through with me, using the evidence'. For the legalistic approach cf. 588n.

593 hic ... domi: cf. 559, 577nn. Cf. 594 *sum profecto et hic et illic.*

594 hoc cuiuis mirari licet 'Have anyone you want wonder at it', i.e. 'I don't care who...'

595 neque tibi istuc mirum ⟨mirum⟩ magis uidetur quam mihi 'and this miracle appears no more miraculous to you than it does to me'; if Spengel's addition (the line as transmitted is two elements short) is correct, another clever instance of linguistic gemination (pp. 15–17).

596 quo modo: 556n.

597–8 'And, I swear to God, at first I didn't believe myself, *me Sosia*, until that Sosia, I mean *myself*, caused me to believe him.' Sosia here is unwilling to surrender his name and identity (cf. 455–62n.), and normal linguistic convention fails him (p. 17).

597 ita me di ament: for the irony cf. 563n. The only divine 'love' bestowed in the play is that upon Alcmena by Jupiter in a very different sense from what is intended in this colloquial oath.

599–600: cf. 410–32.

599 dum apud hostis sedimus 'while we were encamped in the midst of the enemy' (for the technical sense of the verb see *OLD* 4a).   **dum apud:** *b* / *b* (prosodic hiatus).

600 tum formam una abstulit cum nomine: cf. 441–62.

601 neque lac lactis magis est simile quam ille ego similest mei: lit., 'and milk is no more like milk than that other "I" is like me' (cf. English 'two peas in a pod'). Latin has similar proverbs with *aqua*, e.g. *Men.* 1089–90 *neque aqua aquae nec lacte est lactis, crede mi, | usquam similius, | quam hic tui est, tuque huius autem*, and *ouum* (Quint. *Inst.* 5.11.30): Otto (1890) 183. For Sosia's confusion cf. 597–8n.

603 quid igitur?: 62n.   **prius multo ante aedis stabam quam illo adueneram** 'I was standing in front of the palace long before I had arrived there'; language and logic continue to be undermined (cf. 597–8n.).   **illo:** 197n.

604 malum: 403n.

605 huic homini nescioquid est mali mala obiectum manu: lit., 'Some evil has been cast upon this fellow by an evil hand.' Amphitryon offers yet another theory to account for Sosia's tale: black magic. According to popular belief, the mere touch of the practitioner's *mala manus* can cause death (cf. Petr. 63.7). Cf. 782, 830, 1043

606 fateor, nam sum obtusus pugnis pessume 'I second that, since the pounding I took at his hand was totally evil.' Sosia jokingly corrects Amphitryon's claim (605): Mercury had 'touched' him *pessumis manibus* (= *pugnis*).

607 egomet memet, qui nunc sum domi 'I myself beat myself, the "I" who is at home now' (cf. 597–8n.).

610 mihi quidem uno te plus etiam est quam uolo 'Yes indeed, I've actually got one more of you than I want.'   **mihi:** dative of possession.   **uno te:** ablative of degree of difference.

613 faciam 'I'll guarantee you . . .'

614 Davo prognatum patre: Sosia bombastically bestows his lineage on his double (365n.).   **eodem:** with synizesis.

615 quid opust uerbis?: 445n.   **geminus Sosia hic factust tibi** 'You've got a cloned Sosia here' (cf. 787n.).   **hic:** 559, 577nn.

616 nimia memoras mira: the marked alliteration and assonance of *m* suggests that Amphitryon is momentarily intrigued, but he quickly returns (*sed uidistin uxorem meam?*) to his aggressive style of inquiry and dismissal. Whereas Mercury had interrogated Sosia (347–81n.) about his own identity, Amphitryon will now grill him about his double.   **sed uidistin uxorem meam?:** with mention of Alcmena, P. begins to effect a transition to the next scene.

617 quin 'Why . . .' (i.e. 'How could I when. . .').   **licitum est:** in comedy this is preferred to the perfect active.

618 istic: with iambic shortening in the penult.

619 quotiens dicendum est tibi?: the same idiom as English 'How many times do I have to tell you?'

620 sed quid ais?: cf. 364n.   **ais:** monosyllabic.   **num obdormiuisti dudum?** 'You weren't asleep just a while ago, were you?'   **nusquam gentium:** lit., 'Nowhere in the world.' English expresses this idea temporally ('never in a million years') rather than spatially. Cf. 336n.

621 ibi forte istum si uidisses quendam in somnis Sosiam 'Hmm [I'm wondering] if by chance there in your dreams you had seen some sort of "Sosia" . . . ?' (virtual *oratio obliqua*, as Amphitryon is thinking aloud).   **in somnis:** lit., 'in sleep', often of dreams (cf. *OLD* 1c).

622 non soleo ego somniculose eri imperia persequi: Sosia again sententiously assumes the tone of the 'good slave' (590–1n.).   **eri imperi:** a suspect *B* / *C* hiatus (*eri mei* has been proposed).

623–4 Sosia makes his point most emphatically through the repetition of the participle of *uigilo* (five times) and the additional alliteration with *uidi . . . uideo*. For polyptoton of the participle (an Ovidian mannerism) in general see Wills (1996) 231.

623 uigilans: Alcmena likewise will have to insist (698, 726) that she has not dreamt the events of the last night. Cf. 620n. **fabulor:** 201n.

624 uigilantem ille me iam dudum uigilans pugnis contudit 'I was wide awake when that fellow on his watch pounded me just now'; the joke's interlocking word order neatly reflects the notions of conflict (*ille me*) and doubling (*uigilantem ... uigilans*).

625 quis homo?: for the irony cf. 180–4n.   **ego ille:** 597–8n.
quaeso, nonne intellegis? 'Please tell me, you do get it, don't you?'

626 qui, malum, intellegere quisquam potis est? 'How the hell can anyone get it?'   **malum:** 403n.   **ita nugas blatis** 'you babble such nonsense' (*blatio* is onomatopoeic; cf. English 'blah, blah, blah ...').

628 sequere hac igitur me: this clearly indicates that they will continue on toward the house. They could exit via the city wing (i.e. to get home, they must first proceed from the harbour toward the city), but as Alcmena never announces their entrance but simply notices them (660), it is probable that they remain on stage during her monody (633–54). As she sings, they may pantomime their journey.
sequere: 551n.   **mi istuc primum exquisito est opus** 'I must have this matter investigated immediately', virtually repeated by Amphitryon at 790. Cf. 169n.

[629–31] Lines 629–32 have long been suspected of interpolation, and are bracketed by Leo and Ernout. Amphitryon has just ordered (628) Sosia to proceed with him toward the house, but in 629 suddenly tells him to fetch baggage from the harbour. And if Sosia had been drinking this past night (631), we would have expected to be apprised of this at his entrance (cf. his denial at 575ff.). Line 632, however, can stand after 628 (see n. *ad loc.*). Cf. Mariotti (1959).

[629] uide ... efferantur: *uide* in the sense 'see to it' is usually with *ut* or *ne* in P. (this construction elsewhere only at *As.* 755, *Poen.* 578).

[630] et memor sum et diligens: cf. 590–1n.

[631] The image is typically Plautine. Cf. *Pers.* 170 (the source of the interpolation?) *quamquam ego uinum bibo, at mandata non consueui simul bibere una.*

632 utinam di faxint infecta dicta re eueniant tua: lit., 'May the gods see to it that your claims in fact turn out to be false' (Amphitryon refers to Sosia's assertions throughout the entire scene). For the irony – i.e. because of the gods' actions, Sosia's bizarre allegations are indeed true – cf. 563n.   **faxint:** 355n.

633–860 (Scene 5) In the overall structure of the play, this scene finds its 'double' in the almost entirely lost scene 12 (frs. 7–10). As Oniga notes (p. 213), there are also correspondences with the bipartite opening scene, where an opening song similarly was followed by a long scene in recitative septenarii.   METRE: the *canticum* consists of bacchiacs and a few cola reiziana (pp. 70–1). The colometry here generally follows that of Leo and Lindsay; for an alternative organization of these verses see Questa (1984) 293–302.

633	six bacchiacs	(song up to 654)
634	four bacchiacs + colon reizianum	
635–7	six bacchiacs	
638	six bacchiacs with catalexis	
639	four bacchiacs + colon reizianum	
640	six bacchiacs	
641	colon reizianum + four bacchiacs	
641a	bacchiac dimeter catalectic	
642	six bacchiacs	
643	bacchiac dimeter catalectic	
644	bacchiac trimeter	
645	bacchiac tetrameter	
646	colon reizianum + four bacchiacs	
647	bacchiac tetrameter	
647a	colon reizianum	
648	bacchiac trimeter catalectic	
649	bacchiac tetrameter	
650	four bacchiacs + colon reizianum	
651	bacchiac dimeter	
652	bacchiac tetrameter	
653	colon reizianum	
654–860	trochaic septenarii	(recitative)

633–53 The pregnant *matrona* returns to deliver what has become, perhaps for the wrong reasons, one of the most famous songs in P.; for the view that this monody is not inconsistent with the farcical presentation of Alcmena (cf. esp. 633–41) in her first scene see pp. 37–44 and the notes below. The genuine Amphitryon and Sosia are imagined to be fast approaching the house as Alcmena sings, whether frozen on the stage or in animated pantomime (628n.). Sosia, the audience knows, has just informed his master of his failed mission, and Amphitryon is all the more eager to win acclaim in his wife's eyes (cf. 654–7). Viewed within this framework, Alcmena's closing encomium (642–52) of *uirtus*, far from being a spontaneous expression of patriotism, is designed to underscore the comic confusion in the scene that follows. Music and delivery would be essential in establishing tone and nuance throughout, and interpretation is greatly impeded here by our ignorance of these; E. J. Kenney compares Fiordiligi's first aria, '*Come scoglio*', in Mozart's *Così fan tutte*, where the musical syntax undermines any straightforward reception of her moral assertions (see further Ford (1991) 157–64). No less significant is the fact that these lines are delivered by a male actor, who, as he is costumed, is a grotesque parody of female fecundity.

The unifying theme of the entire song is the notion of *satietas*: see notes on 633, 637–9, 647a. Cf. 499–550, 513–14nn.

633–41 Along with 641a–53 (see n. *ad loc.*), one of the song's two major thought units, each of which in turn is made up of two distinct but thematically related sub-sections. Here Alcmena's general reflections on pleasure (633–6) are followed closely by consideration of her own experience in the light of these (637–41); each section is composed primarily in long bacchiac measures with cola reiziana mixed in.

633–4 'Really, in life and living, isn't the matter of pleasure slight in comparison with what is displeasing?' This traditional philosophical commonplace (cf. Pl. *Phd.* 60b) should immediately sound an incongruous note coming from Alcmena; that the brevity of her sexual relations with Jupiter during the long night is foremost in her mind will shortly be made explicit (637–41). For the mock-philosophical tone here cf. the similar musings of the absurdly melodramatic Charinus, *Mer.* 145–6 *dic mihi, an boni quid usquamst, quod quisquam uti possiet* | *sine malo omni*, to which his saucy slave replies, *nescio ego istaec: philosophari numquam didici neque scio*; Plautine comedy, with its popular perspective, has little tolerance for philosophizing. Jupiter later parodies Alcmena's words (937–40).

633 Satin 'So ... really' (*OLD satis* 10); the very first word of her song reintroduces the theme of *satietas*. Cf. 633–53n. **uoluptatum:** the prominent motif of the song's opening, repeated three more times (635, 637, 641). In the prologue, Mercury had explained

(113–14) that the night was lengthened so that Jupiter might 'take his pleasure' (*capit uoluptatem*) with his lover. Given Alcmena's recent appearance, the audience will be alert to sexual innuendo. For the notion of 'pleasure' as a sexual euphemism in Latin see Adams (1982) 196–8; *uoluptas* becomes a technical term for sexual intercourse (*OLD* 5). The genitive with *parua res* is analogous to that with *parum*.   **in uita atque in aetate agunda:** cf. 634 *in aetate hominum*. For similarly sententious language (we should perhaps translate 'Life') cf. *Rud.* 1235 *O Gripe, Gripe, in aetate hominum* ... (with the addressee's mocking reception of the speech in 1249–53). Cf. also 938.

634 cuique: a monosyllable here (syncope); cf. Questa (1984) 296–7.

635 ita di⟨ui⟩s est placitum: ostensibly a phrase of conventional piety, but, given the stress on Jupiter's pursuit of sexual pleasure in the play and the juxtaposition with *uoluptatem* (633n.), highly ironic.   **di⟨ui⟩s:** Leo's correction to yield six bacchiacs. **maeror comes consequatur:** cf. Caec. 168 R = 159 W *consequitur comes insomnia.*

636 quin incommodi plus malique ilico adsit, boni si optigit quid 'Why in fact, it's the gods' desire that more misfortune and trouble be present right at the instant something good happens.' **adsit:** the substantive clause continues from the previous line.

637 domo 'from my own experience', i.e. 'personally', a proverbial usage (Otto (1890) 120); cf. *Mer.* 355 *scio saeuos quam sit, domo doctus* and the similar use of the locative of οἶκος at Soph. *Trach.* 730.

638 uiri [mei] mihi potestas uidendi fuit: *uidere* similarly has erotic overtones at *Truc.* 370 *benene ambulatumst?* :: *huc quidem hercle ad te bene, quia tui uidendi copia est.* :: *complectere.*

639 noctem unam modo 'for one night only' (the supernaturally lengthened night of love!), a resoundingly bathetic conclusion to Alcmena's musings.   **atque** 'Yes, and ...'

640 quem ego: with prosodic hiatus.   **praeter omnis** 'more than all my family and friends'. For the sentiment cf. Cat. 58.2–3 *illa Lesbia quam Catullus unam | plus quam se atque suos amauit omnes.*

641 aegri ex abitu ... ex aduentu uoluptatis: an artful chiasmus.

641a–53 Alcmena's *consolatio* here is bipartite (cf. 633–41n.). First she asserts that Amphitryon's military renown will compensate for the absence of *uoluptas* in her life (641a–47a). This leads into an excursus (648–53) on *uirtus*, the quality that makes such success possible. In contrast to the first major section of the song, the pace is swifter, and shorter bacchiac measures predominate, also combined with cola reiziana.

641a–47a Alcmena's 'self-sacrifice' here is consistent with traditional figurations of gender in Roman society (so Oniga on 642–47), though her substitution of vicarious enjoyment of her husband's success in public life for sexual pleasure is highly farcical. P.'s purpose here is dramaturgical: see 633–53, 653nn. and pp. 41–2.

641a–42 sed hoc me beat | saltem 'But this at least gladdens me.' Alcmena's personal happiness remains the underlying focus as she launches into her encomium of martial valour (cf. 647a, 633nn.) and its relevance to her husband in the public sphere.

642 perduellis: 250n.   **domum laudis compos reuenit:** i.e. worthy of celebrating a triumph (188n.).

643 id solacio est: *sc. mihi* (cf. 641a–42n.).

644–5 absit ... recipiat se 'Let him leave me, provided he comes back home a glorious winner.'

644 absit, dum modo laude parta: a sequence of three bacchiacs, with or without catalexis (cf. 648) is rare in P. (Questa (1967) 215).

645–6 feram et perferam ... animo forti atque offirmato: the elevated language and thought are comically disproportionate to her current situation: her husband, as she believes, is off attending to administrative business for only a short time (cf. 503–5n.). Cf. Perelli (1983) 389.

645 feram et perferam 'I'll endure it, yes I'll endure it to the very end.' For correction (and intensification) through the compound see 43n.

646–7 id modo si mercedis | datur mi 'if only I receive this reward [for my sacrifice]…'

647 belli: locative, as in *belli domique.*   **clueat:** the word belongs to the vocabulary of heroic epic, e.g. Enn. *Ann.* 13 Skutsch.

647a satis mi esse ducam: as her song becomes increasingly melodramatic, Alcmena makes the explicit claim that celebration of Amphitryon's valour will be 'enough'. Cf. 641a–47a, 633nn.

648–53 In P.'s festival of words, designation of Amphitryon as a
uictor uir launches the encomium of *uirtus*, which, like *uoluptas* in the
first half of her song (633n.), is prominently voiced four times in all
(648, 649, 652, 653). In this way P. invites the audience to reflect on
the relationship between the cognates *uir* ('man') and *uirtus* ('manli-
ness', 'manhood'); given the stress on Alcmena's sexual insatiability
(633–53n.), perhaps P. is 'turning a word with usually no perceptible
sexual meaning to a highly sexualized sense' (Phillips (1985) 125–6;
Statius later played on the disjunction between the gender of the
goddess Virtus and the force she embodies: Feeney (1991) 382–5).
For the use of the *uir-* root in general to designate male sexual po-
tency, etc. see Adams (1982) 69–70.

648 uirtus: the very first and last word of the encomium (with
anaphora at 649 and 652).

649 anteit: a spondee; prepositions in compounds often elide
with a following vowel in P. (Lindsay (1922) 149).   **profecto:** the
final position is most emphatic; cf. 1084, *Cas.* 698, *Mos.* 1082.

650 libertas salus uita res et parentes, patria et prognati:
a list reflecting the most revered Roman values.   **libertas:** the
'freedom' from despotism enjoyed by Roman citizens, much more
restricted than modern democratic notions of political and personal
liberty, from which a considerable portion of P.'s audience would be
excluded.   **res** 'property'.   **parentes, patria:** the juxtaposition anticipates Cicero's *patria parens omnium nostrum* (*de Orat.* 1.196).

651 tutantur, seruantur: sc. *uirtute*; each word of this bacchiac
clausula is a molossus, with assonance creating further concinnity.

652–3 omnia adsunt | bona quem penest uirtus 'all benefits
accrue to the man who possesses *uirtus*'.

653 The colon reizianum often serves as a clausula.   **quem
penest:** with anastrophe of *penes* (as often). *penest* apparently is pyrrhic here (cf. Lindsay (1922) 76). Given the emphasis on male sexuality in the song (648–53n.), a pun on *penis* perhaps is intended.
uirtus: the appropriate word to effect the transition to the confused
homecoming of her *uictor uir*; cf. 656 *uictis*, 657 *uicimus*.

654–860 After Alcmena finishes her *canticum*, master and slave
renew their conversation (in recitative) without acknowledging the
song or Alcmena's presence on stage. P. has masterfully set the stage
for the confrontation of the spouses, whose perceptions of the prior
night diverge drastically. As he enters, Amphitryon gloats over his

military success, obviously excited at the prospect of a warm and congratulatory welcome from his wife (654–8). P. delays their meeting until 676, so as to highlight their disparate perspectives. Alcmena shows only moderate enthusiasm at her husband's return (660–3; cf. 679–80). Amphitryon is immediately flustered by this lukewarm reception, and, as each successive detail of Alcmena's and Jupiter's night is brought out through aggressive interrogation, the spectre of a charge of adultery looms larger. Sosia fulfils the conventional function of the interloper (as Mercury had done in 499–550), whose humorous comments and asides help the audience maintain their emotional distance from the characters' plights (as does also the pervasive irony). The audience, which has been assured that the couple will ultimately be reconciled (463–98n.), will enjoy the confused (human) spectacle from the position of superior knowledge it shares with the gods. Alcmena's pregnant state is frequently referred to, most often as the target of Sosia's humour (667–70, 681, 718–19, 723–4, 785–6). The themes of madness, drunkenness and dreams permeate the scene.

654 me: cf. 193n. for the prominence of the first-person pronoun in 654–8.   **uxori exoptatum:** so-called dative of agent with the perfect participle used adjectivally, as regularly in classical Latin.

655–7 Amphitryon describes his victory in the formal diction of a Roman general solicitous of a triumph (cf. Sosia's earlier account and 186–96, 188nn.). Here he easily slips into the role of the *miles gloriosus*, just as Jupiter had earlier in impersonating him (504–5n.), and the audience will take special delight in the braggart's indifferent reception.

655 quae me amat, quam contra amo: for the syntactical juxtaposition of lovers here cf. 134n. Though Roman aristocratic marriages were normally arranged with a view to strengthening political alliances through the procreation of legitimate children, evidence for passionate affection between spouses is not lacking: see Dixon (1992) 83–97.

655–6 re gesta bene, | uictis hostibus: 188n.

656 quos nemo posse superari ratust: 186–7n.

657 eos: a monosyllable.   **auspicio meo atque ductu:** 192n. **meo:** an elided monosyllable.   **primo coetu uicimus:** a terse summary of Sosia's song (219–47).

658 certe enim med illi expectatum optato uenturum scio

'No doubt about it, I'm sure that I'll arrive in accordance with her wishes, since she's long awaited me.'   **certe enim:** 331n.   **illi:** 654n.   **optato:** the adverb.

659 quid? me non rere expectatum amicae uenturum meae?: Sosia's quip deflates Amphitryon's blustery pronouncement and suggests an affinity between Alcmena and his *amica*: cf. 289–90n. We hear nothing further of Sosia's girlfriend; Molière gave his Sosie a wife: p. 73.   **rere** = *reris* (344n.).   **expectatum amicae:** cf. 654n.   **amicae:** ironically, Sosia's girlfriend is described in more positive terms (cf. Adams (1983) 348–9) than Alcmena is in so far as her relationship with Jupiter is concerned: see 287, 288, 288–9, 1136nn.

660 meus uir hicquidem est 'Why, here's my husband', perhaps with exaggerated emphasis on *uir*, so as to deflate further the high-minded content of her song's close; cf. 648–53n.   **hicquidem:** for the (regular) short quantity of the antepenult see p. 64 (enclisis) and Lindsay (1922) 73.   **sequere hac tu me:** Amphitryon and Sosia make a move from the street toward the palace (cf. 551–632, 633–53nn.). Though Alcmena has noted their arrival, and Sosia is about to comment on Alcmena's appearance (664–7), Amphitryon remains squarely focused on Sosia until 676.   **nam quid** 'Why, I wonder …' (= *quidnam*). Cf. *OLD quisnam* and *nam* 7.

661 ille: with iambic shortening.   **me temptat:** Sosia has already told us that Amphitryon is suspicious by nature (555). **sciens** 'intentionally', with *temptat*.

662 id se uolt experiri: for *uolo* + accusative and infinitive cf. *OLD* 6a; *id* is explained by the *ut* clause ('how I lament his going away').

664–7 Sedgwick (n. on 664) objects to the extended preparation for 'a feeble joke' and comments that 'Amphitruo's patience is indeed surprising'. But P. wants to refocus on the pregnant Alcmena, and this particular type of jest is one of P.'s favourites: typically, A makes an enigmatic declaration (often with bizarre imagery), B asks how this can be so, and A delivers the punch-line. P. is much more interested in successfully executing the joke here than portraying Amphitryon realistically. Sosia follows with a second, parallel co-nundrum (665–6). Cf. 357n.

665 prandium: the Roman midday meal (typically fish or eggs, vegetables and wine: see *OCD* 'meals'). In addition to setting up the punch-line (664–7n.), Sosia's concern about lunch here is indicative of his comic perspective: cf. 186–261, 254nn..

666–7 Like professional comedians, Amphitryon and Sosia deliver the joke through the repetition of *qui* and *quia* ('Why?' 'I'll tell you why . . .'). Cf. *Epid.* 33 *qui? :: quia ante aliis fuit.*

666 tibi: iambic (a rare scansion: Questa (1967) 101).   **istuc . . . enim:** both pyrrhic by iambic shortening.   **in mentemst:** Lindemann's correction of *in mentem uenit* (which does not scan). Cf. 180n.   **sero** 'too late'.

667 saturam 'stuffed', indicating that the padding was considerable. Cf. Phillips (1985) 122–3.

668 grauidam: cf. 103, 111 and 681; the adjective is used ten times in the play with reference to Alcmena.   **abeo. :: ei:** *C / D* hiatus (at change of speaker). Cf. 321.

669 quid tibi est? 'What's the matter with you?' (cf. 727, 792).   **ad aquam praebendam:** i.e. to wash the newborn (cf. 1102 and Callim. *Hymn* 1.15–17 for the ancient practice). True to his character type (cf. 153–74, 665nn.), Sosia shirks all labour. **commodum** 'just in time' (sarcastic).

670 d⟨u⟩ctare: a correction of the senseless *dictare*, with the same sense as *rationem ducere* (cf. *OLD duco* 29).

671–3 For his next joke (cf. 664–7n.), Sosia takes his cue from Amphitryon's injunction *bono animo es*. With typically bizarre imagery (156n.), he personifies the well with his claim that his labours will be so vast as to drain it of its 'last breath' (673 *omnem animam intertraxero*).

671 bono animo es 'Cheer up.'

672 numquam edepol tu mihi diuini [quicquam] creduis post hunc diem 'By god, you would never trust me with anything important after today . . .', i.e. 'Believe you me . . .' For the construction without *quicquam* cf. *Bac.* 504, *As.* 459; more fully, *As.* 854 *neque diuini neque mi humani posthac quicquam accreduas* . . . Cf. *OLD diuinus* 1c. **creduis:** 72n.

673 ni ego: *bb* (prosodic hiatus).   **occepso:** for the form see 355n.

674 sequere hac me modo: the series of jokes concluded, Amphitryon repeats the command to approach the house; cf. 660n. **rei:** an elided monosyllable (cf. Questa (1967) 100–1).

675 magis nunc ⟨me⟩ meum officium facere, si huic eam aduorsum, arbitror 'I suppose the more dutiful thing for me to do now is to go to meet him', a flippant reference to the formality that characterizes Roman spousal relations. A genuinely warm (though still formal) welcome would have been bestowed on Jupiter the previous night. The exchange here well illustrates the extent to which P. privileges situation over character. Given her solicitousness at Jupiter's departure in her first scene (499–550), a strictly consistent treatment of character would call for Alcmena to be overjoyed at her husband's arrival; but P. is dealing with a new situation here, and her aloofness sets the comedy of errors in motion (cf. 654–86n.).

676–9 Amphitryon's swagger and pomp is unenthusiastically received, as we immediately learn from Sosia's aside (679–80).

676 Amphitruo uxorem salutat: for the third-person address in affecting a more grandiose tone cf. *Mer.* 713, *Trin.* 435 and 1151–2. The parallel relative clauses (677–8) describing Alcmena's chief attributes are similarly overwrought.   **laetus:** elsewhere in the play only of Mercury's attitude (as god of commerce) toward the audience (2n.).   **speratam** 'longed for', perhaps with erotic overtones.

677 omnium ... unam ... optumam 'the single finest woman of all', the traditional conception of Alkmene (e.g. [Hes.] *Scut.* 4–6). **unam:** for *unus* strengthening the superlative see *OLD* 8b.

678 quamque ... rumiferant probam 'whom my fellow citizens bruit as virtuous' *vel sim.* seems an unnatural thing to say in greeting one's wife in any culture, but consistent with the tenor of this scene (P. is telescoping: pp. 28–9), where it should elicit a malicious giggle from the audience.   **rumiferant:** perhaps coined by P. here.   **probam:** *probitas* is a Roman feminine ideal (cf. *CIL* 1 1809.5 *probisuma femina mater Bruti*) which Amphitryon will eventually claim his wife has breached (810ff.).

679 ualuistin usque 'Have you been well all the while?', a common formula of greeting in P. Cf. 715n.   **exspectatun =** *expectatusne*. P. again strains verisimilitude (678n.).   **haud uidi magis** 'I've never seen anyone more anxiously awaited' (sarcastic). Cf. *Capt.* 561 and *Poen.* 141.

680 expectatum eum salutat: Sosia mocks his master's grandiose style of address (cf. 676, 679); for the comic deflation see 659n.   **haud quicquam** 'in no way at all'.   **canem:** for the dog as a shameless and worthless creature cf. the use of *canis* as a pejorative (Otto (1890) 68).

681 grauidam ... gaudeo: as Jupiter before him (499–500), Amphitryon immediately refers to her (bloated) condition. **pulchre plenam** 'perfectly plump'; the male actor again (cf. 499n.) could emphasize the point by rubbing his protruding belly. For the colloquial use of *pulchre* here see 278n.

685 atque me nunc proinde appellas quasi multo post uideris?: the line is bracketed by Leo and others on the ground that it repeats 683, but Alcmena expresses a single idea from opposing perspectives ('as if you hadn't seen me just now' / 'as if you had seen me after a long time'), as is natural in animated colloquial speech.

686 nusquam ... gentium: 620n.

687 uera ... dicere: cf. 562n.

687–8 haud aequom facit | qui quod didicit id dediscit 'He who unlearns what he has learned does no good'; probably, as Oniga notes *ad loc.*, a proverbial expression; cf. Sen. *Tro.* 633 *dediscat animus sero quod didicit diu*, Cic. *Quinct.* 56 *discat atque dediscat*. For reversals of meaning through the addition of a verbal prefix (cf. English 'destabilize', etc.) in Latin see Wills (1996) 445–6.

688–9 an periclitamini | quid animi habeam? 'Or are you testing out my feelings?' Cf. 661n.

689 quid animi: 58n.

690 an ... an: for repeated *an* in multiple questions see *OLD* 7a. **auspicium:** auspices would have to be taken before a returning army could cross the pomerium. Cf. 192n.   **tempestas** 'bad weather'.

692 dudum? quam dudum istuc factum est? :: temptas. iam dudum, modo ' "Recently"? How "recently" did this happen?' 'You're testing me. Some while back, just now.'

693 qui istuc potis est fieri, quaeso, ut dicis: iam dudum, modo? 'How, please tell me, is what you say possible: "some while back", "just now"?' For Amphitryon as the (doomed) champion of logic cf. 553–4n. and pp. 30–1.

694–5 'Well, what do you suppose? That I'm teasing in kind since you claim you've only now returned when you just left?' (playfully sarcastic).

694 contra: adverb.

696 deliramenta: cf. 581, 727nn.

697 dum edormiscat unum somnum: lit., 'until she sleeps off a certain sleep'. As *edormire* and *edormiscere* are used of sleeping off a hangover, Sosia combines the themes of sleep and drunkenness here to hint that Alcmena is a bacchante. Cf. 702–5.   **unum:** with the indefinite sense of *quidam* (cf. *OLD* 11).   **quaene uigilans somniat?** 'You mean she's a daydreamer?', a proverbial expression. Cf. *Capt.* 848 *hic uigilans somniat* and Otto (1890) 121.

698 uigilo et uigilans ... fabulor: cf. Sosia's similar defence to Amphitryon at 623.

701 quid si e portu nauis huc nos dormientis detulit?: though Sosia among the human characters is the one most apt to acknowledge supernatural influence, 702–5 show that he is just humouring Alcmena here.   **dormientis:** for the theme of sleep see p. 31.

702–5 The jest assumes the audience's familiarity – if only through negative stereotypes – with the mystery cult of Bacchus (Liber), which had probably been introduced into Italy well before the début of *Am.* (cf. pp. 3–4). In 186 BC, the senate, as part of its general backlash against foreign (esp. Greek) influences, declared the cult to be deleterious to public order and morality (Livy 39.8–18) and issued its famous decree. Other references to the cult and its participants by characters in P. similarly reflect the condemnatory and conservative view, e.g. *Bac.* 371 *Bacchides non Bacchides, sed bacchae sunt acerrumae*, *Aul.* 408–9, *Men.* 835. For circumspect discussion of the Bacchanalian affair see Gruen (1990) 34–78.

702 huic: spondaic (a rare scansion: cf. Questa (1967) 110). **quid uis fieri?** 'What do you expect?'

703 Bacchae bacchanti 'a Maenad in her madness'.   **uelis:** pyrrhic (iambic shortening). Scan *B C D A B C D A / B cc D A B c D.*

704–5 'If you make her crazier instead of just crazy, she'll attack you all the more; if you humour her, you'll settle up with just one blow.'

705–6 at pol qui certa res est | hanc est obiurgare 'No, I damn well am going to take her to task.'

705 at pol qui: *atqui* in tmesis with the exclamatory *pol.*

706 obiurgare: Amphitryon takes up a traditionally stern and patriarchal stance toward his wife, who he believes has offended his dignity by failing to acknowledge formalities: cf. 675n. For the full connotations of the verb cf. Cicero's assessment of Herennius' speech against Caelius, *Cael.* 25 *dixit enim multa de luxuria, multa de uitiis iuuentutis, multa de moribus … fuit in hac causa pertristis quidam patruus, censor, magister; obiurgauit M. Caelium, sicut neminem umquam parens.* Cf. *Mer.* 46 *obiurgare pater haec noctes et dies.*

707 inritabis crabrones 'You'll stir up a hornets' nest' (proverbial: Otto (1890) 96). Word-end after the tenth element in septenarii is rare (Questa (1967) 182); scan *B cc D a B C D a B C / D A B c D.*

709 num tibi aut stultitia accessit aut superat superbia? 'Has either foolishness taken hold of you or is your pride overflowing?' The *paterfamilias* concocts yet another explanation for what he perceives to be his wife's mockery.

710 qui istuc in mentemst tibi: 180n. **percontarier:** 13n.

712 itidem ut pudicae suos uiros quae sunt solent = *itidem ut illae quae pudicae sunt suos uiros salutare et appellare solent.* **pudicae:** a wife's failure to greet her husband according to convention should not automatically be taken as evidence of sexual infidelity: P. again is telescoping (678n.). **suos:** with synizesis.

713 'I find on my arrival home that you no longer partake of this custom.' **eo more expertem:** *expers* + ablative is found in archaic (and archaizing) writers (cf. the genitive at 170). The entire sentence has a formal tone, as Amphitryon continues to speak as *obiurgator* (706n.). **eo:** with synizesis.

714 ecastor equidem: Alcmena's increasing indignation is evident in her exclamations (cf. 730 *equidem ecastor*, 812 *obsecro ecastor* and 182n.), which the actor could have rendered ridiculously in falsetto (cf. p. 43). **aduenientem ilico:** *a / B* hiatus. **ilico** = *domi*.

715 et ualuissesne usque exquisiui simul 'and at the same time I asked whether you had been well all the while' (Alcmena is imagined to have given the formulaically correct greeting to Jupiter: cf. 679n.).

716 osculum: a formal kiss in greeting, as those given by a wife to certain of her husband's relations according to the *ius osculi* (cf. Treggiari (1991) 412). To describe erotic kisses P. uses *sauium* (= *basium*, which appears first in Catullus), e.g. *Cur.* 56 *qui uolt cubare, pandit saltum sauiis.*

717 quoque etiam: 30n.

718 tibi parituram: *bb cc D A*; for the rare proceleusmatic see 513n.

719 grauida ... insania: *grauidus* bears both the senses 'pregnant' and 'afflicted with'.　**quid igitur?:** Amphitryon plays 'straight man' as Sosia makes another enigmatic declaration (357, 664–7nn.).

720 deos quaeso, ut salua pariam filium: Alcmena takes Sosia's accusation that she is 'pregnant with insanity' as a bad omen (cf. 722) and ironically calls upon the gods for the safe delivery which she will enjoy on account of Jupiter's assistance (1061ff.).　**deos:** with synizesis.　**filium:** the clear preference in a patriarchal society. The audience knows that she will give birth to *filios geminos* (480).

721 tu malum magnum habebis: perhaps the full expression behind the colloquial interjection *malum* (cf. 403n.).　**malum:** pyrrhic (iambic shortening).

722 istuc: with iambic shortening.　**ominator:** coined here for the play with *omen*.

723 enim uero praegnati oportet et malum et malum dari: lit., 'Yes indeed, a pregnant woman should get both an illness and an apple.' The word-play is difficult to replicate in English (Carrier translates 'But aches are for pregnant ladies, madam – Aches, and lots of apples, a barrel of apples, To nibble on in case she's feeling seedy'). That the second *malum* is the fruit (with long penult) is necessitated by Luchs' law (p. 64). Pliny (*NH* 23.104) notes the general use of *orbiculata* ('round apples') to stop vomiting (cf. 724) and the specific use of the *malicorium* ('pomegranate rind', *NH* 23.107), for nausea brought on by pregnancy.

724 ut quod obrodat sit 'so that there may be something for her to gnaw on'; *obrodat* is probably coined here for the sound-play with *oportet*.　**animo ... male esse:** i.e. 'to be ill-minded', combining the idea of physical sickness in pregnancy with that of Alcmena's ill-disposedness toward himself (cf. 721), as well as continuing the punning on *malum* (723n.).

725 decies dicere: 576n.

726 Scan *B C D A B C D aa B cc D A B c D*.　**in somnis:** cf. 621n. **uigilans uigilantem** = *ego uigilans te uigilantem heri hic uidi*; she agains echoes Sosia's claims in the prior scene (698n.). **uae [misero] mihi!** 'Oh no!' (cf. 741n.).

727 quid tibi est?: 669n. **delirat uxor:** the verb literally means 'to deviate (in ploughing) from the ridge between furrows' (Amphitryon alleges that his wife's mental processes have strayed from their proper course: cf. 696n.). This is the last time in the scene that Amphitryon refers to Alcmena as his *uxor*: cf. 729n. **atra bili:** according to the ancient theory of bodily humours, an imbalance of black bile was the cause of madness; cf. *Capt.* 596 *atra bilis agitat hominem*, Cic. *Tusc.* 3.11, Sen. *Ep.* 94.17.

728 tam ... cito: the hyperbaton, in part motivated by desire for alliteration (*concinnat cito*) is not unusual in P. in the case of such adverbs of degree as *tam, nimis, minus, multo*.

729 ubi primum tibi sensisti, mulier, impliciscier 'When, madam, in your opinion did you first feel it coming over you?' Following up on Sosia's 'diagnosis' (727n.), Amphitryon assumes the attitude of a physician. **tibi:** a vague dative of reference ('so far as you're concerned'); iambic here (666n.). **mulier:** Amphitryon's growing anger can be measured by how he addresses Alcmena; after the formal greeting (676–9), he refers to her once as *Alcumena* (708), thereafter, with seeming contempt, as *mulier* (755, 847 in addition to here; cf. 739), or simply by a pronoun (e.g. 758, 816). He ultimately denies that he is her *uir* and deems her *falsa* (813). **impliciscier:** the inceptive of *implicari*, itself a technical medical term (*OLD implico* 8); *te* is understood.

730 equidem ecastor: 714n. **sana et salua sum:** a common formula, e.g. *Mer.* 174, *Epid.* 563, *Ps.* 1068.

731 me ... qui ... aduecti sumus: Sedgwick cites *Bac.* 1118–19 (*iube ... mauoltis*) for the change of number (the character addressed there also has a double). **hac noctu** 'last night' (cf. 272n.).

732 noctem perpetem: 280n.

733 intuli: apparently with iambic shortening of the ante-penult. **ut** 'from the time that', repeated in 734 (cf. *OLD* 27).

734 eosque: with synizesis.

735 immo mecum cenauisti et mecum cubuisti 'No, indeed, you dined with me and after you reclined with me' (Segal (1987) 180). This playful line probably elicited some whooping and hollering from the audience (cf. 290n.). There is perhaps additional parody in the comic image here conjured of god and mortal happily commingling (as if in the Golden Age). For the presentation of Alcmena as a sensualist by Roman standards cf. 513–14n. For the repetition of *cu* here see 132–5n. **quid est?:** expressive of indignation, cf. 556n.

736 uera dico: cf. 562n. **hercle:** with iambic shortening of the penult. **de aliis nescio:** *c d* + *A B c D*.

737 primulo diluculo 'at the very crack of dawn'; diminutives need not have any special force in P., but *primulo*, in addition to being more euphonic, here is more precise than *primo* (cf. 546–50). **quo modo?:** 556n.

738 recte dicit, ut commeminit: somnium narrat tibi: i.e. Amphitryon 'departed' (cf. 737) along with her dream; cf. Ov. *Her.* 19.66 *nam tu cum somno semper abire soles* and Theoc. *Id.* 11.23–4.

739–40 'But woman, once you awoke, you ought to have prayed immediately to Jupiter of Prodigies, with either salted flour or incense in tow.'

739 mulier: Sosia echoes his master's contemptuous tone ('My dear madam...'): 729n. **prodigiali Ioui:** *prodigialis* is not elsewhere attested as an epithet of Jupiter, but the context makes it clear that Sosia invokes Jupiter in his capacity to ward off ill omens associated with bad dreams; commentators compare his title *depulsor* ('averter of evil'; cf. *CIL* III 895). There is obvious irony in the proposal that Alcmena should have sacrificed to Jupiter.

740 mola salsa ... ture: the *mola salsa* is sprinkled on the back of the victim in Roman sacrifice (cf. *immolatio, immolare*) after wine is poured over its brow; for such a rite (in which incense might also be burned) to expiate the potential evil resulting from nightmares cf. Tib. 1.5.13–14 and Mart. 7.54.5.

741 uae capiti tuo 'Blast your impudence'; *uae* can be 'strongly repudiative' (Gratwick (1993) on *Men.* 512–13) or an expression of anguish (as in 726). **tuo:** disyllabic (as *tua*). **tua istuc refert – si curaueris** 'That's of relevance to you – if you should be so minded.' Sosia impudently throws Alcmena's curse back at her (cf. her outrage at 742) and then pretends to politeness. Cf. *Mil.* 286 *di te perdant :: te istuc aequom – quoniam occepisti, eloqui.*

742 iam hic: *d / d* (prosodic hiatus).   **inclementer** 'rudely'.
atque id sine malo 'and he gets away with it to boot'. Cf. 26–7n.

743 tace tu. tu dic: a tidy chiasmus.   **tace tu:** Amphitryon's
first rebuke of Sosia in the scene. *tace* is *bb* (iambic shortening).

744–59 The first confounding piece of testimony, that Alcmena is
aware of the battle's outcome, has little effect on Amphitryon.

744 uos: Jupiter and Mercury (cf. 747).   **illi** 'on the campaign'.

745 an etiam id tu scis? 'Can it be that you actually know
about this?'   **quippe qui ex te audiui** 'Yes, of course, since I
heard it from you' (the masculine of the relative is used, as *quippe qui*
is already a set phrase); cf. 22n.   **quippe:** the final *-e* does not
count in scansion, as regularly (apocope: p. 62). The line scans
bb c D A B C D A B c D A B c D.

746 expugnauisses … occideris: cf. Lindsay 56–7 for fluidity
in the sequence of tenses in P.   **tute:** the emphatic colloquial
form ('*you* …'); cf. 747, 795, 796, 816, 819.

747 etiam adstante hoc Sosia: there is no contradiction with
132–7, as she refers to Jupiter's announcement of victory upon his
immediate arrival. He is easily imagined to have provided further
details during pillow talk.

748 ubi ego audiuerim? 'Where was I to have heard them?'
(deliberative subjunctive).

**749 me quidem praesente numquam factumst, quod
sciam** 'It never happened in my presence – at least, not to my
recollection.'   **quod sciam:** a relative clause of characteristic in
origin (lit., 'as to what I know').

750 mirum quin 'Big surprise that he doesn't …' (this retort is
always ironic in P.).

750–1 aspice | specto: 209n.

751 uera … loqui: 562n.

752 illi: i.e. Alcmena, as *illa*.

753 quoque etiam: with special stress on the preceding pronoun
(cf. 30n.), i.e. 'don't tell me *you're* insane too'.

755 mulier: 729n.   **ego uero, ac falsum dicere** 'I certainly
do hear him, and he's lying.'

756 neque mihi uiro ipsi credis? 'And you don't believe me,
your very own husband?' Amphitryon suggests that Alcmena should

accept his version of events solely on the basis of his authority as *paterfamilias*, but, to prolong the comic confusion, P. has her trust her own perceptions (756–7).   **eo fit quia** 'Yes because …'   **eo:** with synizesis.

758 tun me heri aduenisse dicis? :: tun te abiisse hodie hinc negas?: Alcmena matches her husband word for word in a playfully rhyming line that is equally divided between them by the central word break of the septenarius.

759 nego enim uero 'I damn well do deny it' (cf. 266n.).

760–1 With this revelation Amphitryon will become increasingly agitated. For the motif of the bowl cf. 534–5n. and the function of the stolen mantle in *Men.*

761 dedisse: scanned as an anapaest, an unexplained but well-attested case of iambic shortening; cf. Gratwick (1993) on *Men.* 689.   **illi:** 744n.

763 ea: with synizesis.   **istuc:** with iambic shortening.

764 ex tua accepi manu: the hyperbaton lends special emphasis to *tua* ('I took it from your very own hand').

765 mane, mane: the former is *dd* (iambic shortening), the latter is *a* (with elision).   **nimis demiror** 'I'm utterly amazed.'

766 qui 'how'.

767 Amphitryon again seeks a logical explanation for the apparent discrepancy regarding the *patera*.

768 istam: with iambic shortening.

769 quid hoc sit hominis?: 576n. (*homo*, unlike *uir*, can refer to women as well as men).   **hoc:** with iambic shortening.

770 ⟨i⟩ tu, Thessala, intus pateram proferto foras: Alcmena presumably turns toward the palace and calls to her maid inside (otherwise we must assume that Thessala has stood beside Alcmena since 633).   **Thessala:** as Thessaly was stereotyped as a haven of witches and sorcerers (cf. 1043 and *OCD* 'magic'), this mute character is significantly named; for the theme of magic see pp. 29–31. The name may be P.'s invention (she need not be named at all): 365n.   **intus** 'from within'.

771 meus uir: the audience will catch a double meaning here; for *uir* = both 'husband' and 'lover' cf. *OLD* 2. For the latter sense (not noted for P. by *OLD*) cf. *As.* 236 *nec quemquam interea alium admittat prorsus quam me ad se uirum.*

772 mira miror maxume: cf. 616n.

773 habet: *cc* (iambic shortening).   **illam:** with iambic shortening in the penult.

773-4 an etiam credis id, quae in hac cistellula | tuo signo obsignata fertur? 'Can it be that you actually [cf. 745n.] believe this, when it's being carried in this chest here, sealed with your signet?' By a kind of *constructio ad sensum*, the relative (referring to the *patera*) is used because *id* here = *haec habet pateram illam.*

774 tuo: with synizesis.

775-6 quin tu istanc iubes | pro cerrita circumferri?: lit., 'why don't you give the order for her to be encircled as one who is possessed by Ceres?' Following up on his earlier diagnosis (727-8), Sosia suggests that Alcmena has gone mad under Ceres' influence and that she must undergo a ritual purification (*lustratio*) in which objects supposed to have curative powers (sulphur or pine torches according to Serv. *A*. 6.229) are to be carried around her.

776 edepol qui facto est opus 'By God, there certainly is need to have that done.' For *qui* (adverb) with exclamations cf. *OLD* 6c, and for *facto est opus* cf. 169n.

777 laruarum plenast 'full of evil spirits'. In popular thought, the *laruae* (cognate with *Lar*) were conceived of as ghosts of the underworld who might torment the living and cause madness. Reflecting the play's careful symmetry, Alcmena makes a similar allegation against Amphitryon later in the play (fr. 8). Cf. the doctor's 'examination' at *Men*. 890 *num laruatust aut cerritus?* In P. *laruae* is always three syllables (*laruarum* is set *BcDA* here).   **quid uerbis opust?:** when attributed to Alcmena, this closing formula (445n.) clashes with her exclamation immediately following in 778; Sedgwick's suggestion to attribute it to Amphitryon is adopted.

778 em tibi pateram, eccam 'Hah, there you are – the bowl' (Thessala has returned carrying the *patera*).   **em:** in origin an imperative of *emo* (cf. *OLD emo* 1).   **tibi:** monosyllabic.   **cedo mi** 'give it to me'.   **sis:** 286n.   **nunciam** 'this very instant' (trisyllabic: cf. 38n.).

779 tu qui quae facta infitiare 'you who deny what you've done' (with *facta* understand *sunt*).   **conuincam palam** 'I will clearly prove wrong' (a quasi-legal usage of the verb; cf. the simplex in 423, 428, 433).

780 estne haec patera, qua donatu's illi? 'Isn't this the cup you were awarded there?' (cf. 433n.).   **summe Iuppiter:** Amphitryon ironically invokes his rival.

781 ea: with synizesis, and so completely lost in scansion, owing to elision here.   **perii:** the colloquial exclamation later will take on a more literal meaning for Amphitryon: cf. 295, 1076nn.

782 praestigiatrix: as with 830 *praestigiator*, the root sense is that Alcmena can dazzle the eyes of others through the creation of illusion (cf. *OLD praestringo* 3a); Sosia means that she must be a magician if the same *patera* can appear in both places at once (cf. 785–6). **multo** 'by far' (= *longe*).

783 agedum: *-dum* intensifies the imperative.

785–6 Sosia's ironic quip is a neat encapsulation of the play's central theme of doubling and features three sets of linguistic 'twins', *peperisti ... peperi,* ⟨*alium*⟩ *... alium, patera pateram*. The repeated verb *parere* here foreshadows the birth of the two boys at the end of the play. This thematic and linguistic playfulness is further underscored by the markedly 'light' rhythm (cf. 42n.) of both highly resolved lines. Cf. p. 16.

785 ⟨alium⟩: Guyet's proposal improves both sound and sense; Ernout's transposition of *ego alium* of the MSS is also adopted.

786 omnes congeminauimus 'we've all twinned together'; *congeminauimus* may be a Plautine coinage. In epic it is used of the redoubling of blows, etc.

787 uide sis signi quid siet 'Please do look at the seal.' Cf. 42!n.

788 aperi modo 'Just open it.'

789 nos delirantis facere dictis postulat: Amphitryon combines the themes of madness and magic; *dictis* in this context probably has the pregnant sense 'chanted spells' (so Stewart (1958) 353 n. 17). For *delirantis* cf. 727n.

791 opus mi est istuc exquisito: cf. 169, 628nn.   **Iuppiter, pro Iuppiter:** Sosia appropriately (cf. 785–6n.) exclaims the god's name twice. Such repetitions of a deity's name are common in (esp.) Greek tragedy, where the language of ritual is often invoked (cf. Bond (1988) on E. *HF* 763), but generally avoided in Latin poetry: see further Wills (1996) 50–2.   **pro:** 376n.

792 quid tibi est?: 669n.   **nulla** = *non* negates the whole sentence ('This cup isn't in the chest at all'); cf. *LU* 80. The libation vessel (538n.) is in fact stolen rather than duplicated (786n.). It inverts the usual function of the token of recognition by only causing further confusion.

793 id quod uerumst. :: at cum cruciatu ... tuo: once again (cf. 370n.) Sosia is physically threatened when he is free of guilt and telling the truth. The hyperbaton here emphasizes *tua* (cf. 764n.). **nisi apparet:** *dd A B* (iambic shortening).

795–7 In response to Amphitryon's insinuations, Sosia proposes a ridiculous and desperate-sounding solution to the 'whodunnit'; cf. *praecucurristi ... exemisti ... dedisti ... obsignasti* and his over-precise use of demonstratives.

795 me captas 'You're trying to trap me.'   **clanculum:** the crucial idea in Sosia's absurd theory, and so repeated in ring composition (cf. 797). For the formation cf. 523n.

795–6 alia uia | praecucurristi 'you took a short cut.'

797 huic: for the spondaic scansion see 702n.; the line begins *B C d+* (a *locus Jacobsohnianus*).   **post:** adverb.

798 iam tu quoque huius adiuuas insaniam? 'You're now encouraging her madness too?'

799 ain ... aio: *B c* and *B*, respectively.

801 iam illud non placet principium de osculo 'Now I don't like that opening part about a kiss.' Although the kiss described is the formal one (716n.) with which Alcmena would greet her husband, Sosia here encourages voyeurism among the audience by reading sexual significance into her words.   **perge exsequi** 'Keep going on.'

802 accubuisti :: euge: *D / A* hiatus.

802–3 euge optume! | nunc exquire 'Bravo, excellent! Now keep pressing!' Sosia's interruption again aims to titillate: *accumbere* (cf. 802) can mean either 'go to bed with' or 'recline at table' (that the latter is Alcmena's meaning is made clear in 804).

803 perge porro dicere 'Keep on going with your story', an animated colloquialism.

804–5 ego accubui simul. | :: in eodem lecto? :: in eodem: with the emergence of the financially independent and therefore relatively 'liberated' *matrona* in the late Republic, we do hear of women reclining with their husbands at Roman dinner parties, but everyday practice probably remained conservative. Excavations at Pompeii and other evidence suggest that men and women normally dined in separate rooms; the women joined the men only to partake in after-dinner entertainments, and would sit rather than recline on the dining couches: see Richardson (1988) 397–8. The effect of pro-viding a precise account here of the previous night's intimate meal is twofold: Alcmena again is farcically depicted as a sensualist and the audience will experience a kind of *Schadenfreude* as Amphitryon ferrets out the salacious details of his wife's evening with a *moechus*.

805 ei, non placet conuiuium 'Oh-oh – the dinner party doesn't have a pleasant ring' (cf. 801).   **ei:** cf. 321n.

806 sine modo argumenta dicat 'Just let her state her evi-dence.' For Amphitryon's legal posturing here cf. 779n.; Bromia, in taking up Alcmena's case with Amphitryon, will adopt a similar approach (1087n.).

807 dormitare 'felt sleepy'. P. teasingly delays the revelation that Alcmena and Jupiter shared the same bed, yet another clear indication that psychological realism is not a goal in P.'s comedy, as Jupiter's casual pretext for going to bed is strictly inconsistent with P.'s portrayal of the lengthened night of love-making.

808 ubi tu cubuisti? :: in eodem lecto tecum una in cubi-culo 'Where did you sleep?' 'Together with you, in our bedroom, in the very same bed.' At a climactic moment of Amphitryon's interro-gation, P. has Alcmena respond in painstaking detail. Cf. 132–5, 804–5nn.

809 perdidisti . . . haec me modo ad mortem dedit: for the theme of Amphitryon's gradual 'death' cf. 781n.

810 quid iam, amabo? 'Oh please, what's the matter now?' (cf. 540n.).   **quid tibi est?:** 669n.

810–11   perii miser, | . . . additum 'I'm done for because while I was away from here her chastity was compromised.' As the result of his interrogation, Amphitryon at last explicitly states his fear that Alcmena's *pudicitia* has been violated (cf. 678n.).

813 uir ego tuos sim? '*I'm* your *husband*?' P. uses the subjunctive or indicative indifferently in repudiative questions (LHS II 338).

814 haeret haec res, si quidem haec iam mulier facta est ex uiro 'This is a sticky matter, if he really has now become a woman instead of a man.' Sosia plays on the two distinct meanings of *uir* ('man' and 'husband') in asserting that Amphitryon has just abrogated his masculinity when he ordered Alcmena not to call him her *uir*.   **haec ... facta est:** attracted to the gender of *mulier*.

815 qua ... propter 'wherefore' (tmesis).   **dicta dicantur:** *figura etymologica*.

816 tute edictas facta tua, ex me quaeris quid delinqueris? 'You make a public proclamation of your misdeeds, and you ask me what you've done wrong?'

817 quid ego tibi deliqui, si cui nupta sum tecum fui?: lit., 'How have I wronged you, if I have been with you, who are my husband?' *esse cum aliquo* is a genteel euphemism for sexual activity: cf. Var. *L.* 6.80 *aeque eadem modestia potius cum muliere fuisse quam concubuisse dicebant* and Adams (1982) 177.   **cui nupta sum:** 99n.

818 tun mecum fueris? 'You were "with" me?'   **quid illac impudente audacius?** 'What creature is bolder than this shameless woman?'; *impudente* points to Alcmena's violated *pudicitia* (810–11n.).

819 saltem, tute si pudoris egeas, sumas mutuom 'If you lack shame, you should at least borrow some', in effect 'You aren't even decent enough to lie to me.' Cf. Ov. *Am.* 3.14.13–14 *sit tibi mens melior, saltemue imitare pudicas, | teque probam, quamuis nos eris, esse putem*; Palmer *ad loc.* compares 'Assume a virtue if you have it not' (*Hamlet* III.4). There is further irony in Amphitryon's enjoinder here in that his *uxor usuraria* has already been characterized as loaning out her sexual favours to Jupiter (pp. 39–40).   **sumas:** jussive subjunctive, to which *egeas* probably is attracted (cf. 961 and *Rud.* 834 *abeas, si uelis*).

820 istuc facinus, quod tu insimulas, nostro generi non decet 'The crime you accuse me of disgraces my lineage.' The institution of Roman marriage was directed toward the production of legitimate children (cf. 655n.).   **insimulas:** sc. *me*; the verb here takes an internal accusative as well (*quod*), as at 859, whereas at 477 and 888 we find the genitive of the charge.

821 tu si me inpudicitiai captas, capere non potes 'If you try to get me on a charge of adultery, you cannot.'   **inpudicitiai:** *D a B cc D A*.

822 cognoscin tu me saltem, Sosia? 'You at least know me, don't you Sosia?' Amphitryon is beginning to become less secure about his identity (cf. 781n.).

823 propemodum 'I'm pretty sure I do' (idiomatically understated).   **in portu Persico:** 404n.

824 testes: for the courtroom atmosphere of the scene cf. 806n.   **illud:** with iambic shortening of the penult.

825–9 Sosia is once again shown to be the the the most flexible of the human characters in his willingness to admit the possibility of suprarational explanation; his strange hypothesis here is in fact the truth.

825 nescio quid istuc negoti dicam, nisi si ... 'I don't know what I should say this whole business is about, unless ...'   **nisi si:** this, in contrast to *nisi* by itself, 'conveys ... an additional suggestion of uncertainty' (Lindsay 104).

826 Amphitruo alius: cf. 785.   **ted hinc absenti** 'although you were away from here'.   **tamen:** 542n.

827 tuam rem curet ... munus fungatur tuom: *munus fungatur* has clear sexual connotations, while *res* can vaguely refer to sexual intercourse; cf. Adams (1982) 164, 203. Cf. *As.* 812–13 *apud amicam munus adulescentuli | fungare, uxori excuses te et dicas senem?*

828–9 'Yes, while the matter of that counterfeit Sosia was shocking enough, this Amphitryon, to be sure, is even more amazing.' **mirum ... mirum:** cleverly self-reflexive (pp. 15–17) as Sosia proposes the possibility of dual sets of doubles. In both cases *mirum* is a substantive (cf. 616).

828 nam quom: Müller's suggestion for the transmitted reading *namque de,* which is awkward in the face of 829 *certe.*   **subditiuo Sosia:** Sosia humorously echoes Mercury's description of Jupiter as *Amphitruo subditiuos* (497).

830 nescioquis praestigiator hanc frustratur mulierem: ironically, Amphitryon is close to the truth in supposing that some magician has enchanted Alcmena into believing that he is her husband; cf. Mercury's apt labelling of his father as a *uorsipellis* in the prologue (123, with n.), and for the connotations of *praestigiator* 782n.

831–4 Though Alcmena's oath – as words printed on the page – may seem 'solemn and serious' (Hanson (1959) 95), the pervasive (comic) irony here argues against sentimentalizing her role. As always, delivery of the lines is crucial. Cf. 831, 832, 833–4nn.

831 supremi regis: for this type of irony see p. 32.

832 Iunonem: for the emphatic delaying of the name cf. 98–9n.   **uereri et metuere:** given Juno's history of revenge against

her husband's lovers, Alcmena should have good cause to be rever-
ential and fearful (elsewhere in the play Juno is comically portrayed
as the jealous shrew: 508, 510nn.). Cf. Mercury's appropriation of
religious language in the prologue (23n.).   **maxume:** i.e. as a
materfamilias (cf. 831) and, ironically, as the goddess's rival.

833 ut: either introducing ('inasmuch as') the reason why she has
sworn so confidently by the gods, or a formulaic phrase such as *ita me
iuuent* ('so may they bless me') is easily understood in this context.
extra unum te mortalis nemo: ironically true; Alcmena cannot
conceive of an immortal *alter tu.*

833–4 corpus corpore | contingit 'has closely contacted his
body to mine', playfully incongruous language in what purports to
be a solemn religious oath (831–4n.), consistent with P.'s emphasis
on the carnality of the affair. Cf. Lucr. 4.1193 *quae complexa uiri corpus
cum corpore iungit* (within the famous exegesis on sexual passion) and,
for 'amorous polyptoton' in Latin poetry in general, Wills (1996)
202–4.

834 quo ... faceret: *quo* + subjunctive (without a comparative)
is used widely in early Latin to express purpose (LHS II 679–80, GL
§545 R.I).   **uera istaec uelim** 'I'd be glad if this were true' (sc.
sint); cf. *OLD uolo* 10.

835 non uis credere 'you refuse to believe me'.

836 mulier es, audacter iuras: Amphitryon inaptly appeals
to the stock notion of female faithlessness and treachery (this and
related misogynistic clichés are collected by Otto (1890) 231–2).

**836–7 quae non deliquit, decet | audacem esse, con-
fidenter pro se et proterue loqui** 'It is appropriate for a woman
who has done no wrong to be bold, and to speak on her own behalf
with assurance and without constraint.' Alcmena and the sisters in
St. are among the most independent-minded female characters in
Roman comedy, but P. was no feminist. Here Alcmena's obstinacy
functions to further the comic misconceptions held by the confused
spouses.

838 satis audacter 'You've already spoken with sufficient bold-
ness' (in divulging what he believes to be her adulterous actions).
⟨**en**⟩**im uerbis proba's** 'Yes, you are chaste in word', adopting
Lachmann's emendation of the senseless *in uerbis probas* of the MSS,
which is one metrical element short.

839–42 Alcmena's often praised words should not be considered outside their dramatic context. The audience will catch the abundant ironies here, above all the fact that this pregnant and sexually insatiable *matrona* who vaunts her possession of traditional Roman feminine ideals is in fact entangled in a web of adultery and deceit. P. is not caught in some sort of a dilemma here, as Sedgwick suggests *ad loc.* ('He had to please his audience with buffoonery, but he can forget it when the nobility of a character appeals to him'), but is merely exploiting his audience's awareness of the real situation for humour at Alcmena's expense.

For the conventional values here, which are abundantly represented in (esp.) Roman epitaphs, see Treggiari (1991) 229–53.

839–40 non ego illam mihi dotem duco esse, quae dos dicitur, | sed ... : lit., 'I don't consider that which is generally said to be a dowry to be my dowry, but ...'; the rejection and usually humorous redefinition of a conventional idea is a Plautine mannerism (cf. Fraenkel (1960) 64).

840 pudicitiam et pudorem et sedatum cupidinem: for the comically inappropriate application of these ideals to P.'s Alcmena see pp. 42–3.

841 deum metum, parentum amorem et cognatum concordiam: in insisting that she reveres the gods, and respects her parents and the mutual interests of her *gens*, Alcmena ostensibly presents herself as a model of Roman *pietas*. The three genitives are objective.   **deum metum:** *deum* is either *B* (synizesis) or *bb* (with iambic shortening). Cf. 832n.

842 tibi morigera atque ut munifica sim bonis, prosim probis 'and that I am obliging to you and dutiful through my good deeds, and of assistance to you by virtuous means': the ideal portrait of the subservient Roman wife devoted to her husband's interests. For the theme of indulgence, ironically invoked here see p. 43; *morem gerere* and *morigera* later are used explicitly of a woman's sexual gratification of a man (Adams (1982) 164).   **morigera:** Williams (1958) argues persuasively that the promise to be *morigera* was part of formal Roman wedding ritual.

843 ne ista edepol, si haec uera loquitur, examussim est optuma 'Egad, if she's really telling the truth, that woman is positively perfect!' The comment of Sosia, our comic centre throughout the scene (654–86on.), suggests that the ideals Alcmena vaunts in 839–42, even if taken at face value, have been pompously over-stated. Perelli (1983) 392–3 believes that Alcmena is being parodied here as a haughty *matrona* who in effect delivers her own funeral elegy.　　**examussim** 'to a T', a term from carpentry; cf. Ernout–Meillet *amussis.*

844 delenitus 'bewitched', < *de* + *lenio* (lit., 'soften down'; for magic as a force capable of emasculating men cf. *Od.* 10.336ff.). **ut me qui sim nesciam:** Amphitryon for the first time explicitly doubts his identity; cf. 781, 1039–52, 1076nn. For the prolepsis see 54–5n.

845 caue sis ne tu te usu perduis 'please take caution lest you lose yourself through someone else's taking possession of you', a variation on Sosia's earlier jest on *usucapio* (375n.). Cf. also the desig-nation of Alcmena as Jupiter's *uxor usuraria* (498, 980–1). Am-phitryon, whose identity as *paterfamilias* is inextricably linked with his control over his wife and his household, is in fact undergoing the process Sosia describes.　　**tu te:** (thematic) linguistic doubling as Amphitryon comes to doubt his unique identity.　　**perduis:** 72n.

846 ita nunc homines immutantur, postquam peregre aduenimus: generalizing from his earlier experience (cf. 456), Sosia concludes that the normal laws of nature may be suspended (cf. 825–9n.).

847 mulier, istam rem inquisitam certum est non amit-tere 'Woman, I am determined not to let the matter under investi-gation slide' (cf. 779, 806nn.).　　**mulier:** 729n.

848 edepol me libente facies 'By all means, that's just fine by me.'　　**quid ais?:** 364n.

849–53 The spouses make a preliminary agreement to proceed with a divorce if Naucrates can verify Amphitryon's version of the events. The audience of course knows the couple will be reconciled (cf. 474–5).

849 tuom cognatum huc a naui Naucratem: the hyperbaton emphasizes that Naucrates is Alcmena's relation (given her recent claim that she maintains *concordia* (841) with her *cognati*, she can expect him to give honest testimony). Scafuro (1997) 234–5 argues that Amphitryon's summoning of a *cognatus* is meant to suggest the convening of a family council regarding the issue of divorce, a dis-

tinctly Roman (but not Greek) practice.   **tuom:** with synizesis.
cognatum huc: *A / B* hiatus at the main break. The entire line has
a 'heavy' rhythm (42n.), as does 850.   **Naucratem:** a common
Greek name (lit., 'commander of the ship'), whose etymology is
alluded to here by *naui* (repeated in 850).

850 una ... una: the adverb and the adjective, respectively
('together with me on the same ship').

851 quid tibi aequom est fieri? 'what is the proper thing to be
done to you?'

852 numquid causam dicis 'Is there any reason whatsoever
you can give?' (*numquid* is adverbial accusative).   **quin te hoc
multem matrimonio:** lit. 'why I shouldn't punish you with the
loss of this marriage'. In addition to divorcing her, under Roman
law Amphitryon could retain a portion of her dowry if a charge of
adultery can be substantiated; cf. Treggiari (1991) 352.

853 nulla causa est 'there's no reason you shouldn't'.

854 duc hos intro: as readers, we have probably forgotten that
the mute baggage carriers have been part of the spectacle since 551.
ego huc ab naui mecum adducam Naucratem: Amphitryon
exits by the harbour wing without entering his palace (which he will
be prevented from doing throughout the entire play).

855 dic mihi uerum serio 'In all honesty, tell me the truth.'
mihi: monosyllabic.

856 ecquis alius Sosia intust: cf. 825–9n.

857 Sosia, in contrast to his master (854n.), does enter the house
and will not reappear until 956.   **abin hinc:** cf. 518n.   **abeo,
si iubes:** exits motivated by the order of a superior are formulaic in
Greek and Roman comedy (cf. Frost (1988) 13).

858–9 'By god it's a remarkably strange thing how that husband
of mine has decided to accuse me wrongly like that, of so vile a
crime!'

858 qui: adverb.

859 insimulare: cf. 820n.

860 Naucrate: either the final *e* is long (cf. Ov. *Met.* 10.608, *F.*
3.729, Juv. 13.98, Lucan 8.358 and Housman (1972) ɪɪ 833–4) or an
unusual *locus Jacobsohnianus* (p. 64).   **cognato ... cognoscam:**
figura etymologica.

861–81 (Scene 6) Just as Mercury had delivered a prologizing address (463–98) after the lengthy confrontation between Sosia and himself, so Jupiter enters and speaks directly to the audience immediately following the long scene of spousal conflict. Sedgwick dismisses the scene as 'unnecessary and repetitive ... clearly added by P. for the benefit of his inattentive Roman audience' (n. on 861ff.), but Jupiter's address here reflects P.'s desire to control the play's reception (cf. pp. 24–7). The god reminds the audience that he and Mercury are role-playing and that the play is a comedy (868), and so domestic harmony will be restored after the birth of the twins. Nor is the content of the address strictly repetitive, as new information is divulged: Alcmena will be granted the boon of a painless birth (879).

Jupiter's address falls into three distinct units: (1) his jocund and metatheatrical *captatio* (861–6); (2) the reassurance that he has come to direct the comedy toward a happy ending in which Alcmena will be exonerated (867–72); (3) an outline of the remainder of the play (873–9). Transition to the following scene is made at 880–1. METRE: after 361 verses of song or recitative with musical accompaniment, Jupiter speaks to the audience in iambic senarii.

861–4 As the stage has been emptied, and Jupiter has not appeared since 550, the god playfully identifies himself, the *torulus* (144) notwithstanding.

863 in superiore qui habito cenaculo 'I who live on the very highest storey'; the expression here invites multiple interpretations. First, Jupiter is probably parodying the lofty metaphors used to designate the sky in epic and tragic poetry, as Enn. *Ann.* 51 Skutsch *cenacula maxima caeli* (cf. Ov. *Met.* 1.176 *Palatia caeli* and 1065 *caeli cultor*). The actor playing Jupiter could also be humorously referring to his own humble status (cf. 26–7n.) in Rome, where he might be expected to live atop one of Rome's notorious *insulae*. Cf. Dupont (1976) 135–6. **qui habito:** *b / b* (prosodic hiatus).

864 Iuppiter: after proceeding in a most roundabout fashion ('I'm the Amphitryon with a slave Sosia, who on occasion becomes Mercury, the Amphitryon who dwells in the uppermost storey and who sometimes becomes Jupiter when I want to'), the god finally identifies himself explicitly. **quando lubet:** 123n.

865 huc 'to the theatre here on earth'. **quom extemplo =** *quom primum*. Cf. 207n. **aduentum adporto** 'I direct my arrival', a stilted phrase; cf. Acc. 554 R = 557 W *quis tu es mortalis qui in deserta et tesqua te adportes loca?*

866 uestitum immuto meum 'I change into my costume', a metatheatrical jest in which the personae of Jupiter and the actor merge (cf. 863n.).

867–8 Lit., 'Now, I've come here out of respect for you, so as not to bring this comedy to an end in an incomplete state' (*incohatam* is predicative); a slightly contorted way of saying 'I'm reappearing in the play to help bring it to a proper conclusion', perhaps with the parallel suggestion 'I'm not here as a *deus ex machina* to tie up the loose ends at this point', as this figure appears *in order to* conclude such a play. The motivations for Jupiter's return as a character are shortly revealed to be threefold: (1) to assist Alcmena (869–72, 877–9); (2) to participate further in the comedy of errors (873–5); (3) and, most farcically of all, to enjoy sexual relations with his 'wife on loan' one more time (891–2; cf. 976–81).

867 nunc: the adverb marks the transition to the second unit of the address, as that to the third in 873: see 861–81n.   **uostri:** Jupiter (as Mercury in the prologue), speaks to the audience in the most familiar terms.

868 hanc ... comoediam: 51–63n.

869–72 Jupiter indicates that he will remain to give aid to Alcmena in childbirth (cf. 1061ff.), and (as *deus ex machina*) eventually appease Amphitryon (cf. 1131–43). He makes his intentions even more explicit at 873–9, which, in typically Plautine fashion, reiterate and clarify the immediately preceding thought.

869–70 simul Alcumenae, quam uir insontem probri | Amphitruo accusat ... : after eight playful senarii, Jupiter focuses on what may be an issue for some audience members (861–81n.).

871–2 Mercury had similarly asserted (492–5) that the gods, despite their obvious delight in carrying out the sex farce, would ultimately be 'fair' and see that the play ended happily.

871 quod egomet contraxerim 'what I myself have provoked', anticipating *id* in 872.

872 Alcumenae innocenti expetat: $A \, / \, B$ (at the main break) and a $D \, / \, A$ hiatus, respectively; the line scans $ABcDA \, / \, BcDABcD$. **expetat** 'come home to' (+ dative; cf. 174n.).

873 nunc: 867n.   **ut occepi semel** 'I as I formerly started to do', i.e. in the play's third scene (499–550).   **occepi:** *dAB* (iambic shortening).

874 adsimulabo atque: *A / B* hiatus at the main break.

874–5 atque in horum familiam | frustrationem hodie iniciam maxumam: there are various character combinations yet to be brought together in the doubles comedy (cf. pp. 13–15), and Jupiter is inviting the audience to revel in the inevitable confusions to follow: cf. Mercury's similar pledge at 470–1. Deception is a central theme of New Comedy that is taken to uniquely self-reflexive extremes in P.; cf. *Mos.* 1149–51 (where the triumphant slave consoles the duped *senex*) *si amicus Diphilo aut Philemoni es, | dicito is quo pacto tuos te seruos ludificauerit: | optumas frustrationes dederis in comoediis.*

875 frustrationem hodie: *a / b* hiatus at the main break.

876 res: i.e. his impregnation of Alcmena, the separate paternity of the boys, and Alcmena's guiltlessness (cf. 1131–43).

876 post igitur demum 'afterwards, only then …'; for temporal *igitur* cf. 210n. The true nature of the *frustratio* will be revealed once the household has been cast into the utmost chaos, i.e. after the doubles comedy has exhausted the possibilities for confusion.

877 atque 'and what is more …' (to emphasize the boon to Alcmena).   **in tempore** 'at the appropriate time'.

878 quod grauida est 'what she has conceived'. For the chiefly archaic use of an adjective with *esse* to approximate a transitive verb see LHS II 34.   **quod:** for the neuter see 501n.

878–9 uiro | … me: perhaps on the analogy of the bare ablative (of source) with such verbs as *genero*. Cf. 111, where Mercury more properly uses *ex*.

881 si 'in case …' (*OLD* 11); *uellem* is a subjunctive in *oratio obliqua* (after 880 *iussi*).   **hanc:** Alcmena's cue to come out of the house.

882–955 (Scene 7) Jupiter humorously effects a reconcilation with the outraged Alcmena so that he may 'borrow her body' once again (891–2, 980–1). Much of the humour in the scene is derived from Jupiter's inversion of conventional relations between gods and human beings as he begs forgiveness from Alcmena: cf. 911n. The reconciliation here sets up another confused encounter between Alcmena and her genuine husband (preserved only in fr. 7–10). METRE: this is the first scene of dialogue in iambic senarii (the earlier encounter of Jupiter and Alcmena (499–550) was in trochaic septe-

narii). The later heated exchange between Alcmena and Amphitryon
likewise will be in senarii.

882–90 Jupiter eavesdrops as Alcmena bursts out of the house
and melodramatically broadcasts her anger over Amphitryon's
charge; she does not notice him until after his aside in 891–6.

882 Scan *A B c dd A B c d+ aa B c D*.   **Durare nequeo in aedibus:** an indication that she has divorce in mind; cf. 928n.

882–3 me . . . argutam: understand *esse* with *argutam* (accusative
of exclamation).   **probri, | stupri, dedecoris** 'shame, illicit
sex, disgraceful conduct', a lively tricolon with crescendo.

883 stupri: in strict legal parlance, *stuprum* is committed with a
woman who is not married at the time of the act, and is distinguished from *adulterium*, the technical term when a man has sexual
relations with another's wife (Treggiari (1991) 263); the two terms,
however, were often used interchangeably.

884 ea quae sunt facta infecta re esse clamitat 'He keeps
shouting that what happened didn't really happen' (Lindemann's
suggestion is printed).

885 quae neque sunt facta neque ego in me admisi arguit
'He alleges what did not happen and I did not commit.'   **in me
admisi:** lit., 'admitted to my person'; the sexual sense of the verb
(*OLD* 2b and c) may be felt as well.

886 id me susque deque esse habituram 'that I will consider
this of no account'.   **susque deque:** lit., 'both up and down'; cf.
Otto (1890) 337 and English 'neither here nor there'. For *-que . . . -que*
and polar expressions in general cf. 7n.

887–8 non edepol faciam 'I most certainly will not consider it
of no account.'   **neque me perpetiar probri | falso in-
simulatam** 'nor will I put up with my being falsely accused of misconduct'. For the participle with *patior*, etc. cf. Acc. 363 R = 359 W
pulsum patimini, and Ter. *Ph.* 304 *egone illam cum illo ut patiar nuptam
unum diem.*   **probri | . . . insimulatam:** 820n.

888 deseram: cf. 928n.

889 satis faciat mi 'apologize to me'.

**888–9 atque adiuret insuper | nolle esse dicta quae in me
insontem protulit:** lit., 'and swear besides that he wishes the
charges he brought against my innocent self had not been uttered'.

891–2 'I've got to do precisely what she demands be done if I want her to take me back as her lover.' Cf. 882–955n.

891 fieri: *bb C.*   **illaec:** with iambic shortening in the penult.

892 amantem: 106n.   **studeam:** subjunctive in *oratio obliqua*.

893–6 Jupiter in effect explains to the audience how a comedy of mistaken identity works.

893 ego quod feci: i.e. his arrival on the prior night and subsequent departure (499–550), resumed by *id factum*.

894 dudum 'of late' (with both *offuit* and *exhibuit*).   **amor** 'love affair'.

894–5 negotium | ... exhibuit 'brought trouble on'.

895 insonti ... insonti mihi: Amphitryon, like Alcmena (cf. 869, 890) is truly 'guiltless', but the application of the adjective to Jupiter, the driving force behind the deception, is highly ironic ('poor innocent little me'), as would be emphasized through delivery. For the doubling here see pp. 15–17.

896 expetent: 872n.

897 sed eccum uideo 'Oh look! I see ...'

898 stupri: 882–3n.   **uxor:** by addressing her as his wife, Jupiter immediately attempts to strike a note of conciliation: cf. 729nn.

899 quo te auortisti?: a stage direction; cf. *Mer.* 433, *Truc.* 358, and Titin. 93–4 R *quor te auortisti? mei fastidis, | meae deliciae.* Alcmena probably does not look directly at Jupiter until at least 935 (cf. 927). Oniga n. *ad loc.* compares the famous scene in the *Aeneid* in which Dido turns away from Aeneas in the underworld (6.469).   **ita ⟨ingeni⟩ ingenium meumst** 'Such is the character of my character'; Seyffert's plausible conjecture, based on the similar polyptoton at *St.* 126 *edepol uos lepide temptaui uostrumque ingenium ingeni*, saves the metre.

900 inimicos: cf. *A.* 6.472, where Virgil describes Dido as *inimica* as she flees to Sychaeus; Oniga notes that *inimicus* became a technical term for divorced parties (Alcmena may again be hinting at divorce: cf. 882n.). There also is irony here in that *inimicitia* is the least desirable state for a human being to be in with respect to a god: cf. *Mil.* 314 *quis magis dis inimicis natus quam tu atque iratis?*   **osa sum:** a deponent form of *odi*.   **obtuerier** < *obtueor* (14n.).

901 heia autem inimicos? 'Come now, enemies indeed!'; *heia* is

often condescending, e.g. *Truc.* 193.   **autem:** for the use in exclamations see *OLD* 6.

903 iracunda: Lambinus' correction of a very early corruption
(cf. Non. p. 269) to *uerecunda*. For the play with religious language see
911n.   **potin ut abstineas manum?** 'Could you possibly keep
your hand(s) off me?' (*potin = potis + ne, sc. est*). One distinction between the two Amphitryons, obvious in performance, is the lecher-
ousness of Jupiter, which no doubt is played to ridiculous extremes.
The god's hands seem to have roamed similarly in the first scene
with Alcmena (cf. 507, 526); for another female character's similar
resistance to such groping cf. *Rud.* 424 *non ego sum pollucta pago* ('I'm
no country buffet'). *potin ut me abstineas manum?*

904 si sis sanus aut sapias satis: cf. the alliterative use of σ
to express Medea's anger at E. *Med.* 476 ἔσωσά σ', ὡς ἴσασιν
Ἑλλήνων ὅσοι. Alcmena's animated speech here is fraught with
doublets (cf. 905 *arbitrere et praedices*, 906 *nec ioco nec serio*, 907 *stultior
stultissimo*).

906 nec ioco nec serio: a universalizing doublet (i.e. 'you
wouldn't speak with her in any manner at all': 7n.) that is thematically apropos. With his usual disregard for verisimilitude, P. has got
ahead of himself: Jupiter will shortly claim that the real Amphitryon's accusations were spoken in jest (916–7). Cf. also Otto (1890)
176–7.

907 tibi 'I tell you' (ethic dative: Woodcock §66, GL §351).
stultior stultissumo 'more foolish than the most foolish man
alive', a common Plautine expression: cf. *Curc.* 551 *stultior stulto.*

908–9 'If I said you were *impudica*, you are none the more so, nor
do I suppose you are, and for this reason I've come back to apologize to you' (no doubt glibly delivered).

909 id: 163–4n.   **reuorti ut:** *A / B* hiatus at the main break.
me purgarem tibi: there is humorous irony in having a god seek
purgatio from a human being. Cf 911n.

911 ted esse iratam mihi: an inversion of divine and human
interaction. It is the prerogative of the gods to be either *propitius* or
iratus toward human beings: cf. 900, 903, 923, 933–5, 1065, 1090.

912 cur dixisti? inquies. ego expediam tibi: skilled rhetori-
cian that he is, Jupiter anticipates Alcmena's line of attack. Cf. 52–
3n.   **expediam** 'I'll clear matters up'; cf. 5n.

913 non edepol quo te esse impudicam crederem 'Good-ness, I didn't say it because I believed that you were unfaithful.' **non quo:** used with the subjunctive, as in classical Latin, to intro-duce a reason to be expressly denied.

915 induceres: understand *animum* ('and how you would find it in your heart to endure this'). Jupiter's vapid and seemingly im-provised explanation has no immediate effect on Alcmena (cf. 918–20).

917 ridiculi causa 'as a joke'; *ridiculi* is a neuter substantive. **uel** 'if you like' (444n.). **hunc:** with iambic shortening. Jupiter gestures toward the palace, which Sosia entered at 857 (as if to fore-shadow his entrance in 956).

918 quin huc adducis meum cognatum Naucratem: the line has a 'heavy' rhythm (42n.). **meum:** with synizesis. **Naucratem:** cf. 854, 1009–10.

920 te huc non uenisse: indirect statement after *testem* ('as a witness to the fact that …').

921 praeuortier 'attend to'.

922 ego illum scio quam doluerit cordi meo 'As for that jest of yours, I know well how it grieved my heart' (cf. 54–5n.).

923 oro obsecro: both verbs are commonplace in divine en-treaties (cf. 934 *quaeso*); for the supreme god's use of them in his desperate plea to his mortal lover see 911n.

924 mihi: an elided monosyllable. **ueniam, ignosce:** *dd / A* hiatus. **irata:** Jupiter's persistent irony (911n.) increases the farcical tone of the scene.

925 ego istaec feci uerba uirtute irrita 'I have rendered those allegations of yours invalid by my *uirtus*.' **uirtute:** the at-tribution of *uirtus* to a woman is otherwise unattested before Cicero; McDonnell (1983) 65 sees a reversal of gender roles. Given Alcme-na's earlier association of *uir* and *uirtus* (648–53n.) and the fact that a male actor plays this most unusual role, an audience might find such a (metatheatrical?) claim uproarious. As always, the actor's delivery would be decisive. Cf. 75n. **irrita:** a legal technical term.

926–7 factis me impudicis … impudicis dictis: the con-ventional opposition between words and deeds is set off in chiastic word-order. For Alcmena's tendency to appropriate philosophical commonplaces cf. 633–4n.

926 abstini = *abstinui*.

927 auorti uolo: 899n.

928 tibi habeas res tuas, reddas meas: a formula for divorce, perhaps already in the Twelve Tables (IV 3). The evidence suggests that a Roman woman married *sine manu* (i.e. without transferring her father's power over her to her husband) already in P.'s time could in some circumstances initiate a divorce: cf. Watson (1967) 48–54, Treggiari (1991) 443–4 (*aliter* McDonnell (1983) 54–80). For the formula uttered here to be binding, Alcmena presumably would have to walk away from Jupiter and their home; instead, they will shortly be reconciled (935n.). See further Rosenmeyer (1995).

929 iuben mi ire comites? 'Are you going to let my attendants accompany me?'   **sanan:** Alcmena's behaviour is entirely rational; for the intentional confusion of sanity and insanity in the play see p. 31.

930 ibo egomet 'I'll go by myself'; cf. *Cas.* 198 *nos sumus* ('we're by ourselves'). The idea of a *matrona* venturing out in public without suitable accompaniment (cf. *Mer.* 401–11), much less alone and without her husband's permission (cf. *Mer.* 821–2), would seem reckless and arrogant to P.'s audience.   **comitem mihi Pudicitiam duxero** 'Pudicitia will accompany me', probably spoken with extreme superciliousness by the male actor. Pudicitia was the personification of women's chastity and was worshipped from an early date. Originally, her cult was open only to *uniuirae* (Livy 10.23.9: cf. Axtell (1907) 39–40). The image conjured here of the goddess of chastity strolling off with the pregnant voluptuary (and unwitting *duouira*) is absurd. For P.'s (sometimes) playful attitude toward such deities see 42n.   **Pudicitia:** the second syllable undergoes iambic shortening in this highly resolved (i.e. 'light') line.

931 arbitratu tuo 'of your choosing' (*tuo* is monosyllabic); Jupiter never gives her a chance to dictate the oath.

932–4 By having the god swear an oath to himself here P. maintains the comic distance farce strives for and keeps the play-within-the-play framework foremost in the audience's mind. Similarly, when Jupiter avers (932) that his wife is chaste, the audience will catch a reference to Juno (cf. 508n.).

933 id ... fallo: *id* is internal accusative ('commit that sort of deception'). *tum* is formulaic in oaths of this type, e.g. Livy 22.53.11 *si sciens fallo, tum me Iuppiter ... leto afficiat.*

934 quaeso: 923n.   **iratus:** 911n.

935 a, propitius sit potius 'No, no – that he be well disposed instead', an abrupt and psychologically unmotivated (so Oniga on 935ff.) change of attitude that is typical of P. The reconciliation will only lead to further confusion.   **propitius:** cf. 1065 and 1090. **confido fore** 'I do trust that he will be so disposed' (with smug irony).

936 nam ius iurandum uerum te aduorsum dedi: Jupiter gives his word with a rhythmically heavy line.   **uerum:** the oath is 'genuine' in that he does believe Juno is chaste (932–4n.). **te aduorsum** 'in your presence'.

937 irata: 911n.   **non sum:** the swift change of attitude is natural in farce (P. for now has wrung as much as he can out of Alcmena's obstinacy). Cf. 935n.

938–43 Jupiter smooths matters over with gnomic reflections that consciously echo those in Alcmena's earlier song on *uoluptas* (cf. 633–6); for their thematic relevance to the doubles-comedy see p. 14.

938 in hominum aetate: cf. 634.   **huius:** with synizesis.

939 capiunt uoluptates, capiunt rursum miserias: Jupiter makes it clear that he is speaking specifically of amorous relationships (cf. 635).   **uoluptates:** with iambic shortening in the ante-penult.

940 redeunt rursum in gratiam: the subject is *homines* (cf. 938–9). Jupiter is also foreshadowing the final reconciliation of Amphitryon and Alcmena; cf. 1141–2.

941–3 The notion that *amor* is only strengthened by conflict between lovers is commonplace: cf. Ter. *And.* 555 *amantium ira amoris integratio est*, Ov. *Am.* 1.8.96 *non bene, si tollas proelia, durat amor*, *AA* 2.447–66, and Otto (1890) 17.

943 bis tanto amici sunt inter se quam prius 'They are twice as much in love with each other as they were before.'

944–5 'You ought to have been careful not to say these things in the first place, but if you also apologize to me for these, I'll have to accept.'

945 isdem 'also' (the archaic nominative singular); some editors change to *idem*.   **purgas:** 909n.   **patiunda sunt:** plural where the impersonal more often is singular (cf. 283n.).

946–8 Jupiter has Alcmena make preparations for a sacrifice to his own *numen* (cf. the ambiguous 946 *mihi*). Amphitryon had offered the usual vows to Jupiter for success in battle (229–30), which the god now humorously fulfils. Cf. 983.

947 uota uoui: *figura etymologica.*

947–8 si ... | rediissem: the protasis of the vow is in *oratio obliqua* after *uota uoui*. The direct form would be *si rediero*, with the simple future in the apodosis.

948 ego exsoluam: *C / D* hiatus, but after the seventh element (54n.).

949–53 As Jupiter instructs her to summon Sosia (949–51), Alcmena heads toward the palace, but does not go directly inside and notices that Jupiter, whom she is imagined not to be able to hear from 952 on, is still talking (954). Her exit is interrupted by Sosia's emergence from the palace and she will not leave the stage until 972. Jupiter briefly (952–3) maps out some of the confusion to follow: Sosia is to be sent off to fetch Blepharo (cf. 1035–6n.) so that *diuinus Sosia* (cf. 976–82) may take his place at the house and abet Jupiter's amours (cf. 1021–fr. 6). Blepharo appears with the real Sosia before Amphitryon (frs. 11–14n.), where he is totally at a loss as an arbiter in the climactic meeting between the two Amphitryons (1035–8). Amphitryon will suffer the physical violence promised by Jupiter here (953; cf. fr. 15–1052n.).

949 euocate: Jupiter turns toward the palace and calls to the slaves whom he had instructed Sosia to lead in at 854.

951 arcessat: hortatory subjunctive.   **qui nobiscum prandeat:** relative clause of purpose.

952 is adeo inpransus ⟨laute⟩ ludificabitur: the transmitted text is two elements short. Lindemann suggested *inpransus lepide ludificabitur* (cf. *Cas.* 558 and *Mil.* 927), but following *Mil.* 1161 we might just as well supply *laute*, which is printed here *exempli gratia*. The general sense at any rate is clear.   **inpransus:** cf. 967–9n.

953 collo ... obstricto 'with his neck roped' (as if a criminal: cf. fr. 15n.).

954 mirum quid solus secum secreto ille agat: for the acknowledgement of another character's aside cf. 381n. and *Mer.* 379 *quid illuc est quod ille a me solus se in consilium seuocat?*   **mirum quid** 'It's strange how ...' (cf. *mirum est qui* 858). The rhythm of the line is heavy.

955 atque 'but look'; often with *eccum* to announce the appearance of a character, especially one just mentioned, e.g. *Rud.* 492.

956–83 (Scene 8) A very brief scene marked by Sosia's appearance and a change of metre. Sosia is apprised of the reconciliation and then dispatched to the harbour (969), Alcmena is sent inside to make final preparations for sacrifice (972), and Jupiter, alone on stage, invokes Mercury (974–83) and informs the audience of his intentions.

In the overall structure of the play, the scene corresponds to 1021–fr. 6.   METRE: 956–73 trochaic septenarii; 974–83 iambic senarii.

956 impera, imperium: *figura etymologica.*

957 ⟨Sosia⟩, optume aduenis 'Sosia, you've come at just the right time' (the supplement is Leo's; the line is two elements short).

958–61 Sosia delivers a sermonette on the *seruos bonus/frugi*: see 590–1n. Sosia's profession of loyalty here is humorously undercut, given both his general character (153–462, 186–261nn.) and the irreverent attitude he displayed toward his master and mistress in his last appearance as a comic interloper (654–86on.). Mercury as Sosia shortly makes a similar speech (991–6).

958 gaudeo et uolup est mihi 'I'm delighted and pleased.' Cf. 993–4.

959 atque ita seruom par uidetur frugi sese instituere 'Yes, and it seems right for a good slave to train himself as follows.' **frugi** 'good', used as an indeclinable adjective (originally *bonae frugi*, predicative dative).

960 proinde eri ut sint: in this generalizing statement, the plural includes *era*, *erus maior*, and (where relevant) *erus minor*.

961 tristis sit, si eri sint tristes: chiasmus.

962 rediistis in concordiam: for the expression cf. 474–5.

964 an id ioco dixisti? equidem serio ac uero ratus 'Is it really so that you said that in jest? I for one believed you said it seriously and sincerely.'   **an id ioco:** *bb c D* (iambic shortening).

965 habui expurigationem; facta pax est :: optume est: scanned *bb C D a B c D A B c D A B c D*.   **habui expurigationem; facta pax est** 'I've cleaned the matter up; we've made our peace'; more play with religious language (911n.).   **pax:** for *pax* of divine blessing see 34n.

966 rem diuinam intus faciam 'I've got some divine business to do inside'; given Jupiter's true intent (980–1), there probably is a sexual pun, though a precise parallel in Latin is wanting. Cf. 'the divine matter' (τὸ θεῖον χρῆμα) in the Cologne papyrus (10) of

Archilochus; for *res* of sexual intercourse see Adams (1982) 203.
uota quae sunt 'with those things which were vowed' (antecedent
omitted).   **censeo** 'Yes, you should' (cf. *OLD* 3b).

967 uerbis meis 'on my behalf'.

969 iam hic ero, cum illic censebis esse me: i.e. 'I'll be
back before you know it.' Given his preoccupation with food (186–
261, 254nn.), Sosia can be expected to carry out this mission zeal-
ously; in the lost portion of the play he presumably complained bit-
terly of missing out on the proposed lunch. There is also irony in
that the other Sosia will arrive shortly (984): cf. 545n.

**970 numquid uis, quin abeam iam intro, ut apparentur
quibus opust?** 'Do you want anything else that would keep me
from going inside now to prepare what is needed?'   **numquid
uis:** 542n.

971 i sane 'By all means, go.'

972 quin uenis quando uis intro: *intro* is separated from *uenis*
to preserve the alternating alliteration of *u-* and *q-*.   **faxo:** 355n.

973 recte loquere et proinde diligentem ut uxorem decet:
scan *B C dd A B c D a B c D A B c D*.   **diligentem ... uxorem:** the
materfamilias is expected to demonstrate *diligentia* in all the affairs of
the household; cf. Treggiari (1991) 425. For Jupiter's highly ironic
use of *uxorem* here cf. 729n. and 980–1.

974–83 Alone on stage, Jupiter addresses the audience in spoken
senarii.

974 hisce: nominative plural (*MHL* 90).   **frustra sunt** 'are
deceived' (= *frustrantur*).

975 errant probe 'they are completely fooled' (Jupiter has completed the first stage of the *frustratio* promised in 875). For *probe* cf.
183n.

976–83 As a demonstration of the gods' supernatural powers,
Jupiter communicates his wishes telepathically to Mercury, who had
left by the harbour wing at 545; as a result, Mercury's frenetic entrance at 984 will be all the more striking.

976 diuine huc: *a / B* hiatus at the main break.   **Sosia:** the
stock comic name (365n.) is amusingly combined with *diuine*.

978 Amphitruonem aduenientem: *a / B* hiatus at the main
break.

978–9 Amphitruonem aduenientem ab aedibus | ... abi-

gas: the pronounced alliteration is perhaps intended to suggest magical incantation (cf. 976–83n.). Just as he was charged to drive Sosia away from the palace in the first scene, so now Mercury is to prevent Amphitryon from entering it so that Jupiter may dally with Alcmena without disturbance.

979 quouis pacto fac commentus sis 'Do it in whatsoever way you think of.'

980 uolo deludi illunc: standard terminology of the clever slave and his cohort in P.: 295n.

980–1 usuraria | uxore: pp. 39–40.

981 mihi morigero: cf. 131n.   **mihi** is a monosyllable here.

982 proinde adeo ut uelle me intellegis 'yes, and according to your understanding of my wishes'.

983 ut ministres: governed by *fac* (982).   **mihi, mihi:** for the linguistic doubling see pp. 15–17 (both are monosyllables here).

984–1008 (Scene 9) With the stage emptied after Jupiter's exit into the palace, Mercury makes an energetic entrance first in the manner of the *seruus currens* (984–90); he then stakes his own (stereo-typical) claim to being a *bonus seruus* (991–6), and finishes with an-other prologizing address (997–1008). For Mercury's versatility as an actor see pp. 24–7.   METRE: 984–1005 are iambic octonarii, 1006–8 senarii.

984–90 The sudden entrance of a *seruus currens* bearing an impor-tant message probably was already a stereotyped scene in Greek New Comedy; cf. Hunter (1985) 80–2, with further references. In P.'s hands, such scenes are taken to burlesque extremes (see *Cur.* 280–98), and, as here, are frequently exploited for metatheatrical humour: with 987 *quam seruolo in comoediis* cf. *Capt.* 778–9 *nunc certa res est, eodem pacto ut comici serui solent, | coniciam in collum pallium, primo ex med hanc rem ut audiat.* That Mercury is merely sporting with comic convention is underscored by the fact that he bears no message at all, but appears in answer to Jupiter's telepathic summons (989) and proceeds to map out his role in the remaining *ludus* (997–1008).

984 Concedite ... abscedite ... decedite: Mercury's bom-bastic entrance is marked by the repetition of the imperative with three different prefixes; cf. *Cur.* 281 *fugite omnes, abite et de uia secedite.* Such an entrance might be made most effectively by passing through the audience; though irrefutable evidence is lacking in the extant scripts, the lowness of the Roman stage and the absence of a formal barrier between actor and audience in Plautine theatre make this plausible: cf. pp. 19–21.

985 fuat = *sit* (archaic subjunctive; here hortatory). Cf. *MHL* 165.   **qui obuiam obsistat mihi:** relative clause of result.

986–7 Lit., 'For, by God, how should it be less permissible for me, a god, to threaten the mob, if it doesn't get out of my way, than it is for a piddling slave in the comedies?' (for the irony that the actor is himself a slave in real life see 26–7n.).

987 seruolo: in marked contrast with 986 *deo*.   **in comoediis:** i.e. 'in comic theatre' (whereas *in comoedia* would indicate a specific play), a formula in metatheatrical contexts (cf. *Mos.* 1151, *Ps.* 1081).

988 ille nauem saluam nuntiat aut irati aduentum senis: both of these typical and sometimes overlapping functions of the *seruus currens* are found in P.'s plays, e.g. *Mer.* 173–4 (safe arrival of the ship) and *Mos.* 365 (arrival of a stern father, the blocking character).   **ille:** the ultima does not count in scansion (apocope: p. 62).

989 ego sum Ioui dicto audiens, eius iussu nunc huc me adfero: the first indication of Mercury's true purpose in appearing now; cf. his similar statement in the prologue (19).   **ego sum Ioui dicto audiens** 'I am obedient to Jupiter'; for *dicto audiens* (as if one word) + dative cf. *OLD audio* 11c.   **eius:** with synizesis.

991–6 Following Sosia's lead (958–61n.), Mercury parodies the 'good slave' *topos*, which he combines with that of the *filius bonus* (992). As Oniga points out on 992ff., the conflation of filial and servile roles is natural in a culture known for its stern *paterfamilias*, who could in fact sell his son into slavery (cf. Twelve Tables IV 2); Dionysius of Halicarnassus (*Ant. Rom.* 2.27.1) noted that a Roman slave had a better chance than his master's son of becoming totally free of *patria potestas* (see further Bettini (1991*a*) 5–13). But to depict, as Mercury does here, the dutiful son as one who aids and abets his father in his adulterous pursuits (993–6) is an absurd inversion of everyday norms consistent with the festive nature of Plautine comedy. Cf. 177–8n.

991 eius: a monosyllable (to be construed with *imperio*). **imperio:** dative with *dicto . . . audiens* (cf. 989n.)

993 amanti subparasitor, hortor, adsto, admoneo, gaudeo 'When he's in love I play the parasite for him, I encourage him, I'm at his side, I give advice, I share his joy.' The five verbs in asyndeton create an appropriately frivolous tone. To appreciate the travesty of social norms here (cf. 991–6n.), we may note that among the Romans there were even strictures on fathers and sons bathing together (Plut. *Quaest. Rom.* 40). In P.'s topsy-turvy world, however, father and son may even become rivals for the same woman (e.g. *Mer.*). **amanti subparasitor:** humorously incongruous after Mercury's declaration of *pietas* in 992. For the role of the *parasitus* see 515n.

994 si quid patri uolup est, uoluptas ea mihi multo maxumast: cf. Sosia's similar claim at 958. **multo:** 782n.

995 amat: sapit; recte facit, animo quando obsequitur suo 'He's in love, he's smart, he does the right thing when he indulges his desire.' **animo ... obsequitur:** 131n.

996 quod omnis homines facere oportet: cf. the similar recommendation of the *adulescens* Diniarchus at *Truc.* 76 *amare oportet omnes qui quod dent habent.* **dum id modo fiat bono** 'provided this is done in proper fashion'; cf. *Mer.* 1021–2 *neu quisquam posthac prohibeto adulescentium filium | quin amet et scortum ducat, quod bono fiat modo.* Sedgwick's translation of *modo ... bono* as 'in moderation' is ill suited to the context, as the behaviour – i.e. Jupiter's incessant philandering – Mercury recommends is anything but moderate (cf. 995 *animo quando obsequitur suo*). Instead, Mercury seems to be endorsing sexual indulgence in general so long as it does not damage one's reputation or finances, a quintessentially Roman notion; cf. p. 44.

997–1008 With considerable detail, Mercury maps out the forthcoming scene (1021–fr. 6) in which he, in the guise of Sosia, will make a *ludus* of the slave's master.

997 deludi: 980n.   **faxo:** 355n.

998 hic deludetur, spectatores, uobis inspectantibus: this rhythmically heavy line could serve as a motto for Plautine comedy in general, where deception and trickery are central, and the audience's essential role in performance is constantly acknowledged. The audience is directly addressed as *spectatores* over 20 times in P., whether in prologues (e.g. *As.* 1), within the body of the play (e.g. *Truc.* 482), or at the final *plaudite* (e.g. 1146): passages collected by

Knapp (1919) 47–9. The audience is more frequently – and more intimately (867n.) – addressed with the second-person pronoun.

999 corona: the garland is standard equipment on festive occasions, and will signal immediately to Amphitryon that his (supposed) slave has been drinking. Cf. (e.g.) *Ps.* 1287, *Men.* 463 (with Gratwick's (1993) note) and 629.

1000 atque illuc susum escendero 'yes, and I'll climb up above there' (Mercury points to the upper level of the palace). For the possible staging of the scene cf. 1021–fr. 6n.

1000–1 inde optume aspellam uirum | de supero 'from up above there I'll drive the fellow away with ease'.

1001 faciam ut sit madidus sobrius 'I'll cause him to be soaked, though sober' (*madidus* = both 'wet' and 'intoxicated'). Cf. fr. 5.

1002–3 Sosia takes the blame for Mercury's actions in the scene represented by frs. 11–14.

1003 eum: with synizesis.   **fecero hic:** *D / A* hiatus.   **quid mea?** = *quid mea refert?* ('What do I care?').

1004 meo me aequomst morigerum patri, eius studio seruire addecet 'It's proper for me to indulge my father; the right thing is to cater to his passion'; traditional morality once again is turned on its head; cf. 991–6, 993nn.   **meo:** with synizesis.

1005 sed eccum Amphitruonem, aduenit 'Oh look – Amphitryon, he's here'; the construction is common in entrances, e.g. *St.* 527 *sed eccum fratrem Pamphilippum, incedit cum socero suo.* **deludetur:** 980n.

1006–8 For Mercury's iambic senarii here see p. 57.

1006 siquidem uos uoltis auscultando operam dare 'If you really want to devote your attention to listening' (the conventional call for attentiveness as in prologues: 38n.).   **siquidem:** the initial syllable is short (enclisis); scan *aa B C D A / B C D aa B c D.*   **uos uoltis:** cf. 1.   **auscultando:** colloquial.

1007 ornatum capiam qui potis decet 'I'll take up the equipment which is appropriate for drunks' (he means primarily the *corona* (cf. 999)). Mercury's new role calls for an altered costume; for the god's self-conscious playing see pp. 24–7. Cf. 1021–fr. 6n.

1009–20 (Scene 10) After entering the house, Mercury would collect any necessary props (cf. frs. 4–5) and, at some point before

1021, ascend by means of a ladder to some sort of scaffolding at the roof of the palace (see pp. 19–21), from which he will harass the returning Amphitryon. In this scene the latter enters from the forum wing and delivers a monologue (1009–14) in the street before directing his attention to the palace. This two-tiered manner of staging is otherwise unattested in New Comedy, but something like it was used in South Italian drama: see p. 52. In Greek tragedy, gods and goddesses *ex machina* appeared on the roof of the scene building. METRE: trochaic septenarii.

1009–14 Naucrates never appears, and remains a mere name with which P. sports: cf. 1009 *in naui non erat* and 849n. The futile search was to keep Amphitryon off the stage during the past four scenes (861–1008). The description of the 'wild-goose chase' throughout the city was a set-piece in New Comedy: cf. Ter. *Ad.* 713–18, *Mer.* 805–8, and *Epid.* 192–200 (where the lead slave feigns having made just such a search). Cf. also Catullus 55, where, in contrast to here, the setting described is distinctly Roman (cf. 1111–13n.).

Amphitryon had exited via the harbour wing (854), but Naucrates' absence at the ship leads him to search the urban centre, and so here he enters by the forum wing.

1009 Naucratem quem ... erat: this type of attraction to the relative is common in P. Cf. Austin (1971) on Virg. *A.* 1.573. Amphitryon's description of his futile search begins and ends with *Naucratem* (ring composition: cf. 1014).

1010 neque ... inuenio quemquem qui illum uiderit: cf. Ter. *Ad.* 716–17 *nec fratrem homo* | *uidisse se aiebat quisquam*.   **domi:** i.e. at Naucrates' house. Cf. *Epid.* 196–7 *utinam conueniam domi* | *Periphanem*.

1011–13 A mix of primarily Greek places (*gymnasia, myropolia,* and *palaestra* would probably suggest foreign decadence to much of P.'s audience) with a few belonging to the landscape of urban Rome (*macello, foro, tostrinis, aedis*).

1011 perreptaui: cf. Ter. *Ad.* 715 *perreptaui usque omne oppidum,* where the verb ('I crept all over the place') suggests the hobbling movement of a *senex* (cf. 1072n.).   **gymnasia et myropolia:** also mentioned in Epidicus' feigned search, *Epid.* 198–9.

1012 apud emporium: if a reference to the Emporium (trade centre) at Rome that was begun in 193 BC (Livy 35.10.12) is meant, this could provide a *terminus* for dating (cf. pp. 2–4); but see Harvey (1981) 482–4. **in foro:** this comes also in the slave Epidicus' list, *Epid.* 198.

1013 in medicinis, in tostrinis: cf. *Epid.* 198 *per medicinas, per tostrinas.* The repetition and rhyme within the first half of the septenarius is a Plautine mannerism: e.g. *Men.* 403 *saepe tritam, saepe fixam,* *Ps.* 695 *scis amorem, scis laborem.* In both Athens and Rome, the doctors' and barbers' stalls were popular meeting places for those interested in gossip or the latest news (cf. Otto (1890) 350). **apud omnis:** not a violation of Meyer's law (pp. 64–5), as preposition and noun constitute a single word.

1014 sum defessus quaeritando: another stock element of the futile search; cf. Ter. *Ad.* 713 *defessus sum ambulando, Epid.* 197 *sum defessus quaerere, Mer.* 805 *defessus sum ... peruenarier* (P. uses *defessus* + the infinitive or ablative of the gerund indifferently). **nusquam inuenio Naucratem** 'I'm not finding Naucrates anywhere.'

1015 uxore hanc: *a / B* hiatus at the main break. Amphitryon's use of *uxore* suggests his anger has subsided somewhat: 729n.

1016 quem propter: prepositions often follow the relative in P. (cf. 653 and Lindsay 82). **suom:** with synizesis. **stupri:** 882–3n.

1017–18 nam ... satiust 'For I'd rather die than let slide today the inquiry which is under way.' For *mortuom satiust* (sc. *esse*) cf. *Truc.* 926 and *Cas.* 111–12; for the foreshadowing of Amphitryon's loss of identity here see 1076n. Cf. also 847.

1018 sed aedis occluserunt 'Well now, they've locked the palace' (especially vexing to the *paterfamilias*). **eugepae** 'Oh, great ...' (ironic).

1020 aperite hoc; heus, ecquis hic est? ecquis hoc aperit ostium?: scanned *bb c D A B c D A / bb C dd a B c D.* **ecquis ... ecquis:** the latter undergoes enclisis, the former does not.

1021–fr. 6 (Scene 11) The promised *ludus* (cf. 997–1008) of the *paterfamilias*, who believes he is being outrageously mocked by his drunken slave. Mercury here assumes the insolence of the triumphant slave in Plautine comedy, who through his clever ruses may gain the upper hand over his master (cf. p. 26).

1021 Quis ad fores est? :: ego sum :: quid 'ego sum'?

'Who's at the door?' '*I am.*' 'What's this "*I am*" talk all about?' (Amphitryon expects to be immediately identified). The highly colloquial nature of the exchange here is evident in the parallelisms of speech: cf. 1023 *quo modo?* :: *eo modo*, 1025–6 *me rogas?* :: *ita, rogo*.   **Quis ad fores:** *bb c D* (with iambic shortening of *ad*).   **quid:** used to quote another's words out of surprise, anger, indignation, etc., e.g. *Bac.* 147 *caue malo* :: *quid 'caue malo'?*

1021–2 tibi Iuppiter | dique omnes irati certo sunt: for the irony see 911n.

1022 qui sic frangas fores: loud knocking on doors is a pervasive sound-effect in P. Cf. 496n.

1023 quo modo?: for the indignant question ('What'?) cf. 556n.   **eo modo, ut profecto uiuas aetatem miser** 'In such a way that you most certainly will live out your life wretchedly.' Mercury deliberately distorts Amphitryon's meaning by answering as if he had been asked (literally) 'In what way?'   **miser:** 2n.

1024 ita, sum Sosia 'Yes, that's my name' (cf. 362n.).

1025 quid nunc uis? :: sceleste, at etiam quid uelim, id tu me rogas? 'What do you want?' 'Scum! Why you even go so far as to ask *me* what I want?'   **sceleste:** the first of several insults traded by the two in this characteristically Plautine exchange; cf. 1026 *fatue* and 1028 *stolide* on Mercury's side of the ledger and Amphitryon's 1029 *uerbero ... ulmorum Acheruns*, 1033 *uerna* and fr. 1 *mastigia*. If the scene were not lacunose, the list of insults no doubt would be extended; for the proposed restoration of one such term see fr. 5n.

1026 fatue 'idiot'.

1027 an fores censebas nobis publicitus praeberier? 'Or were you under the impression that doors are provided for us at public expense?' A topical reference may be lost on us or the joke is metatheatrical (*nobis* = 'for us members of the troupe'), as the stage-building at a public festival might have been financed through a senatorial appropriation. For reference to the details of theatrical production as a source of humour in P. cf. the stage-manager's speech at *Cur.* 462–6 and *Per.* 159–60.   **censebas:** the technical term for making a recommendation in the senate.

1028 stolide 'blockhead' (= *stultus*).   **quid nunc uis tibi?:** 1025n.   **aut quis tu es homo?:** Mercury's pretence of not recognizing Amphitryon is part of the larger scheme to divest him of his identity (1076n.).

1029–30 Amphitryon utters the typical sort of idle threat cast at Plautine slaves by their masters: 518–20n.

1029 uerbero: 180n.   **ulmorum Accheruns:** lit., 'graveyard of elm rods'. The beating of the slave's back will send the branches to their 'death'; cf. *Capt.* 650 *uae illis uirgis miseris, quae hodie in tergo morientur meo.* At *Cas.* 157 Cleostrata refers to her aged husband as *Accheruntis pabulum* ('Hell-fodder').

1030 quem ... faciam feruentem flagris 'whom I'll bring to a boil with blows'.

1031–2 The point of the jest is that Amphitryon has been so spendthrift over the years that in his old age he must beg even for what is least desirable: a beating (*malum*: 26–7n.). The charge of financial prodigality would be especially galling to a *paterfamilias*. For conservative Roman attitudes toward finances see pp. 39–40; for the conundrum style of joke 357, 664–7nn.

1032 senecta aetate: 1072n.   **aetate a:** *a / B* hiatus at the main break.

1033 cum cruciatu tuo: 793n.   **tuo:** an elided monosyllable here.   **uerna:** 179n.   **uerba funditas:** Mercury is about to do some 'pouring' (cf. frs. 4–5) in a more literal sense, as he had hinted earlier (1001).

1034 sacrufico ego tibi. :: qui? :: quia enim te macto infortunio 'I'm sacrificing to you.' 'How do you mean?' 'Why, because I'm "honouring" you with – trouble.'   **macto** = both 'honour with sacrifice, etc.' and 'punish with' (*OLD* 1 and 2); for the negative sense cf. Nov. *com.* 39 R *macto te his uerbenis, macta tu illanc infortunio.*

Fragments 1–19 A substantial section of the play is lost, and only a few lines preserved primarily by ancient grammarians (esp. Nonius) and scholiasts remain. Some of these no doubt are imperfectly reported (cf. fr. 12n.). The vulgate disposition of fragments and scenes is followed here (cf. Fantham (1973)): frs. 1–6 belong to the exchange between Mercury and Amphitryon begun at 1021; frs. 7–10 are from a second confrontation between Amphitryon and Alcmena; in frs. 11–14 Amphitryon, Sosia, and Blepharo are present; and the climactic confrontation between Amphitryon and Jupiter in the presence of Blepharo is represented by frs. 15–19. Modern editors universally reject *non ego te noui, nauilis scriba, columbar impudens*, cited as Plautine by Festus p. 169 (= *incert.* 137 Lindsay), as a line from this last scene. The climactic scene is nearly concluded when the text resumes at 1035. It is possible that additional scenes are completely lost; for a slightly different arrangement see Tränkle (1983).

frs. 1–6 Mercury and Amphitryon continue their argument in trochaic septenarii.

fr. 1 et ego te cruce et cruciatu mactabo, mastigia: in the light of *cruce et cruciatu* (cf. 1033) and *mactabo* (cf. 1034) here, this line may follow 1034 directly. This quotation (as frs. 4–6) is a complete septenarius; frs. 2 and 3 could be the beginning and the end, respectively, of a septenarius. **mastigia** 'whipping-post'. Cf. 446, 1025nn.

fr. 2 erus Amphitruo⟨st⟩ occupatus '*My* master Amphitryon is busy.' Amphitryon presumably has just asserted that he is the master of the house. Mercury continues to treat him as any unwanted visitor, which will only fuel his anger and induce him to assert his identity all the more strongly.

fr. 3 etiam 'still', i.e. Amphitryon may avoid the mistreatment alluded to in frs. 4–5 if he leaves immediately (Mercury may have already brandished one of the props).

fr. 4 optume iure infringatur aula cineris in caput: lit., 'A pot of ashes could be broken over your head with complete justification.' Mercury earlier (1001) had promised only to drench Amphitryon (this threat may be only verbal).

fr. 5 ne tu postules, matula[m], u⟨r⟩nam tibi aquai infundi in caput 'You, jughead, most certainly would be asking to have a pitcher of water poured on your head.' Nonius, who preserves the line (p. 543), gives *matulam unam ... aquam*. Editors generally change *aquam* to a genitive, and interpret *matulam* as an *aquarium uas* (Nonius' gloss). Palmer's suggestion to print *urnam* for the awkward *unam* can be further improved by reading the uocative *matula*, which is applied pejoratively to a person as at *Per.* 533 *numquam ego te tam esse matulam credidi* ('I never supposed you were such an idiot'). For Mercury's predilection in the scene for terms that assail Amphitryon's intelligence cf. 1026 *fatue* and 1028 *stolide*, both of which similarly follow immediately after the verb.

We may presume that the promise to soak Amphitryon was shortly fulfilled.   **ne:** the affirmative particle.

fr. 6 It is tempting to place this before fr. 5 in that it may be a response to Amphitryon's insistence that he is Mercury's master, and this assertion of identity should precede the drenching, which was probably the climactic action of this slapstick scene. But the call to seek a doctor may be Mercury's cue to exit: see further Fantham (1973) 207–8.   **laruatu's:** 777n. The tables are turned on Amphitryon as the (counterfeit) slave accuses his master of insanity (cf. 551ff.); Alcmena similarly is about to judge him to be possessed by demons (fr. 8).   **medicum quaerita:** cf. fr. 8.

frs. 7–10 (Scene 12) Mercury has apparently descended the ladder and gone into the house, leaving Amphitryon alone in front of it. This new scene commences when Alcmena comes out of the house, presumably on the pretext of discovering the cause of all the commotion. The metre switches as the couple enters into a confused and contentious dialogue, the result of the recent scene of reconcilation (881–955). Alcmena cannot understand her husband's apparent change of attitude and, countering his earlier accusations about her sanity, concludes that he is insane (fr. 8). Amphitryon in turn reiterates his belief that Alcmena has committed adultery (frs. 9–10). Tränkle (1983) 232–8 posits the loss of a short intervening scene before frs. 7–10 designed to get Jupiter (and Mercury) out of the palace, but P. probably would not expect his audience to reflect that, from Alcmena's point of view, Amphitryon is both in the palace and out in the street.   METRE: iambic senarii, as the scene of reconciliation between Jupiter and Alcmena (882–955); structurally and thematically this scene primarily corresponds to the earlier confrontation of the spouses (633–860).

fr. 7 exiurauisti te mihi dixe per iocum: cf. 916–17, 920–1, 931–4 (the line is unmistakably Alcmena's).   **dixe** = *dixisse*.

fr. 8 quaeso aduenienti morbo medicari iube 'Please, give the order to cure the disease at its inception.' Alcmena pleads with her husband to seek treatment (for insanity) immediately, a proverbial sentiment (cf. Pers. 3.64 *uenienti occurrite morbo* and Otto (1890) 287). Cf. fr. 6.   **tu certe aut laruatus aut cerritus es:** Alcmena casts back her husband's earlier charges (776–7). The quotation is at least two elements short of being a complete senarius (the only incomplete line among the scene's fragments).

fr. 9 The issue has been brought back to the earlier stalemate: cf. 848–53.   **non causam dico quin uero insimules probri** 'There's no reason that you shouldn't accuse me of misconduct.' **insimules:** sc. *me.* For the charge cf. 820, 859, 887–8.

fr. 10 cuius? quae: Stowasser's plausible correction of *cuiusque* in the MSS; Amphitryon's question would follow on some assertion of Alcmena's *vis-à-vis* her character in which she refers to herself in the third person (e.g. 'Why don't you take the word of your own wife?' 'Whose word? A woman who . . .'). For Alcmena's tendency to objectify herself see 508.   **cuius:** a monosyllable.   **uolgauit** 'prostituted' (cf. 1016).   **suom:** *c D.*

frs. 11–14 (Scene 13) Alcmena, angered over the renewed accusations (frs. 9–10), would presumably re-enter the palace, so as to gather her things and initiate the divorce (cf. 928n.). In the new scene, Amphitryon (left alone on stage) is approached by Sosia, who is accompanied by Blepharo (in accordance with Jupiter's wishes: cf. 949–52, 967–9). Amphitryon will not understand why Blepharo has been summoned, and Sosia, who is expecting only lunch (969n.), will bear the blame for Mercury's mistreatment of his master (1021–fr. 6). METRE: trochaic septenarii, as frs. 11–12 suggest; Sosia similarly had been unjustly accused by his real master at 551–632 (cf. pp. 13–15).

fr. 11 Just as Mercury had promised (1002), Sosia pays the price for the god's actions. The particular threat Amphitryon refers to here is lost (but cf. 1026–8).

fr. 12 ibi scrobes effodito ⟨tu⟩ plus sexagenos in dies 'There you must dig out more than sixty ditches daily.' The promise of hard labour is commonplace in Plautine comedy, where disobedient slaves are frequently threatened with the prospect of the mill or the mines. A similar punishment is described at *Aul.* fr. 3 *ego ecfodiebam in die denos scrobes.*

The line is quoted differently by five different ancient sources (see Leo's apparatus); ⟨*tu*⟩ saves the metre.

fr. 13 noli pessumo precari 'Don't intercede for this scoundrel'; Blepharo's attempt to defend Sosia (e.g. by claiming the two have been together for some time and that Sosia could not have just committed the acts described by Amphitryon) is wholly unsuccessful.

fr. 14 animam comprime: Nonius (p. 233) quotes this as evidence that *anima* can mean *iracundia* or *furor* (cf. *OLD animus* 11); if he is correct, Blepharo would again be appealing to Amphitryon on

Sosia's behalf. But as Leo notes in his apparatus, the placement of the fragment is tentative.

fr. 15–1052 (Scene 14) The climactic scene of the doubles comedy (promised in Argumentum II 6–8 and by Jupiter himself at 953) in which the two Amphitryons square off is regrettably incomplete. Sosia seems to have departed, presumably to escape the punishment proposed by Amphitryon, and left Blepharo behind to arbitrate in the dispute. There is no evidence that Sosia appeared again in the play. It is unclear under what pretence Jupiter leaves the palace; perhaps Amphitryon and Blepharo have charged it and pounded on the doors (cf. Fantham (1973) 211–12).   METRE: trochaic septenarii, as in the corresponding confrontation (263–462) between the other pair of doubles. All the fragments except 18 are complete lines.

fr. 15 manufestum hunc obtorto collo teneo furem flagiti 'I hold this thief caught red-handed in an act of shame and with his neck in a noose', i.e. he claims to have caught Amphitryon trying to break into his house. It is possible to interpret *flagiti* as 'adultery' here and attribute the line to Amphitryon, but Jupiter had specifically foretold (953) that he would drag off Amphitryon *collo ... obstricto* (under either interpretation *flagiti* is genitive of the charge). The fact that Nonius cites the line to illustrate a point about *furtum* has led some editors (e.g. Ernout) to print *furti flagiti*.

fr. 16 The fragment is indisputably to be attributed to Amphitryon and is probably in direct response to fr. 15: cf. *immo* ('on the contrary') and the use of *teneo* to counter Jupiter's claim that he has caught a thief. With the mutual accusations here comes a visual as well as thematic climax as the doubles clutch each other. Amphitryon's anger is most apparent in the alliterative and assonant series *Thebani ... teneo, thensaurum* and *domi uxorem meam | impudicitia impediuit.* **Thebani ciues:** 376n.   **domi uxorem meam** '*my* wife in *my* house'.   **impudicitia impediuit** 'has woven into a web of impurity'.   **thensaurum stupri** 'a heap of lewdness' (in apposition to *hunc*). This proverbial use of *thensaurus* (cf. *Mer.* 641 *thensaurum ... mali* and Otto (1890) 347) seems to originate in the assumption that a treasure trove should be large. Cf. 882–3n.

fr. 17 nihil te pudet, sceleste, populi in conspectum ingredi?: the question could conceivably be asked by either character. Mention of the Theban *populus* (cf. fr. 16) favours attribution to Amphitryon, but it is more humorous to have the general addressed with one of his favourite epithets: with *sceleste* here cf. 1025, 552, 557, 561.

fr. 18 clandestino: presumably part of a vehement accusation of adultery against Jupiter, and of course right on target: cf. *clam* (e.g. 107, 1122).

fr. 19 The fragment reminds us that Blepharo is present and, despite his bewilderment, is called upon to act as an arbiter. The confident tone here befits Jupiter better than Amphitryon, and since Amphitryon will shortly (1037) beg Blepharo to stay on his behalf, the line should probably be attributed to the god.

1035–52 The conclusion of what was probably a substantial scene of confrontation between the doubles.

1035–6 The character named after the Greek word for 'eye' (βλέφαρον) is seeing double; see 365n. for the likelihood that this ironic name is P.'s own invention. Significant names in P. either reflect conventional behaviour associated with the character type (e.g. Pseudolus = 'Liar') or the opposite of these (e.g. the *danista* in *Mos.* is named Misargyrides, 'Son of money-hater').

1035 Vos inter uos partite: an accusative must be understood with the verb. In the lacuna Amphitryon and Jupiter had presumably run through a series of counter claims (e.g. 'This is my house', 'No, it's mine') culminating in 'Alcmena is my wife.' 'No, she's mine', and *uxorem* is the understood accusative. With Blepharo's suggestion that the two 'divide up' Alcmena among themselves cf. Amphitryon's compliance at 1124–5.

For the linguistic doubling here (*uos ... uos*) cf. pp. 15–17.

1036 neque ... censeo 'and, what is more, I don't think ...', a colloquial means of negatively reinforcing a preceding assertion. **uidisse:** for the significance of Blepharo's name see 1035–6n.

1037 quaeso ut aduocatus mihi adsis neue abeas: Amphitryon's confusion as the result of confronting his double begins to show in his desperate plea for Blepharo to stay and assist him.

1038 'Why should I help when I don't know which of you I'm supposed to help?' The promised deception (952) of Blepharo is now complete and he departs utterly perplexed, and (like Sosia) without having had lunch.   **quid opust me aduocato:** lit., 'What need is there for me as an assistant?' (for the construction see *OLD opus* 12b).   **qui utri:** *dd A* (prosodic hiatus).

1039 intro ego hinc eo. Alcumena parturit: an aside. Jupiter hurries into the palace and leaves the stage doors closed behind him.

1039–52 Left alone on stage to ponder his mistreatment at the hands of his wife's paramour, the thoroughly flustered Amphitryon struggles to gain control of himself in the face of the mysterious events (1039–47). After deciding to make a rush into the palace, he ironically blusters that Jupiter and all the gods cannot stop him (1048–52). As he turns toward the palace (1052 *pergam in aedis nunciam*), a loud thunderclap is heard and Amphitryon collapses (cf. 1053–1130, 1073, 1077nn.).

1039 perii miser: for the literal and figurative meanings here cf. 295n.

1040 aduocati ... amici: as only Blepharo has deserted him, the plurals are generalizing. *aduocati* in Roman comedy generally do not straightforwardly provide assistance; at *Poen.* 515ff. they mostly play to the audience as they assist in the deception of a pimp, while at Ter. *Ph.* 441ff. they only further confuse the character who has summoned them for advice.

1041 numquam edepol me inultus istic ludificabit: Amphitryon uses a technical term for deception in Plautine comedy; *ludificabit* (cf. 565n.) here in effect 'adds him to the roster of flimflammed Plautine masters' (Segal (1987) 261 n. 29). There is further irony in his pledge to take vengeance on Jupiter.

1042 me ducam 'I'll go' (*OLD duco* 3).   **resque ut facta est eloquar:** for the indicative in indirect questions cf. 17–18n.

1043 Thessalum ueneficum 'Thessalian sorcerer'. For the traditional association of Thessaly with magic and sorcery see 770n.

1044 peruorse 'like crazy', a colloquial use found only in P. (*OLD* 3).

1045 intro edepol abiit, credo, ad uxorem meam: for the possible sexual *double entendre* cf. Adams (1982) 175–6.

1046 qui me Thebis alter uiuit miserior? quid nunc agam?: the cuckolded *paterfamilias* affects tragic diction.

1047 quem omnes mortales ignorant et ludificant ut lubet 'whom all mortal beings fail to recognize and mock as they please'.

In his confusion and anger, Amphitryon totally miscontrues the situation; *ludificant ut lubet* ironically describes the actions of the two *dei*. Cf. 123, 1041nn.

1048 certumst, intro rumpam in aedis 'I'm resolved to burst right into the palace.' The *paterfamilias* is reduced to assailing his own residence.   **hominem:** still more irony (1047n.).

1049–50 ancillam seu seruom ... uxorem siue adulterum | ... patrem siue auom: the two outer pairs mark the extremes of the Roman social hierarchy; together they constitute a kind of polar expression ('I'll kill any and everyone I see': cf. 7n.). The primary emphasis is on the pair in the middle (for the doublets here see pp. 15–17). For the language cf. *Mil.* 460–1 *intro rumpam recta in aedis: quemque hic intus uidero | cum Philocomasio osculantem, eum ego obtruncabo extempulo.*

1049 siue uxorem siue adulterum: *adulter* occurs here only in P., and apparently is only in process of acquiring the technical sense 'corrupter of a married woman' (Adams (1983) 352) in early Latin. Cf. 135n.

1050 seu patrem siue auom: the absurdly Saturnalian hyperbole that Amphitryon will kill even his father and grandfather (as well as the oblique suggestion that one of them may be having sex with Alcmena) is especially amusing in a patriarchal society such as Rome. For the flouting of *pietas* in Plautine comedy (usually by the lovesick *adulescens*) in general see Segal (1987) 15–41. **obtruncabo:** whereas a husband's slaying of his wife's lover caught *in flagrante delicto* generally constituted justifiable homicide in Greece, the evidence regarding a Roman husband's right to seek immediate redress is inconclusive: Scafuro (1997) 219–23. The use of this particular verb, which elsewhere in the play describes the heroic slaying of King Pterelas (252, 415), underscores the extent to which the *ludus* has effected a role-reversal for Amphitryon.

1051 neque me Iuppiter neque di omnes id prohibebunt: Amphitryon's reckless challenge to the gods and to Jupiter in particular brings one of the central ironies in the play to a climax, and the audience may already anticipate the imminent thunderclap (1039–52n.). Cf. the reported boast of Capaneus, Aesch. *Sept.* 427–9.   **id** 'in this pursuit' (adverbial accusative).   **si uolent:** in that Jupiter is inside the palace, Amphitryon's intention to fly directly in the face of divine will is hopelessly absurd. For the religious formula here see Hanson (1959) 69–71.

1052 No sooner does Amphitryon utter his last word here than he collapses onto the stage (1039–52n.).

1053–1130 (Scene 15) This second 'messenger's speech' includes the play's final song (1053–73). Alcmena's significantly named maid Bromia (1077n.) rushes from the palace to deliver an animated account of the fantastical events that are said to have happened inside. The narrative is crafted so as to highlight the miraculous character of these, and no doubt was to be delivered with breathless enthusiasm. Much is imagined to have occurred since Amphitryon collapsed in 1052 (such telescoping of time is characteristic of nearly all kinds of theatre). Generally speaking, Bromia's opening conforms to a typical tragic situation in which a distraught female character emerges from the *scaena* and relates either her own troubles or those of others inside. After a hyperbolic statement of her astonishment (1053–61), she begins her account with the temporal conjunction that is usual in messenger's speeches (for 1061 *ubi* see 203n.). She then briefly gives an outline of Jupiter's epiphany at the time of the twins' birth, before finally noticing her prostrate master in 1072. After Amphitryon is revived from his death-like state (1076n.), he and Bromia briefly converse (1076–87) until, in keeping with the regular structure of such narratives, she reveals the essence of her report: Alcmena has given birth to twins (1088), and is not an adulteress, at least not in the manner Amphitryon had supposed (1086). Amphitryon asks for further information and the narrative is restarted at 1091, again as a kind of ecphrasis introduced by temporal conjunctions (1091 *postquam*, 1092 *ubi*); this structural doubling is cleverly thematic. Thereafter, Amphitryon frequently interrupts Bromia to express his astonishment and exhort her to continue, and in this way swift pacing and emphasis on the supernatural are maintained throughout, as Bromia supplements her earlier summary with further details. With the revelation of the joint paternity (1123–4), the narrative comes to an end. As Amphitryon reflects on Bromia's account (1125–30), Jupiter suddenly makes his final appearance, this time as *deus ex machina* (1131–45n.). Among P.'s (paratragic) messenger's speeches, Bromia's narrative is most similar to *Cas.* 621–719, where the maid Pardalisca delivers a completely fictional account of Casina's 'bacchic' behaviour. In this play, Bromia's speech finds its counterpart in Sosia's battle narrative (p. 15).   METRE: Bromia's *canticum* (1053–73) is primarily in (sung) iambic octonarii, with a single anapaestic tetrameter (1062) and some trochaic and other iambic lengths mixed in. The rest of the scene is in (recitative) trochaic septenarii.

1053–61	iambic octonarii	(song until 1074)
1062	anapaestic tetrameter	
1063	iambic octonarius	
1064–5	trochaic septenarii	
1066	iambic octonarius	
1067–8	continuous iambic system	
	(= eight iambic metra)	
1069–71	iambic octonarii	
1072	trochaic septenarius	
1073	iambic dimeter	
1074–85	iambic octonarii	(recitative until 1131)
1086–1130	trochaic septenarii	

1053 Spes atque opes uitae meae iacent sepultae in pectore 'The power and prospects of my life lie buried in my heart'; the tragic-sounding language makes for an arresting opening. Bromia's fearful agitation here and in the lines following is strictly unrealistic in that she knows all has come to a happy issue inside; P. is having fun with a stock tragic scene (cf. 1053–1130n.).   **sepultae:** for the prevalence of the theme of death in this scene see 1076n.

  1054 neque ullast confidentia iam in corde, quin ami-serim 'And there no longer is a shred of confidence in my heart that I haven't lost' (slightly tautologous)   **quin amiserim** = *ut non eam amiserim*.

  1055 mare terra caelum: this particular tricolon is found in both poetry (Enn. *Ann.* 556 Skutsch) and prose (Cic. *Tusc.* 5.105). Plautus elsewhere similarly uses asyndetic tricola to affect tragic language: cf. *Trin.* 1070, *Cas.* 623, and *Rud.* 215.   **consequi** 'to bring about' (+ *ut* and substantive clause: cf. *OLD* 8).

  1056 ut opprimar, ut enicer 'that I am being overwhelmed, that I am being killed'; for the tragic anaphora cf. 1062 and Enn. *Andr.* 83 Jocelyn *quo accedam, quo applicem?* For the notion of 'dying' from fear, anxiety, etc. cf. the opening to the similar speech at *Cas.*

621–2 *nulla sum, nulla sum, tota, tota occidi,* | *cor metu mortuomst.* Cf. also 1076n. **me miseram, quid agam nescio:** cf. Pac. 134–5 R = 155–6 W *me miseram* | *quonam clanculum se eliminat?*

1057 ita tanta mira in aedibus sunt facta: cf. the similar exclamation at *Cas.* 625–6 *tanta factu modo mira miris modis* | *intus uidi.* Cf. pp. 29–31.

1058 animo malest 'I'm feeling sick' (cf. 724n.). **aquam uelim** 'I'd love some water', an incongruously homely wish in this context (cf. the English exclamation 'I need a drink!'). **aquam:** the iambic scansion here violates Luchs' law (p. 64). **corrupta sum atque absumpta sum** 'I'm ruined and done for.'

1059 caput dolet, neque audio, nec oculis prospicio satis 'my head hurts, I can't hear, and my eyes are not seeing properly'. Cf. *Cur.* 317 *perii, prospico parum.*

1060 nec me miserior femina est neque ulla uideatur magis: lit., 'neither is there a woman more wretched than I am, nor could any woman be thought to be more so'. For *magis* with a comparative cf. 301n.

1061 ita erae meae hodie contigit 'Such things did happen to my mistress today!' **nam ubi:** cf. 1053–1130nn. **deos [sibi] inuocat:** a conventional formula, here with the usual irony; a woman in Alcmena's condition would be expected to call on *deae* such as Juno, Lucina, Ilithyia, Diana, Venus, or Minerva. **deos:** with synizesis. **inuocat:** in her first narration of the events inside (1061–71), Bromia primarily uses the historic present (as Sosia earlier: 204n.), whereas in her expanded account to Amphitryon (1091–1124) she mixes tenses more freely, e.g. 1093 *inuocat* ... 1094 *contonat* ... 1095 *rebamur* ... 1096 *confulgebant* ... 1099 *audiuimus.*

1062 strepitus, crepitus, sonitus, tonitrus 'there was a crashing, a clashing, a booming and thundering', a masterful climax marked by a change of metre. Each word of this hemistich is an anapaest of like configuration, and the preponderance of *t* here and in the second half of the line (*ut subito ut ... ut ... tonuit*) will perhaps suggest the crack of thunder. Cf. Pac. 336 R = 365 W *strepitus fremitus clamor tonitruum et rudentum sibilus* and *Rud.* 215 (the paratragic song of the shipwrecked Palaestra) *algor error pauor me omnia tenent.* For the homoioteleuton here cf. *Mer.* 639 and Ter. *Hec.* 440. Bromia uses much alliteration and assonance throughout her account, e.g. 1062 *concidit crepitu,* 1063 *Alcumena adest auxilium.*　　**ut subito, ut prope, ut ualide:** close metrical concinnity, with anaphora (cf. 1056n.). For triple anaphora in P. and later Latin poetry see Wills (1996) 367–71.　　**tonuit:** perhaps impersonal, though an appropriate subject is close at hand (1063–5); for the personal and impersonal construction of such verbs see further Wackernagel (1926) I 114–16. The thunderclap she describes as marking Jupiter's epiphany would be the same one that floors Amphitryon at 1052. For epiphany in Roman literature in general see Feeney (1998) 104–7.

1063–7 Commentators have noted the similarities between the scene described here and E. *Bacch.* 594ff., where the chorus, after having collapsed at the bright and thunderous epiphany of Dionysus, is exhorted by the god to cast aside its fears and rise. Cf. pp. 54–5.

1063–4 nescioquis maxuma | uoce exclamat: Bromia hints at the identity of the speaker, who is worshipped as *Iuppiter optimus maximus.* She does not name him until 1121.

1064 adest auxilium: Jupiter delivers on the promise made to the audience at 876–9. Cf. 1131.

1065 tuis: *aB* here.　　**propitius:** a clear sign that the gods' ruse has reached its conclusion and the play's denouement is finally at hand. Divine favour, previously offered only to the audience (2n.) by Mercury, is finally extended to the mortal characters as well. For the motif cf. 935 and 1090.　　**caeli cultor:** cf. *Per.* 581 *di omnes qui caelum colunt.*

1066 '...exsurgite' inquit 'qui terrore meo occidistis prae metu.' 'Rise', he said, 'you who have fallen in dread of me, out of fear.' The extreme fear of the household here reflects a Roman (rather than Greek) sense that *prodigia,* such as those described in 1062–5 and 1067, were necessarily indications of divine anger: cf. Feeney (1998) 81–2.

1067–8 The first four metra of the system run up to and include *confulge-*; for iambic systems in general see Questa (1967) 177–8.

1067 iacui, exsurgo: Bromia's participation in the events described allows her to use the first person (e.g. 1069–71, 1102–3) more freely than Sosia had in his messenger's speech (cf. 203n.). **ardere censui aedis, ita tum confulgebant:** brilliantly supernatural light typically marks divine epiphanies, e.g. *HHAp.* 444–5, E.

Bacch. 596–9, 1082–3. In Theocritus' account of the strangling of the serpents, Zeus provides his ten-month-old son with a guiding light (*Id.* 24.22) throughout the house.

1068 ea res me horrore adficit 'I'm afflicted with utter terror at this event.' Cf. 1066n.

1069 erilis praeuertit metus 'my fear of my mistress prevailed'.

1070 geminos filios pueros 'twin sons, boys!' The birth of twins provides the perfect climax to a doubles comedy! Cf. pp. 15–17.

1071 neque nostrum quisquam sensimus, quom peperit, neque prouidimus: the numinous particulars remain cloaked in mystery (cf. Soph. *Ant.* 407–40).

1072 sed quid hoc? 'But what is *this*?', a formula to indicate the speaker's astonishment (cf. 1130 and Duckworth (1940) on *Epid.* 344). Bromia finally notices her collapsed master; consequently, she will have to restart her narrative (cf. 1053–1130n.). Her surprise is marked by the change of metre.   **senex:** despite the fact that Amphitryon is described as a vigorous warrior in Sosia's messenger's speech, Bromia's description leaves no doubt as to his character type (cf. 1032); in performance, the use of stereotyped masks would make his role immediately obvious. Jupiter, as Amphitryon's double, similarly must be a *senex*. Among the character types of Plautine comedy, an intermediate age-group between *adulescentes* and *senes* is not represented. In amorous pursuits, lovesick young men and their elders are often at loggerheads; when old men themselves pursue *amor* elsewhere in P., they suffer humiliating defeats, as Lysidamus in *Cas.* (cf. *As.*, *Bac.*, *Mer.*; for the general triumph of youth in comedy see Frye (1957) 163–5). As often, *Am.* presents challenging variations on Plautine typologies: while Amphitryon's portrayal as a *senex* can perhaps be explained by his function as a blocking character in his opposition to Jupiter's affair, the lecherous god's unique success as a *senex amator* serves to broaden the sex-farce (cf. p. 37 and Leadbeater (1986)). Casting Amphitryon as a *senex* and making him the butt of the gods' *ludus* would be especially appealing to audience members with overbearing fathers, and may have been intended to poke fun at the ruling elite itself (cf. *senex* and the designation of *senatores* as *patres* and Sutton (1993) 59–60).   **iacet:** with the pregnant suggestion 'lie in death' (cf. 1076n.)

1073 numnam hunc percussit Iuppiter?: Bromia is in effect exclaiming 'he looks as though he's been struck by lightning', but her choice of words ironically points to precisely what happened. Cf. 1039–52n.

1073–4 Iuppiter! | ... Iuppiter: cf. 791 and pp. 15–17.

1074 pro Iuppiter, sepultust quasi sit mortuos: either 'By Jupiter, he's buried as if he were dead' or *sepultus* may possibly mean 'laid out for burial' here (thus Skutsch on Enn. *Ann.* 288). Cf. 1076n.

1075 ibo et cognoscam, quisquis est. Amphitruo hic quidem ⟨est⟩ erus meus: scan *A B C D A B c D / A bb C dd A bb c D*. **ibo et cognoscam** 'I'll go and find out' (he must have collapsed some distance from the doors of the palace).   **quidem ⟨est⟩:** *dd / A* hiatus.

1076 perii ... interii: Amphitryon, like Sosia before him (295n.), undergoes a figurative death and questions his identity as *paterfamilias*. Bromia in effect raises him from the dead in the verses following, where her recognition of him as her master (1082–3) is critical to his resuscitation.

1077 tua Bromia ancilla: P. has purposely delayed revealing Bromia's name; after listening to her frantic *canticum* (1053–1160n.), the audience will be amused to learn that her name characterizes her as a Maenad (Bromius is one of Bacchus' titles). The use of a Maenad to describe these supernatural events is especially appropriate, given the Dionysiac cult's traditional association with miracles (e.g. E. *Bacch.* 704–11), and to the cognoscenti in P.'s audience her name will suggest βρόμος, 'thunder'. For the probable topicality of Bacchic cult at the play's début see pp. 3–4; for the possibility that the name is P.'s invention 365n.   **ita me increpuit Iuppiter** 'so did Jupiter blast me'; cf. 1073n.

1078 quasi si ab Accherunte ueniam: 1076n.   **quasi si =** *quasi*.

1078–9 sed quid tu foras | egressa es?: a natural question for a master to ask a slave that also provides the pretext for restarting the narrative (cf. 1053–1130n.).

1079 nos ... timidas 'us poor women'; Bromia readily slips into the corporate diction of slaves (cf. 362n.).

1080 tu ubi habitas: added to embolden the insecure *paterfamilias* (cf. 1076n.).   **nimia mira uidi:** pp. 29–31.

1081 ita mihi animus etiam nunc abest 'and so my mind is still blown away'.   **etiam nunc:** 408n.

1082 scin me tuom esse erum Amphitruonem?: 1076n. **uide etiam nunc** 'Look at me one more time.'

1083 haec sola sanam mentem gestat meorum familiarium 'She's the only one in my entire household with a sound mind'; the world of the doubles-comedy has truly gone mad when only a Maenad (1077n.) can be said to be in her senses.   **meorum:** *B C* here (synizesis).

1084 immo omnes sani sunt profecto 'No, they all are sane, I swear to it.'

1084–5 at me uxor insanum facit | suis foedis factis: Amphitryon pulls himself together and revisits the issue of his wife's adultery. For the moralizing tone here cf. Caec. 223 R = 227 W *foedis factis facis* (spoken by a typically harsh Caecilian father: cf. Cic. *Cael.* 37).

1085–6 'But I'll make you declare otherwise about that too, and realize that your wife is dutiful and beyond reproach.'

1085 faciam: Bromia playfully picks up 1084 *facit* and 1085 *factis*. **idem:** i.e. in addition to helping him regain a sense of his identity (1076n.), she will restore his faith in his wife.

1086 piam et pudicam: cf. 678n.   **scias:** cf. 1082 *scin ... scio ... scio* and 1085n.

1087 de ea re signa atque argumenta paucis uerbis eloquar: Bromia declares her intention to act as Alcmena's judicial advocate (cf. 806). The pledge to be brief is a rhetorical commonplace (e.g. *Capt.* 53, *Trin.* 4) that, as here (cf. Amphitryon's impatience at 1097), is seldom heeded by the speaker. For the judicial parody see Lage Cotos (1985).   **signa** 'the evidence' (cf. *OLD* 4a).

1088 omnium primum: Bromia attempts to organize her 'defence' carefully, but will shortly begin to ramble again.   **Alcumena geminos peperit filios:** the essential bit of news (1053–1130n.).

1089 di me seruant 'The gods are on my side', a formulaic phrase used by characters who believe they have escaped danger (e.g. *Aul.* 207, *Capt.* 768, *Ps.* 613) that is amusingly ironic in Amphitryon's mouth in that the two gods have just enacted an elaborate *ludus* against him. As he is truly pleased at the news of the twins' birth (cf. 1100), his words should be regarded as sincere here (*aliter* Oniga *ad loc.*, who argues that, in accordance with popular belief, the revelation that Alcmena has given birth to twins in 1089 fuels Ampitryon's suspicions about his wife's infidelity).

1090 tuaeque ... deos: both with synizesis.   **deos esse omnis propitios:** 1065n.

1091 loquere: the deluded Lysidamus similarly tries to accelerate Pardalisca's narrative at *Cas.* 635–6, and 648.

1091–2 postquam ... | ubi: for multiple temporal conjunctions to mark an ecphrasis in a messenger's speech cf. 203n.

1093–4 inuocat deos ... | manibus puris, capite operto: the Romans were notoriously scrupulous in the performance of ritual. In contrast to the Greeks, who made their entreaties with heads bare 'so as to expose the worshipper to divine influence' (Ferguson (1970) 99), the Romans always covered theirs, probably to shield themselves from bad omens.

1093 inuocat: cf. 1061n.   **deos:** with synizesis.

1094 continuo 'immediately', chosen for the jingle with *contonat*. **contonat:** here only; for the intentionally ambiguous subject cf. 1062n.

1096 aedes totae confulgebant tuae, quasi essent aureae: 1067n.   **tuae:** with synizesis.

1097 quaeso, absoluito hinc me extemplo, quando satis deluseris: lit., 'I beg you, release me from this suspense as soon as you have had enough fun' (the tenses are very precise). Lysidamus similarly exhorts (*Cas.* 648 *in pauca confer*) Pardalisca to exercise brevity in her messenger's speech. Cf. 1087n.

1098 quid fit deinde? :: dum haec aguntur, interea uxorem tuam: scan *B C D a B c D a* / *B cc D A B c D*.

1099 nostrum quisquam audiuimus: a common *constructio ad sensum* in Latin (KS 1 22–3).

1100 ita profecto sine dolore peperit: as explicitly promised by Jupiter at 879. In the mythic tradition, Alcmena's labour is cruelly protracted by Juno, e.g. *Il.* 19.119, Ovid, *Met.* 9.281–305. The motif of painless birth may be P.'s innovation, reflecting a deeply held sense among Romans that some compensation (cf. the prayer formula *do ut des*) for Jupiter's treatment of Alcmena is felt to be necessary.

1100–1 iam istuc gaudeo, | utut me erga merita est 'Now that makes me happy, whatever she's done to me.' Though the painless birth of the twins is reasonably taken as a good omen, Amphitryon's sudden and drastic turn of mind is for dramaturgical reasons. For the necessary 'happy ending' see pp. 17–18.   **me erga:** for the anastrophe see 238, 1016nn.

1102 postquam peperit: yet another restarting (1091–2n.) of the narrative. The pace remains frantic (cf. Bromia's mild impatience at 1101) to accentuate the sense of miraculousness.

1103 magnust ... ualet: after the preceding series of perfects (1099–1102), the historic presents vividly mark Bromia's surprise (cf. 1008 *deuolant* ... 1009 *extollunt*). Cf. 204n.

1105–6 diuinitus | non metuo quin meae uxori latae suppetiae sient 'I have no doubt that aid has come to my wife from a divine source.' Amphitryon is bungling his way toward the truth, with the usual irony.

1106 metuo: equivalent to *dubito* here.   **meae:** an elided monosyllable here (scan $B\,cc\,D\,A\,B\,C\,D\,A\,/\,B\,C\,d+a\,B\,c\,D$).   **sient:** 10n.

1107 faxo: 355n.   **postquam:** 1102n.

1108–9 Bromia does not mention that the snakes are sent by the jealous Juno, as regularly in the literary tradition (e.g. Pind. *Nem.* 1.33, Theoc. *Id.* 24.13–16), but P.'s audience would probably be familiar with the story. A wall painting of the event is found in the House of the Vettii at Pompeii.

1108 angues iubatae: the feminine is read (so in 1109, 1111, 1116, 1123) with Nonius (p. 281), whose MSS in this case are older than P.'s, and whose citation is to illustrate the less usual, but attested (see *OLD*) gender. For the illogic of necessarily privileging the direct over the indirect tradition see Timpanaro (1978) 141–2. Crested snakes have a supernatural, dragon-like quality; cf. Williams (1972) on Virg. *A.* 2.206.   **in impluuium** 'into the catchment', a feature of Roman, but not Greek houses, wholly out of place for a Theban palace.

1109 maxumae: in delayed position for special emphasis.   **ei mihi:** in the wall painting of the House of the Vettii (1108–9n.), the fear and shock of Amphitryon, who is present as Hercules clutches the snakes, are obvious; cf. Plin. *NH* 35.36.63 *Hercules infans dracones strangulans Alcmena matre coram pauente et Amphitryone.*

1110 omnis circumuisere 'looked about at all present'. Bromia employs the historical infinitive as the intensity of the narrative increases (cf. 1112 *trahere et ducere*, 1114 *persequi*, and 230n.).

1111 postquam pueros conspicatae, pergunt ad cunas citae: rich alliteration and assonance as the narrative approaches a climax.   **citae:** 244n.

1112 recessim rursum uorsum 'back away towards me', an extreme example of Plautine *abundantia*. Cf. *Epid.* 248 *coepi rursum uorsum ad illas pauxillatim accedere.*   **recessim:** for the formation (<*recedo*) cf. *statim* (239n.).

1113 metuens pueris, mihi formidans: an artful chiasmus, perhaps to parallel the manner in which the twin snakes (the participles are synonymous) might close in on Bromia and the boys.

1114 ille alter puer: cf. 1103.

1115 citus: 244n.   **facit:** *aa* (iambic shortening).

1116 alteram altera prehendit eas manu 'he grabs them, one in one hand, the other in the other hand' (as depicted in the painting in the House of the Vettii).

1117 mira memoras, nimis formidolosum: the alliteration and assonance of *m* here and in 1118 (*nam mihi ... membra misero*) enhance the sense of absolute wonder. For word-end after the tenth element (*formidolosum*) see 707n.

1118 nam mihi horror membra misero percipit dictis tuis 'For utter dread at your words grips the limbs of my poor self'; tragic-sounding: cf. Pac. 224 R = 265 W *horror percipit*; and *St.* 341 *quid ego, quoi misero medullam uentris percipit fames* (a parasite waxes paratragical).

1120 uoce clara exclamat: Bromia has still not explicitly identified Jupiter's role in the strange events: 1063n.

1121 quis homo?: one last opportunity for irony before the god is identified.   **summus imperator diuom atque hominum Iuppiter:** a lofty corrective to Amphitryon's persistent assumption that a human being (1120) was somehow behind the miraculous events, bathetically deflated by the immediately following verse ('he said that he secretly became intimate with Alcmena in bed'). As the comedy moves toward its conclusion, Jupiter's status as the divine *summus imperator* (cf. 504n.) is swiftly restored.

1122 cum Alcumena ... cubitibus: cf. 132–5n.   **cubitibus:** logically plural because Jupiter and Alcmena have in fact had sexual relations twice within the time frame of the play. For the more problematic view that P. meant to suggest a long-standing affair see 481–2n.

1124–5 pol me haud paenitet, | si licet boni dimidium mihi diuidere cum Ioue 'It certainly doesn't bother me to be allowed to divide my largess in half with Jupiter.' Amphitryon's instantaneously positive response to the revelation that Jupiter has had an affair with his wife and fathered one of the twins has troubled some readers, but his compliance brings the play to a sense of final resolution: 'The tendency of comedy is to include as many people as possible in its final society: the blocking characters are more often reconciled or converted than simply repudiated' (Frye (1957) 165).

1125 dimidium: proleptic, as it is Amphitryon's largess (*boni*) that is halved.   **diuidere:** the verb can have obscene connotations (cf. *Aul.* 283–6, Adams (1982) 151 and Cicero's comment on *diuisio* at *Fam.* 9.22.4).

1126 abi: *bb* here (iambic shortening).   **iube uasa pura actutum adornari mihi:** cf. Jupiter's command at 946 *iube uasa pura adornari mihi.* The two Amphitryons ironically share the same words as well as the same woman: cf. 1124–5.

1127 ut Iouis supremi multis hostiis pacem expetam 'so that I may seek the blessing of mighty Jupiter with abundant offerings' (*pacem* has its technical religious sense here: 32n.). Bromia presumably exits here as Amphitryon finishes his instructions, so that the rivals may face each other alone in the finale (1131–46).

1128–9 In the mythical tradition (cf. Apollod. *Bibl.* 2.4.8), Tiresias tells Amphitryon what has happened and what action to take, reflecting the soothsayer's usual role in the Theban plays of Sophocles and Euripides. P.'s gratuitous inclusion of this detail sets up a false expectation and makes the appearance of Jupiter (1131) all the more striking. For the possibility that P. worked directly with a tragedy that featured the appearance of Tiresias at its conclusion see p. 54.

The choice to have Jupiter as *deus ex machina* supplant Tiresias allows for a grand conclusion (1131–43n.), and brings the actor playing him back to the stage for the finale (cf. 1146n.).

1128 coniectorem: lit., 'one who puts things together'. Cf. *Poen.* 444–5 *nam isti quidem hercle orationi Oedipo | opust coniectore.*

1129 hanc rem ut facta est: prolepsis (54–5n.).   **eloquar:** 17–18n.

1130 tonuit: this second thunderclap accompanies Jupiter's arrival. Cf. 1039–52n.

1131–43 (Scene 16) Jupiter appears in the role of *deus ex machina* (presumably in changed costume: pp. 17–18; cf. 861–6) and speaks to Amphitryon directly (Bromia had exited after 1127). The god's appearance is strictly unnecessary in that Bromia has essentially tied up the loose ends, and Amphitryon is no longer angry; to her account Jupiter adds only mention of Hercules' glorious future (1140) and the admonition for the spouses to be reconciled (1141–2). We do not know what kind of device might have been available in P.'s theatre to elevate Jupiter. He may simply have stood on the roof of the stage house (as Mercury had done earlier to mock Amphitryon), though 1143 *ego in caelum migro* suggests movement in some sort of crane. Though the figure of the *deus ex machina* belongs to tragic spectacle, Jupiter hardly behaves like the mighty ruler of the cosmos here, and once again farcically stresses the physicality of his tryst with Alcmena (1135–6).   METRE: iambic senarii.

1131 Bono animo es, adsum auxilio, Amphitruo, tibi et tuis: Jupiter was reported to have addressed Alcmena in a very similar fashion (cf. 1064–5); here he responds gently to Amphitryon's panicked plea for the gods' *fides* (1130). The line scans *a bb c D A bb C dd A bb c D*, with a rare instance of iambic shortening in the next to the last foot (cf. 104n.).   **adsum auxilio:** 92n.

1132–3 hariolos, haruspices | mitte omnes: the god's presence makes these *Iouis Optimi Maximi interpretes internuntiique* (cf. Cic. *Phil.* 13.12) superfluous.

1133 quae futura et quae facta eloquar: the capability to comprehend the past as well as the future is conventionally attributed to soothsayers (cf. 1132). Cf. 1128–9n. and West (1966) on Hes. *Theog.* 32.

1134 multo adeo melius quam illi, quom sum Iuppiter

'I'm so much better than they are, since I'm Jupiter', a light-hearted manner of identifying himself.

1135–6 Alcumenae usuram corporis | cepi et concubitu grauidam feci filio: cf. pp. 39–40.

1136 concubitu: this no doubt suggested *concubina* to the audience.

1136–7 grauidam feci … grauidam … fecisti: one final instance of linguistic doubling.

1138 duos: with synizesis.

1139–40 Hercules and his exploits were so well known to P.'s audience that the hero need not be named.

1139 est susceptus 'was conceived' (cf. *OLD* 4b). The line has a heavy rhythm (42n.).

1140 te immortali adficiet gloria: for the compensation here see p. 37.

1141 antiquam in gratiam: despite all that has happened, Amphitryon and Alcmena are to resume their formerly amicable relationship. This state of ideal harmony in Roman marriage is more often referred to as *concordia* (cf. 475, 841, 962 and Treggiari (1991) 251–3).

1142 haud promeruit quam ob rem uitio uorteres 'She has done nothing wrong to give you cause to blame her.'

1143 mea ui: i.e. because of his powers as a *uorsipellis* (123). **ego in caelum migro:** Jupiter is lifted upward by some device (1131–43n.).

1144–6 (Scene 17) As Jupiter apparently ascends, Amphitryon confirms his acceptance of the situation and signals the end of the play.   METRE: trochaic septenarii, the standard measure for closure in Roman comedy (p. 56).

1144 ita ut iubes … tua: perhaps Amphitryon calls to Jupiter just as he is being lifted above the palace so as to be set down behind it (cf. 1146n.).

1145 ibo ad uxorem intro: the normal order of things is restored for the *paterfamilias*, who can finally enter his residence. By referring to Alcmena as his *uxor* here, Amphitryon explicitly acknowledges complete acceptance of Jupiter's instruction in 1141–2 (cf. 729n.).   **missum facio Teresiam senem** 'I discharge old Tiresias' (for *missum facere* see *OLD mitto* 3b).

1146 spectatores: 998n.   **Iouis summi causa clare plaudite** 'let's have some loud applause for almighty Jupiter'. Jupiter (the leader of the *grex*?) either remains suspended above the backdrop or has been set down behind it. Assuming the latter case, the designation of the actor as 'almighty Jupiter' here is most humorous if he returns to the stage and removes his mask (cf. the similar play on the actor's status at the beginning of the play: 26–7n.). The final *plaudite* in P. is typically very general, and here alone is the audience exhorted to applaud for a particular character/actor (the epilogue of *As.*, where the audience is to give their applause if they wish the *senex amator* to be spared a beating, is not quite parallel). For the possibility that Jupiter was played by Plautus himself see p. 1 n. 5.

BIBLIOGRAPHY

1 Abbreviations

(a) General

Bennett   C. E. Bennett, *Syntax of early Latin*, 1910, Boston.

CHCL   *Cambridge history of classical literature* vol. II, ed. E. J. Kenney and W. V. Clausen, 1982, Cambridge.

DS   Ch. Daremberg, E. Saglio, *Dictionnaire des antiquités grecques et romaines*, 1877–1919, Paris.

Ernout–Meillet   A. Ernout, A. Meillet, *Dictionnaire étymologique de la langue latine*, 3rd edn 1951, Paris.

GL   B. L. Gildersleeve, G. Lodge, *Gildersleeve's Latin grammar*, 3rd edn 1895, London.

KS   R. Kühner, C. Stegmann, *Ausführliche Grammatik der lateinischen Sprache*, 5th edn rev. 1976 A. Thierfelder, Hanover.

LHS   I: M. Leumann, *Lateinische Laut- und Formenlehre*, 1926–8, new edn 1977; II: J. B. Hofmann, *Lateinische Syntax und Stilistik*, 1965; new edn rev. A. Szantyr, 1972 (*Handbuch der Altertumswissenschaft* II 2.1 and 2), Munich.

Lindsay   W. M. Lindsay, *Syntax of Plautus*, 1907, London.

LL   L. R. Palmer, *The Latin language*, 1954, London.

Lodge   G. Lodge, *Lexicon Plautinum*, 1924–33, Leipzig.

LS   C. T. Lewis, C. Short, *A Latin dictionary*, 1879, Oxford.

LU   J. B. Hofmann, *Lateinische Umgangssprache*, 1951, Heidelberg.

MHL   A. Ernout, *Morphologie historique du latin*, 3rd edn 1974, Paris.

OCD   *The Oxford classical dictionary*, 3rd edn 1996, Oxford.

OLD   *Oxford Latin dictionary*, 1968–82, Oxford.

RE   A. Pauly, G. Wissowa, W. Kroll, *Real-Encyclopädie der classischen Altertumswissenschaft*. 1893– , Stuttgart.

Woodcock   E. C. Woodcock, *A new Latin syntax*, 1959, London.

(*b*) *The plays*

Am.	*Amphitruo*
As.	*Asinaria*
Aul.	*Aulularia*
Bac.	*Bacchides*
Capt.	*Captiui*
Cas.	*Casina*
Cist.	*Cistellaria*
Cur.	*Curculio*
Epid.	*Epidicus*
Men.	*Menaechmi*
Mer.	*Mercator*
Mil.	*Miles gloriosus*
Mos.	*Mostellaria*
Per.	*Persa*
Poen.	*Poenulus*
Ps.	*Pseudolus*
Rud.	*Rudens*
St.	*Stichus*
Trin.	*Trinummus*
Truc.	*Truculentus*
Vid.	*Vidularia*

2 Principal modern editions of all the plays by date

Bothe, F. H. (1809–23). Berlin.

Naudet, J. (1830–2). Paris.

Fleckeisen, A. (1850–1). Leipzig.

Ritschl, F., Goetz, G., Loewe, G., Schoell, F. (1871–1902). Leipzig.

Ussing, J. L. (1875–92). Copenhagen.

Goetz, G., Schoell, F. (1892–1904). Leipzig.

Leo, F. (1895–6). Berlin.

Lindsay, W. M. (1910). 2nd edn Oxford.

Ernout, A. (1932–61). Paris.

3 Modern editions of, and/or commentaries on, Am. by date

Lindemann, F. (1834). Leipzig.

Holtze, F. W. (1846). Leipzig.

Palmer, A. (1890). London.
Havet, L. (1895). Paris.
Sedgwick, W. B. (1960). Manchester.
Miller, E. W. (1965). Greenville, PA.
Paratore, E. (1967). Florence.
Cutt, T., Nyenhuis, J. E. (1970). Detroit.
Louro Fonseca, C. A. (1978). Coimbra.
Oniga, R. (1991). Venice.

4 Select English translations of Am. by date

Nixon, P. (1916). Cambridge, MA.
Duckworth, G. E. (1942). New York.
Casson, L. (1971). New York.
Mountebrand, J. H., Passage, C. E. (1974). Chapel Hill.
Roche, P. (repr. 1984). Chicago.
Carrier, C. (1995), in (edd.) Slavitt, D. R., Bovie, P. Baltimore and
    London.

5 Works cited

Abel, K. (1955). *Die Plautusprologe*. Frankfurt.
Adams, J. N. (1982). *The Latin sexual vocabulary*. London.
    (1983) 'Words for "prostitute" in Latin', *RhM* 126: 321–58.
Allan, S. (1996). *The plays of Heinrich von Kleist*. Cambridge.
Allen, W. S. (1978). *Vox Latina*. 2nd edn Cambridge.
Anderson, W. S. (1993). *Barbarian play: Plautus' Roman comedy*. Toronto.
Arnott, W. G. (1975). *Menander, Plautus, and Terence*. Oxford.
Austin, R. G. (1971). *Virgil: Aeneid I*. Oxford.
Axtell, H. L. (1907). *The deification of abstract ideas in Roman literature and
    inscriptions*. Chicago.
Bailey, C. (1947). *Lucretius: De rerum natura*. Oxford.
Barchiesi, M. (1970). 'Plauto e il "metateatro" antico', *Il Verri* 31:
    113–30.
Barnes, H. E. (1957). 'The case of Sosia versus Sosia', *CJ* 53: 19–24.
Barrett, W. S. (1964). *Euripides: Hippolytos*. Oxford.
Barsby, J. (1986). *Plautus: Bacchides*. Warminster.
    (1999). *Terence: Eunuchus*. Cambridge.
Barthes, R. (1972). *Critical essays*, trans. R. Howard. Evanston, IL.

Beacham, R. C. (1992). *The Roman theatre and its audience*. Cambridge, MA.

Beare, W. (1964). *The Roman stage*. 3rd edn London.

Bentley, E. (1966). *The life of the drama*. London.

Bettini, M. (1991*a*). *Anthropology and Roman culture*, trans. J. Van Sickle. Baltimore and London.

  (1991*b*). *Verso un'antropologia dell'intreccio*. Urbino.

  (1991*c*). 'Sosia e il suo Sosia: pensare il "Doppio" a Roma', in (ed.) R. Oniga, *Plauto, Anfitrione* 9–51. Venice.

Bieber, M. (1961). *The history of the Greek and Roman theatre*. 2nd edn Princeton.

Blackman, D. J. (1969). 'Plautus and Greek topography', *TAPA* 100: 11–22.

Blänsdorf, J. (1967). *Archaische Gedankengänge in den Komödien des Plautus* (*Hermes Einzelschriften* 20). Wiesbaden.

Bond, G. W. (1988). *Euripides: Heracles*. Oxford.

Braun, L. (1970). *Die Cantica des Plautus*. Göttingen.

  (1980) *Scenae suppositiciae oder der falsche Plautus*, Göttingen.

Burkert, W. (1985). *Greek religion*, trans. J. Raffan. Cambridge, MA.

Caldera, E. (1947). 'Sulle fonti dell'*Amphitruo*', *RFIC* n.s. 25: 147–54.

Cèbe, J.-P. (1966). *La caricature et la parodie dans le monde romain antique des origines à Juvénal*. Paris.

Chalmers, W. R. (1965). 'Plautus and his audience', in (edd.) T. A. Dorey and D. R. Dudley, *Roman drama* 21–50. London.

Chiarini, G. (1980). 'Compresenza e conflittualità dei generi nel teatro latino arcaico (per una rillettura dell'Amphitruo)', *MD* 5: 87–124.

Clark, J. P. (1980). 'Wordplay at *Amph*. 327–330', *CP* 75: 137–8.

Clausen, W. (1971). '*Duellum*', *HSCP* 75: 69–72.

  (1994). *A commentary on Virgil Eclogues*. Oxford.

Corbett, P. (1964). '*Vis comica* in Plautus and Terence', *Eranos* 62: 52–69.

Courtney, E. (1980). *A commentary on the Satires of Juvenal*. London.

Damon, C. (1997). *The mask of the parasite: a pathology of Roman patronage*. Ann Arbor.

Dixon, S. (1992). *The Roman family*. Baltimore and London.

Dobrov, G. W. (1995). *Beyond Aristophanes: transition and diversity in Greek comedy*. Atlanta, GA.

Dodds, E. R. (1960). *Euripides: Bacchae*. Oxford.

Duckworth, G. (1936). 'The dramatic function of the *servus currens* in Roman Comedy', in *Classical studies presented to Edward Capps* 93–102. Princeton.

(1940). *T. Macci Plauti: Epidicus*. Princeton.

(1952). *The nature of Roman comedy*. Princeton.

Dupont, F. (1976). 'Signification théâtrale du double dans l'*Amphitryon* de Plaute', *REL* 54: 129–141.

(1985). *L'Acteur-roi*. Paris.

(1987). 'Cantica et diverbia dans l'*Amphitryon* de Plaute', in *Filologia e forme letterarie, Studi offerti a F. Della Corte* II 45–56. Urbino.

Earl, D. C. (1960). 'Political terminology in Plautus', *Historia* 9: 235–42.

Easterling, P. E. (ed.) (1997). *The Cambridge companion to Greek tragedy*. Cambridge.

Elam, K. (1980). *The semiotics of theatre and drama*. London.

Enk, P. J. (repr. 1979). *Plauti Mercator*. New York.

Fantham, E. (1972). *Comparative studies in Republican Latin imagery*. Toronto.

(1973). 'Towards a dramatic reconstruction of the fourth act of Plautus' *Amphitruo*', *Philologus*: 197–214.

Fears, J. R. (1981). 'The theology of Victory at Rome', *ANRW* 2.17.2: 737–826.

Feeney, D. C. (1991). *The gods in epic: poets and critics of the classical tradition*. Oxford.

(1998). *Literature and religion at Rome*. Cambridge.

Ferguson, J. (1970). *The religions of the Roman Empire*. Ithaca.

(1979). *Juvenal: the Satires*. New York.

Ford, C. (1991). *Così?: sexual politics in Mozart's operas*. Manchester.

Fordyce, C. J. (ed.) (1961). *Catullus*. Oxford.

Fraenkel, E. (1912). *De media et noua comoedia quaestiones selectae*. Diss. Göttingen.

(1922). *Plautinisches im Plautus*. Berlin.

(1957). *Horace*. Oxford.

(1960). *Elementi plautini in Plauto*. Florence.

Frost, K. B. (1988). *Exits and entrances in Menander*. Oxford.

Frye, N. (1957). *Anatomy of criticism*. Princeton.

Gaiser, K. (1972). 'Zur Eigenart der römischen Komödie: Plautus und Terenz gegenüber ihren griechischen Vorbildern' in *ANRW* I 2.1027–1113.

García-Hernández, B. (1984). '*Nocturnum* (Plaut. *Amph.* 272). Cuestión filológica, solución semántica', *Emerita* 53: 93–101.

Gentili, B. (1979). *Theatrical performances in the ancient world.* Amsterdam.

Gilbert, J. (1995). Review of Taaffe (1993), *BMCR* 95.5.7.

Gold, B. (1998). ' "Vested interests" in Plautus' *Casina*: cross-dressing in Roman comedy', *Helios* 25.1: 17–29.

Goldberg, S. (1980). *The making of Menander's comedy.* London.

Goldhill, S. (1991). *The poet's voice.* Cambridge

Gomme, A. W. and Sandbach, F. H. (1973). *Menander: a commentary.* Oxford.

Gould, J. (1973). 'HIKETEIA', *JHS* 93: 74–103.

Gratwick, A. S. (1973). ' "Titus Maccius Plautus" ', *CQ* 23: 78–84.

(ed.) (1987). *Terence, The Brothers.* Warminster.

(ed.) (1993). *Plautus: Menaechmi.* Cambridge.

Gratwick, A. S. and Lightley, S. J. (1982). 'Light and heavy syllables as dramatic colouring in Plautus and others', *CQ* 32: 124–33.

Gruber, W. E. (1986). *Comic theaters.* Athens, GA and London.

Gruen, E. S. (1990). *Studies in Greek culture and Roman policy.* Leiden.

(1992). *Culture and national identity in Republican Rome.* Ithaca.

Guilbert, D. (1963). 'Mercure-Sosia dans l'Amphitryon de Plaute. Un rôle de parasite de comédie', *LEC* 31: 52–63.

Haffter, H. (1934). *Untersuchungen zur altlateinischen Dichtersprache* (Problemata 10). Berlin.

(1967). *Römische Politik und römische Politiker.* Heidelberg.

Hallett, J. P. (1993). 'The political backdrop of Plautus' *Casina*', in (edd.) R. W. Wallace and E. M. Harris, *Transitions to empire: essays in Greco-Roman history, 360–146 BC in honor of Ernst Badian* 409–38. Norman, OK and London.

Handley, E. W. (1965). *The Dyskolos of Menander.* Cambridge, MA.

(1968). *Menander and Plautus: a study in comparison.* London.

(1975). 'Plautus and his public: some thoughts on New Comedy in Latin', *Dioniso* 46: 117–22.

Hanson, J. A. (1959). 'Plautus as a source book for Roman religion', *TAPA* 90: 48–101.

Happ, H. (1967). 'Die lateinische Umgangssprache und die Kunstsprache des Plautus', *Glotta*: 60–104.

Harris, W. V. (1979). *War and imperialism in Republican Rome*. Oxford.

Hartwig, J. (1972). *Shakespeare's tragicomic vision*. Baton Rouge, LA.

Harvey, P. (1981). 'Historical allusions in Plautus and the date of the *Amphitruo*', *Athenaeum* 59: 480–9.

  (1986). 'Historical topicality in Plautus', *CW* 79: 297–304.

Henderson, J. (1995). 'Beyond Aristophanes', in Dobrov (1995) 175–83.

Herrick, M. T. (1962). *Tragicomedy*. Urbana, IL.

Hirst, D. L. (1984). *Tragicomedy*. London and New York.

Höttemann, B. (1993). 'Phlyakenposse und Atellane', in (ed.) G. Vogt-Spira, *Beiträge zur mündlichen Kultur der Römer* (ScriptOralia 47) 89–112. Tübingen.

Hough, J. N. (1945). 'The *Numquid Vis* formula in Roman comedy', *AJP* 66: 282–302.

  (1970). 'Jupiter, Amphitruo and the cuckoo', *CP* 65: 95–6.

Housman, A. E. (1972). *The classical papers of A. E. Housman* (edd.) J. Diggle and F. R. D. Goodyear. London.

Hunter, R. L. (1985). *The New Comedy of Greece and Rome*. Cambridge.

  (1987). 'Middle Comedy and the *Amphitruo* of Plautus', *Dioniso* 57: 281–98.

Jacobsohn, H. (1904). *Quaestiones Plautinae*. Diss. Göttingen.

Jocelyn, H. D. (1967). *The tragedies of Ennius*. Cambridge.

de Jong, I. J. F. (1991). *Narrative in drama: the art of the Euripidean messenger-speech*. Leiden.

Kassel, R. (1966). 'Kritische und exegetische Kleinigkeiten II', *RhM* 109: 1–12.

Kennedy, G. (1968). 'The rhetoric of advocacy in Greece and Rome', *AJP* 89: 419–36.

  (1972). *The art of rhetoric in the Roman world*. Princeton.

Kenney, E. J. (ed.) (1971). *Lucretius: De rerum natura, book III*. Cambridge.

  (ed.) (1990). *Apuleius: Cupid and Psyche*. Cambridge.

Kerr, W. (1967). *Tragedy and comedy*. New York.

Knapp, C. (1919). 'References in Plautus and Terence to plays, players, and playwrights', *CP* 14: 35–55.

Kroll, W. (1924). *Studien zum Verständnis der römischen Literatur*. Stuttgart.

Lage Cotos, M. E. (1985). 'La Virtud en la Mujer: Nota a PLAVT. *Amph*. 1086–1088', *Euphrosyne* 13: 193–204.

Leadbeater, L. W. (1986). 'Amphitryon, Casina, and the disappearance of Jupiter', in (ed.) C. Deroux, *Studies in Latin literature and Roman history* IV 135–50. Brussels.

  (1987). '*Lubet* and the principle of pleasure in the plays of Plautus', *CB* 63: 5–11.

Lebek, W. D. (1996). 'Moneymaking on the Roman stage', in (ed.) W. J. Slater, *Roman theater and society* 29–48. Ann Arbor.

Lefèvre, E. (1982). *Maccus Vortit Barbare: Vom tragischen Amphitryon zum tragikomischen Amphitruo*. Wiesbaden.

Lehmann, A. (1995). 'Varron biographe de Plaute', *Euphrosyne* n.s. 23: 223–36.

Leo, F. (1911). 'Ueber den Amphitruo des Plautus', *NGG*: 254–62.

  (1912). *Plautinische Forschungen*. 2nd edn Berlin.

Lindberger, O. (1956). *The transformations of Amphitryon*. Stockholm.

Lindsay, W. M. (1922). *Early Latin verse*. Oxford.

Löfstedt, E. (1956). *Syntactica* II. 2nd edn Lund.

Lowe, N. J. (1994). Review of Bettini (1991*b*), *JRS* 84: 221–2.

Luck, G. (1964). *Über einige Interjektionen der lateinischen Umgangssprache*. Heidelberg.

Lucke, C. (1982). *P. Ovidius Naso, Remedia amoris: Kommentar zu Vers 397–814*. Bonn.

MacCary, W. T. and Willcock, M. M. (edd.) (1976). *Plautus: Casina*. Cambridge.

Mankin, P. (1971). *Precious irony: the theatre of Jean Giraudoux*. The Hague.

Mariotti, S. (1959). 'Adversaria Philologica III', in (edd.) H. Dahlmann and R. Merkelbach, *Studien zur Textgeschichte und Textkritik G. Jachmann gewidmet* 123–6. Cologne.

Martin, P. (1970). 'Plaute, *Amphitryon*, v. 292–462. Le dialogue Sosie-Mercure ou la destruction de l'homme par l'appareil totalitaire', *Caesarodunum* 5: 171–7.

McDonnell, M. (1983). 'Divorce initiated by women in Rome', *AJAH* 8: 54–80.

(1986). '*Ambitus* and Plautus' *Amphitruo* 65–81', *AJP* 107: 564–76.

Moore, T. J. (1994). 'Seats and social status in the Plautine theatre', *CJ* 90: 113–23.

(1998). *The theater of Plautus: playing to the audience*. Austin.

Muecke, F. (1977). 'Playing with the play: theatrical self-consciousness in Aristophanes', *Antichthon* 11: 52–67.

(1986). 'Plautus and the theatre of disguise', *CA* 5.2: 216–29.

Nelson, T. G. A. (1990). *Comedy*. Oxford.

Nesselrath H.-G. (1990). *Die attische mittlere Komödie*. Berlin

(1995). 'Myth, parody, and comic plots: the birth of gods in Middle Comedy', in Dobrov (1995) 1–27.

Norwood, G. (1932). *Plautus and Terence*. New York.

Ogilvie, R. M. (1965). *A commentary on Livy, books 1–5*. Oxford.

Olivieri, A. (1946–7). *Frammenti della commedia greca e del mimo nella Sicilia e nella Magna Grecia*, 2nd edn Naples.

Oniga, R. (1985). 'Il canticum di Sosia: forme stilistiche e modelli culturali', *MD* 14: 113–208.

Otto, A. (1890). *Die Sprichwörter und sprichwörtlichen Redensarten der Römer*. Leipzig.

Page, D. L. (ed.) (1938). *Euripides: Medea*. Oxford.

Pascucci (1961–2). 'La scelta dei mezzi espressivi nel resoconto militare di Sosia (Plauto, *Amph.* 186–261)', *La Columbaria* 26: 161–203.

Perelli, L. (1983). 'L'Alcmena plautina: personaggio serio o parodico?', *CCC* 4: 383–94.

Petersmann, H. (1973). *T. Maccius Plautus: Stichus*. Heidelberg.

Petrone, G. (1983). *Teatro antico e inganno: finzioni plautine*. Palermo.

Phillips, J. E. (1985). 'Alcumena in the *Amphitruo* of Plautus: a pregnant lady joke', *CJ* 80: 121–6.

Prescott, H. W. (1913). 'The *Amphitruo* of Plautus', *CP* 8:14–22.

Questa, C. (1967). *Introduzione alla metrica di Plauto*. Bologna.

(1984). *Numeri innumeri: ricerche sui cantica e la tradizione manoscritta di Plauto*. Rome.

Ramsey, W. (1869). *The Mostellaria of Plautus*. London.

Raven, D. (1965). *Latin metre*. London.

Reinhardt, U. (1974). 'Amphitryon und Amphitruo', in *Musa iocosa: Festschrift A. Thierfelder* 95–130. New York.

Renehan, R. (1977). 'Compound-simplex verbal iteration in Plautus', *CP* 72: 243–8.

Ribbeck, O. (1875). *Die römische Tragoedia im Zeitalter der Republik.* Leipzig.

Richardson, L. (1988). *Pompeii: an architectural history.* Baltimore.

Riedel, V. (1993). 'Zwischen Tragik und Komik. Zur Geschichte des Amphitryon-Stoffes von Hesiod bis Hacks', in (edd.) M. Kunze, D. Metzler, and V. Riedel, *Amphitryon: ein griechisches Motiv in der europäischen Literatur und auf dem Theater* 9–23. Münster and Hamburg.

Rosenmeyer, P. A. (1995). 'Enacting the law: Plautus' use of the divorce formula on stage', *Phoenix* 49: 201–17.

Rothwell, K. S. (1995). 'The continuity of the chorus in fourth-century Attic comedy', in Dobrov (1995) 99–118.

Sandbach, F. H. (1977). *The comic theatre of Greece and Rome.* London.

Saunders, C. (1913). 'The site of dramatic performances at Rome in the times of Plautus and Terence', *TAPA* 44: 87–97.

Sblendorio Cugusi, M. T. (ed.) (1982). *M. Porci Catonis orationum reliquiae.* Turin.

Scafuro, A. C. (1997). *The forensic stage: settling disputes in Graeco-Roman comedy.* Cambridge.

Schmidt, K. (1902). 'Die griechische Personennamen bei Plautus', *Hermes* 37: 173–211.

Scullard, H. H. (1950). *Roman politics 220–150 BC.* Oxford.

Sedgwick, W. B. (1949). 'Plautine chronology', *AJP* 70: 376–83.

Segal, C. (1997). *Dionysiac poetics and Euripides' Bacchae.* Princeton.

Segal, E. (1987). *Roman laughter.* 2nd edn Oxford.

Shero, L. R. (1956). 'Alcmena and Amphitryon in ancient and modern drama', *TAPA* 87: 192–238.

Siewert, P. (1894). *Plautus in Amphitruone fabula quomodo exemplar Graecum transtulerit.* Berlin.

Skutsch, O. (1968). *Studia Enniana.* London.

(ed.) (1985). *The Annals of Quintus Ennius.* Oxford.

Slater, N. W. (1985). *Plautus in performance.* Princeton.

(1987). 'Transformations of space in New Comedy', in (ed.) J.

Redmond, *Themes in drama 9: The theatrical space* 1–10. Cambridge.

(1990). '*Amphitruo*, *Bacchae* and metatheatre', *Lexis* 6: 101–25.

(1993). 'Improvisation in Plautus', in (ed.) G. Vogt-Spira, *Beiträge zur mündlichen Kultur der Römer* (ScriptOralia 47) 113–24. Tübingen.

(1995). 'The fabrication of comic illusion', in Dobrov (1995) 29–45.

Sonnenschein, E. A. (ed.) (repr. 1979). *T. Macci Plauti Rudens*. New York.

Soubiran, J. (1966). *L'élision dans la poésie latine*. Paris.

(1988). *Essai sur la versification dramatique des Romains*. Paris.

Stanford, W. B. (1950). 'On the Ὀδυσσεὺς αὐτόμολος of Epicharmus', *CP* 45: 167–9.

Stärk, E. (1982). 'Die Geschichte des Amphitryonstoffes vor Plautus', *RhM* 125: 275–303.

Stein, J. P. (1971). 'Compound word coinage in the plays of Plautus', *Latomus* 30: 598–606.

Stewart, Z. (1958). 'The *Amphitruo* of Plautus and Euripides' *Bacchae*', *TAPA* 89: 348–73.

(1960). 'The god *Nocturnus* in Plautus's *Amphitruo*', *JRS* 50: 37–43.

Styan, J. L. (1975). *Drama, stage and audience*. Cambridge.

Sutton, D. F. (1993). *Ancient comedy: the war of the generations*. New York.

Taaffe, L. K. (1993). *Aristophanes and women*. London and New York.

Taladoire, B.-A. (1956). *Commentaires sur la mimique et l'expression corporelle du comédien romain*. Montpellier.

Taplin, O. (1993). *Comic angels*. Oxford.

Tarrant, R. J. (1983). 'Plautus', in (ed.) L. D. Reynolds, *Texts and transmission* 302–7. Oxford.

Thomas, R. F. (ed.) (1988). *Virgil: Georgics*. Cambridge.

Timpanaro, S. (1978). *Contributi di filologia e di storia della lingua latina*. Rome.

Tobias, J. (1979). 'Bacchiac women and iambic slaves in Plautus', *CW* 73: 9–18.

Tolliver, H. M. (1952). 'Plautus and the state gods of Rome', *CJ* 48: 49–57.

Tränkle, H. (1983). '*Amphitruo* und kein Ende', *Museum Helveticum* 40: 217–38.

Treggiari, S. (1991). *Roman marriage*. Oxford.

Trendall, A. D. (1967). *Phlyax vases* (*BICS* Suppl. 19). 2nd edn London.

Trendall, A. D. and Webster, T. B. L. (1971). *Illustrations of Greek drama*. London.

Wackernagel, J. (1926–8). *Vorlesungen über Syntax*. Basle.

Wallace, R. (1984). 'The deletion of *s* in Plautus', *AJP* 105: 213–25.

Walton, J. M. and Arnott, P. D. (1996). *Menander and the making of comedy*. London.

Watkins, C. (ed.) (1985). *The American heritage dictionary of Indo-European roots*.

Watson, A. (1967). *The law of persons in the later Roman Republic*. Oxford.

Webster, T. B. L. (1953). *Studies in later Greek comedy*. Manchester.

West, M. L. (ed.) (1966). *Hesiod: Theogony*. Oxford.

Westaway, K. M. (1917). *The original element in Plautus*. Cambridge.

Whitman, C. H. (1964). *Aristophanes and the comic hero*. Cambridge, MA.

Wilamowitz-Moellendorff, U. von (ed.) (repr. 1969). *Euripides: Herakles*. Darmstadt.

Wiles, D. (1988). 'Taking farce seriously: recent critical approaches to Plautus', in (ed.) J. Redmond, *Themes in drama 10: Farce* 261–71. Cambridge.

(1991). *The masks of Menander*. Cambridge.

Willcock, M. M. (ed.) (1987). *Plautus: Pseudolus*. London.

Williams, G. (1958). 'Some aspects of Roman marriage ceremonies and ideals', *JRS* 48: 16–29.

(1959). 'Some uses of *gratus* and *gratia* in Plautus: evidence of Indo-European?', *CQ* n.s. 9: 155–63.

Williams, R. D. (ed.) (1972). *The Aeneid of Virgil, books 1–6*. Basingstoke and London.

Wills, J. (1996). *Repetition in Latin poetry: figures of allusion*. Oxford.

Wright, J. (1974). *Dancing in chains: the stylistic unity of the comoedia palliata*. Rome.

Zagagi, N. (1994). *The comedy of Menander*. London.

Zeitlin, F. (1996). *Playing the other: gender and society in classical Greek literature*. Chicago.

INDEXES

1 General

(References in italic are to page numbers; other numbers refer to lines of the play and in most cases to notes in the Commentary.)

ablative: manner, *32*; *qui*, *76*; *cubare* +, 112; means, 161–2; specification (respect), 166, *390*; *adest opus* +, 169; adverbial, *180*; absolute, 188; originally in *-d*, 189; verbs of filling +, 251; cause, 254, 378; comparison, 293, 446; attendant circumstances, 321; in grammatical joke, *369*; time, 548; degree of difference, 610; *expers* +, 713; source, 878–9; *defessus* +, 1014

Accius, *48*

accusative: *clam* +, 107; adverbial, 154, 852, 1051; double, 163–4, 529; after dative, 181; with medial-passive, 238; ellipsis of, 243; cognate, 278; of time, 280; proleptic, 398; with verbal substantive, 519; of exclamation, 537, *882–3*; respect, 564; internal, 820, 933

acrostic, *129*

actors: conspiratorial relationship with audience, *25, 26–7, 32, 34*, 146–7, *153–* 462, 263–92, 470–1; status of, *34*, 26–7, 28, 70–1, 90, 176–9, 863, 986–7, 1146; transvestism of, *38–9*; claques, *40*, 64–96, 70–1, 81–5; *see also* audience

acts: in Menander, *6*; absence of in P., *12, 14*

adultery, *3, 10, 32, 37, 42, 44*, 100–14, 103, 104–6, 132–5, 135, 463–98, 478, 509, 542, 821, 839–42, 996

aediles, *40*, 16, 72

Aeschylus, *48*

Alc(u)mena: costume of, *22*, 667; as 'tragic heroine', *37–8, 40–1, 43*; melodramatic quality of, *40, 43*, 529, 530, 536–7, 542, 639, 645–6, 647a, 882–90, fr. 10; pregnancy of, *16, 38–9, 42, 52*, 100–14, 111, 480–4, 499–550, 499, 654–860, 668, 681, 719, 723, 724; played by male actor, *38–9*, 542, 633–53, 925, 930; sexual insatiability of, *40–4*, 472, 499–550, 509, 512, 513–14, 531, 633–53, 633, 637–9, 647a, 804–5

Alkmene, in Greek myth, *45–6*; prior dramatic treatments of affair with Zeus, *47–50*

alliteration, 1–16, 207, 212, 250, 301, 335, 339–40, 395, 448, 464, 513, 584b–85a, 616, 623–4, 903, 972, 978–9, fr. 16, 1062, 1111

Amphitryon: as *miles gloriosus*, *29*, 193, 654–8, 676; as *senex*, *37*, 1011, 1031–2, 1072; as 'blocking character', *30*, 551–632, 584b, 1072; inflexibility of, *30–1*, 553–4, 586, 693; powerlessness of, *15*, 558, 1046, 1047, 1048; final acquiescence of, *17–18, 44–5*; as *paterfamilias*, 551–632, 756, 845, 1145; in prior drama, *47–9*

anaphora, 1–16, 448, 542, 648, 1056, 1062

anastrophe, 238, 653, 1100–1

archaism, 7, 13, 189, 210, 213, 216, 250, 269, 270, 359, 417, 511, 527, 543, 713

330

2 Latin words